VICTORY WITHOUT TRIUMPH

OTHER BOOKS BY JOHN MICHAEL PRIEST

Published by
White Mane Publishing Company, Inc.

NOWHERE TO RUN
The Wilderness, May 4th & 5th, 1864
Volume I
336 pp • HC • $29.95

ANTIETAM
The Soldiers' Battle
A Military Book Club Selection
463 pp • HC • $34.95

BEFORE ANTIETAM
The Battle for South Mountain
A Military Book Club Selection
456 pp • HC • $34.95

CAPTAIN JAMES WREN'S DIARY
From New Bern to Fredericksburg
Edited by John Michael Priest et al.
148 pp • HC • $24.95

JOHN T. MCMAHON'S DIARY OF THE 136TH NEW YORK, 1861–1864
148 pp • HC • $24.95

ANTIETAM: THE SOLDIERS' BATTLEFIELD
A Self-Guided Mini-Tour
80 pp • SC • $6.95

STEPHEN ELLIOTT WELCH OF THE HAMPTON LEGION
Civil War Heritage Series
107 PP • SC • $12.00

VICTORY WITHOUT TRIUMPH

The Wilderness, May 6th & 7th, 1864

Volume II

ॐ

JOHN MICHAEL PRIEST

 White Mane Publishing Company, Inc.

This White Mane Publishing Company, Inc. publication
was printed by
Beidel Printing House, Inc.
63 West Burd Street
Shippensburg, PA 17257 USA

In respect for the scholarship contained herein, the acid-free paper used in this book meets the guidelines for permanence and durability of the Committee on Production Guidelines for Book Longevity of the Council on Library Resources.

For a complete list of available publications
please write
White Mane Publishing Company, Inc.
P.O. Box 152
Shippensburg, PA 17257 USA

Library of Congress Cataloging-in-Publication Data

Priest, John M., 1949.
    Victory without triumph : the Wilderness, May 6th & 7th, 1864 /
John Michael Priest.
        p.   cm.
    "Volume II."
    Continues: Nowhere to run : the Wilderness, May 4th & 5th, 1864.
    Includes bibliographical references (p.   ) and index.
    ISBN 1-57249-009-8 (alk. paper)
    1. Wilderness, Battle of the, Va., 1864.   I. Priest, John M.,
    1949–   Nowhere to run.   II. Title.
    E476.52.P77   1996
    973.7'36--dc20   96-30236
                                                                  CIP

PRINTED IN THE UNITED STATES OF AMERICA

To the Memory

of the Soldiers of

the Army of the Potomac

and

the Army of Northern Virginia

and

to their descendants this volume

is humbly dedicated.

ᔍABLE OF CONTENTS

LIST OF MAPS

࿎

LIST OF PHOTOGRAPHS

𝒵❧

ACKNOWLEDGMENTS

My special thanks go out to the following individuals and institutions for their cooperation in making this book possible.

Mr. Donald Pfanz, historian at Fredericksburg and Spotsylvania National Battlefield Park, read the first four chapters of the manuscript. His comments and advice were taken to heart. Mr. Pfanz also took my son and me on our first walking tour of the Wilderness. What a tremendous experience!

Mr. Paul Chiles, historian at Antietam National Battlefield, let me wade through the park's microfilm copies of *The National Tribune* and gave me some valuable information on artillery projectiles.

Mr. Ted Alexander, historian at Antietam National Battlefield, generously opened the park's library for my research.

Dr. Richard Sommers and his staff in the manuscripts department at the United States Army Military History Institute (USAMHI) were helpful in supplying me with manuscript material. Dr. Sommers also offered some valuable advice on verifying information which I had some questions about and also guided me to the *Grand Army Scout and Soldiers' Mail* where I found two excellent accounts about the Wilderness.

Mr. Mike Winey and Mr. Randy Hackenburg, photograph division at USAMHI, once again opened their archives for my use. Most of the pictures in this book came from the collection at USAMHI.

Mr. Bryce Suderow generously provided me with his primary material on the cavalry in the Wilderness and lent me a copy of his monograph of the cavalry action there. He also supplied nominal lists of the Federal cavalry's casualties, with their returns for the month of April 1864, and with the newspaper accounts for Confederate casualties.

Mr. John Horn shared his information on the 12th Virginia and Mahone's brigade and on Longstreet's wounding.

I would particularly like to thank Mr. and Mrs. G. B. Catlett of Spotsylvania, Virginia, who showed Mr. Suderow and me where the clash between Stuart and Custer occurred. They also pointed out locations of the Trigg, Stephens, and Rowe farms.

Mr. Wilmer D. Martin graciously gave me permission to use the diary of Thomas Alfred Martin, 38th North Carolina. Marjory G. Blubaugh granted me the use of the William Shaw Stewart reminiscences. Mr. Robert Trout, recognized expert on J. E. B. Stuart, provided information on Alexander Boteler. I am very grateful to all of them.

As always, the staffs of the Special Collections Department at Duke University and the Southern Historical Collections at the University of North Carolina at Chapel Hill went out of their way to make my visits there comfortable and profitable. Their friendly cooperation has always made my days spent with them pleasant.

The following institutions have also provided me with primary documents: Alabama State Archives, Georgia Department of Archives and History, Hampden-Sydney Library, Library of Congress, Michigan State University Press, the Museum of the Confederacy, the University of Georgia, the University of South Carolina, the University of Virginia, the Virginia Historical Society, Virginia Military Institute, and the Virginia State Archives.

Mr. James Kehoe, Antietam Gallery, Sharpsburg, Maryland, generously allowed me to work for him and write at the same time. Friends and employers like him are very rare indeed.

My longtime friend and colleague, William "Bill" Hilton loaned me any book which he had in his personal library as he had done for my earlier battle books. (Bill passed away on August 8, 1993.)

My wife and children deserve particular thanks for forfeiting my time with them so that I could do the research and writing necessary for the completion of this book. The Lord has blessed me more than abundantly with the fine family which He has given me.

INTRODUCTORY REMARKS

Early in 1864 Lieutenant General Ulysses S. Grant, commanding the United States armies, prepared to launch an all out offensive against the Confederate armies. Major General William T. Sherman's Union army in Tennessee was to leave Chattanooga and sweep into Georgia, intent upon destroying General Joseph Johnston's Army of Tennessee before taking Atlanta. That would cut off troop movement and supply shipment intended to support the Confederate forces in Virginia and in the deep South. General Nathaniel Banks, commanding the Department of the Gulf, was to move north and besiege Mobile, Alabama. General Franz Sigel was to move his Federal army through the Shenandoah Valley of Virginia to destroy or capture Robert E. Lee's major base of supply for his Army of Northern Virginia. Farther to the east, Major General Benjamin Butler and his Army of the James were to advance up the James River and invest Richmond and Petersburg. While those movements were occurring, Ulysses S. Grant, traveling with Major General George G. Meade, would take the bloodied Army of the Potomac across the Rapidan River along the Army of Northern Virginia's eastern flank in an effort to keep Robert E. Lee away from Richmond. By positioning the Army of the Potomac between the Confederates and the east coast of Virginia, Grant could maintain a steady supply of materials moving to his army and keep Lee boxed in and on the offensive. That move across the Rapidan began the Overland Campaign—a series of sanguinary battles which would last from the first skirmish on May 4, 1864, through June 12, 1864. The names of the Wilderness, Spotsylvania Court House, and Cold Harbor conjure up bitter memories of relentless combat and butchery similar to those of World War I and rightfully so.

I have reconstructed the fighting in the Wilderness (May 4–7, 1864) from the perspective of the front line soldiers. This book is not about grand strategies or generals. For that type of study I would highly recommend Edward Steere, *The Wilderness Campaign* (Stackpole: 1960). Nevertheless, I believe that it is necessary to explain both how the book is organized and the basic strategies involved in the fighting which took place upon this battlefield. The book is written in chronological order so that the reader will see the battle unfolding as it occurred. Initially this means that the various scenes of the opening actions will switch from one location to the next within each chapter until the different skirmishes develop into full scale actions in their own right. Once the several independent battles erupt they are then followed through until their conclusion.

Battles were seldom fought as neatly as the generals' after action reports tended to report them. I am convinced that Grant had no grand strategy for the Wilderness but that Robert E. Lee precipitated the action and that Grant's strategy was to fend Lee off, then get out of that terrible battleground. I further contend that Grant did not have a very good tactical grasp of the combat situation at the front lines and that he let his generals fight it out on their own.

The Federal cavalry crossed the Rapidan River on May 4 and threw out a protective screen from Chancellorsville to Piney Branch Church, from Todd's Tavern to Payte's Corner and from the Orange Turnpike to Parker's Store on the Orange Plank Road. On May 5, 1864, the Federal army's headquarters ignored the reports from the V Corps' pickets in Saunders Field and started to flank the V Corps toward Parker's Store in an attempt to get past the Wilderness. When it became evident that a large part of the Army of Northern Virginia might be opposite Saunders Field, Grant suspended the flank movement and ordered a general attack along the line from Saunders Field to the Higgerson farm. The formation of the troops suggests that Grant possibly thought that he could envelop Lee's army with the V Corps. Army headquarters ignored reports from the extreme left of the V Corps at Chewning's that there was heavy cavalry action at Parker's Store which threatened the army's southern flank.

While the V Corps attempted to bag the Confederates on the northern end of the field, Getty's division of the VI Corps moved south on the Germanna Plank Road to the Brock Road, intending to support what appeared to be a minor cavalry skirmish at Parker's Store. That division encountered the advance units of A. P. Hill's Corps and became bogged down in a serious action at the Brock Road-Plank Road intersection. The Confederates had flanked the Army of the Potomac. That forced Grant to recall the II Corps which had already reached Todd's Tavern, a few miles south of Getty's division, and send them north to hold back Hill. At the same time, Confederate cavalry successfully harassed the extreme Federal left at

Alsop's Gate and along the Catharpin Road west of Todd's Tavern, forcing Grant to watch his line to the south constantly. Once Grant developed Lee's army, he decided to hammer it out in the Wilderness. This is not a battle known for farsighted planning and brilliant strategy. It was a no-hold-barred Western tussle on a scale of which the armies in the East had never seen before. Grant had men and munitions to waste. Lee did not. If there was a grand scheme behind the Wilderness and the battles which followed, it was one of attrition.

INTRODUCTION

During the predawn hours of May 6, the Army of the Potomac's II, V, VI, and IX Corps prepared for Lieutenant General Ulysses S. Grant's grand assault. The Wilderness was no place to attempt a coordinated frontal attack. Its rough, heavily wooded, and swampy ground would disrupt formations, disorient officers, and create general confusion as it had during the previous day. Grant was not facing the exhausted, underfed, undermanned, and threadbare Confederate army which Major General George B. McClellan had fought during the Maryland Campaign of 1862. The 1864 army was better fed and better equipped than that Army of Northern Virginia. Like McClellan, Grant had a much larger army than Lee, but the past had already shown that size was not as important as maneuverability and the ability to adapt tactics to fit the topography of the battlefield. Grant, however, seemed determined to beat the Confederates into submission. The Army of the Potomac could afford to absorb larger numbers of casualties than the Army of Northern Virginia because it could pull upon a tremendous reservoir of reserves which the Confederates could not muster. Combat attrition, by itself, would accomplish as much as physical victories upon the field. What distinguished Grant from other Federal commanders was that he could distance himself from the human costs of war and was willing to sustain losses which would have made his predecessors resign. He brought to the war the frontier practice of total, unrelenting warfare.

1

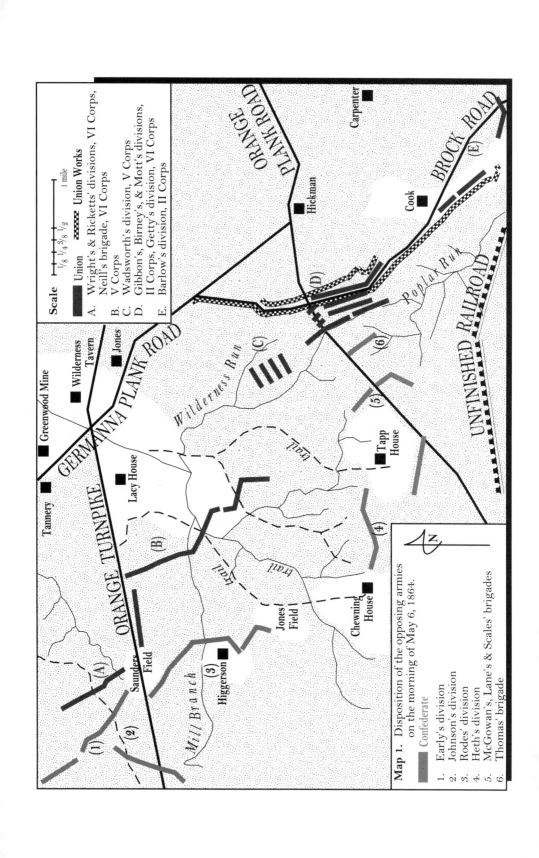

Map 1. Disposition of the opposing armies on the morning of May 6, 1864.

Scale

1/8 1/4 3/8 1/2   1 mile

▬ Union

▨ Union Works

A. Wright's & Ricketts' divisions, VI Corps,
    Neill's brigade, VI Corps
B. V Corps
C. Wadsworth's division, V Corps
D. Gibbon's, Birney's, & Mott's divisions,
    II Corps, Getty's division, VI Corps
E. Barlow's division, II Corps

Confederate

1. Early's division
2. Johnson's division
3. Rodes' division
4. Heth's division
5. McGowan's, Lane's & Scales' brigades
6. Thomas' brigade

Carpenter

Cook

Hickman

ORANGE PLANK ROAD

BROCK ROAD

(E)

(D)

Poplar Run

UNFINISHED RAILROAD

(6)

(5)

(C)

Tapp House

Wilderness Run

Trail

trail

Greenwood Mine

Wilderness Tavern

Jones

Tannery

GERMANNA PLANK ROAD

Lacy House

ORANGE TURNPIKE

(B)

Rail

Rail

trail

Jones Field

Chewning House

Higgerson

Saunders Field

Mill Branch

(A)

(1)

(2)

(3)

(4)

N

THE DISPOSITION OF THE OPPOSING ARMIES

The II Corps occupied the northern and the southern flanks of the Plank Road on the high ground east of and parallel to Wilderness Run and Poplar Run. Brigadier General George W. Getty's division of the VI Corps, less Brigadier General Thomas H. Neill's brigade, supported Major General Winfield Scott Hancock's II Corps along the Brock Road intersection. Brigadier General Horatio G. Wright's VI Corps division with Neill's brigade secured the Federal right wing on a northwesterly unentrenched line parallel to the swampy creek bottom which fed into the center of Saunders Field. Major General Ambrose Burnside's IX Corps, having arrived upon the Federal right and rear during May 5, occupied the ground around the ruins of the Chancellor House and the Widow Willis' farmstead along Flat Run Road. Brigadier General James S. Wadsworth's division of the V Corps, stalled by the thick underbrush in the darkness the day before, remained motionless along Wilderness Run over one half a mile north of the Plank Road.

The Army of Northern Virginia, as in so many previous battles, had held its own on the defensive without yielding any appreciable amount of ground. Rather, by wresting the Chewning and Higgerson farms, and Jones' abandoned field from the Federals, it established a nearly continuous line of log breastworks from a point north of the Orange Turnpike south to the Orange Plank Road near the Tapp farm. Major Generals Jubal Early's and Edward Johnson's divisions (Lieutenant General Richard S. Ewell's Corps) straddled the Turnpike east of the Culpeper Mine Road intersection. Major General Robert E. Rodes' division (Ewell's Corps) held the ground in the vicinity of Higgerson's and Mill Branch. Major Generals Henry Heth's and Cadmus M. Wilcox's divisions of Lieutenant General Ambrose P. Hill's Corps anchored the Confederate right east of the Widow Tapp's along both sides of the Plank Road.

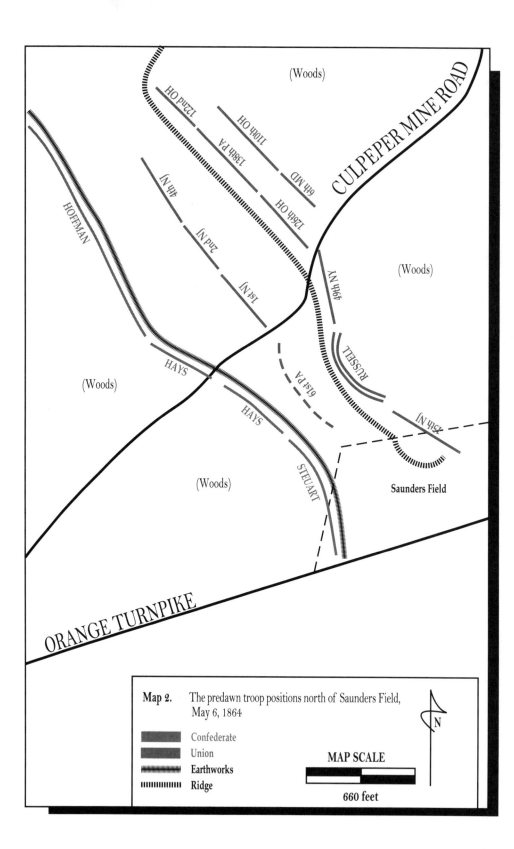

(Woods)

CULPEPER MINE ROAD

122nd OH

138th PA

110th OH

6th MD

126th OH

4th NJ

2nd NJ

1st NJ

49th NY

HOFFMAN

RUSSELL

HAYS

61st PA

(Woods)

45th NJ

(Woods)

HAYS

STEUART

(Woods)

Saunders Field

ORANGE TURNPIKE

Map 2. The predawn troop positions north of Saunders Field, May 6, 1864

N

Confederate
Union
Earthworks
Ridge

MAP SCALE

660 feet

CHAPTER ONE

"I don't believe I ever saw troops behave so badly."

MAY 6, 1864 – BEFORE DAWN

THE SITUATION IN THE WOODS NORTH OF SAUNDERS FIELD
(2.0 miles west of Wilderness Tavern)

Colonel John S. Hoffman (31st Virginia), who took over Brigadier General John Pegram's brigade after the general was wounded during the previous evening, was not considered a military man by his men. Private William W. Smith (Company C, 49th Virginia) said he was "a dull and slow man, unsuited to command such a brigade."[1] Genius was not required, however, to fight a defensive battle in the dense woods of the Wilderness. Hoffman's regiments were entrenched with a field of fire cleared for fifty yards beyond the works. All they had to do was wait for the Northerners to attack them.

Out on the picket posts, Captain Samuel Buck (Company H, 13th Virginia) continued pacing from one end of his line to another. He was exhausted, and distraught, having spent the entire night so close to the Yankee skirmishers that he could distinctly hear them talking to one another. Throughout the evening, he had listened to his brigade entrench and had heard the stretcher parties struggling through the brush with the wounded. The haunting calls of the whippoorwills still echoed in his head. He wanted to return to the regiment where it was safer.

Hoffman, "as brave a man as could be, but no officer," had left him on the line since dark the day before. Captain R. N. Wilson, brigade assistant adjutant general, who was supposed to relieve him at 10:00 P.M., never showed up. Buck walked the posts all night long to keep himself awake more than to superintend his men. Shortly before 4:30 A.M. Wilson finally brought the relief officer out and Buck walked back to his company, glad to be away from such a dangerous position. He later wrote, "I have seen a whole line of battle open fire and keep it up for fifteen minutes, with no enemy within half a mile of them, the only party suffering being their own skirmishers."[2] At the moment he wanted breakfast.

Hoffman's brigade no longer remained on the extreme flank of the Army of Northern Virginia. Shortly after midnight, Brigadier General John B. Gordon's Georgians filed through the woods and went into line on its left. Brigadier General Harry T. Hays' Louisianians and the rest of Early's division still secured the line to the south.[3] Unlike the Federals, the Confederates were securely dug in.

Gordon's men, having robbed their Federal prisoners and the dead during the previous day's fighting, were well provisioned. Squatting down behind the security of their breastworks, they started breakfast fires and feasted upon hard crackers, salt pork and real coffee, sweetened with sugar.[4] While they ate, two guns from Colonel Thomas H. Carter's Virginia battalion were being dragged over a recently cut trail to an open knoll to the brigade's left rear.[5]

UNION LINES

The Federal position in the woods north of Saunders Field remained virtually unchanged throughout the evening of May 5 into the morning of May 6. At 1:00 A.M. Second Lieutenant Joseph M. Waker (Company C, 14th New Jersey) informed Brigadier General William H. Morris, whose brigade was bivouacking in the woods south of the Orange Turnpike, that he was to support Colonel Emory Upton's brigade in an assault against the Confederate position north of the field. At 4:30 A.M. Morris filed his brigade across the pike into the woods on the north side. The narrow, swampy front forced him to deploy his regiments behind Brigadier General Joseph J. Bartlett's brigade, which lay in two lines along the eastern side of Saunders Field.[6] Skirmishers crawled into the brush along its edge. The 151st New York, with its left flank on the Orange Turnpike, went prone in the woods. The remaining four regiments lay down in two more lines behind the New Yorkers.[7] The 15th New Jersey, with Upton's brigade in support, still held the exposed knoll in the northern part of the field.[8] Brigadier General David A. Russell's brigade, in two lines, extended the line to the north along the ridge overlooking the swale which ran into the field. Colonel Hugh Brown's New Jersey Brigade, with Brigadier Generals Thomas Neill's and Truman Seymour's regiments, also on constricted fronts, finished out the formation. Having been issued orders for a grand assault at 5:00 A.M., none of the regiments had entrenched.[9]

THE SKIRMISH LINE OF NEILL'S BRIGADE
(100 yards west of the VI Corps' line)[10]

The 61st Pennsylvania spent a horrible night in the swampy bottom land which separated the two armies. Having tolerated sporadic sniping throughout the night as search parties stumbled through the tangled undergrowth looking for casualties, the men did not care to see the sun rise, knowing that they were going to face a battle before which the one of the day before would pale. All night they listened apprehensively to the Confederates cutting down trees and constructing log works. The soldiers refilled their cartridge boxes and cleaned their weapons. Brush fires flared and crackled all along the line. The smoke stung their eyes and restricted the pickets' lines of sight.[11]

To the north, Seymour's brigade prepared to execute the general orders to engage the Confederates at first light. He arranged his regiments in two lines. The first line (north to south) consisted of the 122nd Ohio, 138th Pennsylvania, and 126th Ohio. The 110th Ohio and the 6th Maryland fell in ten paces behind the 138th and the 126th. The sounds of the Confederates felling trees well beyond the brigade's right front alarmed Colonels William H. Ball (122nd Ohio) and Matthew R. McClennan (138th Pennsylvania). They repeatedly advised Seymour of the urgency of protecting the brigade's northern flank but to no avail.[12] First Sergeant Grayson Eichelberger (Company D, 6th Maryland) crawled into his position on the right front of his company line and assumed the place of First Lieutenant Charles A. Damuth, who had been wounded the day before. He was exhausted to the point of distraction, having spent the last eight hours sitting with his mortally wounded friend, Color Sergeant Jason L. Damuth. Eichelberger had cradled Damuth's head in his lap until 3:00 A.M. and had watched him die in terrible pain. As he lay in the line, Eichelberger consoled himself with the knowledge that his comrade had died with a saving knowledge of Jesus Christ.[13]

4:30 A.M. TO 5:00 A.M.[14]

HOFFMAN'S VIRGINIA BRIGADE
(300 yards west of Seymour's Northern brigade)

Before the first rays of daylight First Lieutenant Robert D. Funkhouser (Company D), under orders from Brigadier General Jubal Early to clear a road for artillery, equipped fourteen of his men from the 49th Virginia with axes and disappeared into the woods on the ridge paralleling Hoffman's line.[15] While they whacked into the trees, Captain Samuel Buck (Company H, 13th Virginia) was sitting next to his breakfast fire of crackling twigs, waiting for his tin cup of coffee to heat up. Without warning, his pickets opened fire. The Yankees quickly responded. Bullets zipped over the headlogs and slapped into the trees behind the line. When the pickets came crashing through the woods, heading for the works, Buck knew that it was not a false alarm. In seconds the men were up and ready to repel the impending attack. He swore that the Yankees were sending no less than five lines against his regiment.[16]

The attack caught Funkhouser and his men on higher ground. Without cover, they made easy targets. The enlisted men suffered 100 percent casualties before they scattered. Private Morgan Snapp (Company D) came out of the woods with two flesh wounds. Gasping for breath, the startled Funkhouser reported to Early and asked if the general wanted him to get another detail together and return to the work. "No, the site is untenable," Early replied. "The artillerymen and horses would all be killed before they could get into position even if it were possible for you to cut the road, and I don't think it is. Report to your company for duty."[17] Dodging the bullets that swarmed past his ears like angered bees, Funkhouser returned to his men who did not understand how he had survived the ordeal.[18]

The skirmishing spread rapidly to the south along the front of the VI Corps. In the flurry of small arms fire, a Confederate sharpshooter in a tree above the 15th New Jersey sent a ball tearing through both thighs of Captain Ellis Hamilton (Company F) who was standing in the open along the picket line.[19] The 61st Pennsylvania, in front of Hays' Louisianians, joined in the melee, firing their weapons as fast as they could. The badly depleted Southern brigade responded fitfully. Seymour's skirmishers added to the din with persistent rifle fire.[20]

For half an hour, the fighting consisted mostly of skirmishers taking pot shots at one another but it was heavy enough to keep the Federals from implementing their 5:00 A.M. assault.[21] By then, Carter's two guns on Gordon's flank had joined the fray.[22] For the next two hours, they pounded the VI Corps with terrible accuracy.

NORTH OF THE PLANK ROAD
MCGOWAN'S SOUTH CAROLINA BRIGADE
(2.75 miles southeast of Saunders Field)

Brigadier General Samuel McGowan straightened his brigade line during the predawn hours by pulling his men back from Thomas' brigade. About one quarter of a mile to the west, they went into position behind a low line of makeshift earthworks which some troops had thrown together during the night. The works paralleled the western bank of another branch of Wilderness Run and continued intermittently south across the pike into a line established by Brigadier General Alfred M. Scales' brigade. McGowan sent his brigade sharpshooters two hundred yards beyond the creek as skirmishers.[23] More than eight hundred yards and another creek bottom lay between the brigade and Lieutenant Colonel William T. Poague's sixteen guns on the Widow Tapp's plateau.[24]

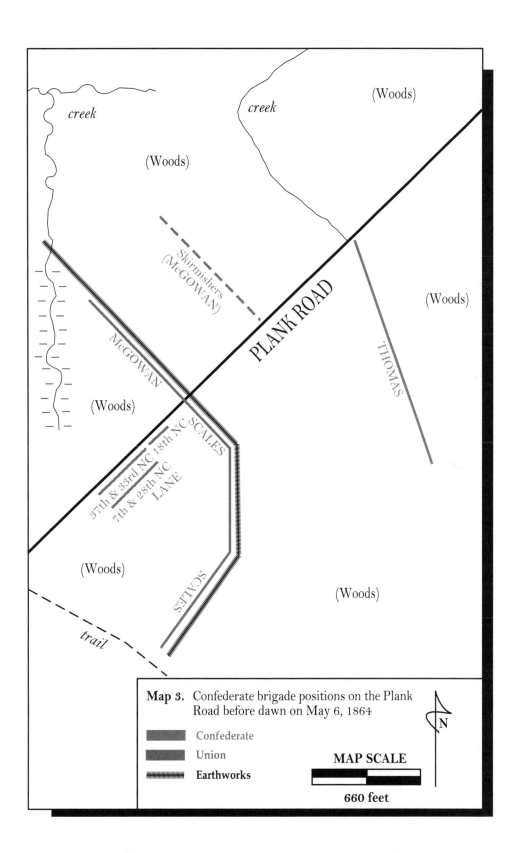

(Woods)

creek

creek

(Woods)

(Woods)

Skirmishers
(McGOWAN)

PLANK ROAD

McGOWAN

(Woods)

THOMAS

(Woods)

SCALES

37th & 33rd NC 18th NC

7th & 28th NC
LANE

(Woods)

SCALES

(Woods)

trail

Map 3. Confederate brigade positions on the Plank
Road before dawn on May 6, 1864

N

Confederate

Union

Earthworks

MAP SCALE

660 feet

SOUTH OF THE PLANK ROAD
THOMAS' BRIGADE

In retiring west, McGowan left Brigadier General Edward L. Thomas' flank hanging in the air about three hundred fifty yards west of Poplar Run. Private George W. Hall (Company G, 14th Georgia) was not alert that morning. As the cook for his mess, he had spent most of the night preparing the day's rations. He then spent an hour in deep prayer and meditation. "I put my whole trust in him," he jotted in his diary, "and I believe He will Shield, guard and protect me from all harm and I believe He will be with me on the field of Battle. Trust in God." When daylight broke "fair and warm" he had no idea just how much he would need his Lord that day.[25]

Few of the Confederate officers along the Plank Road expected any difficulty that morning. The lackadaisical state of affairs alarmed Poague who was riding down to the pike with a detachment to retrieve the gun which the North Carolinians had dragged in the day before. Most of the men were still sleeping in the double ranks of their former battle lines. One brigade had stacked its rifles in the pike. Two regiments had arranged theirs at acute and right angles to the road. Others had stacked their arms without respect to any particular order throughout the woods and brush to the south. The colonel asked an officer what the apparent unpreparedness meant only to be told in a very indifferent tone that the troops expected to be relieved at any minute. When Poague asked the whereabouts of the Federals, the officer lazily drawled that he supposed they were in the woods somewhere to the east. The colonel felt very uneasy about the situation but shrugged it off. He and his men calmly hitched up their gun and rolled back toward the Widow Tapp's.[26]

SCALES' BRIGADE

Scales' North Carolina brigade had no serious thought of entrenching until the first rays of sunlight burst into the men's faces that morning. Private Thomas A. Martin (Company B, 38th North Carolina) intended to share the Yankee eggs which he had picked up the evening before with his two brothers, John and Mack. Colonel John Ashford, however, dashed those hopes when he set the regiment to work building breastworks. The North Carolinians did not overexert themselves. They dragged in rotten logs and fallen tree branches and interlaced them into a dilapidated worm line which barely reached waist height. Scales' men had their works up before 5:00 A.M. and sat behind them taking a breather, intent upon enjoying their breakfasts.[27] A little to the right, First Lieutenant George H. Mills (Company G, 16th North Carolina) anxiously waited for the water fetching detachment, which he had sent out before daylight, to return to the company with the soldiers' canteens.[28] First Lieutenant Rowland S. Williams (Company I, 13th North Carolina) mistakenly thought that Brigadier General James H. Lane's North Carolina brigade was in front of their works.[29]

Major General Cadmus Wilcox, C.S.A.

His failure to thoroughly reorganize his division on the night of May 5, nearly cost the Army of Northern Virginia the battle on May 6.

Massachusetts Commandery; MOLLUS, USAMHI

LANE'S BRIGADE

Lane's North Carolina regiments, instead of being to Scales' front, had been ordered by Major General Cadmus M. Wilcox to bivouac behind Scales' line. For some unexplainable reason the regiments bedded down in formation alongside the Plank Road facing north, rather than east toward the Federal lines. The 18th North Carolina was at the head of the formation, followed to the west by the 33rd North Carolina, then the 37th North Carolina. The battered 7th North Carolina and the 28th North Carolina were in line somewhere near the rest of the command.[30]

WADSWORTH'S DIVISION (V CORPS)

Brigadier General James S. Wadsworth's troops patiently remained in the low ground east of Wilderness Run, awaiting the arrival of Captain Robert Monteith from Lacy's farm with the division's pack mules. The general erroneously believed that the men had shot away too much ammunition during May 5 to continue the action. Monteith, however, while attempting to return to the division with the command's 20,000 rounds of ammunition, was contending not only with ten cantankerous army mules, but with the impressive gaggle of staff officers and the division's servants who were following him. They, in turn, stumbled into the Wilderness with an irksome string of spare horses and pack mules. It did not take long for the weary captain to lose his way in the dense pines below Lacy's. At one point, the sounds of voices and the dancing glimmer of camp fires lured Monteith ahead of his "command" to the edge of a small clearing. Halting his pack train, he dismounted a short distance inside the wood line and reconnoitered the situation. Instead of moving southwest he had inadvertently turned west and had walked into a Confederate outpost near the Higgerson place. Retracing his steps to the base of Lacy's plateau, he reentered the Wilderness and piloted himself forward from picket post to picket post until about 3:00 A.M., when he found the division. He estimated it took about an hour to replenish the men's cartridge boxes.[31]

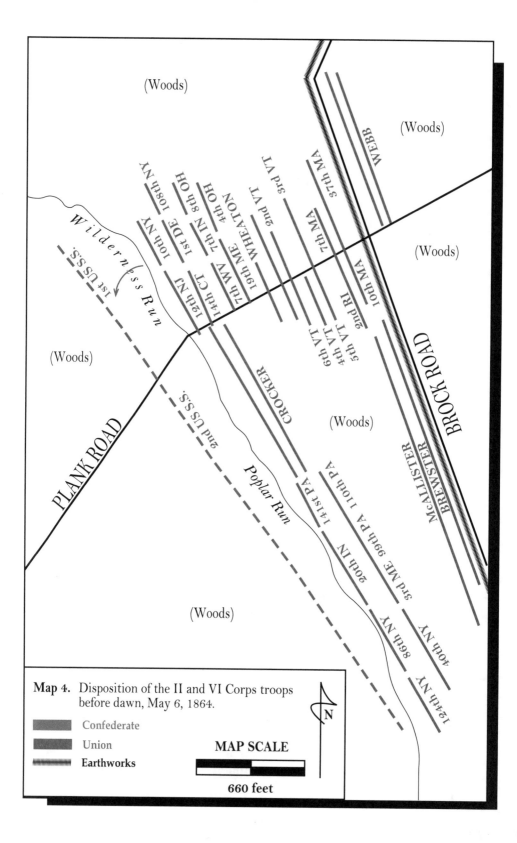

Map 4. Disposition of the II and VI Corps troops before dawn, May 6, 1864.

Confederate
Union
Earthworks

MAP SCALE

660 feet

N

(Woods)

(Woods)

(Woods)

(Woods)

(Woods)

(Woods)

Wilderness Run

Poplar Run

PLANK ROAD

BROCK ROAD

1st U.S.S.

2nd U.S.S.

108th NY
10th NY
1st DE
8th OH
7th IN
4th OH
12th NJ
14th CT
7th WV
7th ME
19th ME
WHEATON
2nd VT
3rd VT
37th MA
7th MA
10th MA
2nd RI
5th VT
4th VT
6th VT
CROCKER
141st PA
110th PA
99th PA
20th IN
3rd ME
86th NY
40th NY
124th NY
McALLISTER
BREWSTER
WEBB

5:00 A.M. TO 6:30 A.M.

THE BROCK ROAD INTERSECTION
CARROLL'S BRIGADE (II CORPS)
(North of the Plank Road)

Around 4:00 A.M. shrill bird calls awakened First Lieutenant Thomas F. Galwey (Company B, 8th Ohio) with a start. Shortly thereafter, occasional shots reverberated along the picket line west of the regiment's bivouac until they blended into a steady patter. Colonel Franklin Sawyer (8th Ohio) forbade the men to light fires for breakfasts. Therefore, Galwey and several of his comrades slipped behind the lines and quietly boiled their coffee in a hole in the ground.[32] In the next line to the west, the officers of the 14th Connecticut cautiously awakened their men.[33] First Sergeant Elnathan B. Tyler (Company B, 14th Connecticut) woke up sore and stiff, with his weapon still by his side. The cold night had left him chilled. He regretted having thrown away his blanket the day before. Most of the men could finish their hard crackers and coffee. The officers were getting them on their feet in preparation for the advance.[34] While the men were shaking out their blankets, the 4th Ohio, which had been stuck at Chancellorsville with the brigade's wagons, came trotting down the Brock Road and fell in on the right rear of the brigade's third line.[35]

At 5:00 A.M., the II Corps' staff officers galloped up and down the narrow road, getting Brigadier General John Gibbon's division to its feet.[36] Colonel Samuel Carroll's brigade formed in three lines. The 12th New Jersey placed its left against the Plank Road with the 10th New York to its right. The 14th Connecticut covered the Jerseymen with 1st Delaware, then the 108th New York, extending the line to the north. The 7th West Virginia, 14th Indiana, and the 8th Ohio completed the third line.[37] Behind them stood the 19th Maine with the 4th Ohio to its right. (Sometime during the night Gibbon had taken the 19th Maine regiment [458 effectives] from Brigadier General Alexander Webb's brigade.) Carroll then ordered the regiment to stay where it was and never issued any further instructions for its deployment. The remaining seven regiments of Webb's brigade went into position somewhere in the vicinity of the Brock Road south of the Plank Road intersection. Without the Maine regiment Webb mustered approximately 1,900 men.

Brigadier General Joshua T. Owen's brigade (Gibbon's division) occupied a line in the Brock Road which extended south from the intersection for about one thousand three hundred fifty feet. His five regiments had no idea about how Gibbon's command had formed for battle. From their position in the works along the Brock Road the men could see no movement beyond the fifty yards wide slashing which separated them from the woods.[38]

Brigadier General George W. Getty's Second Division of the VI Corps straddled the Plank Road between Carroll's and Owen's brigades. Brigadier General Frank Wheaton's five regiments formed in two lines across the pike. (Getty had no contact whatsoever with Owen.) Wheaton's men, however, could see the left flanks of Carroll's three brigades in place along the road a very short distance in front of them.[39] Colonel Lewis A. Grant's brigade fell in on both sides of the road not too far behind Wheaton's men. The 2nd and the 6th Vermont regiments took their places in the front of the brigade (north to south) with the Plank Road separating them. The 4th Vermont covered the 6th Vermont. The 5th Vermont and the 3rd Vermont finished out the third line to the south and the north of the road, respectively. The severe fighting of May 5 had exhausted the enlisted men. The 2nd Vermont came out of the fighting with 63 percent of its original strength. The 4th Vermont lost 40 percent and the 5th Vermont counted 38 percent casualties. The remaining two regiments suffered nearly as heavily.

In the predawn shadows Private Wilbur Fisk (Company E, 2nd Vermont) studied the men around him and noticed how strained and pale their faces seemed. Two days of insufficient sleep and a day of fighting, the likes of which those veteran regiments had never before experienced, had left most of the men too drained to function properly. He dreaded the horror that awaited him.[40]

His brigade commander, Colonel Lewis A. Grant, felt the same way. The order to advance that morning sounded like his death warrant. He could not shake off the feeling that he was going to die. He gave his pocket book to his manservant and his watch to another man with instructions to both on how he wanted them to dispose of his belongings after he perished. He also told them how to look after his horses.[41] The strain affected his concentration. When he placed his brigade upon the field along the Plank Road, he could only remember putting the regiments in two lines.[42]

Brigadier General Henry L. Eustis' brigade went into column behind Grant's Vermonters. The 7th Massachusetts, with the 37th Massachusetts in support, went into line north of the road. The 2nd Rhode Island went into line behind the 10th Massachusetts directly across from them.[43]

Brigadier General Hobart Ward's brigade (Major General David B. Birney's division) had spent an uncomfortable night along Poplar Run, a short distance southwest of Wheaton's brigade. The buglers sounded Reveille along the creek the same as if they had been in a rear line staging area. Coffee fires were soon crackling and snapping along the regimental lines with the smoke lazily ascending into the tree tops above the soldiers' heads. Sergeant Wyman White (Company F, 2nd U.S. Sharpshooters) drank his hot coffee much as he always had without feeling any particular apprehension for the upcoming day.[44] Private Ashbury F. Haynes (Company F, 3rd Maine) awakened in the cool morning air only to discover that his comfortable "log" of the evening before was a stiffened corpse.[45]

Shortly before daylight Colonel John S. Crocker, having assumed command of Brigadier General Alexander Hays' brigade, shoved his men into line on the right of Ward's regiments and forced Ward's command to side-step to the south.[46] Crocker's nine regiments went into formation in two lines very near to the same spot along Poplar Run where they had fought so hard on May 5.[47]

On the north side of the road, the 1st U.S. Sharpshooters, having deployed to the front during the night on the north side of the Plank Road, started the assault in extended order as skirmishers. Corpses, shattered trees, and crushed tanglefoot, but no wounded men, staggered the Berdans' push. (Captain C. A. Stevens assumed that rescue parties had already ventured out in the dark with candles and retrieved those deemed worth saving.)[48]

Farther to the left Brigadier General Hobart Ward dispatched the 2nd U.S. Sharpshooters at the regulation intervals prescribed for skirmishers across the front of Crocker's and his brigades. Their right flank extended to the Plank Road to screen the brigade's advance.[49] The 141st Pennsylvania formed the right of the first line. The 20th Indiana, 86th New York, and the 124th New York, respectively, finished out the formation to the left.[50] The 40th New York held down the left of the second line, with the 3rd Maine, 99th Pennsylvania and the 110th Pennsylvania regiments continuing the formation to the left of Crocker's line.[51]

Brigadier General Hobart Ward, U.S.A.
His II Corps brigade fought very well throughout the day on May 6, but in the afternoon, Ward deserted his troops along the Brock Road.

Massachusetts Commandery;
MOLLUS, USAMHI

Brigadier General Gershom Mott's two brigade division formed in the woods behind Ward and Crocker. Colonel William R. Brewster's brigade fell in line just west of the Brock Road earthworks. Colonel Robert McAllister's eight New Jersey, Massachusetts and Pennsylvania regiments occupied the line to his front. From his position, McAllister could not see Ward's brigade.[52]

Major General Winfield Scott Hancock, commanding the II Corps, had massed an estimated 22,000 men in an area approximately four thousand two hundred feet wide and one thousand two hundred feet in depth.[53] Because of the density of the woods and the distance between the troops many of the individual commands did not have visual contact with the units in front of them. U. S. Grant's grand assault did not get off to an impressive start. The general had not personally inspected the ground to check the feasibility of a massive frontal attack. He left the details of the execution of his plans to his corps commanders, who in turn, allowed their division commanders to implement their instructions. The generals commanding the divisions, because of their limited view of the terrain, relinquished their command control to their brigadier generals who, because of the restricted visibility of the Wilderness, could not exercise adequate command control over their regimental lines. The Federal army could not properly function as a cohesive mass unless it maintained its individual regimental formations. Unlike the Confederates, who had adapted to fighting in extended order—one man every six feet—and who could fight independently with different regiments and brigades, the average Federal enlisted man was not trained to think and function independently. Most of the regimental and general officers had not learned to operate that way either. Maneuvering so many men in lines which ranged from eight hundred to three thousand three hundred feet long was easier to carry out in theory than to execute in the field.[54] From the onset, the dense undergrowth disrupted regimental lines.[55] The advance lurched and surged forward.

Between the two branches of Wilderness Run, Brigadier General James S. Wadsworth's division of the V Corps stumbled toward the right flanks of the II and the VI Corps as they inched west along the Plank Road. The 95th New York and a few companies of the 147th New York dodged through the trees north of the road as skirmishers.[56] The remaining four regiments from Brigadier General James Rice's brigade led the division in column of brigades. Colonel Roy Stone's Pennsylvania brigade came next in the column, then Brigadier General Henry Baxter's brigade, followed by Brigadier General Lysander Cutler's Westerners and New Yorkers.[57]

Wadsworth ordered his brigades to right wheel shortly before reaching the Plank Road. With his men facing west, he then ordered them to file left until their flanks touched the road.[58] The maneuver crossed Carroll's front line a short distance beyond the eastern branch of Wilderness Run and triggered a chain reaction which stymied the assault.

A solitary Confederate shell exploded over Carroll's brigade as the 10th New York stepped into the small clearing on the top of the second ridge, about four tenths of a mile west of the Brock Road and wounded Private James Langstaff (Company D).[59] Farther to the east, the rest of the brigade found itself entangled in the thickets as well.[60] Sergeant Owen T. Wright (Company D, 14th Indiana) glued his eyes upon the green leaves of the stubby trees around him. They were blanketed with white splinters and splattered with dried blood, which, judging from the direction of the patterns, seemed to be Confederate.[61]

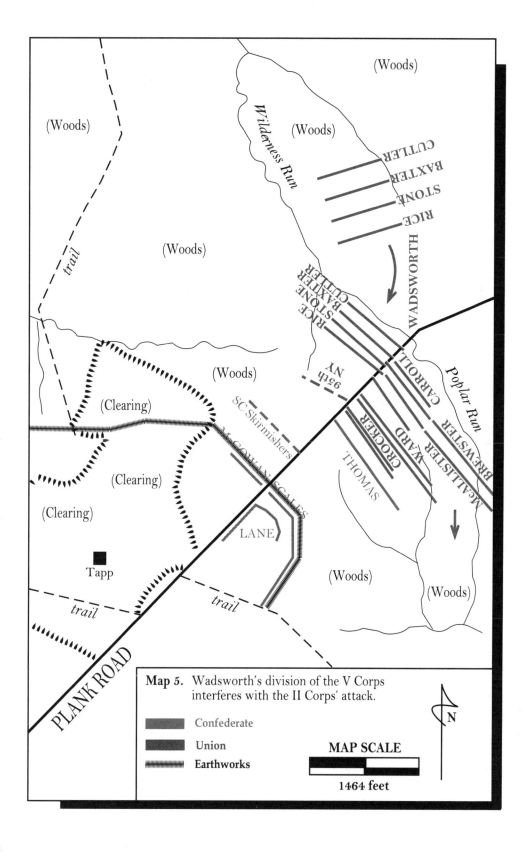

(Woods)

(Woods)

(Woods)

(Woods)

(Woods)

(Woods)

(Woods)

(Woods)

Wilderness Run

Poplar Run

CUTLER

BAXTER

STONE

RICE

WADSWORTH

RICE
STONE
BAXTER
CUTLER

CARROLL

BREWSTER

MCALLISTER

95th NY

SC Skirmishers

THOMAS

CROCKER

WARD

(Clearing)

(Clearing)

(Clearing)

MCGOWAN'S/SCALES

LANE

Tapp

trail

trail

trail

PLANK ROAD

Map 5. Wadsworth's division of the V Corps interferes with the II Corps' attack.

	Confederate
	Union
▓▓▓▓▓	Earthworks

N

MAP SCALE

1464 feet

Carroll ordered his entire brigade to shift to the south side of the Plank Road, across the front of Wheaton's brigade.[62] The 12th New Jersey and the 10th New York moved to the left onto the low ground south of the pike. Simultaneously, Colonel Theodore Ellis (14th Connecticut) directed the 14th Connecticut, 1st Delaware, and 108th New York in Carroll's second line, to flank south of the Plank Road.[63] Carroll's third line without the 19th Maine, which he had ordered to remain in the rear, followed suit.

The movement crowded Crocker's brigade into Ward's regiments. In the shuffle Ward's brigade became entangled and halted to straighten itself out. Crocker moved forward to reorganize his regiments which created a gap between Ward's right flank and the road.[64] Crocker's 1st U.S. Sharpshooters were recalled and placed in the brigade's second line with its right flank on the Plank Road. Private N. Sessions (Company I, 1st U.S. Sharpshooters) objected to the deployment. The Berdans seldom fought in closed ranks. He knew, when firing by command without selecting specific targets, the regiment could expend all of its ammunition within ten minutes.[65] Wheaton's regiments shifted to the left also, blocking the advance of Grant's and Eustis' brigades.[66] Rather than continue the march, Eustis halted his men and realigned them in column of regiments with the 37th Massachusetts in the lead.[67]

Carroll's change of direction placed his regiments across the fronts of McAllister's and Brewster's brigades and behind Ward's command. McAllister, in response to the crowding of his front, obliqued his line to the left, and sent an aide to Ward to find out what he was supposed to do. As his men crashed off to the left, Brewster's regiments moved into line on Carroll's left. In the meantime, Ward shifted his brigade to the right and front until its right flank touched the southern bank of the Plank Road, which temporarily stalled Carroll's brigade.[68]

THE DISPOSITION OF THE CONFEDERATE FORCES
ALONG THE PLANK ROAD
MCGOWAN'S SOUTH CAROLINA BRIGADE

Shortly before the Federal advance started, First Sergeant Berry G. Benson (Company H, 1st South Carolina) assumed his post on the right of the brigade skirmishers, six hundred feet east of the Confederate works. He had not been there more than twenty minutes when one of his men called him over to the Plank Road. He found the man hunched over and nervously pointing toward the east. "Look there!" the fellow blurted. Benson peered toward the darkened tree line to his front. He could not see anything he told the private. "Why, don't you see?" the man whispered in amazement. "It's the Yankee line of battle."

Benson looked harder and in the dim morning light discerned the dark blue of Federal uniforms silhouetted against the blacker backdrop of the woods around them. He was looking at Wadsworth's men moving slowly and deliberately across Carroll's front into a battle line. Despite the temptation to do so, he ordered his men to hold their fire. He did not want to start a Federal charge. He told his men to wait until the Yankees advanced. Benson scurried over to Captain William S. Dunlop, commanding the skirmish line, and reported his observation. The captain ordered the sergeant to relay the information to McGowan. By the time he returned to the skirmishers, Crocker's brigade was slamming into Thomas' brigade and Rice's front line was opening fire upon the South Carolinians.[69]

Captain William S. Dunlop, C.S.A.

Dunlop commanded the skirmish line along Brigadier General Samuel McGowan's front on the morning of May 6.

Dunlop, *Lee's Sharpshooters*, 1899

SOUTH OF THE PLANK ROAD

Very shortly after sloshing through the marshy creek bottom of Poplar Run, the 124th New York (Ward's brigade) stumbled into an isolated nest of dozing Confederates on the right of Thomas' Georgia brigade. The Yankees furiously pounced upon the rattled Butternuts, who scattered like chaff in a breeze.[70] A young captain feverishly attempted to rally his men, thirteen of whom had already been nabbed. Private Henry E. "Rad" Turner (Company I) snatched him by the collar and savagely jerked the frightened captain about before hurling him to the ground.[71] The Rebel thudded unceremoniously onto his rear, the impact jarring his head so hard that his kepi jerked off his head and his hair stood on end. The brigade continued deeper into the Wilderness. All along the way, the New Yorkers continued shooting blindly into the trees at the suspected hiding places of the Confederates. Within minutes, the 124th New York lost twelve men.[72]

To the right front, Crocker's men ran into considerable resistance from Thomas' Georgians. With rounds coming in from the front and right flank, the Confederates held their ground and stubbornly volleyed back into the smoke-laden woods to the east. Colonel Robert W. Folsom (14th Georgia) died in the fighting, but his regiment did not break.[73] The 45th Georgia was also taking a terrible beating. Second Lieutenant Francis S. Johnson, Jr. (Company F) never thought he would get out of the mess alive. A bullet thudded into Private Stapleton Russell's head, killing him instantly. Five other men went down in quick succession with arm and leg wounds. A round smashed into Junior Second Lieutenant Eugene S. Mitchell's thigh, knocking him flat. He quickly administered first aid to himself, only to discover that the tin plate in his haversack had stopped the bullet.[74] They were buying time for the other startled Confederates who were maneuvering into line behind them.

THE PLANK ROAD – NEAR THE WIDOW TAPP'S

Lieutenant General James Longstreet's Corps, having been on the march since 1:00 A.M. from Richard's Shop, struck the Plank Road west of Tapp's shortly before daylight and quick marched toward the front as directed.[75] Longstreet's two division commanders, Brigadier General Joseph B. Kershaw and Major General Charles W. Field, placed their divisions in parallel columns on the Plank Road.[76] Kershaw's old South Carolina brigade, under Colonel John D. Kennedy, led the right column, followed by Brigadier General Benjamin G. Humphreys' Mississippi brigade then Brigadier Generals William T. Wofford's and Goode Bryan's Georgia brigades. The northern column, consisting of Brigadier Generals George T. Anderson's, John Gregg's, Henry L. Benning's, Micah Jenkins', and Colonel William F. Perry's brigades, trailed to the left rear of Kennedy's men by about one hundred yards. On the way down the Plank Road, the veterans swept past Lieutenant General A. P. Hill's field hospital. Hundreds of wounded men lay about the place. Blood-spattered fragments of uniforms, amputated arms and legs, and mangled bodies reminded the men of the grisly work which lay ahead of them. While on the march, they pulled letters and decks of cards from their blanket rolls and blouses and shredded them. Bits of paper littered both sides of the road, Colonel Pinckney D. Bowles (4th Alabama) recalled.[77]

Longstreet and his officers spurred to the front of Kershaw's command. Longstreet shouted above the rhythmic tramp of the infantrymen that, once they reached the works, they were to deploy south of the Plank Road.[78] The columns moved off at the double quick behind the general, who continued toward the front.

Kershaw, in advance of Kennedy's six South Carolina regiments, reached the field first. He found Longstreet on a small knoll on the left side of the road immediately opposite the Widow Tapp's. Since he had not seen Lee, Longstreet immediately took control of the situation. He ordered an aide from Wilcox's staff to escort Kershaw forward. The two officers had barely gone one thousand two hundred feet when Crocker's Federals attacked Thomas' front and flank.[79]

LANE'S BRIGADE

Lane, having heard the firing to the east, was maneuvering his brigade into line along the Plank Road. The 18th North Carolina and the 37th North

Carolina moved into line facing east to the left rear of Scales' brigade. The 33rd North Carolina anchored the line along the road. It faced north and east by battalions to protect the brigade's flank.[80] While Thomas' men blazed away into Crocker's first line, the North Carolinians dragged fallen trees and rotten logs across the 33rd's "L" shaped front and constructed breastworks. As he and his men lay down behind their "works," Major James A. Weston (33rd North Carolina) bitterly resented having not had a chance to enjoy his breakfast of captured Yankee rations. Bullets passing through Scales' positions whacked into the trees around them.

Colonel Clarke M. Avery, commanding the regiment, anxiously paced the line behind his prone Carolinians, trying his best to encourage his men by his example. Every now and then he said something to bolster their spirits. Weston rolled over onto his back. "Colonel, get down behind the breastworks," he admonished him, "you will be killed if you walk about in that way." "No, no," Avery insisted, "it will make the men fight better."[81]

Nothing he could have said or done would have made any of Wilcox's exhausted soldiers fight any harder.

**Major James A. Weston,
33rd North Carolina**

Colonel Clark M. Avery ignored Weston's admonition to take cover during the morning assault on May 6, and it cost him his life.

Clark, *North Carolina in the Great War*, II, 1901

But the Yankees had hit them too quickly. They could not withstand the rapid fire rifles of the Berdans who drilled their ranks seven times faster than they could respond with their muzzle loaders.

The assault upon Thomas took Scales' North Carolinians completely by surprise. Lieutenant Colonel John Ashford (38th North Carolina) panicked at the first burst of small arms fire. Calling his regiment to its feet, he ordered the 38th to about face. He marched the men a few rods west, halted the regiment, turned them about again and walked them back to the breastworks where they took cover. When the rifle fire intensified to the east, Private Thomas A. Martin (Company B, 38th North Carolina) kept as low to the ground as he could and peered into the brush to find out where all the bullets came from. He could not see anything. The volume of musketry drowned out the screams of the regimental officers for the men to retreat.[82]

NORTH OF THE PLANK ROAD
(1,100 yards east of the Tapp house)

The sharpshooters from the South Carolina brigade stubbornly retired before Rice's 95th and 147th New York because they could not hold their position against superior numbers. Rather than press straight ahead, Rice's line veered to the south in response to rifle fire coming in from Thomas' Georgians.[83]

The Federals panicked Thomas' men. Kershaw, having been caught in the open on the pike, did not stand on ceremony either. He spurred his horse back to Kennedy's brigade, which had just reached a point to the right of Poague's artillerymen. He yelled for the regiments to deploy into line of battle. Seconds later the first refugees from Thomas' forward position collided with his column and completely destroyed any semblance of military order.[84]

THE TAPP FARM

General Robert E. Lee and his aides arrived upon the field a few minutes before the Yankees slammed into Thomas' front. They reined to a halt about twenty paces behind Richard's Mississippi Artillery (on the right of Poague's line) to observe the movements upon the field to the east. To the immediate right of the battery a terribly confused mass of infantry, wagons and ambulances clogged the Plank Road. There was a lot of activity but not much rearward movement.[85] Poague listened apprehensively to the fighting southeast of his position with a great deal of concern. A five-foot drop from the eastern edge of Tapp's field blocked his view of the pike but he noticed a large number of Confederate wounded staggering through the scrub oak forest south of his guns. With each passing minute, the roar of battle loomed closer. The colonel ordered Lieutenant Abdon Alexander of Williams' North Carolina Artillery into the pike with a single gun to stay the Federal advance on the southeastern flank.[86] Poague decided to entrench his position. He ordered his gunners to pile up fence rails and logs around each gun to provide minimal protection.

SOUTH OF THE PLANK ROAD

The badly battered 14th Georgia, Thomas' only intact regiment, made a valiant stand against Crocker's Yankee brigade. Their rifle fire shattered one of the regiments in the Federal front line which sent it streaming back into the 1st U.S. Sharpshooters. The Berdans, who had hit the dirt at the first fire, jumped to their feet and cheered. The bulk of the frightened soldiers stopped in their tracks and reformed but their colonel kept on running until several of the Sharpshooters tackled him. One of the men dragged the officer to his feet by his shirt collar. Others screamed at him that he did not deserve the fine regiment which he had. He should be cashiered and

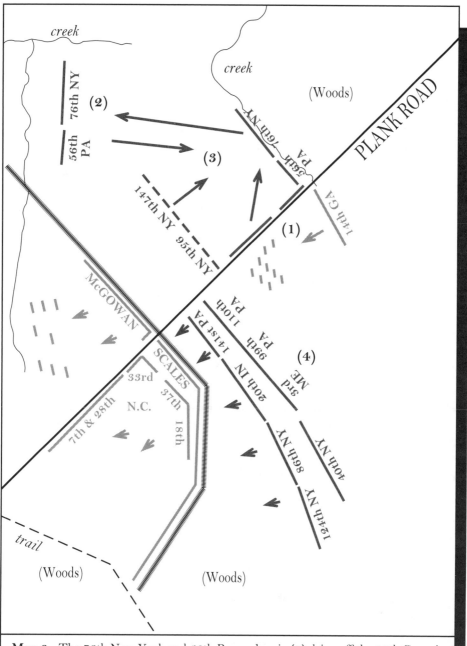

Map 6. The 76th New York and 56th Pennsylvania (**1**) drive off the 14th Georgia then (**2**) neutralize Orr's Rifles (**3**) before being recalled. (**4**) Crocker's brigade (mixed with Ward's) drives back Scales' and Lane's Confederate brigades.

N

MAP SCALE

660 feet

Confederate   IIIIIIIIIIIII **Earthworks**

Union

have his sword taken from him, they yelled. The angry enlisted man let the colonel go and returned to the ranks which the Georgians were quite rapidly thinning.[87]

Casualties were increasing among the Yankees. With each one, the number of men leaving the firing line seemed to double. Many of the soldiers like Corporal William Shaner and Private Samuel Dunham (both Company K) of the 63rd Pennsylvania had promised not to let their friends lie unattended in the woods. When Privates Thomas Shaner and William McMillan (also Company K) went down in the opening exchanges of small arms fire, Dunham and the corporal kept their promise. They abandoned their places in the ranks and carried the two grievously wounded men to the rear.[88] Combat attrition, coupled with the 14th Georgia's stubborn resistance, neutralized any gains that Crocker might have wanted to have made. The Berdans shot away most of their ammunition in record time, as Private N. Sessions (Company I) knew they would.[89] With his brigade's rate of fire rapidly diminishing, Crocker needed help and called upon Ward and his brigade to come to his assistance.[90] Ward's front line advanced into Crocker's ranks. The 14th Georgia, having exhausted its cartridges, retreated west toward Scales' position.[91] The Yankees poured over the haphazardly constructed earthworks, taking prisoners and souvenirs as they reformed.

The Federals caught Scales and Colonel Joseph H. Hyman (13th North Carolina) completely off guard. The two officers were standing behind First Lieutenant Rowland S. Williams' Company I of the 13th North Carolina when a sergeant yelled, "Look in front." Williams poked his head above the low breastworks. The woods were literally blue with advancing Yankees. Ward's brigade had almost entirely flanked the Confederates.[92]

The right wing of Ward's brigade fired blindly into the Confederate lines. The woods roared incessantly with musketry. Scales did not let the ground get warm under his feet. Drawing his sword, he waved it above his head and cried out, "Follow me!" His command to retreat did not get much farther than the few men of the 13th North Carolina who were within the immediate area. Those who heard him jumped to their feet and filed by the right to escape capture.[93] Private Thomas Martin (Company B, 38th North Carolina) popped his head above the breastworks and quickly dropped it down. Incoming Yankee rounds filled the air. He never heard the order to withdraw.[94]

While most of Crocker's brigade retired east toward the brigade's jump off point, Ward's brigade went prone within one hundred feet of the Confederate works.[95] The 141st Pennsylvania suddenly ceased fire and lay down. The order traveled along the line to fix bayonets. Steel clinked against steel, as the veterans quickly slid their bayonets from their scabbards and locked them over the muzzles of their weapons. Sergeant Stephen Rought (Company A) fumbled with his scabbard. He exploded in a rage. His bayonet had fallen out during the advance. Swearing vehemently, he fixed his eyes upon the standard of the 13th North Carolina which hung limply from its staff over the Confederate works. "I'll have that flag!" he screamed. Springing to his feet, with his rifle in his hands, he crashed through the woods. His men followed after him, cheering as they ran. Bullets zipped through the trees around them. Briars snatched at the Yankees' uniforms but did not slow them down.[96] Sergeant John Gross (Company B, 38th North Carolina), who was lying near to Martin, screamed, "Yankees are right here!" Martin grabbed his haversack, which was full of captured Yankee eggs, and started to bolt for freedom when he suddenly realized that the Federals had gotten into the woods ahead of him.[97]

The 141st Pennsylvania spilled over the brush-covered headlogs into the North Carolinians. Rought bitterly demanded the surrender of the North Carolinians' colors. The color sergeant refused. Rought stove in the Confederate's head with his rifle butt. The impact snapped off the stock at the trigger guard. Another Carolinian leveled his weapon upon the sergeant but First Lieutenant Marcus E. Warner (Company D) cut him down with a pistol shot. Wrenching the staff from the dead Confederate's hands, Rought waved the flag aloft, crying, "I've got it! I've got it!" While their comrades rounded up about forty prisoners, Rought and a number of the men studied the newly issued flag. "13th North Carolina Veteran Volunteers" and the names of the fourteen engagements in which the regiment had participated—all stitched in gold thread—filled in the red fields around the Saint Andrew's cross. Lieutenant Colonel Guy H. Watkins, rather than risk losing the prize to the enemy, ordered Rought to take the colors and go to the rear with the Confederate prisoners.[98]

Sergeant Hiram L. Culver (Company B) dreaded going into the battle because of a disconcerting death premonition. A ball thudded into his body seconds after the Pennsylvanians carried the works. He died without uttering a sound.

"Get back to the rear, Johnnies, to the rear," the Yankees told the Rebels as they leaped over the works. Martin and his comrades complied. The Rebels dejectedly shuffled toward the Brock Road in Rought's custody. As he passed through each of Ward's lines, Martin marveled at the frequency with which the Yankees used the term "Johnny." A short distance behind the regiment a stray ball wounded Rought. He stumbled toward the Brock Road, leaving his prisoners to reach the Federal provost marshal on their own. The 40th New York, marching behind the Pennsylvanians, received the credit for their capture.[99]

The 141st Pennsylvania, with the 5th Michigan (Crocker's brigade), blindly charged the next line of works to the front of the II Corps. Corporal Simeon Archer (Company I) crumbled into the thick undergrowth—dead.[100] The Yankees opened fire into Scales' retreating regiments. They wounded a considerable number of the 13th North Carolina. One of their rounds slammed into First Lieutenant Rowland S. Williams (Company I). The bullet struck him in the shoulder blade, knocking the wind out of him. He staggered west through the woods, gasping for breath with each step.[101] The 16th North Carolina extricated itself in rather good order from the melee until it ran into Avery's 33rd North Carolina (Lane's brigade) along the Plank Road. When the 16th had passed around his men, Avery ordered the 33rd to its feet. The colonel cried at First Lieutenant George H. Mills (Company G, 16th North Carolina), as his company filed past, "We will give them one volley before we go."[102]

It was a noble, but futile gesture. Ward's New Yorkers and Pennsylvanians were laying a tremendous fire into the regiment's left wing, along the road, and the apex of the regimental line where it turned to face east. Major James A. Weston (33rd North Carolina) helplessly watched the incoming small arms fire cut down the trees behind their breastworks.[103] The regiment stood up and fired and Ward's brigade promptly volleyed back. Several rounds slammed into Colonel Avery's body and dropped a number of men around him. First Sergeant Joseph Kemp (Company D, 5th Michigan) wrested a Confederate battle flag from the hands of its color bearer for which he received the Medal of Honor seven months later.[104] The small arms fire also thunked into the 16th North Carolina from the rear, killing the color-bearer, Ensign John A. Carpenter, and wounding many others.[105] Private Alfred N. Proffitt (Company D, 18th North Carolina) popped his head over the headlogs a second too late. A bullet hammered his skull just over the right eye. The ball glanced off his frontal bone, cutting a three inch long furrow along his brow. "You can guess if I didn't git away from thare," he wrote to his sister two days later. Dropping his weapon, the thick-headed Tar Heel bolted west into the woods.[106] In all of the confusion scattered Confederate squads returned fire, striking down their own men. The 18th North Carolina fell victim to one such blast before it broke to the rear.[107] First Lieutenant William H. McLaurin (adjutant, 18th North Carolina) managed to get about 75 men through the maelstrom to safety near the Tapp farm.[108]

NORTH OF THE PLANK ROAD

By then McGowan's sharpshooters had retreated into the works along the eastern side of the Widow Tapp's farm, leaving Rice's brigade to contend with the Georgians south of the Plank Road.[109] The 2nd U.S. Sharpshooters, having closed ranks during Ward's advance, drifted to the north side of the Plank Road during the assault. First Sergeant Wyman White (Company F) and a large number of the sharpshooters, during a brief lull in the fighting, noticed an organized body of the Rebels bolt into the road and quick time west. The Yankees pursued them with a shout, firing as they went until they accidentally flanked the 12th South Carolina, which held down the right of McGowan's brigade. The Yankees ordered the Rebels to surrender. Instead, the South Carolinians took cover behind the road bank, which at that point rose five feet above the forest floor on both sides of the pike, and cut loose. The startled Berdans hurled themselves over the opposite road bank and blasted away with a fury. Very shortly the rest of Ward's brigade came to their assistance.

Seconds after First Sergeant Berry Benson (Company H, 1st South Carolina) leaped over the headlog to take cover, he saw the rest of the brigade run as a body to the west. The 12th South Carolina, which had been fighting with its right flank refused, broke first, which exposed the right of the brigade to an enfilade. The 14th South Carolina followed by the 1st then the 13th Regiments peeled away next, dragging any man who could walk with them. (Only Orr's Rifles, which had been detached farther to the left did not retreat.) "It was perfectly disgraceful," Benson lamented. "I don't believe I ever saw troops behave so badly." He did not waste time in joining them. The fear and the speed of the stampede multiplied with each step.[110] The Yankees leaped over the pike to round up the few dead and wounded Rebels which McGowan's men had not taken with them. By some miracle, the Sharpshooters had suffered no casualties.[111]

Rice's brigade in flanking Thomas' Georgians had worked itself into the low ground north of the Plank Road and had exposed its right flank and rear to Orr's Rifles on the northeastern spur of Tapp's farm. A battery from Poague's artillery battalion rolled onto that section of the field which gave the artillerymen a clear view of the right of the Federal line. The battery and the infantry opened fire simultaneously into the backs and the right flank of the 76th New York and the 56th Pennsylvania. Rice ordered the two regiments to face front to rear on the left companies. Despite the confusion of battle, the two regiments about faced, executed a right wheel until they faced east. The veterans then about faced, volleyed and advanced. They succeeded in capturing one Rebel picket and driving the others off but when they closed to within one hundred yards of the guns, the artillerymen limbered up and retreated another four hundred yards. From that more protected position, the gunners loosed a couple of rounds of spherical case at the Federals which brought their charge to a standstill.[112] The rounds burst over Companies H and F of the 56th Pennsylvania, shattering Captain Michael Runkle's arm and killing Lieutenant Henry Eby.[113] The incoming fire stalled Rice's advance on that side of the field. Recalling his regiments, he faced his brigade west with its left flank on the Plank Road.

Meanwhile, the II Corps' lines south of the road had surged ahead and enveloped Scales' North Carolinians. Rice mistakenly assumed that those Federal troops were to his front. When he posted the 76th New York as skirmishers he ordered the men not to fire to the west because their own troops were in that area.[114]

CHAPTER TWO

"Sir, my men are not beaten; they only want a place to reform and fight."

6:00 A.M. TO 8:00 A.M.

WOODS NORTH OF SAUNDERS FIELD
(2.25 miles northwest of Tapp's)

On the northern end of the line the heavy skirmishing still continued. The section of Carter's Virginia artillery was shelling the front of the VI Corps with good effect. Shortly before 6:00 A.M. his artillerymen sent a 12-pounder case shot into the swale between the lines to quiet the noisome skirmishers of the 61st Pennsylvania, and the 1st, 2nd, and 4th New Jersey. The round overshot the Pennsylvanians and hit Company B of the 49th New York (Neill's brigade) which was lying down on the crest of the ridge to the east. While his men were putting their faces in the dirt, Captain John F. E. Plogsted quietly sat down with his back against a huge oak to the right front of the line. Private Christopher G. Funke heard the shell burst a second before a case ball struck Private Christopher Wilken, the man next to him, in the head. The cast iron ball, without losing any momentum, punched a hole through Wilken's skull and kept on going. Funke, too stunned to react, stared mindlessly at the puddle of bone and brains of his comrade. Seconds later a 10-pounder bolt whirled through the woods toward the company. Crashing through the oak tree to the right front of the company, it left Plogsted in a gory puddle. Next, it bored under the ground to the right of Funke. The impact threw men into the air like chaff in the breeze. To the left of Second Lieutenant Julius C. Borcherdt, the bolt struck Private John Weissmantel in the chest and sent him sailing six feet into the

28

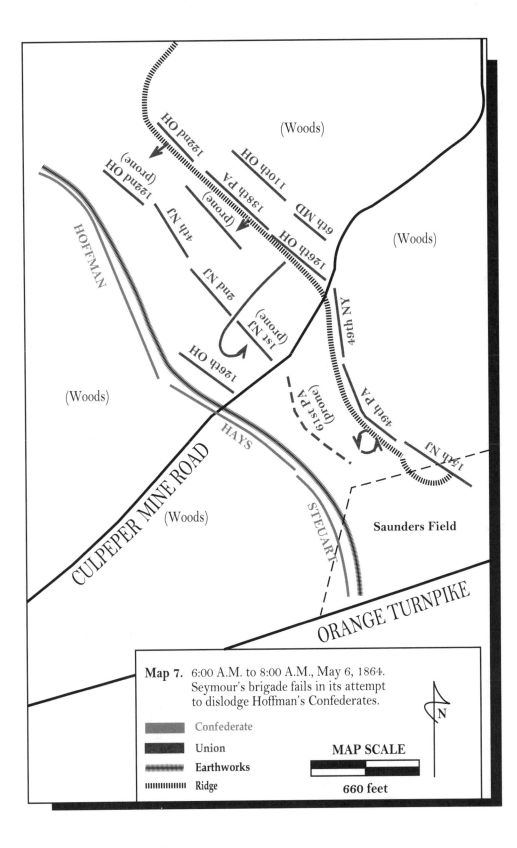

(Woods)

122nd OH

110th OH

138th PA

6th MD

122nd OH
(prone)

126th OH
(prone)

4th NJ

(Woods)

2nd NJ

1st NJ
(prone)

49th NY

126th OH

HOFFMAN

(Woods)

61st PA
(prone)

49th PA

15th NJ

HAYS

STEUART

Saunders Field

CULPEPER MINE ROAD

(Woods)

ORANGE TURNPIKE

N

Map 7. 6:00 A.M. to 8:00 A.M., May 6, 1864.
Seymour's brigade fails in its attempt
to dislodge Hoffman's Confederates.

Confederate

Union

Earthworks

Ridge

MAP SCALE

660 feet

air and rolled First Sergeant Gus Meyer over several times. Weissmantel was dead, and Meyer, shaken but unhurt, did not suffer so much as a scratch.

The startled Borcherdt rushed over to his beloved captain's side. He never forgot the ghastly image of Plogsted's graying face as Funke and three others gathered up his mangled body in a blanket. The bolt, besides ripping off his left arm, had also smashed his right arm and leg. Plogsted knew he was dying and managed to gasp his last message to his wife before the four enlisted men carried him to the ambulance corps, about one hundred yards behind the line.

Borcherdt returned to the company and went prone just as a third round burst directly in front of the line. A searing hot fragment slapped through his hat brim, barely missing his face. Another piece of shell smashed into Private Joseph Klein's hand and arm, mortally wounding him.[1] The artillery shifted their fire along the entire front. For an hour they pelted the VI Corps, taking out men by the handfuls. The shelling killed Lieutenant F. M. Brown (Company A) and several enlisted men in the 61st Pennsylvania, while wounding others.[2]

At 7:40 A.M., the long expected VI Corps attack finally occurred.[3] Originally intended to sweep north on a right grand wheel, the assault quickly dissolved into uncoordinated regimental rushes into the tangled woods along the corps' front. It began on the right with Seymour's brigade and rippled to the left, ending at Saunders Field.

Seymour's two lines moved out against Hoffman's Confederates. Captain James Bumgardner, Jr. (52nd Virginia), who commanded his own Company F and the company to his immediate left, feared that his men would let the Federals get too close to the works before firing. Knowing they could not reload before the Federals would be on top of them with their bayonets, he passed the word not to volley until he gave the command.[4] To the right of the brigade, behind the 13th Virginia, Captain Samuel Buck (Company H) squatted by his crackling fire watching his coffee boil. Overcome with hunger, he had decided to combine breakfast and supper by eating some hard crackers as well. Without warning, the Confederate skirmishers opened fire and Seymour's men responded. The large number of hostile rounds zipping overhead told Buck that this was not a false alarm. Abandoning his coffee, he leaped to his feet, while his men threw themselves against the works. The skirmishers were darting through the trees and hurling themselves over the headlogs. From his post on the berm of the trench Buck again saw five distinct lines of Federals pushing through the woods.[5] Private Jacob Heater (Company D, 31st Virginia) saw them also but counted only four well aligned regiments. He noticed in particular their mounted officers and their heavy looking, well stuffed knapsacks.[6]

Seymour's charge quickly fragmented into separate assaults. The 126th Ohio on the left of his line moved faster than the center and the right. They closed to within thirty to fifty yards before Bumgardner's two companies volleyed into them.[7] Buck's Company H sighted in on their targets, using "unusual care," he later recalled. A conscript whom he had to severely discipline for refusing to do his duty underwent a complete conversion as the blood lust overwhelmed him. "Capt, ain't I knocking 'em?" he cried.[8]

The 126th Ohio took fearful losses. In the first volley, the Confederates unhorsed Lieutenant Colonel Aaron W. Ebright and his acting adjutant, First Lieutenant Thomas Hyatt (Company E).[9] Corporal Francis Cordrey (Company E) saw Color Corporal Daniel W. Welch (Company C) crumble by his side. He grabbed for the flag but another member of the color guard reached them first. Company D lost 27 of its 53 men in seconds.[10] At least one wounded man managed to fall into the Confederate lines before the Ohioans fell back and threw themselves to the ground.[11] They started returning an accurate fire.

The Federals shot down Second Lieutenant William H. Burns (Company B) of the 52nd Virginia. Captain Robert C. Davis (Company A) was aiming a rifle which he had just taken from an enlisted man when a bullet crashed into his head, throwing him onto his back. His weapon discharged, killing Third Lieutenant George W. Moore (Company B) and wounding an enlisted man.[12] First Lieutenant Robert D. Funkhouser (Company D, 49th Virginia) grabbed a rifle and was loading it from a kneeling position behind the works when a bullet struck Private Robert I. Mathews (Company D) in the mouth and exited out the back of his neck. The impact of the round threw him against Funkhouser's back, driving his body into the breastworks. The lieutenant, presuming the man was dead, quickly tossed him against the back of the trench and continued to load and fire. Mathews, who was on his stomach, clawed Funkhouser's hand, gesturing frantically for help. Funkhouser rolled the private over while pulling his pocket knife from his pants, and cut his cartridge box, canteen, and blanket roll free. Placing the folded blanket under Mathews' head, Funkhouser gave him a drink of water, then turned back to his duty.[13]

In the 13th Virginia, Buck was having problems of his own. While the Federals were shooting up the woods behind him, one of his men, the company bully, hurled himself flat onto his back in the trench and refused to shoot at the enemy. Buck, who hated the man, slapped him savagely with the flat of his sword, all the while yelling at him to get up. The man would not budge. Angered beyond reason, the captain hit the man again. The fellow popped up to his knees, fired his rifle into the air and threw himself to the ground. Buck raised his arm, intent upon injuring the coward, when a bullet hit him in the right armpit.

The arm dropped to his side. Reaching over with his left hand, he grabbed his right cuff and jerked the arm to see if it were broken. The moment he released his grip on his sleeve a tremendous amount of blood gushed down his arm, saturating the sleeve and covering his hand. For a second Buck thought he had lost all of the blood in his body. The Federals did not give the Confederates any respite, however. Before the fighting ended, he had two more wounds and four bullet holes in his clothing.[14]

The 138th Pennsylvania, in the center of Seymour's formation, could not work itself through the thickets. The men fell prone and left the 122nd Ohio on its own, which closed to within seventy yards of Hoffman's works before the Confederates cut loose.[15] The regiment went to the ground, and returned fire.

The 6th Maryland and the 110th Ohio, in the second line, rose up but again had to lie down behind a slight rise about thirty-five yards behind the first line, rather than be slaughtered by the hail of bullets. Seymour immediately ordered the regiments to their feet with instructions to close the gap. The Ohioans and the Marylanders covered another forty-five feet before the incoming musketry forced them to their bellies, where they remained throughout the engagement and took a terrible beating.[16] A spent ball glanced off a tree, striking First Sergeant Grayson Eichelberger (Company D) in the right instep. The intense pain convinced him he was severely wounded. He pulled off his shoe, revealing a terrible bruise and nothing more.[17]

A shell sailed over the ridge behind Neill's brigade, exploding in the top of a large tree near Brigadier General Alexander Shaler's brigade which was waiting for its chance to move forward. Captain John M. Dwight (Company I, 122nd New York) went down with a serious leg wound. The branches raining down around Private Edwin Crockett (Company K, 65th New York) scared him. All about him lay the graying corpses of the previous night's fight. The shrill Rebel yell rang through the woods, followed by a tremendous volley, frightening him further. For a few seconds he expected to see the Rebel bullets cut down every tree and person within sight. The artillery barrage triggered a frontal assault by the 49th New York and the 7th Maine into the hollow to the west of the brigade.[18]

In their hurry to get to better cover, the New Yorkers made too much noise. The sound of their equipment rubbing against the brush alarmed Private Christopher G. Funke (Company B). Although the Confederates could not see them, they could definitely hear them. Funke blamed the regiment for drawing as much fire as it did. That one hundred yards into the valley were the longest the 49th had ever run in almost three years of service. Canister and solid shot plowed through the regiment, killing Captain Charles H. Hickmott (Company F) and First Lieutenant Henry C. Valentine (Company I) along with a large number of the men. A case ball sailed over Funke's shoulder, thudding into the soldier behind him. Penetrating the man's right shoulder and chest, it gouged a hole through his knapsack, scattering his letters through the brush behind him. The fluttering papers reminded Funke of frightened white pigeons.[19]

When the New Yorkers reached the 61st Pennsylvania someone yelled, "Halt! Lie Down!" The Federals hurled themselves to the ground in the marshy bottom land. A shell burst ten feet in front of Company B and sent a fragment hurtling through the file to Borcherdt's left. Blood and pieces of raw flesh splattered him before seriously wounding Private Edward Borchard in the left arm. A second piece passed over Borcherdt's right shoulder and struck First Lieutenant Reuben M. Preston (Company K) full in the face, completely removing it. The distressing thought of how he would break the news to Preston's new bride flashed through his mind. But he did not have the time to grieve. Orders came along the line for each company to send three to four men forward as skirmishers. Borcherdt told Funke and a few other soldiers to move out about thirty to sixty feet and not to fire unless the Confederates charged them.[20] The 7th Maine relieved the 1st New Jersey which retired to the eastern slope of the ridge.[21]

The 49th Pennsylvania, near the southern end of the formation, plowed through the brush into the muddy swamp between the lines and dispersed into skirmish parties.[22] While the left wing of the regiment was struggling through the swamp, the Confederates severely wounded Colonel Thomas M. Hulings' horse and shot First Lieutenant Decatur Lytle (Company H) in the head. The Pennsylvanians managed to capture a few Confederates before retreating, but left Private Lewis Kuhn (Company I) stranded in waist deep muck in the bottom land where the Rebels soon captured him.[23]

At Saunders Field the 15th New Jersey stood up to charge when the Confederate artillery on the high ground to the west forced them to cover. A shell caught Private Leonard Decker (Company D) under the arm, destroying his elbow and gouging a terrible hole in his side.[24] The "grand assault" was dying in front of them. By 8:00 A.M., the VI Corps troops were settling down to skirmishing.

6:30 A.M. TO 9:00 A.M.
NORTH OF THE PLANK ROAD
THE TAPP FARM
(About 220 yards west of the Tapp house)

Generals Robert E. Lee and Ambrose P. Hill (Third Corps, Army of Northern Virginia) intercepted McGowan's rattled South Carolinians as they swarmed around Lieutenant Colonel William Poague's artillerymen. "I am surprised to see such a gallant brigade running like a flock of geese!"

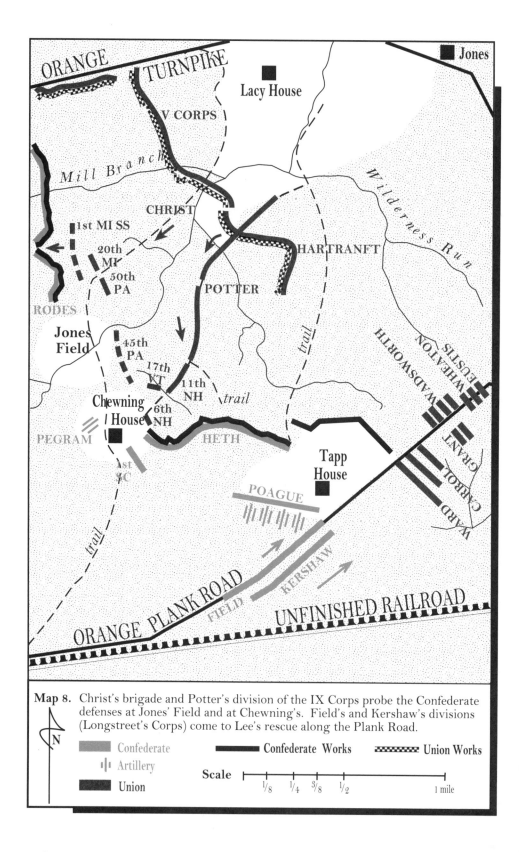

Map 8. Christ's brigade and Potter's division of the IX Corps probe the Confederate defenses at Jones' Field and at Chewning's. Field's and Kershaw's divisions (Longstreet's Corps) come to Lee's rescue along the Plank Road.

N

Confederate

Artillery

Union

Confederate Works

Union Works

Scale

1/8   1/4   3/8   1/2   1 mile

ORANGE TURNPIKE

Jones

Lacy House

V CORPS

Mill Branch

CHRIST

Wilderness Run

1st MI SS

HARTRANFT

20th MI

50th PA

POTTER

RODES

Jones Field

45th PA

17th VT

11th NH

trail

trail

Chewning House

6th NH

WADSWORTH

EUSTIS

WHEATON

PEGRAM

HETH

GRANT

Tapp House

CARROLL

WARD

1st SC

POAGUE

ORANGE PLANK ROAD

FIELD

KERSHAW

UNFINISHED RAILROAD

**Brigadier General
Samuel McGowan, C.S.A.**

When Lee rebuked McGowan's men for running, the general retorted, "Sir, my men are not beaten; they only want a place to reform and fight."

Massachusetts Commandery;
MOLLUS, USAMHI

Lee loudly rebuked the file closers of the 1st South Carolina. Second Lieutenant James F. J. Caldwell (Company B), who could not recall the commanding general's exact words said that Lee "expressed himself rather roughly to us," and he never forgot the general's lack of composure. Both generals were very angry. Lee spurred his horse up to McGowan and exclaimed again, "My God! General McGowan, is this splendid brigade of yours fleeing like wild geese?" McGowan lost his temper and momentarily forgot to whom he was speaking. He shouted back, "Sir, my men are not beaten; they only want a place to reform and fight." The shock of seeing their beloved "Marse Robert" so close to the front and exchanging harsh words with their brigadier shamed a considerable number of the men to a standstill. The regimental officers regained their composure and herded their enlisted men into some semblance of a battle line on the southwestern edge of Tapp's field behind the artillery where they began entrenching.[25]

Lee sent Colonel Walter H. Taylor, his devoted adjutant, galloping back toward Parker's Store to prepare the army's supply train for a retreat should the Federals prove to be more aggressive than usual. He then dispatched an aide to follow Taylor and to intercept Longstreet's column.[26] Hundreds of demoralized and wounded men thronged Tapp's field, the Plank Road, and the woods to the south, making it nearly impossible to locate the position of any particular command.

A. P. Hill decided not to wait for Longstreet's lead elements. Within fifteen minutes he sent McGowan's South Carolinians south toward the Confederate right flank. By the time the lead regiment reached the roadside, Kershaw had galloped some four hundred yards back to the head of his column. McGowan's officers halted their regiments and promptly marched them back to the place they came from.

In the Plank Road

The disorganized elements of Heth's and Wilcox's divisions continued to flow west toward Parker's Store. Once beyond the immediate danger of the front line, the veterans formed into columns and marched away from the fighting. The arrival of Longstreet's Corps did not disturb them in the least. The retreating soldiers split with such precision into files on both sides of the Plank Road that Brigadier General E. Porter Alexander (Kershaw's artillery commander) and a number of the staff officers mistook them for reinforcements who were being deployed north to support Ewell's Corps. Just before Kershaw's command reached the front, a mounted Confederate major galloped into the withdrawing column and feverishly tried to turn some of the men about. Alexander's good friend and staff officer, Captain Joseph C. Haskell, spurred over to the officer, confused about his erratic behavior. "Major, what's the matter?" Haskell asked, "Are not those men being marched back?" "No! God damn 'em!" the major shrieked, "They are running!" Alexander, who overheard the exchange, did not agree. The retreating soldiers did not seem panicked. He surmised that the commands had become too mixed to sort themselves out and that they were moving to the rear to reorganize.[27] Not all of the Confederates were retreating. Colonel John M. Stone's brigade, though fragmented by the attack, was not out of the fight yet. Lieutenant Colonel Alfred H. Belo managed to take what was left of his 55th North Carolina and parts of the remaining three regiments in the brigade and reform them behind Longstreet's forming troops. As Longstreet's men moved around them, Second Lieutenant Charles R. Jones (Company G, 55th North Carolina) heard someone call out, "Boys, get out of the way. We know you did your duty. Let us have a chance and we will finish your job." Belo put his men in reserve on the northern side of the Tapp farm. Stone gathered the few men he could find from the three Mississippi regiments and moved them south along a path which led to a railroad cut south of the Plank Road.[28]

Field's Confederate division arrived very shortly thereafter. By then, the Federals had almost flanked Tapp's field on the south side of the Plank Road.[29] Longstreet ordered him to place his brigades on that flank to meet them. Field managed to get Brigadier General George T. Anderson's five Georgia regiments into position before he received another directive from his corps commander. He recorded that Longstreet wanted him "to form in the quickest order I could and charge with any front I could make."

Brigadier General John Gregg's brigade pushed its way through the stymied mob of wagons, mules, and soldiers which choked the Plank Road and moved past Anderson's men until it arrived at the western edge of Tapp's field. Gregg halted the column, faced it to the left, and gave the command to load weapons.[30] The 3rd Arkansas, with the 1st Texas to its right, formed the left wing of the brigade. The 4th Texas, with the 5th Texas to its right, formed the right wing.[31] The regiments right wheeled through the woods on the northern side of the pike and fronted, facing east, on the open ground behind Poague's artillery battalion.[32]

TAPP'S FIELD

At the same time Sergeant Berry Benson (Company H, 1st South Carolina), who was standing nearby, saw a Union battle line (Ward's brigade) materialize near the edge of the woods about six hundred fifty yards southeast of the guns.[33] The Southern infantrymen quietly stood to arms behind the artillerymen, while they methodically loosed three salvos into the Federals.[34] The canister sent the Federals skedaddling. It did not take long for the South Carolinians to start expanding the works which the artillerymen had already begun. Working feverishly with bayonets, tin plates and tin cups, officers and men alike pitched into the sandy soil.[35] The field pieces suddenly ceased fire. With so many troops cluttering the area, McGowan began flanking his brigade northwest along the trail which led to the Chewning house.

THE CHEWNING FARM

While Birney's division pressed the Army of Northern Virginia from the east, Lieutenant General Ulysses S. Grant personally ordered Major General Ambrose Burnside to send Brigadier General Robert Potter's Second Division and Brigadier General Orlando Willcox's Third Division of the IX Corps against Lee from the north. (Burnside, although commanding the corps, could not make any decisions without Grant's approval.) Colonel Benjamin C. Christ's brigade (Willcox's division) took the same trail which Wadsworth's division had taken to flank Higgerson's during the previous day. Potter, with Colonel John F. Hartranft's brigade from the Third Division in support, marched along the middle trail which meandered down into the Tapp farm.[36]

Potter did not go into the woods without some kind of reconnaissance. Before he put his men on the trail he ordered Colonel Simon Griffin to send a detachment south to scout the line of advance. The duty fell to Lieutenant Colonel Henry H. Pearson's 6th New Hampshire. The colonel took Lieutenants George W. Osgood and Charles F. Winch (both from Company K) with about one hundred men from Companies F and K and headed them southwest. The rest of the division and Hartranft's brigade followed closely after them.

Leaving one third of the company in the ravine east of the plateau, the rest of the detachment ascended the steep ridge into the open field surrounding the Chewning house. Not one hundred fifty yards away, a lone horseman in civilian clothes rode away from the cabin, moving south. The New Englanders quickstepped over to the house without drawing his attention. In the distance, they saw a column of infantry round the bend from the woods to the southeast. With the sunlight glaring in their faces, the Federals could not tell whether they were their men or not. Pearson raised his field glasses to his eyes. "Boys, they are rebs!" he shouted. He yelled at the detachment to fall in and open fire.[37]

McGowan's South Carolinians did not pay any attention to the Federals until bullets slammed into a couple of their men. The round which passed through Sergeant John Wilson (Company K, 1st South Carolina) mortally wounded Private John Davis (Company K) who was walking behind him. The South Carolinians deployed immediately. The stunned Northerners gaped at the approaching Confederate column as an estimated four hundred "Johnnies" faced by the rear rank and while advancing, fell into a battle line. While the Southerners closed to within two hundred yards of his detail, Pearson ordered Privates Albert O. Cutter, Walter W. Smith, and Charles Wright from Company K, and Henry N. Farnum and Joseph Cross (both Company F) and several others into the cabin while he and the rest of the men made tracks for the ravine across from the house.

They ran into the ranks of their own regiment while it was moving into line on the left of the 17th Vermont which had crawled into position along the northern edge of the farm. The 11th New Hampshire remained in reserve.[38] Within short order, six guns from Lieutenant Colonel William J. Pegram's artillery battalion wheeled into the northern end of the field behind the house and unlimbered. To add to the confusion, a cavalry detachment materialized from the south and dashed for the house ahead of the infantry. Canister ripped through the tree tops, showering the men in the ravine with branches and splinters at the same time that Griffin's brigade adjutant general galloped into the clearing. The rattled officer wheeled about and put his spurs to his horse. "The Rebels are coming!" he shrieked. "Colonel Pearson and his men are all gobbled up!" Dashing north along the trail, he rode through the prone 6th New Hampshire and shot past Griffin, who shouted at the officer to come back but to no avail. The infantrymen jeered at his back, "Go it, or the Rebs will have you!" (His days were numbered. The men had no use for cowardly officers.)[39]

The left regiments of McGowan's brigade took cover behind a rail fence near the house while his sharpshooters fanned out along the brigade's right flank and spattered the pines along the lower end of the field. A large white dog burst into the field from the east, zigzagging back and forth between the sharpshooters and the Federals. A couple of South Carolinians deliberately winged the animal and sent it yelping back where it came from.[40] McGowan ordered his brigade forward. The sharpshooters dashed across the spring which drained into the low land and disappeared into the pines. The 6th New Hampshire, after taking about half a dozen hits, withdrew to lower and safer ground. To the north, the 17th Vermont laid down a withering fire which sent the left of McGowan's line reeling. The Confederates returned fire. The Vermonters also took casualties and got lower to the ground. In a matter of minutes, the entire affair was over.[41]

Farther to the south, Sergeant Berry Benson (Company H, 1st South Carolina) saw two dead New Englanders among the pines. He told one of his sharpshooters not to steal a silver watch from one of them. The fellow stole it anyway. Shooting still continued to the left. The Sharpshooters regrouped and fell back to the trail at the southern edge of the farm.[42]

The fracas cost the 6th New Hampshire seven dead and wounded, four captured, and one missing. Most of the missing never escaped the cabin when the Confederates overran it.[43] With the Federals temporarily cleared from their front, most of McGowan's brigade retired to the hillside on the southeastern side of the farm and began constructing earthworks. The rest of his brigade deployed along the right wing of the works, facing north.[44]

JONES FIELD

Very shortly thereafter Christ reached his objective—Jones' field. As the three regiments came into line in the woods on the northern end of the field, Christ deployed the 1st Michigan Sharpshooters to the west to connect with the V Corps. Seven companies sprayed through the woods in skirmish formation while the remaining three maintained the regulation line in reserve. The 20th Michigan and the 50th Pennsylvania deployed into battle front in the woods to support the sharpshooters.[45]

A little over three hundred yards to the southeast, Company K, 45th Pennsylvania stumbled through the dense woods along the right flank of Colonel Zenas Bliss' brigade to cover Potter's march south toward Tapp's. Glancing through the trees to the right, Sergeant Ephraim E. Myers (Company K) saw Burnside and his staff trot onto the ridge in the center of Jones' field. Several rounds from Pegram's six guns sent them dashing to safety. Christ pulled back the 50th Pennsylvania and the 20th Michigan and placed them in line across the trail where it entered the field. He ordered them to dig in.[46] At the same time, the 1st Michigan meandered into the southern end of the Confederate line near Higgerson's and came under fire. The Michiganders exchanged a few shots with the North Carolinians and melted back into the woods around the farm. (They remained there until mid afternoon.)[47]

IN THE PLANK ROAD
(About 200 yards northeast of the Tapp house)

Kershaw placed the 2nd South Carolina in Tapp's field east of Poague's battalion with its right flank resting on the pike. The 3rd South Carolina formed on its right, followed to the right by the 7th, the 15th, the 3rd Bat-

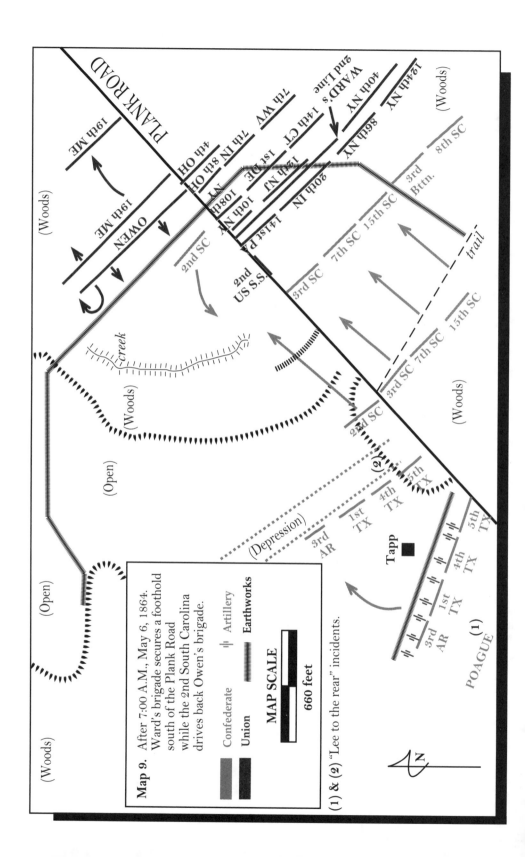

Map 9. After 7:00 A.M., May 6, 1864. Ward's brigade secures a foothold south of the Plank Road while the 2nd South Carolina drives back Owen's brigade.

PLANK ROAD

(Woods)

19th ME

19th ME

OWEN

(Woods)

4th OH

8th OH

7th IN

7th WV

14th CT

1st ME

2nd SC

10th NY

108th NY

12th NJ

40th NY

WARD's 2nd Line

86th NY

124th NY

(Woods)

141st PA

20th IN

2nd US S.S.

3rd SC

7th SC

15th SC

3rd Bttn.

8th SC

creek

(Woods)

2nd SC

trail

(Open)

(Woods)

(Depression)

3rd SC 7th SC 15th SC

(2)

5th TX

4th TX

1st TX

3rd AR

Tapp

4th TX

5th TX

3rd AR

1st TX

POAGUE (1)

(Woods)

(Open)

Confederate   **Union**   ‖ Artillery   Earthworks

MAP SCALE

660 feet

N

(1) & (2) "Lee to the rear" incidents.

talion, and the 8th South Carolina.[48] Once they were organized, he pushed them forward. Lee did not see their advance. Neither did the Federals who had wisely retreated to the southern side of the Plank Road.

SOUTH OF THE PLANK ROAD

Wheaton's and Grant's brigades from the VI Corps had not gotten more than seven hundred yards beyond the Brock Road when their advance stalled. Colonel Lewis A. Grant moved his Vermonters forward by the oblique until they passed beyond Wheaton's left flank. A short distance farther into the woods, the brigade crested a small, relatively open knoll which the Confederates had hastily fortified with a zigzagging line of rotten logs and dead trees. Grant put his men to work to strengthen the position.[49]

Shortly after the Wadsworth's division of the V Corps disrupted the entire II Corps' formation along the Plank Road, Brigadier General Joshua T. "Paddy" Owen marched his brigade by the flank down the south side of the pike, heading for the front lines. On the way he spied Colonel Selden Connor and his stranded 19th Maine. Owen yelled something about Carroll wanting the Mainers to come along with him. Connor, who had no idea where Owen's men came from or where they were going, ordered his regiment to left face and moved it by column of twos into the rear of Owen's men. (By arranging his men in column of twos, he could slip through the commands along the road with more ease than if they marched in a regimental line.)[50]

In crossing a branch of Poplar Run one of the men from the 152nd New York stooped over to scoop up a cup of water. Before he could drink it, a messmate snatched the cup from his hand, gulped the water down, and started up the western side of the bank. A stray bullet slammed into the fellow's body. He tumbled to the forest floor with blood streaming from the corner of his mouth. The soldier who had wanted the drink in the first place continued on with his company.[51]

While approaching Carroll's rear line, Owen heard Poague's sixteen artillery pieces open fire to his right front. Rather than consult any officers about the troop dispositions in the immedi-

**Brigadier General
Joshua T. Owen, U.S.A.**

His brigade was among the first Federals to attack Lieutenant Colonel Franklin Gaillard's 2nd South Carolina during Longstreet's initial push against the II Corps.

Massachusetts Commandery;
MOLLUS, USAMHI

ate vicinity, he cried out, "Let's take those guns," and took off at a gallop, followed by his lead regiment, the 72nd Pennsylvania. The order rippled through the brigade which unfolded like a distended accordion and progressively lost its unit integrity as each regiment stumbled after the one preceding it.[52] Passing through Wheaton's ranks and Wadsworth's division, they reached the front lines shortly before 7:00 A.M.[53]

By the time Ward's brigade had overrun Scales' and Lane's breastworks, Colonels Robert McAllister's and William R. Brewster's brigades had passed around Carroll's left flank to continue their left oblique march deeper into the Wilderness. During the sidestepping, McAllister pulled the 1st Massachusetts and the 115th Pennsylvania from his front line and created a second line with them. A considerable distance into the advance, Brigadier General Gershom Mott and his staff found the brigade crashing about on the Federal left. Mott immediately ordered McAllister to send Colonel William J. Sewell (5th New Jersey) forward with the three regiments on the right of the brigade line. The remaining units were to stay back as the reserve. The 5th, 6th and 11th New Jersey regiments moved forward without skirmishers leaving McAllister with the 7th New Jersey, 8th New Jersey, 26th Pennsylvania and the 16th Massachusetts to come in behind them as support.[54]

To the right, Carroll's first line, consisting of the 10th New York and the 12th New Jersey, advanced with Ward's brigade and disappeared into the woods west of Scales' works, heading toward Lee's position in Tapp's field. The line halted eighty feet beyond the works.[55] In all of the confusion, the men could barely distinguish organized infantry from retreating infantry. The second line—14th Connecticut, 1st Delaware, and 108th New York— occupied the western side of Scales' works. Captain William H. Hawley (Company K, 14th Connecticut), from Carroll's staff, dashed into the woods with the skirmishers from the 14th Connecticut. Almost immediately they came under fire from what they assumed were scattered parties of Confederates. Sergeant Elnathan B. Tyler (Company B, 14th Connecticut) never saw the Confederates who were shooting into the brigade as it struggled through the underbrush.[56] The still smoldering embers of the Confederates' breakfast fires and the scattered corn meal told the veteran William B. Hincks (Adjutant, 14th Connecticut) that his brigade had sprung the Rebels like spooked game. The thick, intertwined second growth of the small trees which laced the more formidable trees together, made further orderly advance nearly impossible. Hincks halted with his regiment and stared into the jungle around him.[57]

Carroll's third line—7th West Virginia, 14th Indiana, and 8th Ohio— had not reached the Confederate breastworks yet. The regiments stood to arms in the woods waiting for something to happen while they attempted to reorganize themselves.[58] To First Lieutenant Thomas Galwey (Company

B, 8th Ohio) it seemed as if the regiment had not gone very far from the Brock Road when a tremendous fire slammed into it.[59] He and a few men were all that remained of the entire 8th Ohio.

Someone shouted, "Hello, 8th Ohio!" "Hey, Carroll's Brigade!" soon followed until everyone was hollering, and unwittingly betraying their positions and their chaotic disposition to the Rebels, who could hear the regiment even if they could not see it.[60] The 4th Ohio remained to the right rear of the brigade. Thomas Galwey noted the time—a little after 7:00 A.M.[61]

McGOWAN'S EARTHWORKS
(About 730 yards east of the Tapp house)

By the time the head of Owen's column came within one hundred yards of McGowan's former breastworks he had left a large portion of his brigade strung out wheezing along his route of approach. The 72nd Pennsylvania, with Colonel De Witt C. Baxter in the lead, dashed across the pike, fronted west, and charged. The Pennsylvanians quickly rounded up several skirmishers from the 2nd South Carolina.[62] The captured soldiers seemed almost relieved to have been taken prisoner. Some appeared quite joyful as they trudged rearward toward the Brock Road.[63]

Lieutenant Colonel Franklin Gaillard (2nd South Carolina) did not let his men open fire until the bulk of Owen's brigade had gotten well within rifle range. Their volley caught the 19th Maine as it crested the bank of the road. Connor brought the line to front, facing northwest and ordered the men to return fire. The New Englanders blazed away at the South Carolinians for several minutes until the 3rd South Carolina enfiladed the regiment's left wing.[64] The single volley escalated into a roar as the rest of Colonel John D. Kennedy's brigade lashed into Ward's front. The 2nd South Carolina successfully rolled up the right of Owen's line, but at a terrible cost. Kennedy went down with a bullet wound in the right shoulder. Unable to staunch the bleeding, he relinquished brigade command to Colonel James Nance (3rd South Carolina) and staggered to the rear. Minutes later, a ball slammed into Nance's brain. Colonel John Henagan (8th South Carolina) took over the brigade.[65]

Nevertheless, its accurate musketry sent the 72nd Pennsylvania streaming to the rear, dragging the rest of the brigade with it. The 152nd New York did not run. Its men fought from tree to tree, trying to desperately save themselves from annihilation. The dried leaves on the forest floor ignited from smoldering cartridge papers. Wounded men screamed for help. With minie balls slapping into the trees around them Private Henry Roaback (Company E) and another man from the 152nd dragged one of the wounded Pennsylvanians to safety. Sergeants George Kidder and George W. Manchester (both Company C) stood back to back, as prescribed in the drill manual for a melee. They chatted in between shots until a bullet threw Kidder forward onto his side. His deathly stare burned itself into Manchester's memory.[66] The 19th Maine retreated with the right of the brigade line. It fell back about one hundred fifty yards to the front of Rice's brigade while the rest of Owen's men filtered back to the security of the entrenchments along the Brock Road. The South Carolinians pursued the Federals a short distance, then disappeared into the woods south of the Plank Road where they rejoined their brigade.[67]

The suddenness of the skirmish attracted Kershaw's attention. He immediately sent to the rear for Humphreys' four Mississippi regiments. He also dispatched a courier along the Plank Road to bring Brigadier General Goode Bryan's four Georgia regiments to the front. The aide found the brigade less than one half of a mile west of the Widow Tapp's where the Georgians had successfully stopped and reorganized a good many of Wilcox's and Heth's stragglers. Bryan's men struggled through the brush on the south side of the road into brigade front, with their left flank resting on the Plank Road. Incoming Yankee rounds pelted the ranks and stragglers from the front continued to sporadically break his regimental formations. Bryan settled the matter quickly. He sent his brigade sharpshooters under First Lieutenant Russell G. Strickland (Company I, 10th Georgia) forward to silence the Federals.[68]

POAGUE'S POSITION ON THE TAPP FARM

While the 2nd South Carolina and the rest of Henagan's brigade were charging into the forest to push Ward's Federals away from Tapp's plateau, Brigadier General John Gregg's brigade maneuvered into position behind Poague's artillery battalion. Seconds later, Sergeant Charles R. Dudley (Richard's Mississippi Battery) glanced to the rear to see Lee and Colonel Charles S. Venable riding behind the battery along the left front of Gregg's brigade.[69] As Lee neared the opening between the 3rd Arkansas and the 1st Texas, the excited infantrymen suddenly realized he was among them. "Go back, General Lee, go back!" the men nearest to him shouted. Simultaneously, Lieutenant Colonel Richard J. Harding (1st Texas), the brigade ordinance officer, Lieutenant Whit P. Randall (Company K, 1st Texas), and First Sergeant Robert White (Company G, 3rd Arkansas) made a dash for Traveller's reins. With the bridle in his hand, White quickly turned the horse's head and tugged his commanding general to a safer position behind the line.[70]

The general then walked Traveller, his famous dapple gray horse, over to Gregg who was mounted farther to the right behind the 4th Texas. (In all of the hubbub, the right of the brigade line had not heard the slight commotion which Lee had precipitated on the left of the line.) Not recognizing

**Brigadier General
John Gregg, C.S.A.**

As he led his veteran brigade into action on the western edge of the Tapp farm, he called out, "Remember, Hood's Brigade, that General Lee's eyes are on you and his heart is with you."

Massachusetts Commandery;
MOLLUS, USAMHI

the regiments in front of him, he queried, "General, what brigade is this?" "The Texas Brigade," Gregg replied.

Brigade couriers Privates Leonard G. Gee (Company E, 5th Texas), and Robert Campbell (Company A, 5th Texas), who were riding by Gregg's side with Quartermaster Sergeant Joseph B. Polley (4th Texas), overheard Lee's conversation with Gregg. "I am glad to see it," Lee said with some relief. "When you go in there, I wish you to give those men the cold steel." He was referring to Ward's Federals who Lee mistakenly believed were in the woods to the east, "They will stand and fire all day, and never move unless you charge them." "That is my experience," Gregg replied. The words had hardly left his mouth when an aide from Longstreet, who did not realize that Lee was upon the field, rode over to Gregg and told him to advance his line.[71] In a more subdued, confidential tone the commanding general reminded his brigadier, "The Texas Brigade always has driven the enemy, and I expect them to do it today." Then Lee added, "Tell them, General, that I shall witness their conduct today."

Gregg spurred to the front of his regiments. Turning his horse to face the line, he shouted, "General Lee wants us to go and drive those people out. Remember, Hood's Brigade, that General Lee's eyes are on you and his heart is with you. Forward! Guide center! March!"[72] When the line moved out at the quickstep, the general wheeled his horse south and took his position behind the right center of the brigade. Lee removed his hat and, standing in the stirrups, exclaimed loudly, as if to reassure himself, "Texans always move them." The Texans who heard him responded with a tremendous Rebel yell. His mere presence electrified the line. Orderly Robert Campbell (Company A) glanced over at his comrade Leonard G. Gee (Company E). Tears of pride streamed down Gee's face. Screaming and yipping at the top of his lungs, he choked back his tears and cried, "I would charge into hell for that old man."[73]

The regiments passed through Poague's artillery position near Captain Arthur C. Williams' North Carolina Battery and leaped over the low gun emplacements which his men had hastily constructed. Bullets zipped in from the woods to their front. One of them broke both arms of Major Joseph C. Webb (27th North Carolina). He was standing not fifteen feet away from Lee and Venable when they rode through an opening in the works and stepped into the barely discernible creek bottom behind the Texans.[74] Hat in hand, Lee slipped undetected into the brigade line between the 5th Texas' left flank and the 4th Texas' right flank. Private John G. Wheeler (Company B, 4th Texas) apparently noticed the general first. "Lee to the rear!" he cried out in astonishment. To the left front, Third Corporal E. J. Parrent (Company D, 4th Texas) turned and pushed the palm of his left hand against the horse's shoulder. "We won't go unless you go back!" someone yelled. Gee, on Lee's right, reached out and snatched Traveller's bridle near the bit. By then, a large number of enlisted men and officers, among them Gregg and his brigade adjutant, Captain John W. Kerr, had converged on Lee. "General Lee to the rear!" and "Go back, General Lee! Go back!" echoed along most of the line. Enlisted men clutched after the general's arms but he shook them off. Gregg repeated the same sentiments while Gee was tugging on Traveller's bridle and started to turn the horse about. Lee quickly took control of his horse and gently urged him toward the rear. "Well then," he said half aloud to Venable, "I will go back." He had barely left the ranks when Venable noticed Longstreet on a knoll near the pike.

"Lee to the Rear."

This 1800's print captures the drama of the moment as three of Lee's soldiers reach out to turn him back from the thick of the battle.

Massachusetts Commandery; MOLLUS, USAMHI

"General," Venable pointed out, "there is General Longstreet." Without saying a word, the commanding general and his aide quietly rode over to Longstreet's side, leaving the Texas Brigade to continue its charge. The two generals briefly discussed the tactical situation along the pike.[75]

SOUTH OF THE PLANK ROAD

As they did so, Humphreys' Mississippi brigade approached them on the doublequick. The 18th Mississippi led the advance. Private W. Gart Johnson (Company C) glanced off to the left through the dust and swore he saw no less than five or six officers gathered along the roadside. In the confusion, he mistook Lee's and Longstreet's staffs as general officers but he distinctly recognized the commanding general and his own corps commander.

"General," he heard Lee command, "you had better form your line a half mile back and bring it up." "I think we can form here," Longstreet called back. He twisted in the saddle and ordered Humphreys, who had just halted his brigade in the road, to form his regiments where they stood. Johnson recalled, "We...were panting like lizards."

**Captain David A. Dickert,
Company H, 3rd South Carolina**

David Augustus Dickert, who enlisted in 1861 when he was fifteen years old, saw more South Carolinians hit at the Wilderness than he remembered seeing Federal casualties at Fredericksburg.

Dickert, *Kershaw's Brigade*, 1899

Humphreys faced his column, stood in the stirrups, and screamed, "Battalion front! By company, right half wheel, doublequick, march!" The four Mississippi regiments broke formation by companies and wheeled to face southeast. All the while Federal bullets thunked into the Confederate regiments who had not had a chance to load their weapons. They stoically absorbed the rounds from Ward's front regiments, who had moved into the woods between the Plank Road and the left flank of Henagan's South Carolinians.[76] The South Carolinians took a fearful beating within the first few minutes of the action. Captain David A. Dickert (Company H, 3rd South Carolina) saw Carolinians cut down in gory heaps which rivaled the scores of Federal dead before the stone wall at Fredericksburg.[77]

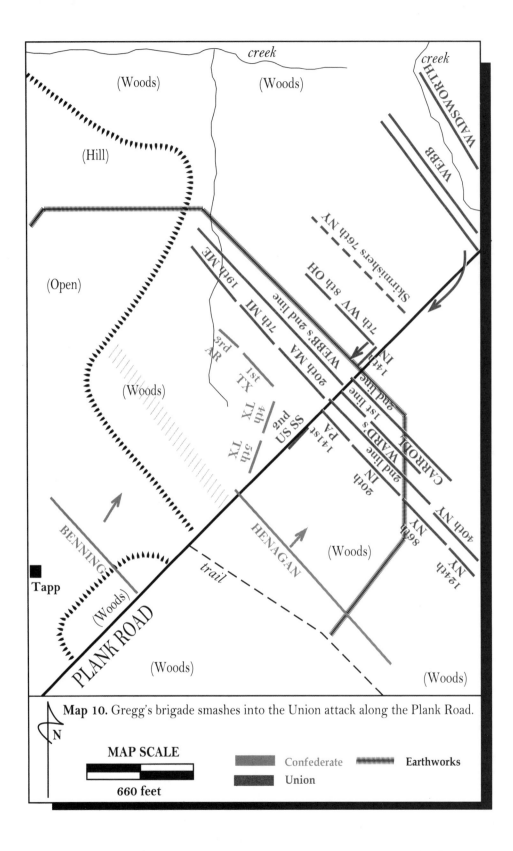

Map 10. Gregg's brigade smashes into the Union attack along the Plank Road.

MAP SCALE

660 feet

Confederate   Earthworks

Union

N

North of the Plank Road
(About 250 yards east of McGowan's earthworks)

The rallied 19th Maine never contacted Rice's brigade (Wadsworth's division) while it waited for a counterattack which did not occur. Colonel Selden Connor took the time to review the situation east of his regiment. "While the troops were all in good order," he wrote much later, "confusion and uncertainty seemed to prevail among their leaders."[78] Connor did not linger near Wadsworth's division. Before too long, Webb came marching along the Plank Road with the rest of his brigade. He was operating under direct orders from Birney to relieve Getty's division (VI Corps), which Birney believed was on the north side of the Plank Road.[79] (Neither of them realized that Getty's three brigades were already on the south side of the road and were nowhere near the direction in which Webb was heading.) Once Webb cleared Wadsworth's front, he maneuvered his brigade into battle formation north of the road. The 20th Massachusetts anchored the left of the front line. The 7th Michigan fell in to its right.[80] The 19th Maine secured the right flank.[81] The remaining five regiments comprised the second line.[82] The brigade crunched through the woods unobserved by Carroll, who was south of the road, and crossed over McGowan's abandoned works.

Carroll, because he had seen no troops beyond his right flank and had no idea what was transpiring farther west along the road, sent his third line into action. Colonel John Coons flanked his 14th Indiana to the right and sent it in column of fours down the Plank Road with orders to sweep the Rebels out of the woods along the front.[83] The 8th Ohio and the 7th West Virginia went into line in the woods, faced west, then stepped off in line of battle.

In the meantime, Lee had ridden a few paces north of Longstreet's knoll, heading for the base of Tapp's hill. His conscientious aide, Venable, took the opportunity to apprise Longstreet of what had transpired with Gregg's Texans. Longstreet slipped away from Humphreys' men, rode over to Lee, and firmly told him, as only he could, that his place was not on the front lines. Lee respectfully listened to his "Old War Horse" and urged Traveller to the safety of Poague's artillery battalion.[84]

Gregg's three Texas regiments and the 3rd Arkansas did not lose any time getting onto the field. Seconds after Lee withdrew from their front ranks, they closed up their formation and pressed forward. Webb's brigade, which had ascended the hill a few yards beyond McGowan's old line picked off about a squad of men from the 4th Texas as they approached the pines in the southeastern corner of Tapp's field. "Some of our best men were killed and wounded before a chance was given them to fire a shot," Quartermaster Sergeant Joseph Polley lamented years later. Fat Private Jim

Summerville (Company F), staggering under the impact of a direct hit in the belt buckle, dropped his rifle, clutched his belly in his arms and spun from the onrushing line. The men nearest him roared with laughter as Summerville, who was howling in a pitch that ran up and down the scale, whirled around a couple of times before he could stop himself. With the guffaws of his comrades echoing around him, he quickly unbuckled his waist belt. The bullet, which bored through his buckle and tunic, barely broke the skin near his navel.[85]

The Texans surged ahead another hundred yards into the edge of the woods.[86] The sight of a waiting Federal battle line startled the Confederates but did not slow their pace. Webb, who was just as surprised, did not yield either. His soldiers stood their ground and volleyed into the 4th Texas and the 5th Texas regiments as they swept past them and made straight for Ward's right flank in hopes of crashing through the Federal lines.[87] The 2nd U.S. Sharpshooters, on Ward's right, sniping from tree to tree, dropped many Texans in their tracks. Very few of the Southerners penetrated the Yankee lines. They came so close to the Federals, however, that their muzzle blasts literally singed the Sharpshooters' faces. Sergeant Wyman White (Company F, 2nd U.S. Sharpshooters) wrote, "Men on both sides stood until they fell...killed or wounded. More men were lost during that hour than had been lost all the morning before."[88]

The Confederates drove the Berdans back upon the right angle of Lane's former line of works which paralleled the Plank Road. The 141st Pennsylvania stood its ground behind the north-south line created by the eastern leg of the works and unleashed an horrific volley into the 4th and the 5th Texas at a distance of less than one hundred yards. A bullet hammered Sergeant Major George Robinson (5th Texas) in the head. The ball bored through one side of his face, severed his tongue, and shattered his jaw before exiting through the opposite cheek. Acting Major J. J. McBride (5th Texas) was shot through both legs.[89] A bullet knocked the color bearer of the 4th Texas off his feet. Nevertheless, he held onto the colors until Private A. A. Durfee (Company B) pulled the staff from his hands. A minie ball shattered Durfee's hip before he had gone fifty yards. He passed the colors to Sergeant Major Charles S. Brown, whom the Federals felled the second he laid his hands upon the flag. The sergeant major gave them to a fourth man who escaped the fighting unscathed.[90] The brigade ordnance officer, Second Lieutenant Whit Randall (Company K, 1st Texas) collapsed in the ditch alongside the road, pierced by no less than five bullets.[91] The Berdans' hellish, continuous rapid fire brought the charge to an abrupt halt. The badly mauled Confederate regiments closed ranks and tried to slug it out with the numerically superior Federal forces.

To the north, the 3rd Arkansas and the 1st Texas found themselves squaring off against Webb's brigade and suffering equally heavy casual-

**Brigadier General
Alexander S. Webb, U.S.A.**

His Federal brigade fought Brigadier General John Gregg's 1st Texas and 3rd Arkansas to a standstill north of the Plank Road.

Massachusetts Commandery;
MOLLUS, USAMHI

ties.[92] A minie ball knocked Colonel Van H. Manning (3rd Arkansas) off his feet. He lay on the ground with a shattered thigh. His second in command, Major William K. Wilkins, died in the fighting. Before the regiment could quit the action, the Federals had cut down eight of the ten officers present for duty and had killed or wounded 83 enlisted men out of an effective strength of 155 officers and men.[93] The 1st Texas lost just as heavily. The 20th Massachusetts split its fire between the 1st Texas and the left flanks and the backs of the 4th Texas and the 5th Texas. The 7th Michigan and the 19th Maine steadily hammered the 1st Texas and the 3rd Arkansas until the Mainers ran out of ammunition. Upon receiving permission to pull his men out of the line, Connor retired his regiment from the fighting. Captain Charles H. Banes, the Assistant Adjutant General of the brigade, led the 19th Maine to the ammunition crates which were about one hundred fifty yards behind the firing line.[94]

A Yankee bullet zipped into Company F, 4th Texas and snapped Corporal Bob Murray's leg in two just below the knee. He crumbled to the forest floor in a great deal of pain. Looking up, he spied Quartermaster Sergeant Joseph Polley and his clerk, Private William "Ole Pap" Morris (Company F), coming toward him at a run. "Dad gum it, Joe," he painfully pleaded, "I beg; you and 'Ole Pap' help me to the rear!" Polley hesitated momentarily, still fuming over the way Murray had cheated him at cards two days before. Nevertheless, leaving the field was a more viable option than staying with the regiment. Grabbing the wounded corporal by the arms, the two veterans hauled him up between them and dragged him away. Murray's dead leg flopped from side to side as they pulled him through the woods toward the Plank Road. Occasionally it wrapped itself around a sapling or snagged on some underbrush, which staggered their retreat. In the rush to escape, Polley, who kept his eyes glued upon the ground to see where his feet were heading, ran into a low hanging tree branch which snatched his hat from his head. He cried out, "Hold on, Morris, and let me get my hat!" "Ole Pap" refused to slow down. "A great time to pick up a hat!" he shot back, as he kept making tracks.[95]

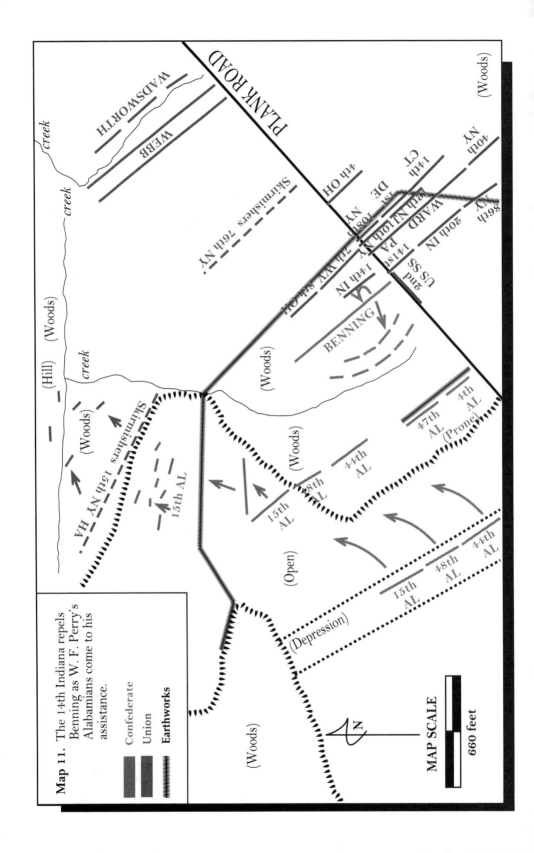

Map 11. The 14th Indiana repels Benning as W. F. Perry's Alabamians come to his assistance.

Confederate
Union
Earthworks

MAP SCALE

660 feet

N

(Woods)

(Depression)

(Open)

15th AL
48th AL
44th AL

15th AL

44th AL

48th AL

47th AL

4th AL
(Prone)

(Woods)

Skirmishers 15th NY HA

15th AL

(Woods)

(Hill)

creek

Skirmishers 76th NY

BENNING

14th IN

8th OH

7th WV sharps

14th NY

141st PA

20th IN

86th NY

WARD

US SS

2nd

40th NY

1st US SS

DE

14th CT

4th OH

WEBB

WADSWORTH

creek

creek

creek

(Woods)

PLANK ROAD

Within half an hour, it was all over. When Gregg noticed the 14th Indiana doublequicking up the Plank Road, heading directly for the left rear of his two regiments, he yelled for the 4th Texas and the 5th Texas to pull out. The Texas brigade ran from the field, leaving over fifty percent of their original eight hundred effectives dead or wounded between the lines.[96] The Texans and the Arkansans streamed around Brigadier General Henry L. Benning's Georgia brigade as it charged into the woods on the eastern side of Tapp's farm. Benning, whom the men referred to as "Old Rock," spurred his horse from one end of the brigade line to the other to hurry his men along. As Benning rode behind the 15th Georgia, Private William A. Flanigan (Company G) saw one of Gregg's badly wounded men take off his battered felt hat and flag the general down with it. "Drive up, Rock," the injured man rasped, "Old Tige's treed over yonder." The general, appreciating the wounded fellow's concern for General George T. Anderson and his brigade, called back, "Attend to your wound. I'll attend to Tige." Second Lieutenant Thomas Culver and Private Joseph H. Hines (both Company K), who overheard the general, laughed.[97] The Georgians ran pell-mell toward the Yankee lines.

While the 14th Indiana was flanking right and filing onto the low ground east of the Widow Tapp's, the 7th West Virginia and 8th Ohio were crossing over the captured Confederate works and relieving Webb's fatigued brigade from the firing line. The two disoriented regiments had walked only a few yards beyond the Confederate rear line entrenchments when Benning's Georgians sprang upon the left flank of the 14th Indiana. Colonel John Coons (14th Indiana) quickly recovered from the unexpected attack. Fronting the regiment, he commanded the men to open fire, then called at the top of his voice to Lieutenant Colonel Franklin Sawyer to bring his 8th Ohio into line by files to strengthen his position.[98] At the same time Benning reeled under the impact of a ball which broke the bones in his left shoulder. Turning the brigade over to Colonel Dudley M. DuBose (15th Georgia), he headed to the rear. Lieutenant Tom Culver and Private Joe Hines (both of Company K, 15th Georgia) perished in the volley.[99] Caught in a deadly fire from the front and the right flank from the 141st Pennsylvania, which had just driven Gregg's Texans away, Benning's Georgians collapsed. His badly mauled brigade reeled from the field.[100]

WILLIAM F. PERRY'S ALABAMA BRIGADE IN TAPP'S FIELD

No sooner had Benning's brigade disappeared into the woods east of the Tapp house than Brigadier General E. McIver Law's Alabama brigade, under the command of Colonel William F. Perry, doublequicked up the Plank Road. The 15th regiment brought the brigade on to the field, followed by the 48th, 44th, 47th, and the 4th regiments. Obliquing to the left as they came abreast of the Tapp house, the 15th Alabama swept behind

Lee and his staff officers. The general's full black cloak caught Colonel William C. Oates' attention.

Lee wore it over his shoulders as if he had a chill. His face was livid. His mouth moved nervously. ("Full of animation..." was how Oates described it.) Bullets zipped overhead from the east and the southeast. Lee ignored them, his gaze fixed upon the fighting south of the Plank Road. Turning in the saddle, the general shouted at his chief of staff, "Send an active young officer down there." The appearance of Confederate infantry behind him stunned him a little. "What troops are these?" Lee blurted. "Law's Alabama brigade," a private in the 15th regiment shot back. "God bless the Alabamians!" Lee shouted.[101]

Once the 15th Alabama gained enough room for the entire brigade to clear the Plank Road, it fronted and bolted east toward the cover of the small fold in the ground which crossed the field about two hundred yards beyond General Lee. It waited there for the rest of the brigade to come into line on its right. The Alabamians stood in place. Not long after, litter bearers carried the severely wounded Benning through their ranks.[102] The 48th Alabama fell in to the right, followed successively by the 44th, 47th, and the 4th regiments.

The brigade momentarily rested in the depression. Major General Charles W. Field trotted his horse along the length of the line. He halted behind the 4th Alabama and called Colonel Pinckney D. Bowles to his side. He rapidly told Bowles to send out skirmishers and to keep his right flank against the Plank Road. The 4th was to be the directing (guide) battalion for the entire brigade.

Skirmishers leaped into the open, skittered forward about fifty yards and threw themselves down in a dense thicket. For several minutes they anxiously watched Federal bullets clip through their perimeter. The brigade rushed to their assistance and the attack spilled into the woods in response to the volleys from the 141st Pennsylvania which were driving Benning's Georgians from the front.[103]

Help for the 14th Indiana came too late. Perry's Alabamians loosed a wild volley into the woods and charged. The loud crashing noise which the balls made in the forest to the west told First Lieutenant Thomas Galwey (Company B, 8th Ohio) that the front lines had run into fresh troops with full cartridge boxes.[104]

The oncoming Alabamians pushed about one hundred yards onto the wooded plateau on the eastern side of the Tapp farm. The 4th and the 47th Alabama, having gotten ahead of the rest of the command, went prone behind a temporary line of piled up tree trunks and rubbish along the brow of the hill. They scattered their skirmishers toward the creek bottom along Wilderness Run, where they ran into the fitful musketry of the 14th Indiana as it peppered the fleeing remnants of the previous assault. Bowles, who had also been given command of the 47th Alabama, listened to the tempo of the firing pick up on the far right of his line. He incorrectly assumed that "Tige" Anderson's Georgians had come up on the south side of the Plank Road. (Humphreys' Mississippians were on his flank.) The 14th Indiana forced Bowles' skirmishers to retire to the works. The Alabamians responded with two volleys, then charged.[105]

The Northern End of W. F. Perry's Line

The remaining three regiments on the left of the brigade inadvertently walked into flank fire from Colonel J. Howard Kitching's two regiment brigade which had just arrived on the field north of Wadsworth's division. The huge 15th New York Heavy Artillery, having crossed Wilderness Run from the north, posted skirmishers in the fringe of woods about two hundred fifty yards beyond Perry's left. The 6th New York Heavy Artillery, an equally large regiment, formed its reserve on the crest of the wooded hillside behind the 15th. Fresh from the defenses of Washington and armed as infantry, neither regiment had ever fired a hostile round before that morning. They outnumbered the Alabamians by almost seven to one and clearly had the opportunity to roll up Longstreet's corps from the north.

As soon as the first incoming shots passed harmlessly over the Alabamians, Perry quickly ascertained that the Federals were on the high wooded ground to his left. He immediately ordered Colonel William C. Oates to take his 15th Alabama after them.[106] The colonel shouted the command and the line officers picked it up. The 450-man regiment executed a sixty-degree wheel without seeming to break step and charged.[107] The northern face of McGowan's abandoned earthworks destroyed the regiment's formation as the veterans madly clawed their way over the headlogs. The Rebel yell resonated across the plateau.

The artillerymen in the 15th New York Heavy Artillery, having never heard the Confederate battle cry, broke ranks and skedaddled at a crouch back across the creek and up the hillside. They marked their rout with their discarded haversacks, blanket rolls, and knapsacks. Private William C. Jordan (Company B, 15th Alabama) gazed in awe at the tremendous quantity of accouterments which the frightened Federals were throwing aside. "This certainly was the richest battle field that I ever beheld," he mused.

By the time the 15th Alabama reached the far edge of the clearing and the swamp at the base of the hill, its formation had dissolved into a skirmish line. The Confederates snared about eight frightened Federals and cut down a handful of New Yorkers who were trying to escape. Every now and then a Federal shot back. Private Thomas White (15th Alabama), on the far left of Company B, went down with a shattered leg. Word of mouth

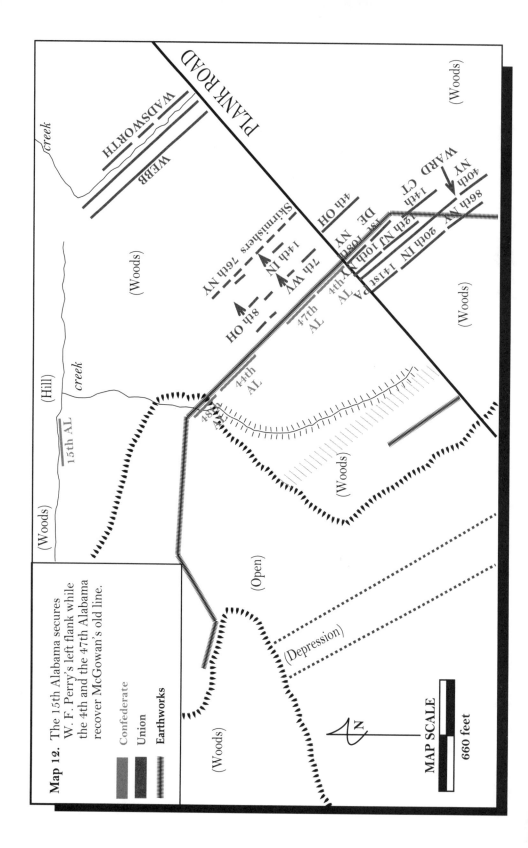

Map 12. The 15th Alabama secures W. F. Perry's left flank while the 4th and the 47th Alabama recover McGowan's old line.

Confederate
Union
Earthworks

PLANK ROAD

WADSWORTH
WEBB

creek

(Woods)

(Hill)
creek

(Woods)

15th AL

76th NY
14th IN
Skirmishers
7th WV
8th OH
47th AL

44th AL

48th AL

WARD
40th NY
14th CT
86th NY
4th OH
DE
98th NY
108th NY
2nd NJ
9th NY
20th IN
141st PA
4th AL
141st PA

(Woods)

(Woods)

(Woods)

(Open)

(Depression)

(Woods)

MAP SCALE
660 feet

N

carried the news to the far right of the line to his uncle. There being nothing he could do for White, Private William C. Jordan splashed across Wilderness Run with his company and cautiously started up the hillside.

The Confederates advanced in extended order. Jordan spied a rolled Yankee gum blanket lying in the brush about a foot to his right front. He deftly sidestepped and snatched up the rubber ground sheet, tossed off his own wool one, and slipped the Federal one across his body before continuing his advance. By then a large portion of the 15th Heavies had rallied on the top of the hill and were firing wildly down upon the Confederates. The surprised Southerners instantly dove to the ground and began throwing tree limbs in front of themselves for protection. While most of the Yankee rounds went high, a number of them found their marks. Before the shooting stopped they managed to kill two Alabamians and wound ten more. Jordan, who had lain down with several other men, while returning fire, felt something tug on one of his ankles. He hastily pulled his pants leg out of the top of his sock only to find that the bullet had cut through his sock and pants without striking meat. The skirmish lasted several minutes. The heat and general exhaustion from having become engaged in combat began to tell upon him. He broke into a cold sweat. His throat became exceedingly dry. He called Captain DeBurnie Waddell (Company G) to his side and asked if he could borrow his tin cup. The captain handed it to him. With his rifle at trail arms, the private took off at a dog trot down the hill toward the creek. On the way, a spent bullet smacked into the stock of his weapon without disabling it. He reached the creek, drank a cup of muddy water, then refilled it to take some of it back to Waddell.

By the time he returned to the firing line the 6th New York Heavy Artillery was in line behind the 15th New York. It appeared that the Federals were moving toward the Confederate left. The Confederates did not hang around to be "gobbled up." They broke and ran to the open ground south of the creek branch where Oates hastily shoved the regiment back into formation.[108]

THE SOUTHERN END OF W. F. PERRY'S LINE

Meanwhile, on the far right of the brigade along the Plank Road, the 4th Alabama dropped an estimated twenty men in the 14th Indiana.[109] At least eighteen officers and enlisted men were also hit in the 8th Ohio. Captain James E. Craig (Company E) died instantly. Captain David Lewis (Company G), who, despite the warm weather, had gone into battle wearing a great coat with half cape, crashed to the ground with a shattered thigh. One of his men grabbed his cape and dragged him from the firing line. Colonel John Coons (14th Indiana) frantically rode over to Lieutenant Colonel Franklin Sawyer (8th Ohio). Being on horseback, they could see the woods in front of them swarming with Confederates, and they decided to withdraw their colors to keep them from getting captured.[110]

Their men, however, did not stand on orders. The 14th Indiana streamed rearward, taking the 7th West Virginia, on the left of the line, with it. Private John R. McClure (Company G, 14th Indiana) peeked out from behind a tree, only to find himself staring down the muzzle of a Rebel's musket. He threw himself behind cover and awaited the shot, which did not come. Snatching up a nearby stick, the boy stuck his hat upon it and cautiously poked it into the open. At the same time he swung around to the opposite side of the tree. When the Confederate popped his head out of the thicket in which he was hiding to better identify his target, McClure squeezed off a well aimed shot. The Confederate toppled into the brush.

Sickened at heart, the startled Yankee ran over to his prey. He had never seen any of his "kills" die before. He rolled the dead soldier over and saw how youthful the "man" seemed. For a moment, McClure contemplated rifling the boy's pockets for identification so he could send word home to the fellow's parents. When he saw the dead soldier's face and heard the death groan escaping from his lungs, he changed his mind. He did not have the stomach to rob him. Leaving the Confederate alone, he went back into the fight only to be grazed in the right arm and seriously wounded in the right breast.[111]

Sergeant Owen T. Wright (Company D, 14th Indiana) was "gobbled up" in the assault. While the Alabamians were herding him to the rear past Poague's artillery battalion, he peered at the gunners, who were standing in front of their field pieces and straining to look over the tree tops to see what was going on. "Which is the direct route to Richmond, boys?" the sergeant shouted at them. They apparently did not hear him over the hellish rifle fire which thundered through the woods to the south.[112]

A disconcerting alarm rippled through the 8th Ohio from the left that its flank was up in the air. Galwey darted a glance across the road to his left. A large body of Confederate troops was pushing, almost at a run, through the small clearings behind the regiment. The Western officers screamed at their men to "change front—left to rear" but the command came too late and the dense hazel broke up the 8th Ohio. The recruits in the regiment panicked and bolted rearward—in ones, twos, and threes until the larger part of the line shattered. The Confederates, upon seeing the fleeing Federals' heads bobbing up and down among the stubby trees, frightened the recruits more with their fierce Rebel yells. The veterans in the 8th Ohio swore mightily at the recruits to come back and fall in, but to no avail. All they could do was fend for themselves. The Ohioans ran in squads—east—toward the Brock Road.

The retreat nearly accomplished what the Rebels' bullets could not. The hazel trees ripped and tore the men's clothes and gouged their arms

and legs. Time and again the men in front trampled over pliant chinqua-
pins which, when let go, viciously slapped the faces of the men. A clump
of bushes savagely ripped the seat out of Galwey's trousers. A staff officer, while galloping by, guffawed and pointed at the lieutenant's exposed rear, then spurred away. Embarrassed, he snatched up a discarded
shirt as he ran and stuffed it into his pants.[113] He was determined to retreat with dignity.[114]

THE 15TH ALABAMA ON THE NORTHERN END OF W. F. PERRY'S LINE

Private William C. Jordan (Company B) found Colonel William C. Oates
on the open plateau south of the swamp firmly reforming his tired men.
The enlisted man bluntly told Oates that he was too overheated to go back
into the fray. The colonel patiently told him that the regiment was going to
stack arms because they were going to be relieved by other troops. Jordan
immediately thrust his rifle at Private William M. Callaway, his messmate,
with orders to stack it, whereupon he walked over to a nearby cherry tree
and plopped down to rest.[115]

WADSWORTH'S DIVISION, V CORPS
(About 140 yards east of McGowan's abandoned works)

A picket from the 76th New York tore into the regiment's skirmishers
shouting something about the Rebel regiments being four lines deep and
heading their way. Private Francis M. Norton (Company C, 76th New York)
did not put any credence into the fellow's report until he heard the musketry from Perry's Alabamians crashing through the woods in front of his
regiment and saw panting refugees from Carroll's three regiments breaking for the rear. A number of those men rallied on the 76th New York. Every now and then one of the nervous New Yorkers opened fire despite the
warnings of their officers to the contrary. Disregarding the impressive volume of rounds which zipped and thudded through the woods around them,
the officers insisted that there were no Confederates to the west. The New
Yorkers became more anxious. Again, handfuls of men snapped off shots
into the smoke-obscured woods to their front. Norton could not handle the
stress any longer. Orders or not he pulled off a round in the direction of the
shooting. While he brought the weapon down to reload he noticed that
nearly everyone around him was running toward the rear. He did not hesitate to join them. A few steps behind the old firing line, a bullet struck his
arm, staggering him, but he kept on running.[116] The 76th New York created
a stampede. Webb's brigade collapsed behind them.[117] In turn, a large portion of Stone's Pennsylvania brigade fragmented and fell back into Baxter's
which had maneuvered to the northwest. Baxter was wounded and the
11th Pennsylvania lost 157 men before leaving the field. In the confusion,
the 12th Massachusetts split apart. Some of the men crossed to the south

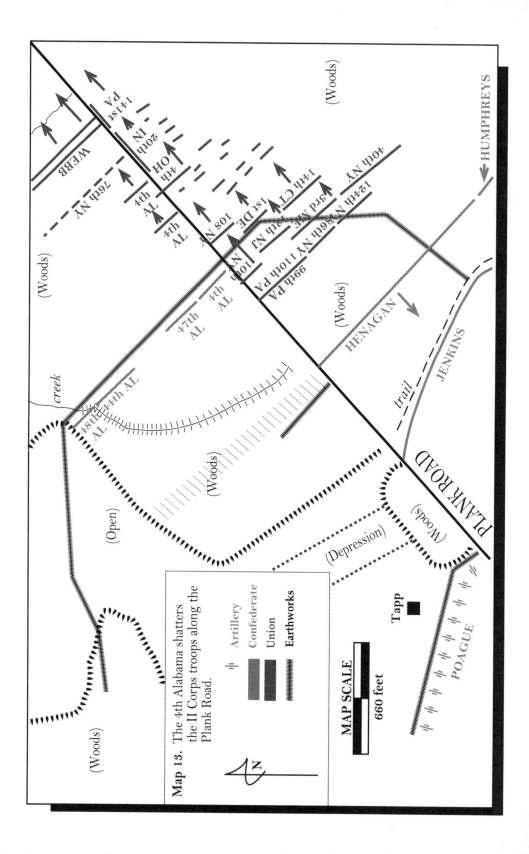

Map 13. The 4th Alabama shatters the II Corps troops along the Plank Road.

Artillery
Confederate
Union
Earthworks

Tapp

MAP SCALE

660 feet

N

(Woods)

(Woods)

(Woods)

(Woods)

(Woods)

(Open)

(Depression)

creek

WEBB

141st PA

76th NY

20th IN

4th OH

4th AL

4th AL

108 NY

1st DE

14th CT

3rd NJ

126th NY

124th NY

10th NY

40th NY

66th NY

110th PA

99th PA

101st NY

4th AL

47th AL

48th AL

44th AL

HENAGAN

JENKINS

trail

HUMPHREYS

PLANK ROAD

POAGUE

side of the Plank Road while the rest followed the brigade. By then, Cutler's brigade had been shattered by the Federal soldiers in front of them.[118] The frightened soldiers scattered north and east with most of them not stopping until they reached the Brock Road or Lacy's farm.[119]

SOUTH OF THE PLANK ROAD

Across the road from Bowles' attack, Ward's first and second lines were engaged in a stubborn stand up fight against Humphreys' Mississippians and Henagan's South Carolinians. For a brief time, the Confederates surged forward before being driven away. Again they pushed ahead only to be stubbornly forced back to their original jump off point. About one hundred yards to the rear, the Carolinians literally collided with Brigadier General Micah Jenkins' five South Carolina regiments from Field's division which had gone prone in the trail which ran south from Tapp's. Henagan's men rallied in front of Jenkins' troops and forced the Federal line back.[120]

In less than five minutes Company C of the 18th Mississippi, Humphreys' lead regiment, lost one lieutenant and sixteen enlisted men out of two officers and thirty-four enlisted men engaged. Private W. Gart Johnson (Company C, 18th Mississippi) later estimated that the other companies in his regiment suffered just as severely. The Federals' deadly rifle fire and the dense woods having completely destroyed whatever Confederate regimental formations existed, the Southerners were forced to fight in small clusters from mixed commands.[121] To the right rear of the two brigades Bryan's Georgia regiments struggled through the Wilderness to deploy farther south along their flank. Jenkins rode into his left regiment, the 1st South Carolina, and issued orders to nineteen-year-old Colonel James R. Hagood to advance his men to the front whenever he deemed it necessary. The young colonel wisely let his men stay prone.[122]

Shortly before Bowles' Alabamians slammed into the 14th Indiana, the 141st Pennsylvania and the 20th Indiana, having nearly exhausted their sixty rounds per man, filed right into the Plank Road and headed east toward the ammunition wagons to the rear.[123] The 99th Pennsylvania and the 110th Pennsylvania from Ward's second line moved into the space which they left vacant. The 10th New York and the 12th New Jersey, standing in Carroll's line some distance behind them did not, in turn, advance to replace them on the right of the 3rd Maine. This left a gap in the Federal formation and exposed the right flank of the 3rd Maine to any incoming volleys from that area. While Humphreys' and Henagan's Confederates kept the front line regiments busy, Bowles made his attack against Carroll's three regiments north of the pike.

What happened next cannot be attributed to any preconceived plan. When the 14th Indiana and the 7th West Virginia collapsed and fled to the east, they simultaneously uncovered the flank of the 8th Ohio north of the road and exposed the rear of the Federal troops south of the road. The 4th Alabama poured into the gap and created a general panic through the center of the Federal columns. By throwing themselves into McGowan's old earthworks, they flanked the Yankee line south of the Plank Road.

Their riflery struck the 3rd Maine first. A spent ball thunked into Private Ashbury F. Haynes' (Company F) thick skull, knocking him flat. "Haynes is killed!" a comrade called out. A minute or two later, the stunned and badly bruised enlisted man "resurrected" himself from the dead and groggily assumed his place in the firing line.[124] Officers frantically screamed at their men to retreat, but in the din of small arms fire not everyone heard their pleas. Eighteen-year-old Private George G. Russell (Company E, 3rd Maine) suddenly turned toward his right to check upon the regimental colors. They had disappeared. Scared out of his wits and lonesome beyond belief he wheeled about and trotted but a few paces when he realized that he had been surrounded. Rebels swarmed the woods between him and the regiment. He instinctively dropped his rifle to the ground to see what would happen.[125] The hard headed Haynes did not realize he was alone either until he cast a glance to both sides and saw that the line had fled. He ran faster than Russell. Bounding down the hill, he stumbled across his messmates—Privates Condon and William H. Ham. They had both gone down with thigh wounds. A hasty glance told the pragmatic New Englander he could not save either one of them. Despite Ham's plea to carry him off, Haynes kept on running. He saw no need to rescue the dying.[126]

The Alabamians also fired into the right of Carroll's brigade south of the Plank Road. The 10th New York's skirmishers, in their distinctive Zouave uniforms, darted into the line from the smoky woods across the road with word that the Confederates were not far behind. Captain George M. Dewey (Company A), who commanded the battalion of 298 officers and men, ordered Companies A and D, on the right of the regiment to wheel until they faced the Plank Road. The two companies fired by flies from the right into Bowles' Alabamians who responded immediately. A number of the hostile rounds struck home. First Sergeant Jack Hannigan (Company A) went down with a bullet through his heart. The same musketry also killed Private Jesse W. Chace (Company A) and Corporal John Meeks (Company F), whose company formed the angle of the line. On the left of the regiment Captain Joseph La Fiura's Company E, which consisted mostly of recruits, nearly panicked the rest of the battalion. Some of the newly enlisted Frenchmen in the company, in accordance with European custom, stepped back from the firing line to reload. The men around them misinterpreted their actions as a prelude to a rout. One by one, the four companies from the road to the left of the line wavered and began to lose their cohesion. Color Sergeant Edward Harrison (Company B), the color guard, Captain Dewey (Company A), Second Lieutenant Charles W. Cowtan (Company K) and several officers halted the rout by advancing the colors forward of the line. The frightened soldiers returned to the ranks and marched about fifty feet beyond their original line. At this point, the Confederates lashed into the New Yorkers with a vengeance. Their well aimed volleys knocked down an estimated 60 officers and men. Twenty-year-old Second Lieutenant George Hackett (Company A) lost his right arm as a result.[127] In going forward, the 10th New York exposed the right flank of the 12th New Jersey to incoming rounds. The 12th, having already absorbed enough rounds, collapsed and retreated rearward, the regiment breaking into harried squads. "We tried to stand it [the enfilade] but it was more than human power could do," First Lieutenant George A. Bowen (Company C) wrote in his diary.[128]

When Carroll's first line folded, it collided with the 108th New York, the 1st Delaware, and the 14th Connecticut. Adjutant William B. Hincks (14th Connecticut) watched his men pitch from the firing line as Confederate rounds struck home. Without orders, the New Englanders replied with a terrific volley, to which the Rebels responded in kind. For half an hour the forest roared and flamed as the opposing forces tried to blast each other into eternity. Once again Hincks found himself in a conflagration reminiscent of his first combat at Antietam where he could not hear the screams of the men standing near him. The regiment was taking an horrific beating. Captain Samuel Fiske (Company G) went down in the tumult—mortally wounded in the shoulder.[129] The noise unnerved First Sergeant Elnathan B. Tyler (Company B). When the man standing next to him pitched to the ground Tyler could not synchronize the man's death with the sickening thud he normally associated with a minie ball impacting flesh. The firing was simply too loud. His mind inadvertently fine-tuned itself to pick up the "zip" "zip" of the individual bullets which sang past his ears. Each one seemed to tell him that his time had come.[130]

The 1st Delaware, its ammunition expended, retired from the fighting. Its

First Lieutenant William B. Hincks, Adjutant, 14th Connecticut

This youthful looking veteran compared the fighting in the Wilderness with his first engagement at Antietam. The fighting was so intense in both battles that he could not hear the screams of the men around him when they were shot.

withdrawal stampeded the 108th New York. Neither regiment stopped running until they reached the Brock Road.[131] The 14th Connecticut, rather than be captured, was slowly retiring from the fight. Crawling back over the Rebel breastworks, which were nothing more than a few felled trees with dirt thrown over them, the Connecticut soldiers lay down around their colors and returned fire. About fifty men under the command of Captain James R. Nichols (Company I) and Lieutenant J. Frank Morgan (Company C) fought Indian fashion from tree to tree on the regiment's left. Their riflery quickly drove the Confederates back into the woods.[132]

The Confederates forced Colonel Lewis A. Grant to refuse the right of his brigade line.[133] Bowles' attack, however, expended itself just before it reached Wheaton's VI Corps brigade. Wheaton walked his regiments into line on Grant's right and proceeded to lay a destructive fire northward across the pike.[134] A number of the Alabamians pursued some of the Federal refugees to the swale in front of Wheaton. One of his Pennsylvania regiments had formed on the level ground about three to four hundred yards east of the crest. The men went to their knees and peppered the brush-covered creek ridge across from them, hoping to strike down an enemy whom they could not see. Their bullets caught the fleeing Private Ashbury F. Haynes (Company F, 3rd Maine) in the creek bed as he attempted to scale the bank. Rebel bullets spattered the hillside around him. Yankee riflery pruned the scrub trees and overgrowth above his head. He fully expected to die from both incoming fires. Skittering over the hilltop on all fours while the minie balls clipped the bushes off at their bases, he rushed through the Pennsylvanians to their colonel, whom he found standing by the regimental colors.

"Is the first line of battle all in?" the colonel demanded. "All in, Colonel, but the dead and dying," Haynes panted. "I am the last man to leave the Third Division of the II Corps." "How far away are the Rebels?" the colonel persisted. "About 100 rods, coming down the hill." "I've got no orders to charge," the officer blurted, somewhat confused, "what would you do?" "I would charge upon the Rebel line, orders or no orders." At that, Haynes dashed to the left wing of the regiment and attempted to rally that end of the line. It was too late. Minutes later, the formation broke and streamed back toward the Brock Road, dragging Haynes with it.[135]

During the brief encounter, a minie ball wounded Getty, forcing him to turn the division over to Wheaton. Wheaton watched in amazement as the Confederate attack stopped and retreated back toward Tapp's field. The general noted, "The enemy, on account of the dense woods, could not see the advantage gained, and his weak reconnoitering force following the II Corps was obliged to retreat as soon as they came in view of our front."[136] That "weak reconnoitering force" was the 4th Alabama. During its brief half hour of hell raising the regiment had gallantly nearly spent itself in a "forlorn hope" against no less than three Federal divisions, the better part of which the Alabamians routed or disorganized.[137]

NORTH OF THE PLANK ROAD

The sudden rush of his scattered regiments to the rear sent Wadsworth down the Plank Road toward the first organized troops which he could find. He clattered to a halt in front of the 150th Pennsylvania and the 143rd Pennsylvania (Stone's brigade). The Pennsylvanians anxiously clutched their weapons. Their own men streamed rearward, skirting around the regiment's flanks or shouldering through its ranks to seek refuge behind their line. "Give it to them, Bucktails!" The two Pennsylvania regiments emptied their rifles into the Alabamians, staggering their charge. Wadsworth could hardly contain himself. "Boys, you are driving them," he screamed. "Charge!"[138] The Alabamians withdrew, taking prisoners as they went.

Back at Scales' abandoned earthworks, a Confederate soldier got the drop on Private George G. Russell (Company E, 3rd Maine). "Take off your cartridge box," the soldier demanded. Russell was nervously fumbling with the harness straps of his knapsack. His quaking fingers repeatedly slipped off the harness' buttons. Fishing his hand into his pants pocket he yanked out his pocket knife intent upon cutting the cartridge box free. The Rebel snapped his rifle to his shoulder and pulled the hammer to full cock. "If you cut them 'ere straps I will shoot you," he snarled. He turned the confused private over to two of his comrades who rushed Russell rearward with his hands raised and his knapsack still on his back. Bullets clipped the trees around them and the Yankee feared for the safety of his hands and arms with every second. Breaking into a clearing, they stumbled across another Confederate who was tending to the severely wounded Lieutenant Holman M. Anderson (Company I, 3rd Maine). The Confederates turned Russell over to the kindly Rebel with instructions to take the two Federals to Lee's headquarters. On the way to the rear, the fellow allowed Russell and the badly bleeding Anderson time to stop and rest. He even shared his meager rations of hoecakes and bacon with them for which Russell gave him his good shaving set.[139] It was only a few minutes after 9:00 A.M.[140]

Gregg's, Benning's, and Perry's brigades, despite their severe casualties, had successfully shattered most of Wadsworth's division and had swept away about half of Gibbon's and Birney's commands. In sacrificing themselves, they gave Kershaw and Field enough time to deploy the balance of their divisions for the telling blow upon the Army of the Potomac. The 124th New York with the 86th New York, 99th Pennsylvania, and the 110th Pennsylvania to its right, still held on to Ward's first line. The men did not realize that the Alabamians had driven back all of the brigade's second line except the 40th New York which was isolated some distance to its left.[141]

CHAPTER THREE

"Remember your wives, your sweethearts, your sisters at home."

8:00 A.M. TO 10:00 A.M.

THE WOODS NORTH OF SAUNDERS FIELD
(2.25 miles northwest of Tapp's)

While the skirmishers between Early's division and the VI Corps sporadically popped off rounds at one another, Brigadier General John B. Gordon's Georgians were stuffing themselves on captured Yankee rations. His pickets, under Captain Benjamin F. Kellar (Company F, 60th Georgia), having not been involved in the morning fight, because the Federals had concentrated upon Hoffman's brigade to the south, were doing excellent work reconnoitering the VI Corps' flank. They reported the woods to the front of Gordon's line clear of all troops. The outposts, consisting of one man every thirty to forty feet, were warned before daylight not to fire upon any horsemen approaching them, whether singly or in squads, unless close identification revealed them to be Federals. Not too long after Hoffman repulsed Seymour's brigade, a lone cavalryman from the 1st North Carolina rode into Gordon's line from the north. After conferring briefly with the trooper, Gordon turned to his staff and told them, "I am going to scout with a cavalryman in the woods. We will have to run for it, if discovered, and the fewer, the better in the crowd."

Turning their horses north, the two walked toward Flat Run and disappeared in the woods. Lieutenant Thomas G. Jones, Gordon's aide de camp, followed them with his glasses for as long as he could until the forest swallowed them. Jones took a squad of skirmishers down to the creek

66

to cover the general and the scout should they run into any Federals. The party veered east, following the general's supposed route. After going about half of a mile, they turned back and waited.[1]

Gordon and his escort galloped about one and one half miles behind the Union right without seeing any of their men. Coming across another cavalryman who had been near Germanna Ford, he learned that besides a great number of wagons, guards, and a thin line of cavalry videttes, the Federals had nothing of consequence in the area. While returning to their own lines, Gordon's escort directed him toward a hill to the south. The two dismounted and crawled up the slope until they could see Seymour's brigade at their breakfast fires on the crest of the ravine across from them. From his vantage point, Gordon could see no Federal supports in the woods to the east.

An hour after he departed on the reconnaissance, Gordon was back in his own lines, looking for Jones. "He told me to go with him, and take particular note of what he said and of the lay of the ground, so that I could inform General Early or General Ewell, whichever I met first...," Jones later wrote. As they studied the ground north of Flat Run, Gordon told Jones that he believed he could pull enough troops unobserved from the breastworks to flank the Federals and overrun their right wing.

Around 9:30 A.M. Jones left Gordon near the creek and rode back toward the Turnpike.[2] He asked repeatedly about Early's location and was told to keep heading south. He was approaching the northwestern corner of Saunders Field when he saw his corps commander, Lieutenant General Richard Ewell, approaching the corner of the clearing. A field officer stepped out from behind the works and curtly yelled at Ewell to stay out of the open ground. He said that the Federals had a sharpshooter trained upon that spot who had just shot a man there several minutes before. Ewell reined his horse in and Jones skirted around the field. Introducing himself, he began relaying Gordon's information to the general when Early, who had been looking for Ewell, rode up to them.

At Ewell's request, Jones retold his story, adding for emphasis that Gordon and his "good scouts" had personally observed no Federal troops within supporting distance of their northern flank. Early grilled Jones before turning to Ewell to remind him that he had sound intelligence reports which said the IX Corps was moving up to bolster the VI Corps. He expected the Federals to attack the Confederate left and he was disposing troops to meet the threat. Turning to Jones, Early, speaking for Ewell, as he had so often done before, told the aide to tell Gordon to stay where he was and that they would visit him later to investigate the situation.

Discouraged, Jones reined his horse to the north. A short distance up the trail he came across Gordon. After listening to Jones' story, Gordon took Jones back to the generals. The young officer maintained his distance

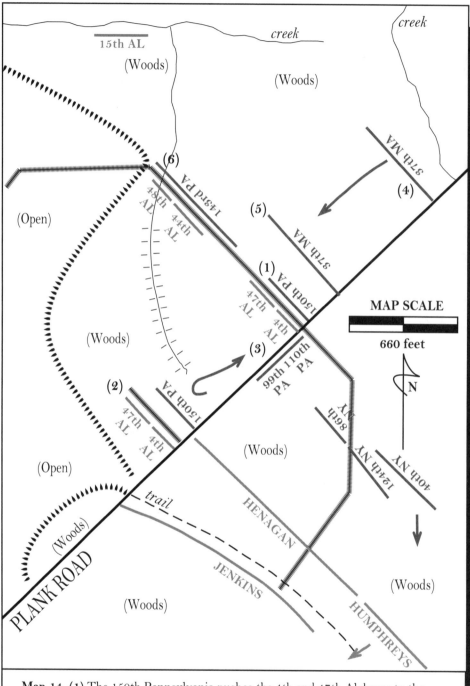

Map 14. (1) The 150th Pennsylvania pushes the 4th and 47th Alabama to the works at the top of the hill (2). The Alabamians recover their works (3) and stop the charge of the 37th Massachusetts (4)-(5), while (6) the 44th and the 48th Alabama hold off the 143rd Pennsylvania.

| Union | Confederate | Earthworks |

while Gordon was arguing his case. Fifteen to twenty minutes later a highly perturbed Gordon rode back to Jones. "General Early, evidently didn't believe a word of what I told him of what I had seen myself," Gordon said in disbelief. Dejected, they rode back to their brigade.[3]

9:00 A.M. TO 11:00 A.M.
MCGOWAN'S ABANDONED EARTHWORKS
(About 730 yards east of the Tapp House)

The panting survivors of the 4th Alabama were regrouping behind the Confederate earthworks along the western branch of Wilderness Run. "Behind this second line we felt quite secure and we all congratulated ourselves on our capture," First Lieutenant Robert T. Coles (4th Alabama) later recalled. Colonel Pinckney D. Bowles used the brief respite to send Coles running to the left to check the alignment on the northern end of the brigade.[4] He found the 47th Alabama in its allotted place in the line but could not see any of the other regiments. The 44th and the 48th Alabama had strayed too far to the left. With bullets cutting through the brush around him, he stumbled back to the 4th Alabama exhausted and gasping for air. Fearing capture more than death, because of Grant's discontinuance of the old prisoner exchange system, he suggested a withdrawal to Bowles.[5]

The Alabamians, who were outnumbered by the 143rd and the 150th Pennsylvania by two to one, stubbornly loaded and fired to the front heedless of the increasing volume of rounds which thunked into the trees and headlogs. The 99th Pennsylvania and the 110th Pennsylvania on the south side of the road emptied their rifles into the 4th Alabama's flank. The right wing of the regiment collapsed, retreating back to the flimsy works near the western face of the woods. At the same time Lieutenant Colonel L. H. Scruggs bolted up to the colonel and reported that the Federals had pressed back the 47th Alabama. The colonel shouted for the rest of his command to retreat. The 150th Pennsylvania followed them over the works, then abruptly stopped about thirty yards from their lines.[6]

The large 143rd Pennsylvania found itself involved in a firefight with William F. Perry's "lost" 44th and 48th

Colonel Pinckney D. Bowles, 4th Alabama

His intrepid regiment punched a hole through the center of the II Corps along the Brock Road which nearly destroyed the Union hold there.

Courtesy of Morris Penny

Alabama regiments. The dense brush along the Federals' front masked the gap in Perry's brigade line. Perry had no idea what was transpiring along the southern flank of his command. Having witnessed Oates' assault upon Kitching's heavy artillery brigade, he sent word for the 15th Alabama to come forward before racing over to the supposed position of the 44th Alabama, which, to his chagrin, was not there. Riding to the left, he discovered that the two regiments were veering northeast through the swampy creek bottom and were fighting their way up the eastern slope of the stream toward the 150th Pennsylvania's right flank and the front of the 143rd Pennsylvania. The thick vegetation magnified the numbers of invisible Federals upon the field in the Confederates' minds. The two regiments were waging a battle with the shadows.

The Pennsylvanians wounded Lieutenant Colonel John A. Jones, leaving the command of the 44th Alabama in the hands of Major George W. Carey. The very young officer with the regimental colors in his left hand and brandishing his large infantry sword in his right hand gallantly advanced to the front center of the line. The Alabamians behaved beautifully. Their ranks were well closed with every available man in his appointed place.

It was a different story a short distance to the left where the smaller 48th Alabama was not doing as well. The regimental front gradually disintegrated as clusters of men abandoned their posts and cowered behind trees. They needlessly dodged the Federal bullets, most of which passed well over their heads.[7]

To the south along the Plank Road, Bowles rallied his 4th and 47th Alabama regiments behind the makeshift works near the crest of the Tapp plateau. The 150th Pennsylvania continued to blaze away at will into the Confederates on the hillside above them. Bowles could see the Federals closing up their line preparatory to a charge and ordered his two dwindling regiments to attack. The outnumbered Confederates leaped over their temporary breastworks and with the Rebel yell dashed into the muzzles of the Pennsylvanians.[8] Within minutes, they had retaken their old position.

Wadsworth, upon seeing his men break, galloped down the Plank Road, desperately looking for fresh troops to feed into the smoky meat grinder. Nine hundred yards to the east, he clattered up to Brigadier General Henry L. Eustis' inactive brigade as it stood in column of regiments south of the Plank Road along the eastern side of Poplar Run and screamed for the regiments to come to his support. Colonel Oliver Edwards, commanding the lead regiment, the 37th Massachusetts, flanked his regiment to the right into the woods on the north side of the road, while the rest of the brigade stayed in place. With its left flank against the road bank, the 570-man regiment faced left and charged blindly through the woods, firing as they went.

Brushing aside fleeing Federals and bayoneting an occasional stray Confederate, the 37th battled the cat thorns, saplings, and tangle foot under a hail of Confederate bullets which were knocking men out of the ranks. A minie ball bored into Color Sergeant John W. Field's forehead. His flag tottered a moment in his death grasp until another man pulled the colors from his hands and pressed forward with them. The 37th Massachusetts suddenly halted in the smoky woods a short distance in front of the Alabamians. While the men strained their powder-blackened eyes to gaze through the clouds of smoke, trying to see what stood in front of them, Wadsworth trotted up to them. "You have made a splendid charge!" he shouted at Edwards. "Your regiment has done all that I wished and more than I hoped. I will now go to reform my lines and you must fight your way back as best as you can." Wheeling his horse to the left, the general disappeared into the woods behind the regiment, headed, they supposed, toward the left flank. Lieutenant Colonel George L. Montague suddenly realized that the regiment was almost on top of the Confederate breastworks.[9] Turning to Edwards, he blurted, "We must go at those with a rush!" The colonel never had a chance to give the order. Captain Rufus P. Lincoln (Company C) rushed up to the colonel, reporting that the Confederates seemed to be closing in on the regiment's right flank. "Refuse your right and hold your position," Edwards told him.[10]

THE BROCK ROAD INTERSECTION

Brigadier General Thomas G. Stevenson's division of the IX Corps turned off the Germanna Road onto the Brock Road intersection shortly after Perry's attack had died away. Colonel Sumner Carruth's brigade led the column.[11] The 4th and the 10th U.S. Regulars led the brigade, followed respectively by the 57th, 56th, and 59th Massachusetts regiments.[12] The 56th Massachusetts intercepted the 7th Massachusetts, which, having sustained heavy losses, was being pulled from Eustis' brigade and sent north. Several of the officers and men saw Captain Z. Boylston Adams (Company F, 56th Massachusetts), their former assistant surgeon, and warned him that he would get what he was looking for if he kept going where he was heading. The captain shrugged it off. One mile farther down the road, the brigade forked west onto the Plank Road. The weary soldiers mindlessly filtered around the pair of silent brass 12-pounders which Captain Edwin P. Dow (6th Maine Artillery) had left standing in their way. Adams glanced up as he brushed against one of the cannons to find himself standing next to Major General Winfield S. Hancock. The image of the general sitting bolt upright in the saddle etched itself indelibly into his mind as did most of the events of that day. He studied the sun-bathed road as it gently dipped into the swale several hundred yards to the west. Everything seemed deceptively pleasant.[13] Lieutenant Colonel Stephen Weld (56th Massachusetts) noted the time. It was 8:45 A.M.[14]

To the southwest, the sounds of the Alabamians' dying forlorn hope resonated ominously among the trees like a distant storm. The veterans, like Adams, tended to mentally block out the musketry and concentrate instead upon the tranquillity of their immediate area. To the newer men the small arms fire seemed too uncomfortably close.[15] The brigade continued about half of a mile down the pike until it came abreast of what was left of Wadsworth's concealed division.

The battle-scarred woods were too dense for the approaching IX Corps troops to see very far into the thickets on both flanks. Suddenly Wadsworth with his aides de camp, Captain Robert Monteith (Company H, 7th Wisconsin) and Second Lieutenant Earl M. Rogers (Company I, 6th Wisconsin) broke into the road near the front of Carruth's brigade. The regimental commanders shouted their men to a halt and Adams stepped away from his company, straining his ears to hear what the bareheaded general was telling Carruth. He heard something about falling in by echelon in the woods north of the road.

The 10th and the 4th Regulars, being the smallest regiments in the brigade, disappeared into the woods to form the first line.[16] The 57th Massachusetts, numbering 579 officers and men, led by Colonel William F. Bartlett, filed into line behind them. The 56th Massachusetts moved into the third line with the 59th Massachusetts completing the formation. First Lieutenant Isaiah Hoyt (Company B, 32nd Massachusetts), who was on detached duty with Wadsworth, spurred up beside Adams as he started to leave the road. He asked Adams if he had anything to eat. "No," the captain quietly replied. While turning his horse, about to ride away, Hoyt told him matter-of-factly, "Before this day is over, you will be hungry; I guess I shall find you here half an hour hence." Adams watched his friend trot toward the Brock Road, then joined his men on the rise of ground between the two branches of Wilderness Run.[17]

Once the regiments' left flanks disappeared into the cover of the Wilderness, they faced west and broke into battalions (halves). Instead of advancing in four lines, the brigade was going to move forward in eight staggered battle lines. A short distance to the front, on the western side of the middle branch of Wilderness Run, the order traveled through the column to dig in. The regiments closed up by bringing their right wings on line with the rest of their companies. Hoyt caught up with Adams and his company while the enlisted men were dragging in rotten logs and tree stumps to construct breastworks. The lieutenant passed the captain a box of sardines which he quickly stuffed into the blanket roll he wore across his shoulder.[18]

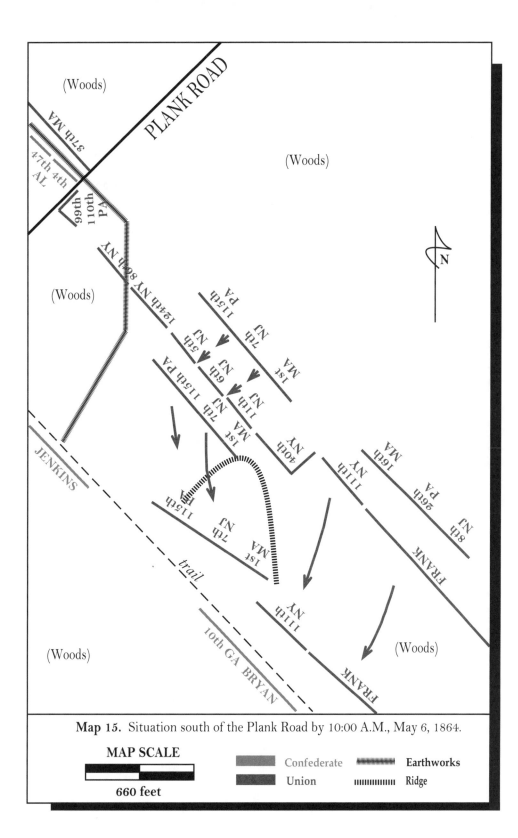

Map 15. Situation south of the Plank Road by 10:00 A.M., May 6, 1864.

MAP SCALE

660 feet

Confederate   Earthworks

Union   Ridge

(Woods)

PLANK ROAD

(Woods)

N

37th MA

47th AL   4th

69th   110th PA

148th NY   98th NY

(Woods)

115th PA

3rd NJ

7th NJ

1st MA

6th NJ

11th NJ

13th NJ

7th 115th PA

1st MA

40th NY

16th MA

11th NY

26th PA

8th NJ

JENKINS

trail

115th PA

7th NJ

1st MA

11th NY

FRANK

10th GA BRYAN

(Woods)

FRANK

(Woods)

SOUTH OF THE PLANK ROAD

About three hundred yards to the southwest Henagan's and Humphreys' Confederate brigades began to slacken their fire. Word filtered back to Jenkins' waiting brigade to move forward and relieve Henagan's South Carolinians, who had expended most of their ammunition. Brigadier General E. Porter Alexander, whom Longstreet had ordered south to check upon Stuart's cavalry, found the South Carolinians standing along a trail, loading their weapons. He rode up to the young brigadier and, extending his hand, said, "Old man, I hope you will win that next grade this morning." "Well," Jenkins replied as he twisted in his saddle to face his men, "we are going to fight for old South Carolina today, aren't we boys?" On the left of Jenkins' line, Colonel James Hagood pushed his 1st South Carolina through the tangled woods until he came upon the 2nd South Carolina which had taken cover behind a makeshift breastwork of toppled pine trees. While the 2nd regiment retired, the 1st South Carolina stole into the works. Unable to see anything but the flashes of the Federals' rifles through the thick vegetation and the smoke, Hagood decided not to waste his men in a frontal assault against the 86th New York. Instead, he dispatched Company's F and C, with Company E in support, forward as skirmishers to harass the Federal line. Hagood reasoned, "...a line of skirmishers, darting from tree to tree, could approach so close to the enemy's masses as to make their position untenable." The ploy worked. The Confederate skirmishers forced the New Yorkers to cease fire and pull back to safer ground. Hagood believed that if his plan were adopted by the rest of the line, where the firing had not abated, Longstreet's Corps could retake all of the ground lost by A. P. Hill. He sent a messenger with his plan to the rear to find Jenkins with the recommendation that the general quickly implement it.[19]

While his Company E covered the front of the regiment, Orderly Sergeant Frank M. Mixon bellied over to Hagood's side and asked permission to crawl forward to loot the Federal dead. The boy colonel told him it was mighty dangerous, but if the sergeant wanted to risk his life while staying close to the

**Brigadier General
Micah Jenkins, C.S.A.**

This promising young officer, who until the Wilderness had begun to lose hope in the cause of the Confederacy, did not live to see the end of the battle.

Battles and Leaders, 1:IV
Grant-Lee Edition, 1888

works, he could do so. The plucky sergeant skittered through the leaves like an ant, always taking care to keep a corpse in front of him to avoid getting shot. After robbing eight bodies, Mixon crawled back to the colonel. "What have you got?" Hagood anxiously asked. Lying on his back, the sergeant hurriedly emptied his pockets. He spilled some rations, a few trinkets, several knives and six watches into the leaves between them. The colonel carefully selected a timepiece for himself, then went about his business. Mixon later gave a watch to Captain Patrick H. Wood (Company E) and sold another to his messmate Private Sid M. Key.[20]

Farther to the south, the 10th Georgia, on the left of Bryan's brigade line, ran into a tremendous fusillade. A minie ball whistled into Company E, striking Private David I. Walden in the center of the forehead. Walden said he saw flames, followed by streaks of lightning, then shooting stars as he collapsed face first to the ground. He lay semiconscious, his face buried in a hollow in the ground, awaiting death. His friend, Captain Andrew Jackson McBride (Company E) saw his face immersed in a puddle of blood and decided to leave him alone. Walden was in a world of his own creation. Opening his eyes, he could see nothing but his own blood. Before the war he had heard an aged politician say he would drink all of the blood spilled during the war. All the desperately wounded Confederate could see was the "old man" lapping blood from his private puddle. [21]

When the Federals wounded Colonel Willis C. Holt, McBride took over the regiment. He took his post next to Private James E. Hudson (Company E), who was firing prone from behind a tree. A loud crack told McBride that Hudson was out of commission. The captain decided to step to the right rear behind Captain O. Sid Kimbrough (Company A) who had taken cover behind a four-inch sapling. A tremendous hail of bullets stripped the bark from Kimbrough's tree. McBride unceremoniously hurled himself to the ground and shouted at Kimbrough to do the same. The other captain spat that he would be damned if he would. He was going to hold out his arm and get a furlough. Kimbrough had barely straightened his arm when a ball hit it with a resounding whack. Saying good-bye to McBride, he dashed toward a large tree a few steps to the rear. Finding the severely wounded Private William Leonard Waterson (Company E) behind it, Kimbrough began cursing and berating him as a skulker. The private was in no mood for the captain's shenanigans. Dry up or he would get a stick and beat the life out of him, Waterson yelled back. Kimbrough kept heading toward the rear.[22]

The firing became so severe that Captain Daniel Sayer (Company E, 124th New York) ran over to Lieutenant Colonel Charles Weygant, whom he found ten paces behind the center of the regiment's right wing, to tell him that his company was out of ammunition. Weygant, struck by the captain's obvious lack of protocol, curtly told him to tell Colonel Francis

M. Cummins about his predicament. "Why," the harried Sayer gasped, "Colonel Cummins was carried to the rear fifteen minutes ago, and I am afraid, mortally wounded." Weygant's mouth fell open. He could hardly believe what he heard because the colonel had been standing only a few feet to his left during the entire fight.[23] The regiment, having lost contact with Lewis A. Grant's Vermont Brigade, was on its own hook.

Perry's charge had not penetrated the Northern lines deep enough to affect McAllister's brigade as it worked itself south and west of Lewis A. Grant's position. The brigade was lurching fitfully through the smoky forest when the woods suddenly exploded with small arms fire to the right and the left of the brigade. In response, McAllister's front line blazed away into the shadows for several minutes. Lieutenant Colonel John Schoonover (11th New Jersey), once he realized that his regiment was not receiving any incoming rounds, yelled at his men to cease fire. The 5th and 6th New Jersey regiments to his left did not follow suit.[24]

Colonel Francis M. Cummins, 124th New York

During the height of the fighting south of the Plank Road, Cummins was severely wounded and taken to the rear fifteen minutes before his lieutenant colonel, Charles Weygant, realized that the command of the regiment had devolved upon him.

Massachusetts Commandery; MOLLUS, USAMHI

Instead, Sewell fed his three regiments into the gap between the left of the 124th New York and the 40th New York. Shortly thereafter, McAllister brought his six regiments (in two lines) into position behind Sewell. A colonel, whom McAllister did not know, asked for permission to retire his regiment because he needed ammunition. McAllister secured the officer's assurance that he would return soon. As the other regiment slipped east, McAllister moved the 8th New Jersey, 26th Pennsylvania, and 16th Massachusetts regiments into line too far south of the 40th New York to be seen by anyone in that regiment. He pushed skirmishers forward and secured the position.[25] Eventually, while the shooting ebbed along the front, the 1st Massachusetts, 7th New Jersey, and the 115th Pennsylvania passed over the position held by the 5th, 6th, and 11th New Jersey, who retired to a safer spot in the woods and went prone while the men who relieved them secured a small hill closer to the Confederate lines.[26]

The battle seemed to have temporarily fought itself to a standstill while both armies deployed for more action. Stevenson's Division of the IX Corps massed in column of regiment north of the Plank Road to support what was left of Wadsworth's and Birney's division. Five regiments from Ward's brigade and nine regiments from Mott's division (II Corps) secured the Union line south of the Plank Road. Grant's Vermont Brigade from the VI Corps still occupied its section of breastworks behind the left wing of the II Corps. To bolster the left flank, Hancock dispatched Colonel Paul Frank's six regiments to assist McAllister's brigade. At the same time, Colonel William R. Brewster and his eight regiments, in two battle lines, crashed through the woods to the left and rear of the New Jersey troops without making contact with them.[27] At one point McAllister believed he saw a regimental line facing his left flank but it disappeared before his reconnaissance party could verify its existence.

While Frank and his men were approaching McAllister's position from the rear, he sought out McAllister and asked him to open ranks to let his men pass through. McAllister protested because he had skirmishers in front of his own brigade. He told Frank to protect his left flank and would not let him disrupt his Jerseymen's line. Frank nastily shot back that he had orders "to find the enemy wherever he could find him and whip him." Pulling his horse aside, he spurred back to his brigade. The regiments flanked south and passed around McAllister's left before deliberately turning north across his line of march.[28] Frank connected with the refused left flank of the 40th New York in front of the New Jersey brigade.[29]

While Frank disappeared deeper into the woods, Brewster's large brigade went into line east of the Jerseymen facing south. The two commands were not in sight of each other.[30] Lieutenant Colonel John Leonard (72nd New York) yelled for five volunteers to head south and locate the Confederates. Sergeant Major John M. Lyon, Private James M. Young (Company B), and three others stepped forward.[31]

LONGSTREET DEPLOYS FOR BATTLE

The Confederates were not idle but were jockeying into an assault position south of the Plank Road. The Federals lost their combat initiative the moment Frank's men slipped around McAllister's left wing. No sooner had they deployed than they ran into Colonel John M. Stone's entrenched Confederates along the trail from Tapp's to the unfinished railroad line. Frank chose his smallest regiment, the 125th New York, to move forward as skirmishers. (The balance of the regiment had been detached that morning for picket duty on the southern end of the Brock Road.) The Federals did not see the Confederates until the woods in front of them exploded in a blast of flame and smoke. Color Sergeant Harrison Clark, in an act of careless bravado, was advancing well ahead of the regiment to within ten

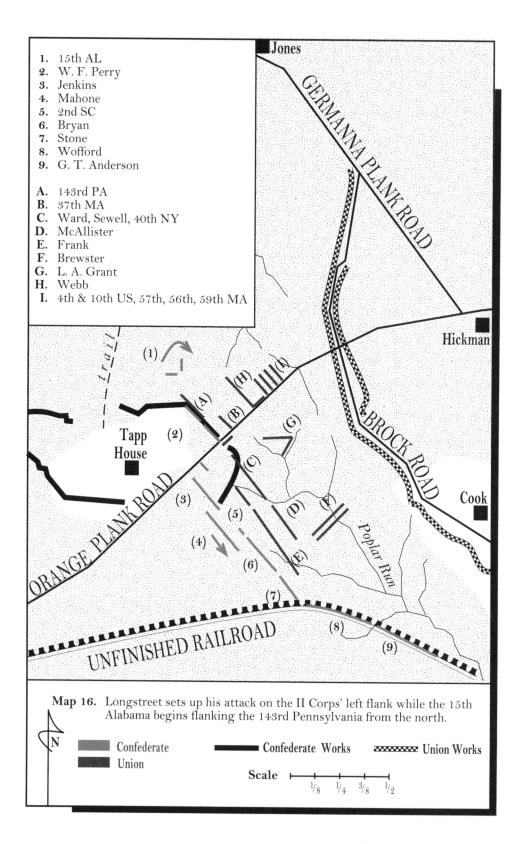

Map 16. Longstreet sets up his attack on the II Corps' left flank while the 15th Alabama begins flanking the 143rd Pennsylvania from the north.

1. 15th AL
2. W. F. Perry
3. Jenkins
4. Mahone
5. 2nd SC
6. Bryan
7. Stone
8. Wofford
9. G. T. Anderson

A. 143rd PA
B. 37th MA
C. Ward, Sewell, 40th NY
D. McAllister
E. Frank
F. Brewster
G. L. A. Grant
H. Webb
I. 4th & 10th US, 57th, 56th, 59th MA

Jones

GERMANNA PLANK ROAD

Hickman

BROCK ROAD

Cook

Tapp House

ORANGE PLANK ROAD

Poplar Run

UNFINISHED RAILROAD

N

Confederate
Union

Confederate Works

Union Works

Scale 1/8 1/4 3/8 1/2

feet of the concealed Confederates when a minie ball shattered his leg. He staggered to the rear about sixty feet into the arms of Private Philip Brady (Company I), who snatched the standard from the sergeant as he collapsed. Lieutenant Colonel Aaron B. Myers trotted over to the sergeant's side and promoted him to second lieutenant on the spot. Very shortly after that, a round killed Brady. Corporal Charles S. Davis (Company B) took the flag from the private and carried it throughout the remainder of the action. Minutes later, a bullet cut down Myers. First Lieutenant Merritt Miller (Adjutant) caught the unconscious colonel as he fell and yelled for a couple of volunteers to haul him away.[32] The suddenness of the assault forced the New Yorkers to step back toward McAllister's brigade.

Stone sent his skirmishers, under the command of First Lieutenant Robert F. Ward (Company B, 42nd Mississippi), over his breastworks to secure his front. They stepped over a number of the 125th New York's casualties and began exchanging shot for shot with them. Stone did not want to precipitate a general engagement. Isolated and as outnumbered as he was on the Confederate right, he did not want to risk getting overrun and exposing the army's rear to an envelopment. He commanded Ward to cease fire. The Mississippians obeyed him but the Federals refused to recognize the informal truce.[33] The right of Frank's line showed signs of driving a wedge into the woods between Jenkins' right flank and Bryan's Georgia brigade. Colonel John Bratton, commanding the 6th South Carolina, sent a courier crashing through the woods looking for men to plug the gap. He happened upon the 2nd South Carolina which had just been relieved from the front and ordered it forward.[34]

The muzzle flashes of the opposing skirmishers ignited the leaves on the forest floor. At first the ground around them smoldered, then intermittent flash fires ignited along the Confederates' position. No one could see anything through the pall of smoke created by the burning leaves and saplings. Within minutes the woods turned into a Dantean landscape. The screams of the wounded men, as the flames lapped at their bodies, horrified Sergeant Minard McDonald (Company H, 111th New York, Frank's brigade). They seemed to materialize from everywhere. "It was like stepping into Hell," he recollected.[35]

Without warning, the woods flashed and roared as the newly arrived 2nd South Carolina loosed a deadly volley into the New Yorkers from about forty yards away. A large number of the Federals went down in the blast.[36] By the handfuls, demoralized soldiers in Frank's line slipped from the ranks and trickled back through McAllister's New Jersey regiments. At one point, Frank sent a personal order for McAllister to relieve his men. But, McAllister refused to comply, insisting that he had to advance with his own line.[37]

Meanwhile First Lieutenant Robert F. Ward (Company B, 42nd Mississippi) told his men to prop slightly wounded New Yorkers up against the trees along their front, facing the Federals. The wounded men protested the Rebels' inhumanity but Ward told them matter-of-factly that the Federals would not shoot their own men and all the Confederates wanted was a cease fire. While being dragged into the line of fire, the mortally wounded Sergeant Charles H. Perry (Company F) asked the lieutenant if he knew Colonel Reuben O. Reynolds of the 11th Mississippi. He knew him, the lieutenant replied. The sergeant asked to be taken to see him. Ward agreed to have Perry removed. As the stretcher crew carried Perry off, he tended his watch to the Confederate. Ward refused it, saying the sergeant might need it in prison, whereupon Perry handed him his pocket testament in thanks for saving his life.[38]

The Yankee skirmishers suddenly ceased fire. Ward mistakenly thought it was because they had decided to honor the informal truce.[39] Its ammunition expended, the 125th New York retired from the skirmish line. A couple of men dragged their crippled color sergeant by his arms to safety seconds before the flames reached him.[40] The rest of the brigade mistook the withdrawal for a rout. Panicked by the limited visibility from the fires, choking on the asphyxiating smoke which blanketed their area, and unnerved by the piteous cries of the wounded, the regiments turned about and streamed rearward into McAllister's men who met them with a wall of leveled bayonets. While his rattled men regained their composure, Frank spurred up to McAllister. "I want to get ammunition," Frank spat. "Where?" McAllister retorted. "Away back in the rear," the distressed colonel blurted. McAllister told him that supply mules had just come up on the right of his line and if Frank would send a small detachment with one of his sergeants he could be resupplied in a few minutes.

Rifle shots from the skirmish line suddenly echoed across the New Jersey brigade from the west. Rather than waste any more time with Frank's sorry lot, McAllister yelled for his men to open ranks. Frank's brigade disappeared into the woods behind the Jerseymen and never returned.[41]

By 10:00 A.M. Longstreet received word from Brigadier General William T. Wofford that his Georgia brigade had discovered the left flank of the Federal II Corps.[42] Wofford sent his aide, Major James M. Goggin, to the corps commander requesting permission to slip his brigade east in the railroad bed so he could left wheel his six Georgia regiments north to roll up the Federals. Wofford specifically asked to have his brigade on the extreme right, the post of honor.[43] Without hesitating, Longstreet consented to the move.

Turning to Goggin, he commanded, "See General Anderson and direct him to *report* to General Wofford." Goggin was in an awkward spot. Brigadier General George T. Anderson and his Georgians belonged to Field's

Division—not Kershaw's. "General Anderson, knowing I am *not* on your staff may hesitate to obey the order," the major respectfully suggested. At that moment Major General Martin Luther Smith, Lee's chief engineer, Colonel G. Moxley Sorrel (Longstreet's adjutant general), and several staff officers returned from a reconnaissance to the south and confirmed Wofford's report.[44] Longstreet told Sorrel that if he could pull several brigades together along the southern end of the line, keep them in contact with each other and swing north against the Federals he believed a "splendid success would follow."[45] Longstreet's staff officers quickly spread the word of the impending attack through the right wing of the Army of Northern Virginia. He dispatched Brigadier General E. Porter Alexander south to check on Stuart's cavalry operations.

Jenkins trotted into the prone 1st South Carolina. His immaculate appearance left an indelible impression upon Colonel James Hagood. He later recalled, "Elegantly dressed (as he always was), superbly mounted and his face lit up with a martial fire such as I have never seen in anyone else, he realized all that I had ever dreamed of in the true soldier."[46] The general trotted his horse behind his soldiers, who rolled over onto their backs to hear him. Sergeant Frank M. Mixon (Company E) quickly noticed, while Jenkins spoke, that blood dripped from the broken little finger on the general's right hand. The youthful brigadier ignored the bullet wound as he talked to his soldiers. "Men of the First, we are going to charge. Now I want each and every one of you to remember that you are South Carolinians. Remember your wives, your sweethearts, your sisters at home. Remember your duty." Turning toward the colonel, he said, "Colonel Hagood, get your regiment ready."[47] He rode off while the colonel steadied his line for the attack.

Meanwhile Sorrel headed south along the trail that ran into the unfinished section of the Orange Railroad. He found Wofford's Georgians on the trail with their right flank on the northern lip of the railroad cut. Anderson's Georgia brigade was in line, facing east, on the opposite side of the cut. Sorrel immediately sent Anderson left wheeling northeast into the track bed.

**Lieutenant Colonel
G. Moxley Sorrel, C.S.A.**

The distinguished looking Sorrel organized Longstreet's flank attack against the II Corps and personally led the regiments into the action.

Bernard, *War Talks*, 1892

Wofford, for the sake of military expediency, quietly surrendered the post of honor to his fellow Georgian.[48] The two brigades moved east by the flank until Wofford's left flank cleared the trail crossing.

At the same time, Brigadier General William Mahone's Virginia brigade was preparing to slip south toward the Confederate right flank along the same wood road. First Lieutenant James E. Phillips (Company G, 12th Virginia) glanced into the tree tops and suddenly became aware that the sun had risen, shining an ominous bright red. The regiment took off by files at a trot onto the narrow path to its right front. A short distance into the tangled woods, the 12th Virginia, leading the column, stumbled across the site of a recently abandoned surgical field station. Arms and legs lay in a grisly pile near the route of march, the sight of which unsettled Phillips. Turning toward his second lieutenant, Pat Kelly, he whispered, "Pat, if this don't demoralize our men, nothing on earth will do it."[49] The Virginians went into position below the right of John M. Stone's brigade line. (Stone, who was preoccupied watching McAllister's Federals, did not know anything of Mahone's movement.) The 12th Virginia held the right of the line at a point near where the path crossed over the trail but not within sight of the crossing. The 41st Virginia fell in to the left rear, followed respectively by the 61st, 16th and the 6th Virginia. Lieutenant Colonel Everard M. Field (12th Virginia) disappeared with his 170 hand-picked sharpshooters into the woods one hundred fifty yards east of the brigade to cover whatever action might develop. In the relative silence of his sector, it never occurred to him to check his watch.[50]

The sudden quiet along McAllister's brigade disturbed him. He sent the command down the line for his regiments to lie down. Crawling from tree to tree, he worked his way south until he came to what he referred to as an open ravine which was bordered on the far side by some very large trees. He spied several Rebel pickets crouching low in the ravine and others darting their heads around from behind those trees. Beyond the trees he clearly saw the railroad cut and behind it, the southern embankment and the heads of more Confederate soldiers. The colonel scurried back to his brigade and immediately sent an aide to the rear with orders to report his observations to Mott.[51]

NORTH OF THE PLANK ROAD

The 4th and 47th Alabama regiments forced Colonel Oliver Edwards (37th Massachusetts) to yield ground by executing a maneuver which, under the pressing circumstances, only seasoned veterans would have attempted. He ordered his regiment to volley and retreat by ranks. His front rank fired, then withdrew through the rear line, loading as it went. Twenty-five paces behind the rear rank, the front rank about faced and returned fire while the second rank passed to a point twenty-five paces farther behind.[52]

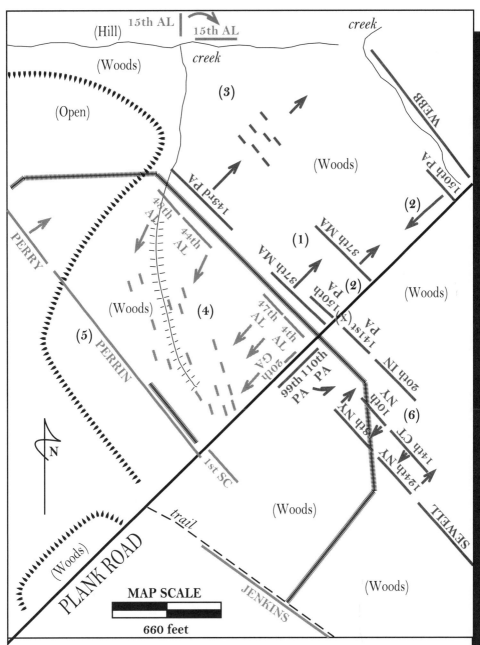

Map 17. Situation before 11:30 A.M.

(1) The 37th Massachusetts is forced to retire. (2) The 150th Pennsylvania makes three attempts to take the works. (x) The 4th Alabama drops Wadsworth in the Plank Road. (3) The 15th Alabama drives off the 143rd Pennsylvania. (4) W. F. Perry's Alabamians and the 20th Georgia quit the field as Perrin and E. A. Perry (5) arrive upon the field. (6) The remnants of Ward's and Carroll's brigades reshuffle their positions.

| Union | Confederate | Earthworks |

Their precision volleying to the west and the northwest in conjunction with those of the 143rd Pennsylvania kept Perry's Alabamians at bay. Colonel William C. Oates, whose 15th Alabama was advancing to the support of Perry's left wing, marveled at "the regularity and effectiveness" of the Federals' shooting. He knew his men were not moving in on green troops.[53]

Along the Plank Road the 4th Alabama and the 47th Alabama held their own long enough to repel the 37th Massachusetts and to allow the 150th Pennsylvania to regroup. While Edwards' New Englanders were retiring from the field, the Pennsylvanians surged forward only to be driven back. Three times they charged the breastworks. Each time the Alabamians stalled their attacks. With each attempt, Wadsworth, nervously pounding his hat upon the pommel of his saddle, galloped into the fray with his "Bucktails." The charge cost him a horse.[54] Borrowing a mount from a nearby officer, he spurred back along the road to find troops to flank the Confederates.

The Federals had exacted more than a "pound of flesh" from the Rebels. First Lieutenant Robert T. Coles (4th Alabama) remembered, "Our ammunition was becoming dangerously low and it appeared that either one side or the other would soon have to give way." He and his men sincerely believed the Federals would carry the works.

The Alabamians were taking hits. The regiment dwindled in size with each charge. The very devout Major William M. Robbins, while waving his large sword around his head, continually urged his men to aim low and to keep under cover. Without warning, he whirled about. His sword flew from his grasp and he collapsed face first to the forest floor. The shock of seeing his dear friend crumble right near him stunned the young adjutant. He screamed at Colonel Pickney D. Bowles and frantically pointed at the major's seemingly lifeless body. Seconds later Coles and several others were at the major's side. They gently rolled him over expecting the worst and discovered that he had a severe scalp wound, nothing more. Bowles denied the major's request to be taken to the rear because he did not want to lose litter bearers to the horrendous Federal rifle fire. They left Robbins lying on his back. Nearby lay Stephen D. Quinley (Company E), one of Coles' closest friends, face down in the leaves. The adjutant vividly recalled Quinley's prediction at Chickamauga about a bullet and not a rope was predestined to snuff out his life. Coles rolled his friend over onto his back. Like the hard headed major, a spent ball had glanced off his skull and knocked him out.[55]

Wadsworth, who desperately needed more men, rode back a short distance into the forward position held by Webb's brigade, which had formed an "L" behind a hastily erected barricade of logs. While Wadsworth was telling Webb to relinquish the command of his own brigade and of Carruth's five-regiment brigade from the IX Corps to him, a mass of fully armed

Yankee soldiers came milling across the road from the south, just east of Webb's position. Every now and then a panicked fellow raced across the road as if the Rebels were on his heels. For the most part, the retreating Federals acted like a herd of cattle meandering home to the barn. Line officers from nearby regiments yelled and hollered at the mob who coldly ignored them and kept moving rearward. Frank's brigade left the battle with far less grandeur and bombast than when it had entered it. Wadsworth continued his conversation with Webb by commanding him to ride south and bring up four regiments to stop those men. Webb could not believe that Wadsworth was relieving him of command to round up skulkers. But he obeyed him, nonetheless.[56]

Brigadier General James S. Wadsworth, U.S.A.

The fearless Wadsworth, despite the loss of a couple horses, personally led his regiments and the 20th Massachusetts into the fighting along the Plank Road. His bravery cost him his life.

Massachusetts Commandery; MOLLUS, USAMHI

Once Webb disappeared down the road, Wadsworth turned to the seasoned 20th Massachusetts which occupied the southern leg of the brigade formation. He told Colonel George N. Macy to wheel his regiment to the west and follow him. Macy refused. His regiment alone held that front, he argued. The impatient general, half frenzied from seeing his men slaughtered, shrieked that the New Englanders were cowards. Without saying a word, he leaped his horse over the regiment's works right into the blazing rifles of Perry's Alabamians. A soldier on the right of the 4th Alabama took deliberate aim at the general and squeezed off a round. The horse went down in a heap, throwing the general into the packed dirt of the road near the base of a large tree. A couple of Alabamians watched him lay there, sprawled in the road, stunned, then ran back to their adjutant blubbering something about having killed a Yankee general.[57]

The Northern End of Colonel W. F. Perry's Line

The dense, overgrown woods and the hillside on Perry's northern flank slowed the advance of the 15th Alabama to a walk. While the 143rd Pennsylvania was hammering the 44th and the 48th Alabama, Oates' men were groping up hill, looking for Kitching's large Federal brigade which they had run into over an hour earlier. The Federals were gone. Unknown to Oates, Colonel J. Howard Kitching had withdrawn his two large regiments during the supposed flank movement which had caused Oates' initial retreat that morning.[58]

With no one to fight, Oates wheeled his regiment south toward the sounds of the firing. The 15th Alabama reached the creek bottom on the flank of the 143rd Pennsylvania in time to keep the 48th Alabama from retreating. His men went into line along the southern bank of another branch of Wilderness Run at right angles to the right flank of the 143rd Pennsylvania. A single volley into the smoke-enshrouded side of the Yankee line sent it scattering for safety. The 143rd Pennsylvania broke to the rear and carried the battered 150th Pennsylvania with it.

The Federals literally disappeared along Perry's front and he congratulated himself, rather prematurely, for having whipped Wadsworth's entire division single handed. Unable to report to Lee in person because the Federals unhorsed him, he sent Second Lieutenant Leigh R. Terrell (Company D, 4th Alabama) to the right of the line to check their condition.[59]

THE 4TH ALABAMA ALONG THE PLANK ROAD

The 20th Georgia (Benning's brigade) came up on the rear of the 4th Alabama minutes before Oates struck the Federal right. Right wheeling into line along the bank of the Plank Road, the Georgians became engaged for a second time that morning. They laid a desultory fire into the 99th Pennsylvania and the 110th Pennsylvania who promptly responded and drove them away. For some unexplainable reason, the Federals ceased fire and Bowles ordered the 4th Alabama to retreat to the works on the brow of the hill. The Southerners pulled back, dragging their wounded with them. The Federals fired a few scattered volleys after them but did not try to pursue. The 47th Alabama followed very shortly thereafter.[60] A noticeable lull settled over the battlefield.

THE NORTHERN END OF COLONEL W. F. PERRY'S LINE

Terrell returned to Perry with discouraging news. He could not find either the 4th or the 47th regiments. Prior to the captain's return an officer from Lee arrived with a promise of reinforcements. The colonel, who had not informed the captain about how he had previously sent another officer to Lee with a status update on his brigade, dispatched the weary Terrell back to army headquarters with the following response. The general need not send reinforcements. Perry's men had resupplied from the Federal casualties. His Alabamians could still fight on but he did need flank support.[61]

South of the Plank Road
11:00 A.M. to 11:30 A.M.

A Captain Nash and one of Brigadier General Hobart Ward's staff lieutenants rode up to the hard-pressed 124th New York, which anchored the brigade's left. With their orderlies, Private Norman Sly (Company D) and Corporal John R. Post (Company H), they rode up to Lieutenant Colonel Charles Weygant (124th New York) to exchange pleasantries before passing farther to the south. Weygant never saw the two officers again.

Finding a fifty-foot-wide gap between the regiment and the troops on its southern flank, they trotted through the opening, and found themselves facing off against a squad of Rebel infantry. The two enlisted men, who were riding behind the officers, did not wait to be captured. Leaving the officers to their fate, the orderlies wheeled their horses about and made a hasty escape.[62] Weygant noticed the riflery had suddenly waned to almost nothing.

Presently, the 14th Connecticut and the 10th New York from Carroll's brigade came up behind the right wing of the 124th New York. They halted a few feet away, and since the area had quieted down, they started scrounging around for firewood. Before long, small camp fires crackled and flamed, and the invigorating aroma of brewing coffee mingled with the sulfuric odors of the Wilderness. Weygant's New Yorkers begged him to let them break ranks and cook breakfasts but he refused.[63]

When the Connecticut men finished their coffee, he asked Colonel Theodore Ellis (14th Connecticut) if his men could swap places with his regiment. The colonel raised no objections to the switch.[64] At this juncture, the 141st Pennsylvania and the 20th Indiana, having replenished their cartridge boxes, came up behind Colonel Samuel Carroll's two remaining regiments. They were moving forward to relieve the 99th Pennsylvania and the 110th Pennsylvania. Ward, who had ridden back to place his two regiments in the line, found Carroll near his men. Ward told Carroll to advance with his brigade. The colonel retorted that it was not possible. He had less than five hundred effectives present on his line. They had just come out of a severe fire fight and he did not want to walk into an ambuscade. The general, even though he did not have the authority to do so, vehemently insisted upon Carroll's support. Carroll yelled at the men to get to their feet.[65] The 141st Pennsylvania and the 20th Indiana passed through the 14th Connecticut. Adjutant William Hincks (14th Connecticut) watched the red diamonds upon the kepis of the 141st Pennsylvania bob into the woods in front of the regiment, quietly noting they must have just been transferred from the defunct First Division of the III Corps and had not been issued the blue trefoil of the Third Division, II Corps. As soon as the Keystone men cleared Carroll's formation, he told his men to lie down. They were not going any farther.[66]

NORTH OF THE PLANK ROAD

In the tumult and confusion of Oates' Alabamians stampeding the 143rd Pennsylvania and the 150th Pennsylvania, Wadsworth regained his feet and stumbled back to his staff officers. Two horses down in one day was not a good omen.[67] The men in the 56th Massachusetts, the second regiment in Carruth's brigade, heard the last violent bursts of the 4th Alabama's riflery before it quit the field. The few veterans in its ranks began throwing dirt upon their log breastworks. The newer men in the regiment dove for cover with each discharge, then sheepishly resumed their work while the old hands scoffed at them. The longer the firing continued the more the green troops became keenly aware of the suffering of the casualties who lay strewn throughout the woods. Their piteous groaning and screams strained their nerves.[68]

Minutes later Wadsworth ordered Carruth's five IX Corps regiments forward to recover the ground lost by the 150th Pennsylvania. They passed over the prone Pennsylvanians. Private Charles A. Frey (Company D) of the Bucktails noted, "...several lines of raw troops were moved to the front."[69] The New Englanders stubbornly maintained their drill manual formations despite the horrible terrain. Carruth's brigade halted. The acrid smoke from thousands of discharged weapons draped the trees in a suffocating veil. The sickening sweet smell of fresh blood, mingled with the stench of human waste, permeated the woods. Wounded men limped away from the fighting. Some dragged themselves along with their hands. Others hobbled rearward under their own power. A recruit in Company F of the 56th Massachusetts turned around in the rear rank and started after the wounded men. Captain Zebulon Boylston Adams snagged him not twenty paces from the line. When the man showed no blood, Adams grabbed him by the shoulders and rattled him from his head to his ankles before sending him, downcast, back into the ranks, where he fainted. The captain and a file closer dragged him to a tree behind the line and splashed his face with cold water.[70]

Captain Zebulon Boylston Adams, Company F, 56th Massachusetts

Adams, a surgeon turned warrior, served in two other regiments before joining the 56th Massachusetts. He left behind an extremely vivid account of the Wilderness.

Massachusetts Commandery;
MOLLUS, USAMHI

Closer to the front, Wadsworth stood alone with Captain Robert Monteith, his aide. The white haired officer looked worse for wear. He felt totally exhausted, he confessed to the captain. The day's fighting had worn him out, leaving him totally unfit to command. In justice to himself and his men, he said that, perhaps, he should turn the division over to Cutler, who commanded his First Brigade. Brushing the notion aside, he asked Monteith to fetch him a hard cracker.[71]

THE EASTERN EDGE OF THE TAPP FARM

Major General Charles W. Field rode into the badly shot up 4th Alabama, 47th Alabama, and the 20th Georgia. Their losses took him aback. To Colonel Pinckney D. Bowles (4th Alabama) he blurted in disbelief, "This is all of my command that I can find." Lee did not have many brigades left to feed into the battle. He sent forward Brigadier General Abner Perrin's Alabama Brigade (R. H. Anderson's Division, A. P. Hill's Corps) which fell in on the eastern side of the Tapp Farm a few rods north of the Plank Road. He also dispatched Brigadier General E. A. Perry's small Florida brigade farther to the left with orders for Colonel William F. Perry's Alabamians to regroup and connect with E. A. Perry's left flank.[72]

Perrin had all of his line officers dismount before moving them quietly into the ramshackle breastworks just below the crest of the hill. The 8th Alabama, which held the right, on the Plank Road, went prone as did the remaining four regiments to its left. Lieutenant Colonel Hillary A. Herbert (8th Alabama) remained upright, admonishing his men with the words of General Israel Putnam at Breed's Hill, "We must not open on them until we can see the whites of their eyes." A second later, a Yankee sharpshooter sent the colonel sprawling to the ground, severely wounded. Major Duke Nall immediately stepped into the colonel's spot to assume command. The marksman cut him down also. Captain H. C. Lea (Company C) took over the regiment. The veterans still withheld their fire.[73] The brigade's sharpshooters trickled down the slope and took cover on the hillside and in the bottom land near the Plank Road and bided their time.[74]

SORREL'S FLANKING MOVEMENT

Brigadier General William Mahone contacted Lieutenant Colonel Everard M. Field's skirmish battalion in the woods southwest of McAllister's brigade to brief him about Longstreet's intended strike from the south. Wofford's and Anderson's brigades were waiting in the railroad cut to the southeast prepared to hit the Federals on their left flank. Their own brigade (Mahone's) would lead the assault. Mahone instructed the colonel to quietly and slowly take his skirmishers east until Field could hear the cheers of the flanking brigades at which point he was to charge.

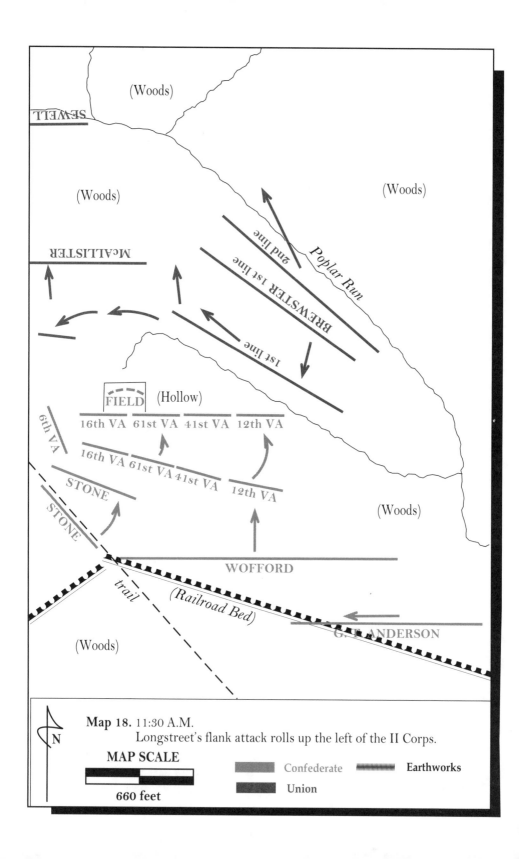

(Woods)

SEWELL

(Woods)

(Woods)

McALLISTER

Poplar Run

BREWSTER 1st line 2nd line

1st line

FIELD (Hollow)

16th VA   61st VA   41st VA   12th VA

6th VA

16th VA   61st VA 41st VA   12th VA

STONE

STONE

WOFFORD

trail

(Railroad Bed)

(Woods)

G. T. ANDERSON

(Woods)

Map 18. 11:30 A.M.
Longstreet's flank attack rolls up the left of the II Corps.

N

MAP SCALE

660 feet

Confederate   Earthworks

Union

The colonel followed the orders explicitly. His sharpshooters inched their way through the overgrown forest.[75]

At the same time, to the south and the southeast, Sergeant Major John M. Lyon and his four volunteers from the 72nd New York got their first glimpse of Wofford's and Anderson's Georgians. The five Federals, having left Brewster's brigade between two branches of Poplar Run several hundred yards behind them, came to a rise of open wooded ground and walked right into the Georgians' heavy skirmish line. The sight of two lines of Confederate infantry quick marching toward them brought the Federals to an abrupt halt but the Rebels fired before they had time to respond. Sergeant Major Lyon caught a bullet in the left side and collapsed to the ground. Private James M. Young (Company B), heedless of his personal safety, dashed across the bullet-swept ground to retrieve his sergeant's body. Hoisting the unconscious Lyon over his shoulder, the private disappeared through the woods, making tracks for his own lines. He left behind the other three men. (No one in the regiment ever learned what happened to them.)[76]

The sounds of the riflery reverberated over the rear rank of McAllister's New Jersey brigade. He glanced at his watch. It was about 11:30 A.M. Knowing the Rebels had flanked him, he sent word to Colonel William J. Sewell to take the second line, behind him, to "change front on the right company, right regiment." Sewell yelled his three regiments to their feet and wheeled them rearward to face south. McAllister also commanded his three regiments to "about face, left half wheel by regiments." Within short order, Mott and his staff galloped into the brigade.[77]

By then, Young was staggering into the ranks of the 72nd New York. Lieutenant Colonel John Leonard sent several men into the brush to relieve the heaving private of the severely wounded sergeant before ordering his regiment forward. The brigade fragmented into at least two lines, losing its cohesion. The regiments fell in wherever they could. Brewster's brigade jumped over the lower branch of Poplar Run to fill the gap between McAllister and the railroad cut. Bullets zipped through the trees. One severely wounded Captain John A. Krom (Company I, 120th New York) seconds after he crossed the creek.

Field, having forced his sharpshooters "some" distance into the tangled woodland north of the railroad cut, heard a thunderous, reassuring Rebel yell resounding through the forest to the south. The colonel screamed at his men to charge. The riflemen muscled their way through the briars and the tangle foot as fast as humanly possible until they broke into a rectangular, open hollow in the woods. Measuring about two hundred ten feet by one hundred twenty feet, Field assumed it to be an old pond bed. A large Federal regiment on the eastern lip of the depression attracted the colonel's attention. Brewster's right regiment, having walked into riflery from

Wofford's and Anderson's skirmishers, broke to the north in column of fours and was crossing the Virginians' front.[78] Unable to resist such an opportune time to snag a moving formation, Field yelled for his men to open fire. The officers and noncommissioned officers repeated the command loud enough for everyone, including the Federals, to hear.

Four Federals fell out of their formation. Field distinctly saw them bring their weapons to full cock. About three feet to the side, he saw a tree which seemed as wide as his body. He was sidestepping toward it when a bullet ripped through the back of his tunic, scraping his spine. He dropped behind the tree, his body screaming with excruciating pain. Simultaneously, a sergeant from the 61st Virginia fell dead at the colonel's feet with a bullet in his brain. The colonel momentarily fiddled

Lieutenant Colonel Everard Field, 12th Virginia

Despite a painful bullet wound across his spine, Field led Brigadier General William Mahone's sharpshooters against the II Corps' flank on May 6, 1864.

Bernard, *War Talks*, 1892

with the idea of quitting the field until he discovered that he had only been grazed. A slight grin flickered across his face. He could not go to the rear with such a trifling injury because his men would mock him for all eternity were he to do so.

The accurate Confederate rifle fire disrupted the Yankee column. Part of them ran. The greater portion of the Northerners remained upon the field and returned fire. All the while the two sides exchanged shots, Field listened intently to the rhythmic clanging of canteens against the brush behind him. When it grew loud enough to convince him that the rest of the brigade was very close at hand, he gave the command to charge. The order rippled across the depression and his men bolted forward. They reached the eastern lip of the hollow about the same time that Mahone's brigade struck the western side of it. The brigade opened fire through the skirmishers at the Federals. With his men trapped between the opposing lines, Field hastily pulled them back.

In the meantime several groups of Federals worked their way around the Confederates' left and at a range of about seventy-five yards blazed away into the flank of the 6th Virginia. Caught in the open, the rattled Confederates began to mill like cattle. The left wing of the regiment tried to face the Federals but in doubling back upon itself created more chaos until the line devolved into a confused herd some thirty ranks deep. Mahone rode into the jumbled mess. "What regiment is this in this confusion?" he asked in a voice loud enough for everyone to hear. Someone shouted the regimental number at him. "The 6th Virginia regiment," he responded in astonishment, "of *my brigade—that splendidly drilled regiment—in this condition?*" His remonstrance shamed the men into formation. Before too long, he had the entire brigade in line and left wheeling toward the north.[79]

Mahone's Virginians led Longstreet's counterattack with Wofford's and Anderson's men trailing behind them. The Virginians took McAllister from the front. His first line stalled the attack with several well executed volleys. By then, however, Wofford's Georgians had enveloped his left flank and rear. No less than three musket balls slapped into McAllister's black horse but the dying animal refused to fall. The Jerseymen streamed rearward. Unable to stop them, the colonel turned to the northeast and slowly urged his horse after them.[80]

**Brigadier General
William Mahone, C.S.A.**

The diminutive Mahone, who weighed under 125 pounds, rallied the 6th Virginia when it buckled under pressure from the II Corps during Longstreet's flank attack.

Bernard, *War Talks*, 1892

Brush fires were spreading across Mahone's front, slowing down his charge. The hideous screams of those wounded who could not escape the flames rose above the musketry. "All of the dead in some parts of the field were charred. Truly war is terrible in all [of] its phases," Sergeant John F. Sale (Company H, 12th Virginia) entered in his diary.[81] The 12th Virginia veered to the right to pass around the flames and pushed its way north. A mounted officer pranced his horse along the front of the regiment's right wing, catching the attention of Sergeant William C. Smith (Company B), brother of the regimental adjutant. He was Lieutenant Colonel G. Moxley Sorrel. "Follow me, Virginians!" he exclaimed. "Let me lead you!" As the colonel spurred into the undergrowth ahead of the regiment, he caught up with Private D. M. Bernard (Company E). The enlisted man passed a new pair of discarded officer's gloves to Sorrel, who received them with a smile. "They are the very things I need," the colonel told him. Occasional incoming rounds pattered the Virginians. One of them glanced off Smith's right ankle. In a great deal of pain, he limped away from the firing line. Two rounds thunked into Private Jim Farley (Company E). One hit him in the shoulder. The other slammed into his face. But, he refused to quit the field. He continued in the advance, with blood streaming from his terrible injuries. Riding ten paces behind the line, Mahone calmly admonished his men, "Steady in the 12th!" First Lieutenant John R. Patterson (Company E), from his position as a file closer, instinctively twisted his head to the left to see why the general would have to say something like that. His heart sank as Sergeant George G. Morrison (Company A) violently threw his rifle to the ground and headed rearward. It suddenly occurred to the lieutenant, that, "if such a man as George Morrison was going to the rear, the bottom of the fight must be out on that part of the line."[82]

To the right rear and the east, Wofford's and Anderson's brigades plowed deeper into the Wilderness, trying to catch up with McAllister's and Brewster's brigades which were fleeing toward the Brock Road. Wofford's men crowded Anderson's front, which forced "Tige's" brigade to slow its pace and to yield ground.[83]

CHAPTER FOUR

"...the enemy ceased firing and stopped damaging the trees."

6:00 A.M. TO 4:00 P.M.

WICKHAM'S PICKET OUTPOSTS ON THE BROCK ROAD
(2.3 miles southeast of Todd's Tavern)

By 6:00 A.M. Brigadier General Williams C. Wickham had pulled his four Virginia cavalry regiments together along the Brock Road. Dismounting them, he sent them forward in skirmish formation toward the 2nd Pennsylvania's Federal videttes south of Todd's Tavern.[1] Their advance did not cause any serious alarm to Brigadier General David McMurtrie Gregg, who commanded the Second Division of the Federal cavalry corps. He had Brigadier General Henry E. Davies' four regiments mounted at 3:00 A.M. and waiting in the large field west of the tavern.[2] With the exception of the 2nd Pennsylvania, he had retired Colonel J. Irvin Gregg's remaining five regiments to the tavern before daylight and had them deployed along a two thousand six hundred fifty yard line, stretching from the tavern along Piney Branch Run to the Piney Branch Church Road.[3] Wickham's Confederates herded the 2nd Pennsylvania to within one mile of the tavern. At that point the Confederates went prone in the woods on both sides of the road and banged away at the Yankees, who were nearly five hundred yards away.[4]

Companies G, E, K, and F from the 8th Pennsylvania came to the 2nd Pennsylvania's assistance.[5] The 4th Virginia, on the right of the Confederate line just northeast of the road, took cover behind a rail fence on the northern edge of the woods. An extensive, open field separated them from the Yankees. "...it was all excitement and little danger," Private Alexander

95

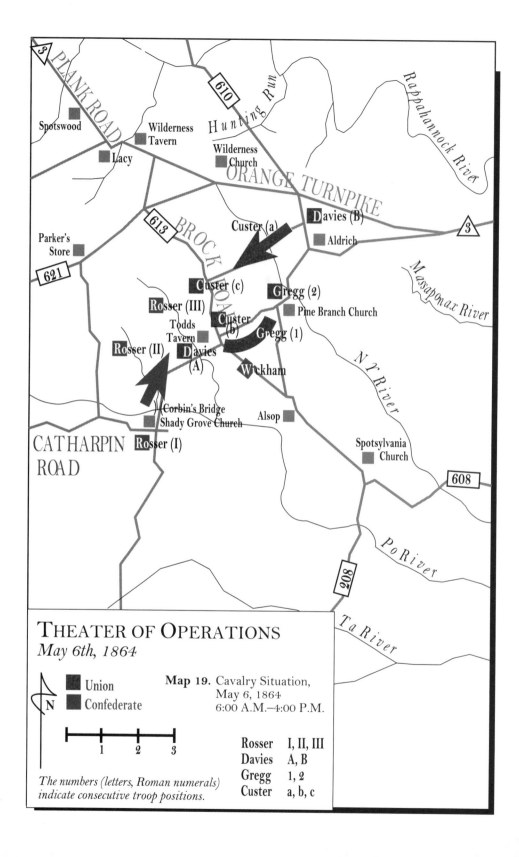

THEATER OF OPERATIONS
May 6th, 1864

N

■ Union
■ Confederate

Map 19. Cavalry Situation,
May 6, 1864
6:00 A.M.–4:00 P.M.

| | | |
| 1 | 2 | 3 |

*The numbers (letters, Roman numerals)
indicate consecutive troop positions.*

Rosser   I, II, III
Davies   A, B
Gregg   1, 2
Custer   a, b, c

**Brigadier General
Williams Wickham, C.S.A.**

Wickham's Virginia cavalry brigade opened the fighting south of Todd's Tavern on May 6, 1864.

Massachusetts Commandery;
MOLLUS, USAMHI

Hunter (Company H) recollected. A veteran, who had seen action as an infantryman since 1861, he paid little attention to the long range potshots. He listened to the regiment's other infantrymen turned cavalrymen grouse about how much more dangerous it was to fight on foot than to dash in and out of a fight. The recruits provided him with the most amusement. "They changed color and flattened themselves to the earth not daring to look up," he mused. "Others became hysterical, danger affecting them like a strong stimulant."[6] Second Lieutenant John A. Holtzman (Company D) snapped a round off into the open, then rolled over onto his side to write in his diary, "I am now lying behind an old log, shooting, and a ball has just cut the top of the log a little."[7]

By the early afternoon the 16th Pennsylvania relieved the 1st Maine near Piney Branch Church Road. The New Englanders' officers had to awaken a number of their men who had fallen asleep on the picket line. From there, the Mainers wandered east onto the Couse farm, on the north side of the road which ran southeast from Piney Branch Church to the Gordon Road. Despite the pleas of Katherine Couse and her family, the troopers stole most of the corn and chickens from the farm until they came under rifle fire from dismounted Confederate cavalry. Unsnapping their carbines, the troopers rattled the trees on the southern side of the farm yard and galloped back toward the church.[8]

The long distance skirmishing continued throughout the day until 4:30 P.M. when the Yankees retired from the fight. Gregg's brigade went to Piney Branch Church and the 1st Maine went on picket.[9] Davies' Brigade pulled back to Aldrich's, about four and a half miles northeast of Todd's Tavern.[10] The entire day's fighting resulted in six men wounded.[11]

Private R. H. Peck (Company C, 2nd Virginia) estimated that the regiment expended about 115 rounds per man and had nothing else to say about the fight. It lost only one man killed and one wounded in the process.[12] The fighting cost the 3rd Virginia Cavalry Private Phen Loran (Company B)—killed. Lieutenant John P. Puryeard (Company A) was shot through the right lung and the spine while Private William A. Cooke (Company F) was slightly injured.[13] The 4th Virginia counted ten wounded. In referring to the recruits, Hunter noted, "Their relief must have been great when at dusk the enemy ceased firing and stopped damaging the trees."[14]

CUSTER'S BRIGADE NEAR CHANCELLORSVILLE
(5.2 miles northeast of Tapp's)

Before dawn Major General Philip H. Sheridan ordered Brigadier General George A. Custer's and Colonel Thomas C. Devin's brigades to march down the Furnace Road to reinforce Gregg's cavalry division at Todd's Tavern. Custer's brigade left its bivouac one mile below Chancellorsville at 2:00 A.M., taking the Catharine Furnace Road toward the Brock Road. The 7th Michigan led the column, followed by the 5th, 6th, and 1st Michigan regiments. Averaging a little over one mile an hour, Custer and the 7th Michigan reached Todd's Tavern by 7:00 A.M., where they halted to await further instructions.[15] An hour later, the 5th Michigan joined them. Within the next two hours, the rest of the brigade arrived.[16] Lieutenant Colonel Peter Stagg and his 1st Michigan had barely reined in at the Tavern when Custer ordered him to turn about and ride north to relieve the 1st Vermont Cavalry, which had been shot up the day before along the Catharpin Road, because it was the only regiment patrolling the Brock Road above Todd's Tavern.[17]

Arriving at the Furnace-Brock Road intersection, the 1st Michigan replaced the Vermonters on the picket lines. Captain George R. Maxwell (Company K) led his company into the pine forest west of the Brock Road.[18] Passing through the forest for about twelve hundred yards, his men dismounted along the northeastern side of a rugged sedge field south of the Rowe Farm.[19] Rectangular, it measured about five hundred sixty yards along its northeastern and southwestern sides and four hundred yards along its northwestern and southeastern edges. A washout cut through the farm yard at a diagonal from about the southwest corner to a point one hundred eighty-three yards from the northeast corner. The trail from Corbin's Bridge split at the northwest corner of the farm. One branch ran one thousand two hundred yards north to Trigg's Farm. The other followed the northeastern side of the field to the point where the washout crossed its path. Then it turned northeast.[20]

Very shortly after the skirmishers deployed, Custer arrived with the rest of the brigade. While Major James H. Kidd (6th Michigan) ordered Captain Manning D. Birge (Company A) to join Maxwell's pickets, Custer positioned his brigade back in the woods, facing southwest along the long side of the field, to keep any approaching Confederate cavalry from seeing his regiments. The 1st Michigan, on regimental front in a single line, held the right of the brigade two hundred yards below the fork in the road. The 6th Michigan, also on regimental front in a single rank, supported it. The brigade band fell in on the left of the 1st, with the 5th, then the 7th Michigan finishing out the formation. The men dismounted, standing at "in place rest" in front of their horses. Custer and his staff rode out to the picket line to superintend their operation.[21]

10:00 A.M.
ROSSER'S BRIGADE AT CORBIN'S BRIDGE
(4.3 miles southeast of Tapp's)

Brigadier General Thomas Rosser's Confederate cavalry regiments were awake at dawn but by daylight they were still in their bivouac on the southern side of the Po River. Shortly before 10:00 A.M. Major General J. E. B. Stuart and his staff rode into Rosser's brigade and ordered him to take his regiments down the same back road which the Yankees had used the day before to escape from Craig's Meeting House. He was to strike the Yankees' left flank and to determine their troop dispositions.[22] Leaving the 7th Virginia behind to guard Captain Philip P. Johnston's guns while the battery turned its horses out to graze, Rosser took the remaining three regiments in the brigade and crossed the Po River.[23] With the sounds of the infantry fighting echoing over their heads from the north, the cavalrymen moved a little over half of a mile northeast of the bridge before turning north across the field of the previous day's battle. A short distance into the woods, they struck the back trail which led to the Trigg farm, two miles to the northeast.

Colonel Elijah White's 35th Virginia Battalion (about 150 men) was in the front of the brigade when the order came from Rosser for White to "send his best squadron to the front." White halted the column and sent Captain Frank Myers (Company A) back to Rosser. Myers never forgot the general's instructions. "Myers," he said, "move your people down this road and run over everything you come to. I'll send a pilot with you." With his guide alongside, the captain wheeled about and reported back to White who asked, "How far must I go?" Unable to answer, Myers returned to Rosser who bluntly replied, "Tell him to drive him as far as he can." Myers followed the command to the letter and took his men forward. Companies A and D, finding the road and wayside littered with the discarded equipment of the 18th Pennsylvania, spurred their horses into a gallop and left the brigade and their pilot far behind them.[24]

About half an hour into the advance, Stuart, who was trapped at the rear of the column by the narrowness of the track, sent Lieutenant Theodore Garnett, his aide de camp, ahead to instruct Rosser to attack the Federal outposts on sight. Forcing his way through the pines paralleling Rosser's

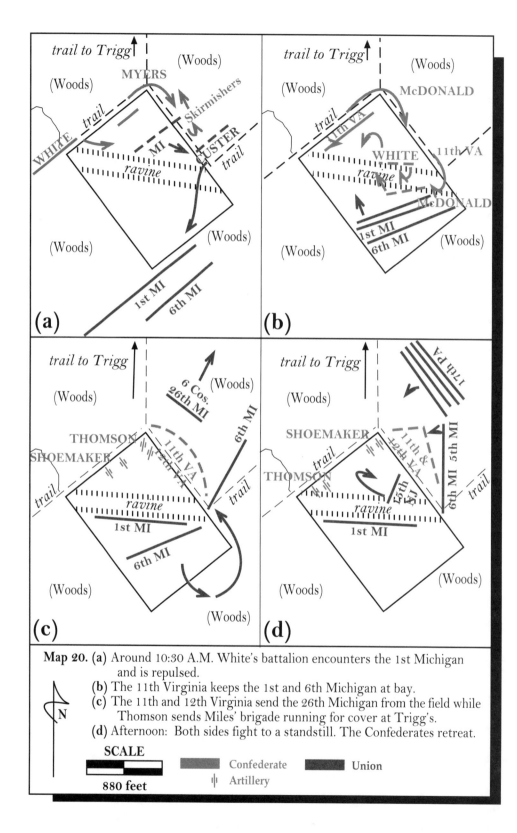

Map 20. (a) Around 10:30 A.M. White's battalion encounters the 1st Michigan and is repulsed.

(b) The 11th Virginia keeps the 1st and 6th Michigan at bay.

(c) The 11th and 12th Virginia send the 26th Michigan from the field while Thomson sends Miles' brigade running for cover at Trigg's.

(d) Afternoon: Both sides fight to a standstill. The Confederates retreat.

SCALE

880 feet

Confederate   Union

Artillery

distended column, Garnett reached White's battalion "in good time" and warned White that he would be running into the Yankee pickets before too long.[25]

Rosser hurried a messenger to Myers and his squadron to slow their pace and give the brigade a chance to catch up. By then Myers had come to the swampy stream bordering the southwestern corner of Rowe's field. Turning with the trail along the upper edge of the field, the squadron came under fire from Custer's skirmishers who were popping out of the grass about one hundred fifty yards to his right. They cracked off a couple of ineffectual rounds, before running back to the shelter of the woods.

Myers ignored them and continued riding with his squadron to the far corner of the field where the road forked north and east. The column halted there. He called over his shoulder for his guide. Private Jim Harper (Company A), who was riding nearby, snorted that the "dam 'scape gallus" was last seen running toward the rear like the devil, with a captured Yankee saddle.[26] Turning to Second Lieutenant Benjamin F. Conrad (Company A), the captain asked him which road to take. It did not matter, Conrad drawled, just so they got to the Yankees.

Myers turned the head of the column to the right along the fence row and shouted, "Forward, boys; and get ready to fight." Twisting about in the saddle he saw White filing the rest of the battalion into the field. Three hundred seventy-seven yards from the corner, where the lane turned northeast into the woods, Company A walked into the 1st and 6th Michigan's waiting skirmishers. Muzzle flashes stabbed through the pines not twenty feet in front of the unsuspecting Confederates. Privates Joseph Hendon and Henry Moore were knocked from their horses—dead. Private Samuel Crumbaker went down, mortally wounded. A carbine bullet smashed Conrad's thigh. Rather than retreat, the Rebels shouted the Rebel yell, and fired back. The blast killed the sergeant major of the 1st Michigan, Private Lucius F. Handy (Company F) and another enlisted man. A round struck Private James D. Rowe's horse (Company H) in the breast, killing it instantly.[27] The Rebels charged, sending the Federals reeling back upon their supports.[28]

At the first Confederate yelps, Custer, who was riding in the woods on the left end of the picket line, galloped across the front of the woods from the southeast, heading for the 1st Michigan. The troopers were mounted by the time he reached the tree line in front of them. Reining his horse about, he drew his saber and shouted for the band to play. With the strains of "Yankee Doodle" mingling with the rifle shots on his right flank, he swirled his sword in the direction of the attack and commanded, "Forward, by divisions!" The 1st Michigan broke into battalion front (six companies per line) as it charged. The 6th Michigan was right behind it. The two regiments became jumbled together as they bolted into the open ground.[29]

Myers, unable to stop the attack, yelled for his men to retreat. By then White was leading the rest of the "Comanches" at the charge toward the woods across from him.[30] Some troopers on the left of the battalion jumped the shallow end of the ravine and crashed head long into the right wing of the 1st and the 6th Michigan. Second Lieutenant Cortez P. Pendill (Company K, 6th Michigan) was cut down in hand to hand combat. On the southern end of the line, Custer's men reached the eastern side of the ravine seconds before the Confederates did. Reining to a halt, they fired point-blank into the "Comanches." A bullet whistled into Company C, breaking Color Sergeant Thomas N. Torreyson's leg. In the wild exchange of carbine fire, the Yankees killed Privates John Douglass and Hugh S. Thompson (Company C) and wounded several other troopers.[31]

The left wing of White's battalion gave way under the pressure and broke to the rear with the Michiganders close behind them. The Yankees shot the mount out from under the Virginians' adjutant, First Lieutenant Richard T. Watts. Dismounted, he was pulling the saddle bags with the regimental papers from his horse when the Yankees captured him.[32] The attack caught the 11th Virginia on the right flank while it was riding toward White's support. The regiment halted near the southwestern corner of the battlefield awaiting orders when a stray ball wounded Colonel Oliver R. Funsten's horse. He immediately rushed a courier toward the rear of the regiment to bring Major Edward H. McDonald forward. The major, seeing the orderly coming toward him, assumed the message was for him and rode to the front without receiving it. As his horse struggled through the pines bordering the road, he told the men, who were mounted in column of fours in the trail, to remain steady.

Funsten turned the regiment over to McDonald who immediately ordered the men to charge. The formation stretched out into an unraveling column as it progressed. Splashing across the swampy creek, the 11th Virginia swept along the western side of the field and rounded the corner, making for the Michiganders' right flank. The column burst through the few Yankees in the road, and rounded the ridge where Myers' squadron had begun the fighting. McDonald glanced to the left as he crested the ridge at the turn. Over the tree tops, he briefly caught a glimpse of Federal infantry milling along the high ground near Trigg's before the impetus of the charge carried him into the woods.[33]

Major James H. Kidd incredulously watched the 11th Virginia thunder by the 6th Michigan's right flank and disappear into the woods to his right rear.[34] Like Myers, McDonald suddenly found himself running straight for a waiting line of Federal cavalry. He looked over his shoulder to see that only two companies had managed to keep pace with him. Rather than halt, which would have presented the Federals with plenty of stationary targets, McDonald cocked his revolver and led his men full tilt toward the Westerners.[35]

Custer's men did not budge. Despite the pistol balls which slapped into the trees around them, they waited until the Confederates swept to the south along their front. Then they opened fire with their carbines. The volley startled the untried Private William S. Ball (Company I) as he blindly raced past the Yankees. The man next to him reeled in the saddle as two bullets struck him, destroying the elbow of one arm and the wrist of the other.[36] The squadron of the 11th Virginia, having run the gauntlet, flanked west in column and charged through the field toward the right rear of the 6th Michigan, which was engaged with the rest of the regiment along the ravine. "...like the French army that marched up a hill and then marched down again, [the Confederates] turned and charged back without attempting to turn their head of column towards the place where Custer was standing at bay," the amazed Kidd recalled.[37]

McDonald and his Virginians were too busy trying to save their lives to notice the troopers who were gathered around Custer. "The Yankees [were] at our backs," McDonald later wrote. It was each man for himself. With every stride of his horse, McDonald watched the ravine grow deeper and wider. Raising his horse's head, he laid the spurs into the animal's flanks and leaped a span which, in his mind, had grown to canyon proportions. Several of his men followed after him and left the Yankees, whose mounts were not trained jumpers, clattering to an abrupt halt along the eastern side of the gully.[38]

While McDonald's squadron rallied upon the rest of the regiment along the western side of the field, White attempted to lead the rest of the 11th Virginia in a countercharge. Spurring his horse into a gallop, he dashed right up to the Federal line, pistol in hand. Within seconds, he was hit by no less than five rounds. Two or three went through his hat. A bullet snatched the revolver from his hand. One cut his cheek and another grazed his tongue. Turning around in the saddle, he suddenly realized that no one had followed him into battle. Wheeling his horse about, he ran several steps when his horse crashed to the ground—dead.

**Colonel Elijah V. White,
35th Virginia Cavalry Battalion**

"Lige" White, a Marylander, whose horse was shot out from under him, owed his life to Private William H. Viers (Company B).

McDonald, *The Laurel Brigade,* 1907

Pulling himself free, he was limping back toward the Confederate lines when, off to the left, he noticed some Confederate troopers in full retreat.

White shouted at them to "rally and charge." A few of them turned about but would not advance to their certain deaths.

One of them, Private H. William Viers (Company B, 35th Virginia Battalion), galloped over to White. "Take my horse, and get out," Viers cried as he jumped from the saddle. White swung onto the horse and reached down to Viers. "No," the colonel insisted, "get behind the saddle." With a couple of the intrepid Yankees very close behind, the two cavalrymen escaped. "Why they did not kill us, God only knows," White later wrote Viers.[39]

Meanwhile, Lieutenant Colonel Thomas B. Massie's 12th Virginia with Lieutenant Carter's gun from Captain James W. Thomson's battery bolted toward the Federal right. Riding ahead of his piece, the lieutenant dismounted and tore down a section of fence to allow men onto the hill on the western side of the field.[40] While the gun was rolling into battery, the 12th charged blindly into the woods for a short distance. The Yankees shot back, wounding at least four horses.[41] The Virginians quickly cleared the remaining Federals from their front, then returned to support the guns. With Carter's gun firing over their heads, the Confederate cavalrymen came out of the woods in a justifiable panic, which Captain William N. McDonald, Rosser's ordnance officer, misinterpreted as a rout.[42]

From his position on the knoll Carter, who had just been joined by the rest of Thomson's Battery, could see Federal infantry moving out of the woods behind the ridge east of the Trigg farm. Four regiments from Colonel Nelson A. Miles' brigade (Barlow's Division) were moving west to support the left of the II Corps beyond Poplar Run. The 140th Pennsylvania and the 183rd Pennsylvania, being the two larger regiments, were on the flanks with the smaller 81st Pennsylvania and the 61st New York between them. When the regiments crested the open hill overlooking Trigg's, the four Confederate guns struck the unsuspecting 140th Pennsylvania with case shot which killed or wounded 13 officers and men. Panic stricken, the regiment peeled back toward its jump off point. The 183rd Pennsylvania shattered and also fled the field, leaving the unprotected 61st New York and the 81st Pennsylvania at the mercy of another blast from the Virginia artillerymen which took out three enlisted men, including Orderly Sergeant Kelly who was struck in the groin with a half inch lead ball. They also wavered and retreated to the eastern base of the hill.[43]

By then the 12th Virginia Cavalry was dismounting and running into the pines north of the guns, heading for Custer's right flank.[44] Noticing that the rifle fire had slackened along his front, Custer told Kidd to take his 6th Michigan Cavalry north and "Flank that battery." The regimental bugler sounded the "Rally." Those troopers who heard the call assembled around the colors in the low ground east of the ravine. Within a few minutes, they were dismounted and moving by the rear into the woods.[45] At the same time, six companies from the 26th Michigan Infantry were racing through the woods south from Trigg's to investigate the cannonading and the small arms fire.[46] The sight of the 12th Virginia milling around Thomson's guns and spraying into the forest in front of them brought the Michiganders to an unexpected halt. Believing they were outnumbered, Private Newton T. Kirk (Company E) and a few of the men around him loosed a disorganized volley into the Rebels, "to stir them up a little." Before the Virginians could respond, Kirk recollected, "...[we] turned in retreat, and came back thru' the woods with a celerity that surprised ourselves."[47]

Moving his men through the woods after the infantrymen, Massie ran headlong into the equally surprised dismounted 6th Michigan. A nasty firefight echoed throughout the woods. The Confederates unhorsed Major Charles W. Deane while he was directing the Federal line of advance.[48] The Yankees, who were armed with the seven shot Spencers, peppered the woods around the Virginians and dropped their men in disconcerting numbers. In very quick order, they wounded Privates M. Glover and Robert Painter, and Captain Sipe. Private David Danner died in the melee.[49] The Confederates, despite their inferior weapons, gave the Yankees a stiff fight.

It was around noon and neither side was gaining any appreciable advantage.[50] Devin's Federal cavalry brigade with Lieutenant Edward Heaton's Companies B and L, 2nd U.S. Artillery, deployed along the Brock Road, east of Custer's position. Devin sent the 17th Pennsylvania north along the road to connect with the II Corps. The 6th New York stretched south to connect with Gregg's brigade at Todd's Tavern. The 9th New York Cavalry remained in the center, connecting with both wings of the brigade. Devin, having reconnoitered the position before his men arrived, had seen only three of Thomson's guns. Believing he had fire superiority, he ordered Heaton to unlimber his eight guns and roll them by hand to the wooded crest behind Custer's men.[51]

At the same time, Rosser was trying to secure his own position. Captain John J. Shoemaker's Virginia artillery rolled into battery on Thomson's right.[52] For the next hour the batteries slammed away at each other. The Federals responded with a "desultory fire," Lieutenant Theodore Garnett, Stuart's aide de camp, noted.[53] Private George M. Neese (Thomson's Battery) stared at the midday sun. "I could just make out to see the sun, and it looked like a vast ball of red fire hanging in a smoke-veiled sky," he wrote in his diary. With visibility cut to under twenty-five yards it made it nearly impossible for the Confederates to hit their targets.[54] With most of the Rebels' shots sailing over the Federal position, the Yankees gained enough time to place their guns in a semicircle across the Confederate front.[55]

The long shots provided a tremendous amount of sport for Custer's 7th Michigan which was covering his left rear and protecting the brigade's remuda along the Brock Road. The leader of the brigade's servants and black contrabands, who were herding the horses, was a skinny fellow named Malachi. Troopers derisively nicknamed him "Bones," and allowed him to have a horse with a lame leg. He rode his crippled horse bareback without the aid of a bridle and used a hickory club to goad the animal along. As the first rounds showered the road side with branches, Malachi panicked. Beating his animal into a stilted gate, he was leading the "column" a short distance north along the road north toward the II Corps when a Confederate round burst in the tree tops in front of him. Malachi about faced and counter marched his frightened drovers back toward their starting point when another round sent them careening north again. The Michiganders watched the entire folly for several minutes until it became apparent that the brigade was going to lose its entire herd unless someone put a stop to it. Shouted commands were of no avail. Finally, the white officer in charge of the entire caravan galloped up to Malachi in an attempt to calm down the confused civilians and their horses. Using the flat of his saber, and much to the amusement of his troopers, he unhorsed Malachi with several hard blows upon his head and shoulders. With their leader unconscious in the road, order was quickly restored and the horses were led to a much safer location.[56]

By 1:00 P.M. the field, with the exception of the skirmishing in the woods north of the field, had become relatively quiet. Rosser ordered Thomson's Battery to shift to the northwest corner of the battle ground, near the lower end of the ravine and sent Major Edward H. McDonald and about 150 of his men from the 11th Virginia into the woods to reinforce the 12th Virginia. Colonel Elijah White had managed to reorganize about thirty of his officers and troopers behind the guns. Nearby, another dozen from the 11th Virginia were rallied around Third Lieutenant Isaac Parsons, Jr. (Company D).[57]

McDonald's troopers closed in on the left of the 12th Virginia, extending their line another two hundred feet. The seemingly larger number of Confederates alarmed Major James H. Kidd (6th Michigan). Looking to the northwest, he could see nothing but Rebels. He refused his right flank and sent a man to Custer for help.[58] Custer pulled the 5th Michigan from his left, behind the ridge, and ordered it and the 17th Pennsylvania to side slip to the right to reinforce the 6th Michigan. They fell in beyond the Virginians' left flank in column of battalions with their carbines at the ready. At the same time, a squadron from the 1st New Jersey arrived to support one of Custer's batteries. Captains Walter R. Robbins (Company G) and Garrett V. Beekman (Company L) went into line to the left rear of the guns, waiting for the signal to advance.[59] McDonald watched the veteran troopers slowly, deliberately left half wheel their four lines toward his flank.[60]

He refused the left of his command to meet them and prepared for the worst. The Yankee cavalrymen poured a tremendous fire into the Confeder-

**Major Edward H. McDonald,
11th Virginia Cavalry**

McDonald and his 11th Virginia anchored the Confederate cavalry's left flank against the better equipped 5th and 6th Michigan and the 17th Pennsylvania.

McDonald, *The Laurel Brigade*, 1907

ates. Third Lieutenant Edmond Pendleton (Company C) was killed at McDonald's side. Twisting about, the major noticed that Captain Hugh H. McGuire, Jr. (Company E) was lagging too far behind his company, and yelled at him to assume his place on the line. With McGuire dodging from tree to tree, McDonald turned around to face the Northerners when he heard the distinct thud of a bullet striking a person nearby. He looked around. McGuire lay on the forest floor with a bullet wound in his left arm. McDonald was telling one of the captain's men to take him to the rear when Private Charles B. Riley (Company D) stepped up and volunteered to do the work. "Let me take him," Riley pleaded. "I am scared to death—can neither load or fire my gun." Realizing he needed men who could fight on the line, the major consented. Riley helped McGuire a short distance to the rear before the severe volume of carbine fire got the better of him. Abandoning the captain in the brush, he took off running and never returned to the regiment.[61]

To the south, the Federal artillerists loosed a deadly barrage upon the Confederates in front of them, with most of their rounds taking effect among Shoemaker's crews. Their rapid, accurate fire killed one man and wounded nine others besides killing three horses and disabling eight more.[62] The hellish landscape burned itself into Private George M. Neese's memory. "...a thousand fires blazed and crackled on the bloody arena, which added new horrors and terrors to the ghastly scene spread over the battle plain," he entered in his diary.[63] The ferocity of the attack appalled Garnett. "...the [Federal] batteries on both of our flanks opened on us, their own shell crossing each other in mid-air, and spreading considerable alarm in our ranks," he recollected.[64] The cavalry in the woods behind the guns suffered terribly from the Federal shells and case shot falling among them. The Virginians panicked and raced toward the cover of the creek bottom and the relative safety which it offered while Rosser remained mounted among Thomson's gunners, valiantly trying to inspire them by his courage.[65] "He is no General at all," Myers later informed his family in a bitter letter. "As brave a man as ever drew a breath, but knows no more about putting a command into a fight than a school boy."[66] Captain William N. McGregor's battery came up on Shoemaker's right, rolled into position, and quickly dismounted one of the Federal guns with its first fire, then limbered up and charged to a more advanced position.[67] Stuart also arrived. With his bared sword resting in the crook of his left arm he persistently rode his horse back and forth along the road behind the guns. "You *must* go back, boys," he urged them. "The Yankees can't no more than kill you if you fight them—and if you don't go back I'll kill you myself—better [to] be shot by the enemy than by your own men—go back, boys!" A few stalwarts did return to support the artillerymen but most did not. Captain Frank Myers (Company A, 35th Battalion) who witnessed the entire incident later reflected, "...the murderous cross-fire had such a demoralizing power that even Gen. Lee himself could not have kept the majority of the runaways on the smoking field."[68]

Brigadier General
Thomas Rosser, C.S.A.

Captain Frank Myers bitterly criticized Rosser when he wrote, "He is no General at all. As brave a man as ever drew a breath but knows no more about putting a command into a fight than a school boy."

Battles and Leaders, 1:IV, Grant-Lee Edition, 1888

With their guns mercilessly pounding the Confederate artillery, Custer's soldiers advanced as a body. The 11th and the 12th Virginia collapsed and ran from the woods toward the low ground behind the guns. Captain George R. Maxwell's squadron (1st Michigan) and Robbins' squadron from the 1st New Jersey surged toward the gap between Shoemaker's and Thomson's batteries. A shell burst over the Jerseymen and a fragment knocked the foreleg from under Beekman's horse. Robbins, who passed him in the charge, never forgot how forlorn he looked.[69] The Confederates limbered up and retired to safer ground farther to the rear before the Yankees reached them.[70] With their own artillery dropping rounds in front of them, the Yankees retired to their original position and claimed the victory for the day.[71]

White tried with minimal success to bring his frightened skulkers out of the woods to the road. When he ordered Captain Marcellus French (Company F, 35th Virginia Battalion) to run into the swamp to bring them out, the captain initially refused, saying that if the men saw him going to the rear, it would further demoralize them. He went anyway and managed to bring some men back.

Meanwhile, White found Captain Frank Myers standing on a mound of dirt in the swamp. Leaping over the muddy water between them, he landed almost face to face with the captain. A low flying shell screamed close by their heads, forcing White, who had never reacted to artillery fire before, to duck. With Myers doing everything to suppress a laugh, the embarrassed White sheepishly raised his head and blurted, "I golly! I believe I am demoralized myself."

He had every reason to be. As the rifle fire waned into nothing, the artillery attack intensified to the point that White ordered his men to lie down in the woods behind the road. A handful of troopers hurled themselves into a hollow when an incoming shell howled into them. Ripping the head from Corporal James F. Broy (Company F, 35th Virginia Battalion), it splattered his comrades with his brains before it exploded and killed a horse behind them. The shells created total havoc among the battalion's horses. Plunging and rearing as the searing chunks of iron tore ghastly holes in their bodies, the animals were more dangerous to the men who were lying nearby than the projectiles. To worsen matters, a soldier in the 11th Virginia stole Private Edwin R. Oxley's clothes and saddle from his dead mount while he was asking Myers what he was to do since his horse had been killed. Oxley (Company A) left the field, swearing vehemently that "any man who would steal at such a time as that ought to be hung." The counter-battery fire ceased around 2:00 P.M.[72] The Confederates left their dead on the field between the lines for the Federals to look after. By 4:00 P.M. the Yankees had retired to the woods on the eastern side of the battlefield, and Stuart decided that the place was secure.[73]

Had Stuart and Rosser not been where they were at that particular stage of the battle, it would have been quite possible for Miles' infantry and Custer's cavalry to have caught Wofford's, Anderson's, and Mahone's brigades from the flank and the rear while they were preparing to turn the II Corps along the railroad cut. The Confederate cavalry, nevertheless, lost control of the field and suffered the heavier percentage of casualties. (Rosser lost about 19 percent of his men engaged compared to a Federal loss of 2 percent.) But, with three cavalry regiments numbering about 650 officers and men and 12 guns, Stuart successfully kept one infantry brigade (1,995 effectives), two cavalry brigades (3,654 effectives) and two Federal artillery companies (141 effectives) fully occupied for at least three hours, thereby depriving the II Corps of their services.[74]

CHAPTER FIVE

"Face the enemy; no Bull Run here."

11:30 A.M. TO 12:00 NOON
WADSWORTH'S POSITION ALONG THE PLANK ROAD

Minutes before Longstreet's flank attack began, Wadsworth was tightening up his mixed organizations from the II, V, and IX Corps troops. Shortly after Captain Robert Monteith (Company H, 7th Wisconsin) brought him a hardcracker, the general asked Major Edwin S. Osborne (149th Pennsylvania), a member of his staff, for his horse. Again the general rode into the ranks of the stubborn 20th Massachusetts and this time successfully goaded the regiment forward. The New Englanders flanked south across the road until their right flank rested against the berm. Then they advanced. The field had become relatively quiet since the 86th New York backed off from the 1st South Carolina.[1]

To the north, the 10th and the 4th U.S. Regulars went to ground in front of their brigade and refused to go any farther.[2] Behind them, Colonel William F. Bartlett (57th Massachusetts), who had lost a leg to a sharpshooter at Yorktown in 1862 and now sported a cork one in its place, dismounted and limped over to Sergeant Edwin D. McFarland (Company I). He asked for a drink from the sergeant's canteen. Bartlett was worried about his men and how they would behave under fire for the first time. A veteran of the Peninsula and Port Hudson, he knew that he had not had enough time to train them adequately for any action of this magnitude. "It will be a bloody day," he wrote in his journal that morning, "I believe I am prepared to die." After taking a swig, he faced the regiment and gave the order to advance. A spent minie ball struck him in the temple, knocking him to the ground. Eager hands quickly bore him to the rear. As the order car-

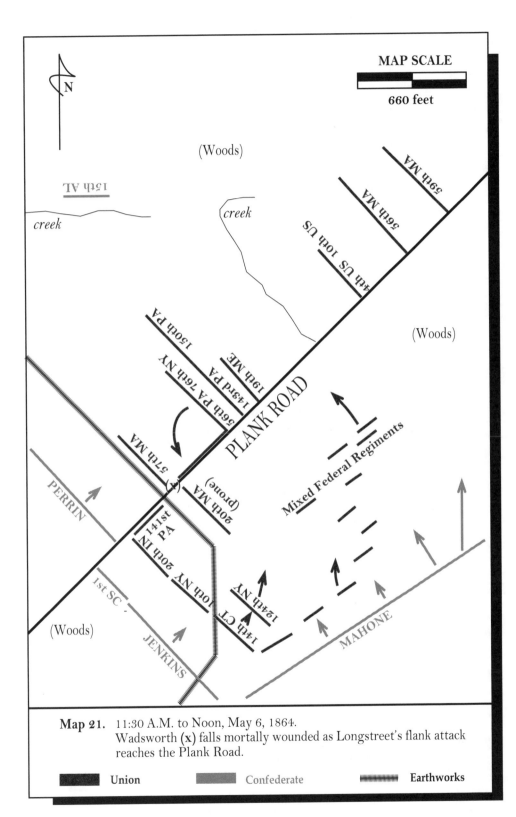

MAP SCALE

660 feet

(Woods)

13th AL

59th MA

creek

creek

56th MA

4th US 10th US

150th PA

(Woods)

143rd PA

19th ME

56th PA 76th NY

PLANK ROAD

57th MA

Mixed Federal Regiments

(x)

20th MA (prone)

PERRIN

141st PA

14th CT 40th NY 20th IN

124th NY

1st SC

(Woods)

JENKINS

MAHONE

Map 21. 11:30 A.M. to Noon, May 6, 1864.
Wadsworth **(x)** falls mortally wounded as Longstreet's flank attack
reaches the Plank Road.

Union　　　Confederate　　　Earthworks

ried down through the line, Captain Joseph W. Gird (Company B) stepped out in front of his men and quickly admonished them to keep cool. He warned them not to break formation and not to fire until so ordered and then to fire low. While stepping back into his post in the front rank on the right end of the company, a bullet hit him in the skull. His arms flew up in the air and he crumbled to the ground—dead. Lieutenant Colonel Charles L. Chandler assumed control. The regiment moved out.[3] It stubbornly struggled to maintain its regimental formation despite the dense undergrowth.

The rumor of Bartlett's alleged death quickly traveled back through the woods to the 56th Massachusetts. "Poor Bartlett is killed," Colonel Charles Griswold told his lieutenant colonel, Stephen Weld. (Weld had no way of knowing that his good friend Charley would never speak to him again.)[4] The 57th Massachusetts continued to move ahead leaving the 56th Massachusetts very far behind it.

Captain Z. Boylston Adams (Company F, 56th Massachusetts) brushed past a wounded Confederate sergeant who was propped up against a tree. Ignoring the soldier's plea for water, he continued forward and went to the ground with his men about fifty yards ahead. An enlisted men however fetched the Rebel a cup of water from Wilderness Run before rejoining his men. Without warning, the Confederate fired into the backs of the Massachusetts men, whereupon several of the New Englanders, without orders, broke from the ranks and mercilessly dispatched the fellow.[5]

SOUTH OF THE PLANK ROAD
THE SOUTHERN FLANK OF WARD'S BRIGADE

McAllister's collapse forced the 40th New York to pull back its line to face south. The New Yorkers laid a heavy fire into the left of Mahone's brigade, briefly stalling its advance. The Virginians, nevertheless, swarmed past the regiment's left flank. Rattled Federals behind the 40th emptied their rifles into its ranks, forcing the New Yorkers to retire to a partially rallied line from Mott's Division. They made a very brief stand, then ran toward the Brock Road.[6]

THE VERMONT BRIGADE

The Southern counterattack flowed around the fragmented regiments of the II Corps and struck the inverted "V" of log works held by the Vermont Brigade. The Rebels' shots came in at chest height, chinking the headlogs on the breastworks. Most of the Vermonters, like Private Wilbur Fisk (Company E, 2nd Vermont) preferred to lie on their backs to load. Others, like the intrepid fellow next to Fisk, tried to pop off rounds from a kneeling position. "I am killed," the fellow exclaimed as a ball ripped into his chest, just missing his heart. He stood up to step to the rear when he suddenly dropped—lifeless—across Fisk. Someone shouted to retreat. The

Vermonters scattered, every man for himself for the Plank Road, where they had been ordered to rally. "So much hard fighting, and so many killed and wounded for nothing," Fisk later complained. At the time he did not care where he was heading just so it was far away from the slaughter.[7]

THE 124TH NEW YORK AND CARROLL'S BRIGADE

The 124th New York had barely begun their cooking when bullets started zipping around them from the left flank. Lieutenant Colonel Charles Weygant rushed his startled regiment into position, facing it to the left, nearly perpendicular to its original line.[8] An intense storm of small arms fire east of the earthworks broke Ward's left wing. McAllister's brigade, on Ward's left flank, rapidly disintegrated and, in its flight, swept the 124th New York from the field.[9]

Adjutant William Hincks (14th Connecticut) immediately yelled at his men to fall in to meet the assault.[10] The shrill Rebel yell resounded above the small arms fire. The Connecticut men, many of whom were armed with Sharps breech-loading rifles, slammed away at the onrushing Confederates with a tremendous fury. Men raised themselves to their knees to get steady aim. No one but the officers and the file closers stayed afoot and they were frantically admonishing the "boys" to aim low. Wounded men fell out to go to the rear. Their comrades snatched up their arms to keep the rate of fire up. (They later estimated a firing rate of four rounds per minute.)[11] Private Charles House (Company D) caught a bullet in the foot which temporarily disabled him. He tried to stay at his post despite his painful injury.[12]

The Confederates went around the regiment's flanks, nearly enveloping it in a complete circle. They were so close that the Federals could distinctly see the butternut of their uniforms as they dodged between the trees. Their musketry became increasingly accurate. A color bearer, Corporal Henry K. Lyon (Company G), absorbed a round. As he dropped to his knees, he stabbed the end of the staff into the ground and attempted to hold the U.S. colors upright. Seconds later a bullet knocked down Sergeant Elnathan B Tyler (Company B), who was next to him. When a couple of men took the sergeant to the rear, the dying Lyon handed the U.S. colors to Lieutenant Colonel Samuel A. Moore, gasping he had done his best.[13]

Men were quitting the line, and the regiment's volume of fire waned considerably. Many of the men, like Corporal John Billson (Company D), assisted wounded comrades to the rear. He had just hoisted House onto his back and was struggling through the thickets toward the rear when the regiment abandoned its position. The Confederates seemed too close for House's liking. He slid off Billson's back and skittered toward the Brock Road faster than the corporal could run with two good legs.[14] Sergeant Charles G. Blatchley (Company I) suddenly glanced to one side only to discover that he was alone. The colors were gone and he was not staying around to find out why.[15]

The New Englanders retreated several hundred yards with the Rebels right behind them. All the while the Southerners called at them to surrender. The threat of languishing in Andersonville Prison spurred the Federals to new speed. It did not take the bulk of the 14th Connecticut long to get to the freshly reinforced breastworks along the Brock Road.[16] It seemed as if every Federal along the entire front had taken to his heels in flight.

ALONG THE PLANK ROAD

In short order, Wadsworth learned that the Confederates (15th Alabama) still remained upon the northern end of his line. Twisting in the saddle to face Monteith, he pointed toward the remnants of the 56th Pennsylvania and the 76th New York, which were lying in formation facing west, and shouted, "I will throw these two regiments on their flank and you hurry forward the First Brigade (Cutler's)." The captain dug his spurs into his horse and clattered down the Plank Road.[17] Within seconds a courier from Hancock galloped up to the general, blurting a warning to watch out for his left flank. Wadsworth darted in behind the Pennsylvanians and the New Yorkers and hollered for them to change direction to the south.[18]

At that instant, the Rebel yell echoed from the brush along the eastern face of the abandoned Confederate works. The 8th Alabama, near the top of the hill on the edge of the Tapp farm, sent a volley hammering into the right flank of the 56th Pennsylvania and the 76th New York and into the front of the 57th Massachusetts.[19] The 8th Alabama's first fire caught Wadsworth completely off guard. The distraught general and his aide de camp, Second Lieutenant Earl M. Rogers (Company I, 6th Wisconsin), stood in the road, transfixed, as the 8th Alabama unleashed two more volleys into the Federals.[20] Hundreds of rounds smashed into the unsuspecting ranks of the 57th Massachusetts which had just halted within ten feet of the Confederate front line works. The untried Federals returned fire.

The Alabamians' sharpshooters found themselves in a bad fix. They were lying in the hollow caught between two fires—their own line near the crest of the hill and the Federals in front of them. Private William Berry (8th Alabama) defiantly stood up in the open and took deliberate shots at the Federals until a bullet snuffed him out. Skinny Private Joe Shuttlesworth, who barely weighed one hundred pounds, did the same and a round mortally wounded him also.[21]

The Confederates leaped to their feet about three yards in front of Wadsworth and Rogers. The general snapped out of his daze and wheeled his horse about to run when a bullet crashed into the back of his head. Brains and blood splattered Rogers' tunic. Wadsworth toppled from his horse which frantically bolted eastward and Rogers' horse crumbled in the

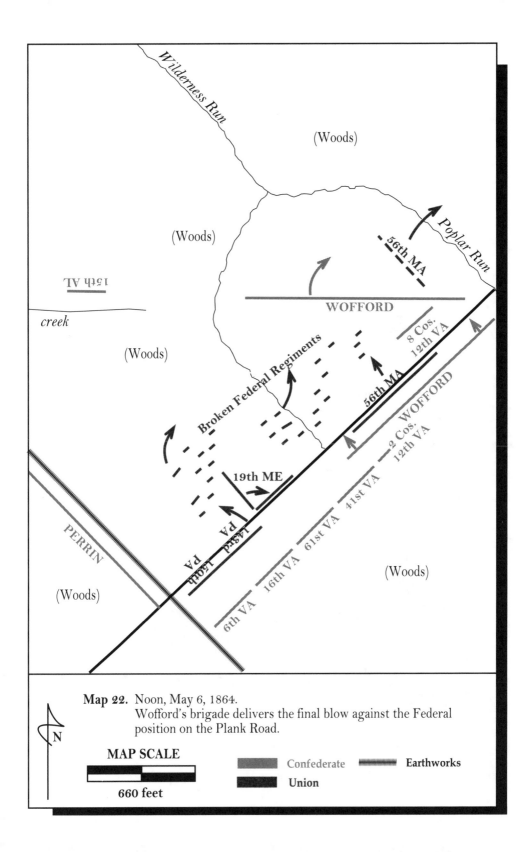

Map 22. Noon, May 6, 1864.
Wofford's brigade delivers the final blow against the Federal position on the Plank Road.

MAP SCALE

660 feet

Confederate
Union

Earthworks

N

(Woods)

(Woods)

(Woods)

(Woods)

(Woods)

(Woods)

Wilderness Run

Poplar Run

creek

15th AL

56th MA

WOFFORD

8 Cos. 12th VA

56th MA

Broken Federal Regiments

2 Cos. 12th VA

WOFFORD

19th ME

41st VA

61st VA

16th VA

6th VA

143rd PA

150th PA

PERRIN

road, throwing him in a heap next to the general. The frightened aide fumbled with the general's coat, desperately trying to snatch Wadsworth's gold watch from the inside pocket when a bullet passed uncomfortably close to his head. Rogers' eyes caught the deathly glint of leveled bayonets rapidly approaching him. Forgetting the watch, he ran several yards down the road where he found the general's horse with its reins snagged in the brush. Pulling the reins free, he threw himself onto the horse's back, leaned forward in the saddle, and raced toward the Brock Road.[22]

SOUTH OF THE PLANK ROAD

The suddenness of the attack startled the 20th Massachusetts as it neared the eastern side of the depression in front of the abandoned Confederate works. Without orders, the veterans dove to the ground as a body. A stray bullet dropped Colonel George N. Macy. Major Henry Abbott, who immediately took over the regiment, refused to lie down. He paced the line admonishing the men to remain steady.[23] At the same time Colonel James R. Hagood yelled his 1st South Carolina to its feet, "First Regiment, forward." The South Carolinians stepped over their slight breastworks and reformed. "Charge!" The Rebels shattered the 86th New York. It streamed rearward without firing a shot, dragging the 99th Pennsylvania and the 110th Pennsylvania with it.[24]

Colonel George N. Macy,
20th Massachusetts

These two photographs show how the war aged Macy. The left one shows him early in the war before he lost his left hand and was wounded again at the Wilderness. The right one shows an aged veteran.
Massachusetts Commandery; MOLLUS, USAMHI

Confederates swarmed through the woods at will. They shot down Abbott. His men managed to carry him to the rear minutes before the regiment broke and ran.[25] While Perrin's Alabamians were clearing the field of opposition north of the Plank Road, the 1st South Carolina was sweeping due east on the south side. Mahone's Virginians were moving toward the road in a northeasterly direction while Wofford's and Anderson's Georgians were closing in from the south. Regiments everywhere, Northern and Southern became jumbled beyond control.

Major Henry Abbott,
20th Massachusetts

The youthful Abbott, who had risen to major from lieutenant, had served with his regiment since 1861. The Wilderness was his last battle.

Massachusetts Commandery;
MOLLUS, USAMHI

12:00 NOON

NORTH OF THE PLANK ROAD

The right of the 57th Massachusetts wavered. Men started to leave the line by squads.[26] The left of Company H quit the field, carrying with it part of the color guard and the right of Company C. The men streamed past First Lieutenant Charles Barker (Company F), who immediately stepped behind his men and ordered them to retire. Two minie balls thunked into his body in quick succession and he went to the ground with an arm wound and a shattered thigh. The lieutenant fumbled in his tunic for his handkerchief. He needed to stop the profuse bleeding. Captain Levi Lawrence (Company F) dropped to the ground beside him, tore the handkerchief from his shaking hands and tied off the wound above the knee before returning to the company where he caught a load of buckshot in the neck.

Grabbing a nearby musket, the severely injured Barker pulled himself to his feet and tried to hobble away from the Confederates. But, his leg could not take the strain. He crashed to the ground. Rolling onto his behind, he sat up and, using his arms as crutches, inched himself toward the rear. An enlisted man and the wounded Lawrence soon found him and dragged him toward the Brock Road.[27]

The Confederates took out over two hundred of the New Englanders in a matter of minutes. Lieutenant Colonel Charles Chandler, not knowing what was going on, shouted at Sergeant Leopold Karpeles (Company E), "Color Sergeant, what's the trouble?" Karpeles, with the colors in hand, leaped up onto a shattered tree stump to look around. "Colonel, the Rebs are around us," he replied. The colonel and Karpeles with a handful of men started running for the Plank Road. Near the side of the road, the colors, which Karpeles had left unfurled, got caught in the brush. "For God's sake, boys, don't forsake your colors," he cried. First Lieutenant Henry C. Ward (Company G) ordered Karpeles to conceal the flag. While the sergeant was feverishly rolling them around the staff, Sergeant Edwin D. McFarland (Company I), Lieutenant Charles Royce (Company C) and 32 other enlisted men rallied around him. The colonel, realizing that they were the only members of the 57th who remained upon the field, told everyone to lie down. They threw themselves onto the forest floor and hoped no one would find them there.[28]

THE 19TH MAINE

Perrin's Alabamians drove the 57th Massachusetts from the field north of the road. The 1st South Carolina, with all of Mahone's brigade, except eight companies of the 12th Virginia, herded the remainder of Ward's brigade from the field. About one hundred fifty yards from Wadsworth's front, the Confederates ran headlong into the 143rd Pennsylvania, the 150th Pennsylvania, and the 19th Maine—three veteran regiments. The two Pennsylvania regiments successfully left wheeled and crossed to the south side of the Plank Road just as the Alabamians volleyed into the 57th Massachusetts. Taking cover in the drainage ditch the two regiments bought at least five minutes more time for the Federals along the Plank Road.[29]

The 1st South Carolina took quite a few hits. The regiment's charge stalled about one hundred yards from the Federal position. "While out there in front of the Yankee works we were subjected to the most deadly fire," Frank Mixon (Company E) later wrote. The plucky Carolinian carried a worm-eaten, rotted oak stump with him into the action. Propping it up with a stick, he threw himself down behind it. Within a minute or two, his brother, Joyce, crawled up on his left. Lieutenant Hair joined him on the right. The lieutenant twisted his head to speak to Mixon when a minie ball bored through his right temple and exited through his left cheek. The lieutenant's head thunked on the ground. The startled sergeant quickly lifted it up. Blood gushed from Hair's mouth and nose. It trickled from his eyes and his ears as well. Mixon cradled the officer's head in the crook of his arm until the hemorrhaging nearly stopped before wiping the blood from his face with a handkerchief.

Mixon asked whether he could get back. Hair believed he could. The stalwart lieutenant raised himself up to his full height. A bullet cut the tobacco pouch from his coat. Hair took off at a very wobbly run. Mixon followed his progress for about one hundred yards when something lifted Hair off his feet and hurled him head over heels into the brush. Believing his friend was dead, the sergeant busied himself with what was going on in front of him. (Hair survived the war.)[30]

The Pennsylvanians expended about ten rounds of ammunition per man before Perrin's men took them on the flank and the rear. Lieutenant Colonel John D. Musser (143rd Pennsylvania) died in the fighting. When the Pennsylvanians retreated, his body remained upon the field.[31]

To the east, completely out of contact with any regiments, Colonel Selden Connor of the 19th Maine broke off a conversation with Captain Banes, the adjutant general of Webb's brigade. Telling Banes to inform Webb that he was not going to wait upon orders, Connor faced the regiment to the east, then right wheeled it into line along the northern side of the Plank Road. Individual stragglers, then squads of demoralized men, raced across the Plank Road across Connor's line of fire. Without warning, the Vermont brigade, en masse, bolted into the road on the left of Connor's men, heading east. He recognized Colonel Lewis A. Grant in the middle of the mob. Confederate rifle fire cracked out in the woods behind the Vermonters and a color bearer frantically raced up and down the road trying to rally the demoralized troops but to no avail.

The moment the fleeing Federals cleared his front, Connor stepped into the road and commanded his men to volley by files. By twos, the soldiers leveled their weapons and cut loose. The barking rifles sounded like a huge string of very loud fire crackers bursting on the Fourth of July. By the time the last file fired, all of the others were loaded and the staccato of riflery repeated itself.[32] The Virginians staggered under the blast. For several minutes they engaged the Federals in a vicious firefight.[33] The colonel's body shuddered under the impact of a slug which struck his thigh with the force of a sledge hammer and knocked him into the dirt. "Are you hit, Colonel?" Connor glanced to the north and saw Webb's head poking above the brush along the side of the road. "I've got it this time, General," he winced as Captain Nehemiah Smart (Company E) shoved him onto a blanket. A small squad of willing volunteers hoisted the two hundred pound officer off the ground and struggled toward the Brock Road.[34] While the Federals to the west were streaming through the woods behind them with the Alabamians in pursuit, Wofford's Georgians were spilling over the road on their left flank. The Mainers fled to the east.[35] Using the easternmost branch of Poplar Run to mark their right flank, Wofford's Georgians crowded to the left, and, completely unobserved, overlapped the front of the 12th Virginia.[36] Anderson's brigade, having run into very little opposition, fell back on the right flank, leaving the field to Wofford and the Virginians.[37]

THE 56TH MASSACHUSETTS

Two hundred twenty yards west of the eastern branch of Wilderness Run, the 56th Massachusetts detached skirmishers from every company to the west. Captain Boylston Adams (Company F) left his men to check the skirmishers' placement. He found Private John Buckshot, a sharpshooting St. Regis Indian from Company F, standing behind a tree and scanning the woods around him. The thick underbrush and the impenetrable smoke greatly restricted his line of sight. Adams warned Buckshot not to snap any rounds off to the front for fear of hitting their own men. (The 19th Maine was about one hundred twenty-five yards beyond the 57th's regimental line.)

The captain walked back to the regiment as it was filing south across the Plank Road into the drainage ditch on the other side. The men went to their knees behind the brush-covered berm of the ditch while their officers remained in the road. Having learned early on to utilize makeshift cover, without orders, they dragged tree trunks and branches along the southern lip of the ditch. The New Englanders anxiously held their fire despite the unnerving zips and whistles of incoming slugs. The acrid smell of burned powder stung their eyes and parched their throats.[38]

Captain Warren B. Galucia (Company E) was anxiously waiting for Color Sergeant Robert C. Horrigan (Company E) to return from the 57th Massachusetts where he had sent him (with the colonel's permission) to bring back a sixteen-year-old musician from that regiment, Charles F. Everett (Company D). Both men hailed from Worcester. The captain had known Everett since the day he was born. The boy had begged Galucia to lend him a weapon and accouterments so he could go into the fight with his regiment. When the captain told him off, the boy shouted back that he would go anyway. He disappeared for a few minutes, then returned with a musket and his pockets stuffed with cartridges. "I am going, Warren," Everett snarled, "and no thanks to you." The captain, who knew the boy's family very well, pleaded with him not to go to the front for the sake of his mother and sisters but Everett paid him no heed. He went anyway. When the firing erupted on the right flank Horrigan hurried back to the regiment to assume his place with the color guard. Hurrying past the captain, he called out, "I will tell you of your boy later."[39]

Captain Warren B. Galucia, Company E, 56th Massachusetts

Galucia, who had seen Musician Charles F. Everett (Company D) grow up in his home town of Worcester, sent the color bearer to the front to check on the boy's condition. Everett was killed.

Massachusetts Commandery; MOLLUS, USAMHI

From his position behind the second company to the right of the colors, Adams felt extremely vulnerable. One or two shots, close together, cracked through the air a short distance to his left. Presuming they came from the company to his left, he was turning on his heels in that direction when a batch of frightened Federal soldiers bounded through the brush and leaped into the road. "For God's sake don't fire in here, these are our own men," one of them cried. Within moments, hundreds of Federals, most of them wearing the trefoil of the II Corps upon their caps, swarmed over and around the 56th Massachusetts.[40] Lieutenant Colonel Stephen M. Weld waited for the retreating men to clear his front then yelled the command to open fire.

Wofford's Georgians responded with a withering blast. Adams watched several of his men keel over while others limped away from the firing line. A bullet slammed into First Sergeant Sanderson, Adams' acting lieutenant. The sergeant threw his arms up in the air and fell flat on his face by the captain's side. Second Sergeant Frederick G. Weale, British Crimean War veteran, stepped up to Adams and formally saluted. Pointing to the bullet wound in his chest he asked permission to quit the field. The stunned captain told him to head back.

Presently, Colonel Charles E. Griswold raced to the right of the line with Color Sergeant Robert C. Horrigan. Confederates by threes, then squads dashed to the northern side of the road right in front of the two New Englanders. Griswold jerked out his pistol and snapped off rounds at the Rebels at point blank range while Horrigan, with the flag in one hand, attempted to punch out any Confederate who got too close to him. A bullet sliced through the colonel's jugular vein. He collapsed onto the road, bleeding to death. Horrigan retreated to the line.[41]

South of the Plank Road

Squads from remnants of shattered regiments attempted to rally along the eastern bank of Poplar Run. In the bottom land, Colonel Charles Weygant (124th New York) pulled together his color guard. Unsheathing his sword, he gallantly leaped to the western side of the creek, while simultaneously calling for Color Corporal George Washington Edwards (Company A) to unfurl the flag. An unexpected volley from the 12th Virginia on higher ground in front of the small line sent the half-hearted Federals clamoring up the eastern slope to safety. Being no fool, Weygant sheathed his blade and took off after them.[42]

Wofford had his hands full trying to take the 56th Massachusetts by frontal assault. The New Englanders were dropping men in Cobb's Legion. A minie ball zipped through Company G, and struck Captain Charles W. Baldwin in the left elbow, causing his arm to flop heavily against his side. He felt no pain despite the tremendous amount of blood which saturated his sleeve. The captain, having seen enough wounds, knew that if he did not get help he would bleed to death on the field. He wheeled about and staggered several paces to the rear to search out Lieutenant George F. Pierce. He found the lieutenant doubled up in a heap in the brush. What was the matter? Baldwin gasped. Shot in the abdomen, Pierce winced, believing he was going to die. The lieutenant carefully straightened himself up, fearing the worst. Opening his tunic, he unbuttoned his fly only to find a bloodied minie ball trapped in his shirt. The blood was not his. It was his captain's. Baldwin's elbow had slowed the bullet's velocity enough to knock the wind out of him but nothing more. Pierce plopped the ball into the captain's good hand and they staggered back toward the rear lines.[43]

Wofford diverted his brigade to the left. At about one hundred fifty yards, the Federal bullets slammed into the eight stray companies of the 12th Virginia, the right flank of which had gotten bogged down in the marshy creek bottom of Poplar Run. The 56th Massachusetts' battle flag waved momentarily above the thicket. First Lieutenant James E. Phillips (Company G) remembered seeing one of the standard's tassels flying through the air before the colors suddenly disappeared.[44] The New Englanders stopped the Virginians in the hollow to the south.

Ensign Benjamin H. May (Company A, 12th Virginia), with the regimental colors in his hands, sank to his knees in the oozing muck and stubbornly tried to plow himself free. The flag snagged on the brush and the trees. Lieutenant Colonel G. Moxley Sorrel urged his horse into the mire until he came alongside of May. Noticing that the sergeant was having a difficult time, the colonel reached for the colors and insisted on leading the charge. May jerked the standard back. He refused to let the officer have the staff. "We will follow you," May insisted. Not too far to the west, Private Leroy Edwards (Company E), who had overheard the entire incident, saw his good friend, Private John Lee, go to the ground, wounded.[45] The Virginians remained in the low ground in front of the 56th Massachusetts for a few minutes but they seemed more like hours.

56TH MASSACHUSETTS

Lieutenant Colonel Stephen M. Weld (56th Massachusetts), being on the north side of the road in the trees near the center of the regiment, had no idea what was transpiring to the west. Adams, who also had not seen the colonel go down, bound across the road to the Weld's side and shouted something about the regiment being flanked. Weld twisted about on his heels, looking for someone in authority who would tell him what to do. He spied Webb a few paces behind him. The young colonel asked the general whether he should retreat or not. Webb, who had just witnessed the collapse of Wadsworth's front, shot back, "Get out of there as damned quick as you can!" Weld faced about still confused about what to do. Adams remained at his side trying to yell above the din to get him to react to their predicament. A soldier raced up to the colonel from the north, saluted and shouted a message in Weld's face which Adams could not hear. Weld turned to Adams. "The colonel is killed," he exclaimed. "I am in command. Call off your men."[46]

Adams, bending low, recrossed the road and slipped into the ditch with his company. One by one he jerked men by their shoulders and pointed his thumb over his back. The silent message swept from one end of the company to the other like an electrical current as the New Englanders leaped to their feet and followed their captain across the open road into the woods. In crossing the high road bed they caught their first brief glimpses of the Confederates, who by this time were swarming around both ends of the regiment.[47]

12TH VIRGINIA

Ensign Ben May, having cleared the edge of the swamp, took off at a run ahead of the regimental line seconds before the 56th Massachusetts shattered. The screaming Confederates leaped over the impromptu earthworks, climbed onto the road bed and dashed into the woods on the opposite side. Privates Leroy Edwards, George S. Bernard, and another

**Colonel David A. Weisiger,
12th Virginia**

During Longstreet's counterattack, Weisiger led eight of his companies across the Plank Road, too far in advance of the rest of the brigade.

Bernard, War Talks, 1892

member of Company E, at a distance of about forty yards, fired simultaneously at a frightened Yankee. "I hit him," Edwards shouted gleefully. They all thought they had. Dashing up to the injured man's side, they discovered he was more scared than hurt. Edwards tenderly reached down and helped the quaking man to his feet. "I hope you are not hurt!" the Virginian exclaimed. While those three stopped to "check their kill," the rest of the company pressed a few yards beyond them after a small group of demoralized Federals. Not too far away, Second Lieutenant John R. Patterson (Company E) and an enlisted man cornered a Yankee in a small clearing. The private raised his rifle to drop the Yankee when the lieutenant yelled at him, "Don't shoot! We will catch him!" The Federal ducked behind a tree, then took off running.

Patterson changed his mind. "Let him have it!" he said. The private coldly shot the man down while the Federals disappeared from their front.

Colonel David A. Weisiger (12th Virginia) suddenly realized that the rest of the brigade had not kept up with his regiment. He called off the assault on a flat piece of ground about fifty yards north of the Plank Road. Quickly reforming his eight companies, he faced them south. Five to six feet above where they stood, the road bed of the Plank Road crossed their front.[48]

56TH MASSACHUSETTS

Adams and a few of his men retreated about one hundred ten yards and rallied with about 75 men around Lieutenant Colonel Stephen Weld and the colors. The forest being more open, the Northerners popped off shots at Wofford's Confederates who were darting through the woods around them.[49] Bullets materialized from every quarter but the rear. Adams heard a loud crack. His leg seemed to be on fire and his body shook from his ankles to his shoulders. He cried at Weld, "I'm hit, sir." "Get off to the rear as soon as you can," Weld replied. Adams stayed until the men, as if by mutual consent, decided to retreat. Weld commanded them to fall back.

Private Elijah Beals (Company B) stayed back with the captain. Pulling Adams' arm over his shoulder, he helped him escape. Another one hundred or so yards brought the two to Wilderness Run. The private eased the captain across the marshy bottom land and through the creek bed. Halfway up the opposite bank, Adams heard a second loud crack, a ball having shattered the knee cap of his wounded leg. At the same time, Beals fell forward, knocking the captain down. Raising himself up on his hands, Beals said, "They've broke my leg but we can go it I guess."

Adams could not get himself to his feet. He felt weak. Beals begged him to get up. "No use, no use!" Adams insisted, "I can't go any more, save yourself." Beals tried to pull the officer to his feet. "Save yourself, Beals," the captain ordered. Beals stared briefly at Adams, then picking up his rifle like a staff, he limped over the rise. Shortly thereafter, Color Sergeant Robert C. Horrigan splashed across the stream, dragging the flag after him. Adams attempted to get up a couple of times but collapsed each time. Propping himself on his elbow, he unholstered his pistol and decided to await his fate.

A few minutes later, two Confederate soldiers came across the captain. One of them ordered Adams to surrender his watch and his money. The plucky captain cocked his revolver and pointed it at the man. "Look here," he weakly said, "I'm ready to surrender but I'm not going to be robbed." One of the men calmly stepped into a firing position, cocked his weapon and brought it to his shoulder. Adams knew they meant business. "Hold on," he pleaded, "Where's your officer? I'll surrender to him." The words had barely escaped his mouth when he spotted an officer climbing the bank and waved him over. "I surrender to you, sir. Your men were just going to shoot me."

The officer told the two men to move on, whereupon Adams tendered his sword and pistol to the Confederate and explained that the two men, considering the circumstances, were not behaving abnormally but he did not want to be robbed. Captain Henry H. Smith (Company D, 24th Georgia) cordially identified himself to Adams. Taking Adams' weapons with him, he ascended the hill behind his men and disappeared over the brow of the bank.

A thunderous volley, followed by a dense cloud of sulfuric smoke and terrible shrieks sent the Rebels scampering down over the bank. (Unknown to Adams, Smith died in that blast.) One of the Rebels snatched Adams' hat from his head and kept on running while rifle fire, in a northerly sweep, clipped the top of the hill behind him.[50]

THE BROCK CROSSROADS

The Confederate infantry had herded the 7th West Virginia, 14th Indiana, and 8th Ohio up to the edge of the earthworks north of the Brock Road intersection. The Rebels, First Lieutenant Thomas Galwey (Company B, 8th Ohio) recalled, were right on their tails.[51] Galwey jealously eyed the earthworks, which bristled with the burnished rifle barrels of "green" troops and he longed to hurl himself behind them while leaving the battle to the untried troops. Unfortunately, as the three regiments reached the fortifications, the Federal soldiers behind them fled.[52] The 8th Ohio formed a diagonal line (northwest to southeast) across the intersection. Troops choked off the Brock Road, making passage nearly impossible.[53] First Lieutenant Charles Myerhoff (Company D, 14th Indiana) marveled at how many men cluttered the road, most of whom would not respond to their officers' orders or their pitiful pleas to stand fast.[54] Climbing over the headlogs, the wheezing Federals turned about and prepared to stymie the suspected Confederate drive in the open while the men who were supposed to rescue them regrouped.[55]

Immediately south of the crossroads, the 14th Connecticut scrambled over the works into the Brock Road. Major General Winfield S. Hancock trotted up to the wounded Colonel Samuel Carroll and told him to retire the men he could find to the woods east of the road to take a twenty-minute breather. They had done their fair share for the moment. The 14th Connecticut, apparently being the only organized regiment from the colonel's command which he could locate, fell back as ordered and kindled coffee fires.[56] The New Englanders found the 1st Delaware three hundred yards east of the Brock Road. That regiment had already stacked arms and had begun accounting for its casualties. The 14th Indiana also fell back to their position.[57]

First Lieutenant George A. Bowen (Company C, 12th New Jersey) and his detached squad took cover behind the works along the western side of the Brock Road, which he described as a pile of "Rotten logs and a little earth." The panting captain and his handful of men readily threw themselves in with the hodgepodge regiments along the road to defend it against the suspected counterattack. It did not take too long for more rattled Yankee soldiers to clear the woods and to join the men behind the barricades.[58] The 14th Connecticut had barely gotten their coffee heated when bullets thunked into the trees around them.[59] Terrified soldiers poured through the woods all around them.[60] Hancock, fearful of another rout, galloped into the regiment.

"For God's sake, Carroll, form your men and give us something to fall back on." The New Englanders hurled their coffee cups into the leaves on the forest floor and fell in. They fixed bayonets and charged into the battle along the front of the works. The 8th Ohio joined in the mess also.[61] A pair of caissons and guns under the command of Lieutenant William H. Rogers (6th Maine Battery) rumbled through the two regiments, totally disrupting their closed formations.

First Lieutenant Oramel G. Daniels (Company I, 8th Ohio) in command of the color company found himself and the left wing of the regiment completely cut off. Carroll waited until the guns had cleared the front before continuing his assault. As the bulk of his company bolted forward to assist their comrades south of the intersection, Daniels screamed at them to fix bayonets and rally all of the stragglers who were escaping to the rear. He collared a very rattled captain from the 40th New York, who drew his sword to defend himself. "Captain, none of that," Daniels sternly warned him. "Face the enemy; no Bull Run here."[62] A volley at one hundred yards, coupled with a sudden blast of canister, sent the Confederates reeling back into the woods across from the earthworks.[63]

At the same time the frightened Federals returned to the defenses north of the Brock Road intersection and relieved that part of Carroll's line.[64] The 8th Ohio marched into the woods east of the road to reform itself. Galwey had never seen such a fear of surrendering as he did in those woods. Death was preferable to internment in Andersonville prison. Throughout the afternoon, Ohioans kept drifting back into the regiment.[65] The rifle fire along the southern end of the line slackened as Daniels and his squad approached their regiment.

Ammunition bearers were working their way through the woods from the Brock Road to resupply the 12th New Jersey's and the 10th New York's depleted cartridge boxes. No wind was stirring in the forest and a foul, eye-burning cloud of burned powder hovered over the troops. During the respite, Second Lieutenant Charles Cowtan (Company K, 10th New York) glanced over his shoulder to the right rear of the line. A continuous column of wounded men, most of whom were being borne on blankets by their comrades, snaked its way toward the field hospitals east of the Brock Road. The 10th New York started fires to boil coffee.[66]

In the confusion, Lieutenant Colonel Charles Weygant (124th New York) and his motley command staggered across a narrow woodland trail which ran almost parallel to the works. Once into the "road" the fleeing Federals gradually slowed to a walk. Again, he told Color Corporal George Washington Edwards (Company A), who was the only man from the regiment with him, to unfurl the colors. Within a few minutes the lone officer and his coterie had swollen to some fifty men from various regiments.[67]

ON THE PLANK ROAD, NEAR THE CONFEDERATE WORKS

As soon as Longstreet became aware of the Federal rout he ordered Major John Cheves Haskell, his assistant inspector general, to bring up a battery to rush the Federals along. The colonel hurried the four guns east toward Wilderness Run. On the way, he happened upon a Federal general, in full, uniform lying in the dirt alongside of the road. The colonel stooped over the unconscious Wadsworth. Realizing that he was still alive, Haskell ordered two of his orderlies to drag him out of the dirt and to get him shelter. The two made a square—four muskets, stuck bayonets first in the ground—around the general, then draped a discarded blanket over the butts to keep the sun off his face. They commandeered a surgeon who forced water and morphine down Wadsworth's throat before leaving him to tend to those whom he could save. Meanwhile, Haskell left two guns limbered in the road and pushed the remaining two farther east toward Wilderness and Poplar Runs. Along the way he directed the gunners to drop sporadic rounds into the woods at the oblique.[68]

SOUTH OF THE BROCK CROSSROADS

Looking down the trail, Weygant spotted Major General David Birney and his staff trotting toward him. He quickly shuffled his men into the regulation column of fours and got them into step by the time Birney and his people recognized their presence. About ninety feet from the stragglers, the general pulled his horse to one side, his officers following him. Weygant was wheeling about to bring his men to shoulder arms to deliver a rifle salute when a solitary artillery shell from one of Haskell's guns screamed in from the northwest. Too startled to react, the colonel helplessly watched it impact and explode in the trail almost under Birney's horse. The sudden flash with its sulfuric yellow cloud blinded the frightened infantrymen who were standing transfixed in the open. The general's officers scattered before the smoke cleared, leaving him at the mercy of his terrified mount,

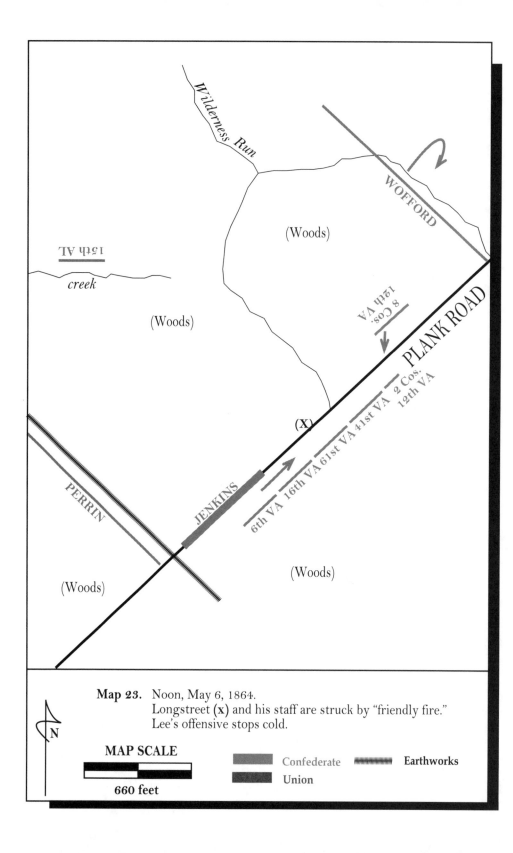

Wilderness Run

(Woods)

WOFFORD

15th AL

creek

(Woods)

8 Cos.
12th VA

PLANK ROAD

(X)

6th VA 16th VA 61st VA 41st VA 2 Cos.
12th VA

JENKINS

PERRIN

(Woods)

(Woods)

Map 23. Noon, May 6, 1864.
Longstreet (**x**) and his staff are struck by "friendly fire."
Lee's offensive stops cold.

N

MAP SCALE

660 feet

Confederate

Union

Earthworks

which was wildly bounding from one side of the road to the other, carrying Birney out of sight.

Undaunted, Weygant led his band half a mile farther until they walked into the slashings between the Brock Road earthworks and the woods. Union battle flags fluttered above the headlogs. An old "salt" among the colonel's men jubilantly hailed, "Ship ahoy, land ahead, boys, land ahead!" They had returned home. As the column passed through an opening in the line, Weygant marveled at the distance to which the works extended along the road to both flanks.[69]

When Haskell finally realized that his rounds were being wasted upon nonexistent targets, he told his artillerymen to cease fire.[70] In the meantime, Brigadier General Micah Jenkins hastily assembled his brigade in column of fours in the Plank Road. The youthful general, in going to the front, passed by the 5th South Carolina and asked Lieutenant John D. McDonnell how Company E intended to fare that day. "The same as usual," McDonnell replied.[71] In their new, dark gray uniforms the South Carolinians seemed almost black, like a formation of Yankee infantry on the move.[72] Longstreet and his staff were personally leading them east. Mahone reorganized four of his regiments in battle line in the woods fifty yards south of the road and was marching them by files toward Poplar Run. Lieutenant Colonel Joseph P. Minetree (41st Virginia) rushed over to Colonel V. D. Grovner (61st Virginia) to report that the 12th Virginia, excepting the two left companies, could not be found anywhere. Grovner arbitrarily halted the brigade about three hundred yards west of Poplar Run and hunted out Mahone to personally relay Minetree's information to him. The woods to the north between him and the Plank Road were an inferno with the flames crackling and licking at a sky already dark with smoke. "I have never seen a battle-field where there was more destruction and more horrors than that of the Wilderness," Grovner bitterly remembered.[73]

Unobserved by Mahone's brigade, Lieutenant Colonel G. Moxley Sorrel turned his horse west in the road and galloped several hundred feet back to Longstreet and his entourage who were about four hundred yards east of the reclaimed Confederate breastworks. The general's standard bearer was flying an impressive, new headquarters flag. Through the pall of thick smoke, some of the enlisted men said it resembled a Federal regimental flag. When one of the general's aides de camp, Lieutenant Andrew Dunn, suggested that Longstreet was needlessly exposing himself to danger, the general curtly shut him up with, "That is our business."[74]

Kershaw and Jenkins, Major Osmun Latrobe and Lieutenant Colonel G. Moxley Sorrel, Lieutenant Alfred E. Doby (Kershaw's aide de camp), at least two other officers, and an orderly, Private Marcus Baum (Company E, 2nd South Carolina) escorted Longstreet toward the front.[75] Lieutenant Colonel Everard M. Field, commanding Mahone's sharpshooters, who had a clear view of the general and his party, distinctly saw the mounted officers veer off toward the woods north of the road. The colonel was reforming his men on the left of the brigade when he heard a soldier nearby shriek the alarm, "Look out, boys, they are coming back! There they come! There they come!" Mahone, who was standing to Field's right, fully anticipated a counterattack from the road. He calmly ordered, "Steady, Men, steady! Get in your places! Get in your places!"[76]

Jenkins pulled his horse up beside Longstreet and joyfully clasped the general's hand. "I am happy," he exclaimed. "I have felt despair for the cause for some months, but am relieved, and feel assured that we will put the enemy back across the Rapidan before night." Wheeling his horse about to face the column, he shouted. "Why do you not cheer, men?" The South Carolinians rent the air with a vigorous outburst.[77]

Without warning, a shot or two reverberated over the road. Field glanced to the east, suspecting that they came from the regiments on the right of Mahone's brigade. Kershaw swore they came from the north side of the pike.[78] The scattered rounds erupted into a rolling volley from the right of the 41st Virginia which rapidly carried west toward the 61st Virginia. The initial blasts caught the detached color guard from the 12th Virginia full in their faces as they ascended the road bank from the north. Private John Mingea (Company B) died instantly as did Private Billy Pucci (Company A), who, at his mother's urging, had just accepted Christ as his Savior that morning.[79] A minie ball smashed Corporal Ben White (Company C) in the side of his head, tearing away a portion of his skull. First Lieutenant James E. Phillips (Company G) winced at the sight of the corporal's brains running out through the wound. "We left him on the ground going around & around on his elbow not knowing what he was doing," the lieutenant wrote.[80] "The enemy are in our rear, and we are in a bad box," the frightened Private George S. Bernard (Company E) thought as the panicked Virginians went to the ground. "You are firing into your friends! Show your colors! Show your colors!" they cried.[81]

One hundred yards east of the 5th South Carolina, time stopped for Captain Francis W. Dawson, on Longstreet's staff. Upon hearing the first reports, Jenkins stood in the stirrups. "Steady, men!" he shrieked. The volleying rapidly worked toward his back. "For God's sake, steady!"[82] The racket caught Sorrel completely off guard. He had moved a few steps ahead of Longstreet when he heard the shooting and had no time to react before a hail of bullets slammed into the staff officers.[83] One struck Longstreet from the front. Barely missing his larynx, it skidded under his skin, carried away part of his right scapula and exited behind his right shoulder.[84] The impact jerked him out of the saddle and sat him down again. With his right arm limply slapping against his side, he attempted to ride forward unaware that with each breath he was spurting blood over his tunic. Jenkins toppled into the road—unconscious

The Wounding of Lieutenant General James Longstreet, C.S.A.

Longstreet, *Manassas to Appomattox*, 1908   Massachusetts Commandery;
                                                              MOLLUS, USAMHI

and dying—with a bullet in his brain. Doby and his orderly, Baum, lay in the dirt nearby—dead—along with four wounded orderlies.[85] The front files of Jenkins' brigade faced right. Most of the Carolinians hit the dirt to avoid a second volley which they instinctively knew would follow. Company E of the 5th South Carolina dropped as a man to its knees and prepared to fire. Thinking quickly, McDonnell ordered his men to keep steady. No one had been hit, he insisted. Kershaw clattered into the South Carolinians' ranks. "They are friends," the general hollered. Lieutenant Colonel Robert Simms stepped out in front of the 5th South Carolina and repeated the plea not to open fire.[86]

His useless right arm dangling by his side, Longstreet waved his left arm in the air and rode toward the south side of the road. He suddenly realized the seriousness of his injury when he felt the blood soaking through his coat. Three of his staff officers, Captain Francis W. Dawson, Lieutenant Colonels Peyton Manning, and G. Moxley Sorrel, seeing him wobble unsteadily in the saddle, dismounted and surrounded his horse.[87] The three officers eased him from the saddle and propped him against a tree. Captain Andrew Jackson McBride (Company E, 10th Georgia), who was sitting against the tree offered his own canteen to one of the aides. The general could not swallow the water. McBride believed his general was dying. With bloody froth bubbling from his mouth, the general gasped to Major John W. Fairfax, "Tell General Field to take command, and move forward with the whole force and gain the Brock Road."[88] Young Dawson, believing that Longstreet was dying, did not wait to gape at his beloved general. He mounted up and dashed down the Plank Road toward Tapp's, intent upon bringing up a surgeon.[89] With his good arm, Longstreet reached up and, one by one, pulled each man's head close to his mouth. In blood choked whispers, he dispatched Major Osmun Latrobe, Major John C. Haskell and a few more officers to inform Lee of the Northern rout and to advise him to press the attack if he wanted to have them all by nightfall.[90] Colonel Ashbury Coward (5th South Carolina) walked back to his regiment in tears. As he broke the terrible news of Longstreet's and Jenkins' woundings to Lieutenant John D. McDonnell (Company E) it suddenly dawned upon the lieutenant that he was probably the last man from York County to speak to Jenkins.[91]

Meanwhile, about one hundred yards to the east, Captain Hugh R. Smith (Adjutant, 12th Virginia) stuck his white handkerchief on the point of his sword, and leaped onto the northern side of the road where he frantically wigwagged the "flag" back and forth, trying to get the attention of the 41st Virginia. Ensign Ben May, heedless of his personal safety, jumped onto a stump alongside the road and coolly waved the regimental colors from one side to the other. Smith spied Major William H. Etheridge (41st Virginia) approaching the road from the south. Running at a crouch, he bound into the ditch on the south side and told him they were killing their own men. The major quickly called out for his Virginians to cease fire.[92] The shooting died away like a receding wave as the command was shouted down the line in both directions. When the eight "lost" companies of the 12th Virginia stepped into the open, they were surrounded by mournful squads from the 41st Virginia. Private George Bernard (Company E, 12th Virginia) and his comrades were touched by the genuine sorrow of their fellow Confederates. He repeatedly heard the men of the 41st lament "Boys, we are so sorry! We are so sorry! We did not know you were our friends!"[93]

**Ensign Benjamin May,
12th Virginia**

When Mahone's brigade opened fire upon Longstreet and his staff, May leaped onto a stump along the Plank Road and signalled the men across from him to stop shooting.

Bernard, War Talks, 1892

WILDERNESS RUN

The severely wounded Captain Boylston Adams (Company F, 56th Massachusetts) watched in horror as the 16th Georgia mechanically filed into battle formation along the creek bottom in front of him. Before he could react he heard, "Halt! Commence firing!" Adams hurled himself onto his face, covering the back of his head with his clasped hands. Bullets zipped back in reply. For a few tense seconds, he listened to the balls spat the ground around him and thud into rotten tree stumps. Peering uphill to his left, he mentally latched onto a hole created by the exposed root of an upturned tree. With an unexpected surge of energy, he crawled up to the fallen tree and stuck his head into the hollow at its base. For several minutes, he lay motionless, hoping not to get shot again.

When the field became quiet, he sat up. Shouting to the prone and kneeling Rebels he waved at them and called down for them to fetch him. An officer sent two men scampering up the hillside. The soldiers laid him on the ground next to the creek and he introduced himself to Lieutenant Colonel Benjamin E. Stiles, who, to Adams' surprise, offered the captain some of his own cornbread and sent an enlisted man to get Adams a hat. The two officers talked for several minutes, during which time Stiles told his New England prisoner that in addition to graduating from Yale, he had a law firm in Savannah. The soldier returned with a badly damaged red kepi and before long quite a gaggle of enlisted men crowded around Stiles to listen to the two men converse. Their polite informality when in the presence of their social superiors left a permanent impression upon Adams, who did not realize how democratic the Confederate service really was. "I was somewhat amused by the camaraderie between the colonel and his men. It seemed so different from the reserve and distance which in our army was always shown between soldiers and their officers," he vividly recalled many years later.

After fifteen minutes of casual chatting, orders came down the line for the Georgians to pull out. Stiles jumped to his feet and commanded, "Attention! Forward, Right wheel!" The well disciplined Georgians fell in, crossed the creek and right wheeled toward the Plank Road. Two more lines followed after them. Adams noticed that all of the rebel officers were dismounted. He also noticed how all of the enlisted men seemed to stare at his attractive light blue great coat. Within minutes, he was alone.[94]

ALONG THE PLANK ROAD

Following Longstreet's wounding, Lee reformed his lines. In the process the rank and file of the Army of Northern Virginia helped themselves to the spoils of war. Mahone's clerk for the brigade ordinance officer, Private Westwood A. Todd (Company E, 12th Virginia), having swapped his fagged horse for a fresher mount from a captured trooper of the 5th New York Cavalry, galloped down the Plank Road to join Lee and his staff near the forward works. The Virginian loved the spirited horse. It came fully equipped with a new McClellan saddle, saddle bags and a bright red saddle blanket. Stray shots still whistled down the road from the retreating Federals when Todd reined in next to Private Hamilton "Jimmy" Blakemore (Company E, 12th Virginia), courier for Major General Richard H. Anderson, who was not ten feet from Lee and his generals. A bullet thudded into the front shoulder of Blakemore's horse and for a brief moment—a very brief moment—Todd feared for the general's safety. All around him lay brand new Federal equipment. In short order, he dismounted, snatched up two Federal overcoats and rolled them inside of a captured Yankee blanket.

Death was no respecter of persons. Back near the Confederate works, the 6th Virginia hurriedly plundered the unconscious Wadsworth. They stole his boots and silver spurs. They cut the buttons off his coat but left his shoulder boards alone. Corporal Bob Archer (Company G), whom the men called "Nosey," took the general's wallet and the ninety dollars in Yankee greenbacks he found in it. Private John W. Belote, Jr. (Company C) snatched the general's gold watch.[95] The enterprising Orderly Sergeant Frank M. Mixon (Company E, 1st South Carolina) jerked a pair of brand new high top boots from the feet of a neatly dressed Yankee officer who had no further need for them. He quickly handed them over to Colonel James R. Hagood, who immediately swapped them for his worn-out pair.[96] With a Federal overcoat, sans cape, and a large Yankee gum blanket draped over his arm, Surgeon Spencer G. Welch (13th South Carolina) slowly walked down the smoky Plank Road numbed by the carnage and amazed at the amount of discarded equipment. He wrote to his wife, "I have never before seen woods so completely riddled with bullets. At one place the battle raged among chinquapin bushes. All the bark was knocked off and the bushes are literally torn to pieces."[97]

While the doctor helped himself to Yankee booty, Major General Charles Field had reached Longstreet. When he asked the general how he was doing, Longstreet told him that others would take care of him and Field was to assume command of the corps. By then, Surgeons J. S. Dorsey Cullen and Randolph Barksdale had arrived upon the field. After stanching Longstreet's wound, they loaded him onto a stretcher and started down the Plank Road with his staff gathering around him. One of his officers placed his hat over his face as they neared Jenkins' column. "He is dead, and they are telling us he is only wounded," Longstreet heard one of the soldiers exclaim. His mind always concentrating upon his duty to his men and his country, he weakly raised his hat from his face with his left hand. "..the burst of voices and the flying of hats in the air eased my pains somewhat," he recalled.[98]

An ambulance came down the road to them. The surgeons quickly pulled the general's boots off and removed his coat before placing him inside. Very shortly thereafter, Major Robert Stiles, having arrived from Ewell's Corps, happened upon the general. He could not get through the ring of mounted officers who had surrounded the ambulance. One stood on the rear step of the vehicle. All were in tears. Stiles reined in alongside one of the staff officers, who had been severely wounded in the accident. The man paid no attention to his wound as the major pestered him for information. Longstreet was severely wounded, maybe dead, was the only response he received. Stiles pulled behind the wagon and stared into the shadows at Longstreet. The general's white socks caught his attention first, then his blood-drained face which shone almost white. His forehead seemed more massive than usual. Dark red blood, almost black in appearance, covered his neck and shoulder. The wagon jolted Longstreet into a fleeting consciousness. The general silently raised his unwounded left arm and pulled his shirt away from his chest. Stiles sighed with audible relief at seeing Longstreet's bright blue eyes peer weakly at his ghastly wound.[99] The entourage passed Lee farther west along the Plank Road. But, he said nothing. He did not have to. Major Osmun Latrobe from Longstreet's staff had already informed him of the tragedy. His face darkened with genuine sadness, bordering on despair, Lee anxiously wrung his hands, trying not to break under the strain of the day's events.[100]

CHAPTER SIX

"This is the meanest thing I have ever seen..."

**Major General
Richard H. Anderson, C.S.A.**

Following Longstreet's wounding, R. H. Anderson assumed command of the Army of Northern Virginia's First Corps.

Massachusetts Commandery;
MOLLUS, USAMHI

12:00 NOON TO 3:00 P.M.

THE PLANK ROAD

With Longstreet on his way to the rear, Lee turned his horse toward the east and in a short time was on the front lines near where Longstreet had been shot. After discussing the situation with Major General Charles Field, he decided to turn the command of Longstreet's Corps over to Major General Richard H. Anderson from A. P. Hill's Corps. Field complied, saying that he did not have enough experience to accept such a promotion. Major John Cheves Haskell, one of Longstreet's artillery battalion officers, accurately recorded the dilemma in his memoirs. He wrote, "The wounding of Longstreet and Jenkins was even more disastrous than the death of Jackson, for he [Jackson] had, to a large extent, accomplished his objective and left his position such that Stuart could and did complete the victory, but Longstreet fell just as his move had utterly routed and demoralized the enemy...there

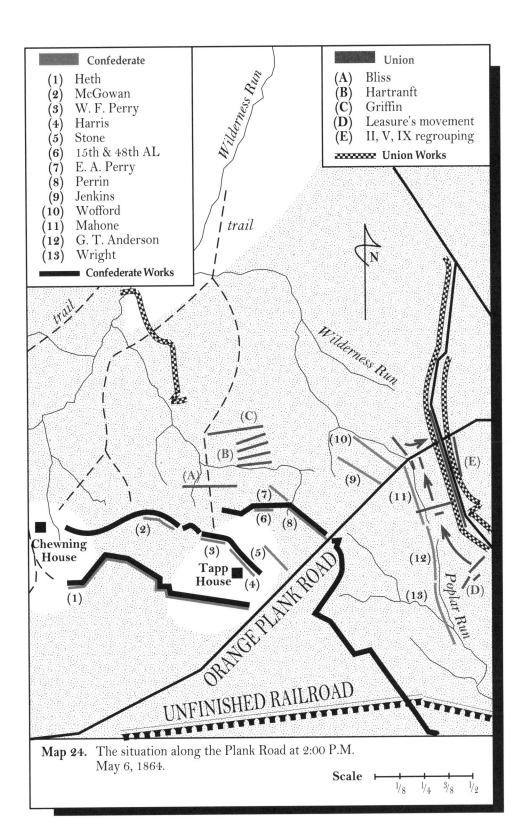

Confederate

- (1) Heth
- (2) McGowan
- (3) W. F. Perry
- (4) Harris
- (5) Stone
- (6) 15th & 48th AL
- (7) E. A. Perry
- (8) Perrin
- (9) Jenkins
- (10) Wofford
- (11) Mahone
- (12) G. T. Anderson
- (13) Wright

Confederate Works

Union

- (A) Bliss
- (B) Hartranft
- (C) Griffin
- (D) Leasure's movement
- (E) II, V, IX regrouping

Union Works

N

Wilderness Run

trail

trail

Wilderness Run

(C)

(B)

(A)

(10)

(9)

(E)

(7)

(6) (8)

(11)

Chewning House

(2)

(3) (5)

(12)

Tapp House

(4)

(13)

Poplar Run

(1)

(D)

ORANGE PLANK ROAD

UNFINISHED RAILROAD

Map 24. The situation along the Plank Road at 2:00 P.M.
May 6, 1864.

Scale 1/8 1/4 3/8 1/2

was no one to carry it on." While orderlies sought out Anderson, the commanding general ordered Field to straighten out the corps' lines to stave off any counterstroke.[1]

POPLAR RUN

The sudden press of panic stricken Federal refugees along the Brock Road sent Hancock into motion. His excellent corps had disintegrated into milling herds of confused and demoralized soldiers. Squads from mixed commands threw themselves behind the breastworks of rotten logs which the engineers had constructed along the Brock Road. Hancock and his staff trotted up and down the dirt track, all the while throwing handfuls of cartridges from their saddle bags at the troops. The general ordered the soldiers to reform where they were, First Lieutenant George A. Bowen (Company C, 12th New Jersey) recollected. Hancock did not want them to hunt out their regiments or brigades. They were to stay put and "whip" the Rebs as they had at the copse of trees at Gettysburg. Bowen and a handful of his men rallied, determined to make a stand.[2]

Fearing a breakthrough on his southern flank, which had been vacated when Frank's brigade disappeared into the Wilderness earlier in the day, Hancock sent Colonel Daniel Leasure's three IX Corps regiments into the gap. Under orders to sweep north along the face of the Brock Road breastworks, Leasure marched his regiments west into the woods at a point about one thousand yards south of the Plank Road. The 21st Massachusetts sent Company H forward to cover the front and the left flank as skirmishers, while the rest of the regiment held the left of the line. The 100th Pennsylvania went into formation on its right with its right flank against the works. The 3rd Maryland, its men still wearing their XII Corps badges, fell in behind the Marylanders and Pennsylvanians.[3] The Federals moved out at the quickstep through the Dantean landscape which the day's fighting had created. The woods around them crackled and flared. The leaves on the forest floor were smoldering and burning. The air was thick with white smoke and the acrid smell of burning pine wood. About one half of a mile into the advance, the skirmishers and the left flank of the 21st Massachusetts had a close brush with the Confederates along Poplar Run. They drove them into a smoke-clogged thicket. At that point, Sergeant Marcus M. Collis left Company H to find the regiment. When he did not return, Sergeant James H. Damon went after him. The Rebels snatched him up as well. Shots struck the New Englanders' ranks. A bullet hammered Captain George C. Parker (Company F) in the face. The bullet glanced downward into his neck, but he refused to leave the field. Another slapped into Company G and clipped a finger from First Lieutenant George E. Davis' left hand. Private Herbert Joslin (Company G) never knew what hit him. He collapsed with a bullet in his brain. Sergeant Major P. Frank Gethings took off from the regiment toward the skirmishers. But, he walked into the Confederate line and was captured.[4]

Leasure's brigade halted and left wheeled into line which threw the 100th Pennsylvania into the more heavily timbered ground on the north side of the Plank Road. Brigadier General Gershom Mott and an orderly rode into the rear of Company D and confronted Sergeant William Hoffman. "Who commands these troops?" Mott asked. The sergeant pointed toward Leasure, who was standing very close by. "Colonel, for God sake get your men out of here!" Mott yelled. The colonel shouted at his brigade to retire. The three regiments individually filed from the north then the south into the Plank Road before turning east toward the Brock Road and the Federal breastworks.[5] Company A, 21st Massachusetts left the dying Private Asa Piper in the hands of Corporal Albert J. Osgood and Private Wilbur A. Potter. The Confederates "gobbled up" those three and six other enlisted men.[6]

The Disposition of Lee's Right Wing

Lee had a great deal more to worry about than Leasure's half hearted foray along his front. He had to get his lines reorganized before Hancock's II Corps attempted another assault. By 2:00 P.M. his right wing stretched along the eastern branches of Wilderness and Poplar Runs—the same positions it had held the day before. Wofford's Georgians anchored the north side of the Plank Road with Jenkins' brigade, under Colonel John Bratton, in support. Mahone swung into line on the south side of the road on the western bank of Poplar Run, followed respectively by Brigadier Generals George T. Anderson's and Ambrose Wright's brigades. Kershaw's battered division was in position behind them.[7]

His northern flank was not as well organized. Perrin's Alabama brigade held McGowan's old line running north from the Plank Road. Brigadier General E. A. Perry's very small brigade of Floridians continued the line for about another five hundred feet beyond the northern face of the works. Colonel William C. Oates with the 15th Alabama and the 48th Alabama occupied a section of the works about one hundred yards to the west.[8] The rest of the Alabamians' battered brigade was building works in the woods about two hundred yards behind them at a point where a second line of breastworks turned west toward Chewning's.[9] To their left, McGowan's South Carolina brigade, less its sharpshooters, occupied the balance of the works.[10] Brigadier General Nathaniel H. Harris' Mississippi brigade was standing in reserve near the Tapp house.[11] Colonel John M. Stone's exhausted brigade, having finally been reunited, was close at hand between Tapp's and the rear of Perrin's brigade.[12] Most of Wilcox's division had reassembled behind a thin line of works which paralleled the trail from Higgerson's to the southern edge of Jones' field. Heth's battered division had assembled in the low works on the southern and southwestern side of the Tapp house, north of the Plank Road.[13]

NORTH OF THE TAPP FARM

It seemed as if the Federals were not going to give the Confederates any respite. Brigadier General Robert B. Potter began his flanking movement around 11:00 A.M.[14] Colonel Zenas Bliss' brigade led the division, followed by Colonels John Hartranft's then Simon Griffin's regiments. In the dense, burning woods Potter's brigades lost their bearings. Crashing back and forth through the woods consumed more time than originally anticipated. His brigade officers insisted that the division tramped at the least one mile to the east. Nevertheless, it took until 2:00 P.M. to reach and deploy across the easternmost trail which ran into the Tapp farm from the north.[15] Quite by accident, they were in the woods directly opposite the Confederates' entrenchments. Unable to see anything along his front except trees and undergrowth, Potter maneuvered his three brigades for an assault. Bliss's regiments formed the head of the column. Hartranft's fell in to his left rear. Griffin's brigade went prone in the woods behind the first two lines.[16]

The 81 men of Company K, 45th Pennsylvania took the right flank and front as skirmishers under the direction of a Captain G. H. McKibben from Potter's staff. A branch of Wilderness Run crossed their path nine hundred forty yards above the Tapp house. Sergeant Ephraim E. Myers (Company K) and his men unsuccessfully tried skipping over the creek to keep their feet from getting wet, while McKibben shuffled them south.[17]

THE CONFEDERATE LINES—NORTHERN SIDE OF THE TAPP FARM

With the Federals stumbling about in the woods, Colonel William F. Perry sent word to Lee that he feared an attack from the north and that he wanted to conduct a strike in that direction. A staff officer countermanded his decision. The colonel was to wheel to the right behind Brigadier General E. A. Perry's men and take part in a general advance which the staff officer expected to commence at any time.[18] Perry trotted behind the left of his brigade, riding northeast toward his two advanced regiments. He found First Lieutenant Robert T. Coles (Adjutant, 4th Alabama) lying on his back with his head and shoulders propped against a tree. Reining his mount to a halt, the colonel straightened himself in the saddle and cockily said, "Well, Bob, I propose this evening to make a spoon or spoil a horn." The adjutant, having no idea what the colonel meant by his remark, idly wished him well and Perry rode on.[19] He headed directly to the 15th and the 48th Alabama. Calling Colonel William C. Oates from his regiment, he introduced him to General E. A. Perry, whose Floridians anchored the northern flank of Lee's second line.

The two Perrys decided to "feel for the enemy," Oates recollected, to "see what they could develop." Colonel Perry instructed Oates to advance

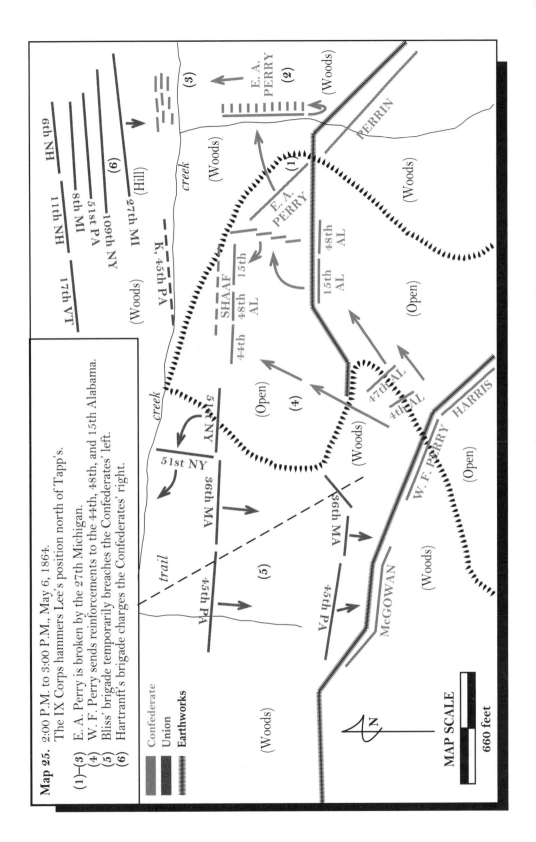

Map 25. 2:00 P.M. to 3:00 P.M., May 6, 1864.
The IX Corps hammers Lee's position north of Tapp's.

(1)–(3)   E. A. Perry is broken by the 27th Michigan.
(4)   W. F. Perry sends reinforcements to the 44th, 48th, and 15th Alabama.
(5)   Bliss' brigade temporarily breaches the Confederates' left.
(6)   Hartranft's brigade charges the Confederates' right.

Confederate
Union
Earthworks

MAP SCALE

660 feet

N

17th VT
11th NH
9th NH
8th MI
51st PA
109th NY
27th MI

(Hill)
(Woods)
creek
(Woods)
(Woods)
(Woods)
(Woods)
(Woods)
(Woods)
(Open)
(Open)
(Open)
(Open)

K, 45th PA

E. A. PERRY
(2)
(3)

(1)
E. A. PERRY
PERRIN

SHAAF
15th
48th
AL
15th
AL
48th
AL
44th
48th
AL

47th AL
4th AL
W. F. PERRY
HARRIS

(4)

51st NY
51st NY
36th MA
45th PA
36th MA
45th PA

trail

(5)

McGOWAN

in echelon of battalions with his own 15th Alabama to the left front of the 48th Alabama. Instead of making a right wheel in a solid line, Perry wanted each regiment to wheel by battalions (halves) and advance with forty paces between each line. Instead of striking the Federals with one solid line, he would hit them successively with four smaller lines. Oates objected to the maneuver, saying that not an hour earlier he had lost the lieutenant in charge of his regimental ambulance corps in the very creek bottom which his men had taken that morning. The moment his men crested the open hill south of that creek they were going to catch flank fire. Both Perrys brushed the colonel's statements aside as unfounded.

Colonel Perry placed the 48th Alabama under Oates' command with permission to react as he saw fit should the situation warrant it. Oates hurriedly shuffled his two regiments into formation as instructed and immediately hastened his skirmishers under Captain F. Key Shaaf (Company A, 15th Alabama) to the left with instructions to move by the right flank as the regiment marched east. The Florida brigade stepped out. The left wing of the 15th Alabama right wheeled, followed at the required distance by the right wing. The 48th Alabama repeated the maneuver. Almost instantly, Shaaf's skirmishers opened fire upon Company K, 45th Pennsylvania, who had moved into the ravine on Oates' northern flank.[20] Their rounds harmlessly spattered into the trees over the heads of the 27th Michigan, Hartranft's lead regiment, which was working its way up the northern slope of the hill to the east of the Pennsylvanians.[21]

McKibben, leading the Pennsylvanians, went down with his dead horse. In short order, the Rebs wounded Sergeant Reuben E. Fillis and Private Thomas Kelley. Company K veered farther to the left in response to the firing. An unarmed squad of Federal soldiers unexpectedly emerged from the cover of the oak forest in front of the skirmishers and silently brushed past them, heading for the rear. The Pennsylvanians kept moving south without saying a word to them.[22] Privates William A. Roberts, Frank P. Swears and Simon Sanders (Company K) were strung out at six-foot intervals and had proceeded a very short distance when Sanders crumbled into a heap. Major Edward A. Kelsey, commanding the skirmish line, told Roberts and Swears to check him out. The two enlisted men repeatedly called Sanders by name while they were darting to his side. They rolled him over. He was dead—a bullet through his heart. Kelsey ordered the men to return to their posts. Roberts expected to die at any moment because the Confederates were rapidly spattering the trees around them. Roberts stood his ground in the open and shot away four rounds before a Confederate bullet slammed into his left arm, just below the shoulder. Kelsey told him to head to the rear. As he cleared the brigade line, the fighting picked up in earnest. Minies clipped the branches and the leaves from the trees around him, while he was walking back toward the field hospital clutching his dead arm with his right hand. Blood saturated his sleeve and rolled over his hand. All the while he kept thinking about his friends on the firing line, heedless of the fact that he might lose his arm.[23] Company K slipped southeast, leaving Myers and two other enlisted men in the oaks to keep the Rebels busy. From where he stood, Myers could see the Confederates flitting from tree to tree. At one point a minie zinged uncomfortably close to his skull.[24]

At the same time, E. A. Perry's line crossed the creek bottom in front of the 27th Michigan, which had just gone prone in the brush on the military crest on the southern side of the hill. The Michiganders, many of whom had never seen combat, were pulling logs and brush along their front, trying to protect themselves from an enemy whom most of them could not see. Their company officers were standing above the cover, staring down into the swampy valley. Perry's veterans left wheeled in what appeared to be close column of companies and started up the slope. The Federals mistakenly assumed the Confederates were going to surrender and foolishly allowed them to close within hailing distance. At one hundred yards they cried out for the Rebels to come on in, at which point the Floridians deployed into line of battle. "Fire!" Major Samuel Moody (27th Michigan) yelled. "Give it to them! Aim low!"

Rather than scatter, Perry's veterans returned the riflery, volley for volley. A headquarters aide wandered into the Michiganders as the shooting reached a crescendo. Stopping near the firing line, he quietly studied the situation for a few minutes then, just as coolly, walked away. All the while, he never lost his composure, despite the bullets which zipped by his head and splintered the tree bark around him. Sergeant Charles T. Jeffers (Company K) admired the officer's courage, knowing full well that had he panicked he would have stampeded the regiment's recruits.[25]

At the first bursts of musketry Oates halted his two regiments and ordered them to change front by the rear rank which placed the 48th Alabama on the left where they fronted, facing north. His skirmishers bought the Alabamians a precious three minutes—enough time for them to drag enough logs along their front to create some kind of cover. Perry's Floridians, one hundred yards to the east, did not have time to refuse their left wing before Bliss' Federal brigade, lead by skirmishers from the 36th Massachusetts, caught them full on the flank.[26]

The 45th Pennsylvania held the Federals' right with the 36th Massachusetts in the center. The 51st New York completed the formation to the left. (The 58th Massachusetts formed the reserve.)[27] Oates' rifle fire smacked into their right front. The New Englanders and the New Yorkers executed a partial right wheel to face the Confederate works and to maneuver around the Alabamians' blazing rifles. Instead of passing the 48th Alabama, the

51st New York ran into the 44th Alabama, which had just gone into line on the left of the 48th. The 51st New York pulled back their line until they faced east, at right angles with the rest of the brigade.[28]

The maneuver uncovered the front of Hartranft's brigade which was coming through the woods behind the New Yorkers. The 27th Michigan led the assault, followed by the 109th New York, the 51st Pennsylvania, and the 8th Michigan.[29] The Michiganders ran into E. A. Perry's smashed brigade only to come under severe flank fire from Oates' Alabamians. Their line collapsed and fell back on the two regiments behind them, who in turn panicked and broke to the rear. Colonel Frank Graves (8th Michigan) ordered his men to open ranks and let the three regiments run through them.[30] Hartranft immediately called his two smallest regiments, the 2nd and the 17th Michigan, from his right flank and reserve to stay the rout.[31] By then, the 8th Michigan was taking off through the woods toward Oates' two regiments. The Westerners did not get very far before the Alabamians sent a deadly fire crashing through their ranks. Graves collapsed to the forest floor—dead. Before the smoke had fairly cleared, the regiment lost an estimated forty men killed and wounded.[32]

The Pennsylvanians and the New Englanders to the west rushed through the brush in a forlorn hope, intent upon carrying the Confederate works which rested on a rise of ground to the southeast. The left wing of the 36th Massachusetts breached the Confederate line. The 45th Pennsylvania also spilled over the works and ran headlong into McGowan's right wing. A severe hand to hand fight erupted. The Pennsylvanians dragged a number of prisoners into the woods with them as both sides recoiled from the melee.[33]

The 51st New York streamed to the rear in a panic. Major William F. Draper (36th Massachusetts), in the center of the line, leaped upon the works and shouted at Captain Thaddeus L. Barker (Company A), who commanded the left wing, to refuse the regiment's flank. Barker ran through the woods toward Hartranft's brigade and vainly tried to get one of his reserve regiments to come forward in support.[34]

Meanwhile, Major General Ambrose Burnside, who had been with Potter's division throughout the day, rode into Griffin's brigade. The 109th New York and the 51st Pennsylvania lay to his front, trying not to absorb rounds from the Alabamians. The 8th Michigan was valiantly trying to hold its own. "Let Griffin attack," the general commanded. The colonel formed the 17th Vermont, 11th New Hampshire, and 6th New Hampshire (west to east) in line in the open woods. "Forward!" he shouted. The brigade tramped through the woods, over the top of Hartranft's two rear lines, who rose in succession and cheered the backs of Griffin's soldiers. In squads, then by companies, they thronged his formation, cutting him off entirely from his command. A couple of solid shots bounded through the trees, followed closely by a bursting shell or two and destroyed the morale of the 8th Michigan. The Westerners abandoned their position in a dead run. They slammed into the onrushing 6th New Hampshire and stalled its advance. The 6th momentarily wavered and showed signs of scattering. Lieutenant Colonel Henry H. Pearson (6th New Hampshire) hurriedly slipped off his horse and elbowed his way through the regiment. Jerking one of the regimental flags from a stunned color bearer, he screamed at the top of his voice, "Come on, Sixth New Hampshire! Forward!" A cheer erupted from nearby and traveled through the regiment to both flanks like an electric current. With their colonel in the lead, the New Englanders pushed through the woods toward E. A. Perry's position on the crest in front of them.[35]

To the west, Captain Leander Cogswell (Company D, 11th New Hampshire) heard the command to "Charge!" A second later, a minie ball thudded into Lieutenant Colonel Moses N. Collins' forehead. The impact hurled the colonel against Cogswell's left shoulder, almost knocking the captain off his feet. The regiment moved out, leaving its dead colonel in a crumpled heap at the base of a pine tree.[36]

The 11th New Hampshire struck the fronts of the 44th, 48th, and the 15th Alabama regiments about the same time that Colonel William F. Perry fed his remaining men into the right of the line. The 47th Alabama reached the front seconds ahead of Colonel Pinckney D. Bowles' 4th Alabama, which was rushing to support the right flank. By the time Bowles' men arrived upon the field, Brigadier General E. A. Perry's battered brigade was quitting the fray. The general and his color bearers trotted past Bowles, crying out that the brigade had expended all of its ammunition. The 9th Alabama (Perrin's brigade) did not get the word to pull out. The Floridians put up a tremendous resistance. With their regimental formation shattered, they fought individually from whatever cover was available. Bowles admired their spunk.

The colonel noticed that two of E. A. Perry's men were still cracking off rounds at the advancing Federals who were only forty paces away. When the Federals got too close for comfort, the two Rebels calmly backed away from their cover and headed toward the rear. One of the them dropped with a bullet in the leg. His friend quietly walked back to his side, lowered himself down upon his haunches, pulled the wounded man's arms around his neck, and calmly dragged him away from the firing line. "It was one of the most heroic acts I ever witnessed," the colonel recollected.[37]

Heroism alone could not sustain the hard pressed Confederate brigade. The 44th Alabama, on the left of the 48th Alabama, collapsed under the flanking move by the 36th Massachusetts. It quit the field in a literal rain of lead, dragging with it the 48th Alabama. Colonel William F. Perry frantically pulled the 47th Alabama from the left of the 4th Alabama to shore up

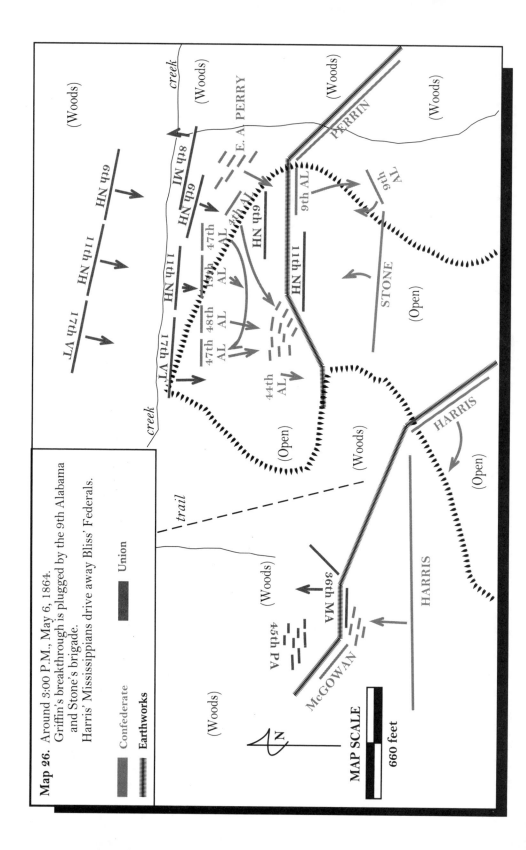

Map 26. Around 3:00 P.M., May 6, 1864. Griffin's breakthrough is plugged by the 9th Alabama and Stone's brigade. Harris' Mississippians drive away Bliss' Federals.

Confederate
Union
Earthworks

MAP SCALE
660 feet

N

(Woods)

creek

(Woods)

(Woods)

(Woods)

(Woods)

6th NH

11th NH

17th LA

17th LA

11th NH

6th NH

8th MI

E. A PERRY

47th AL

48th AL

13th AL

47th AL

6th NH

44th AL

47th AL

11th NH

PERRIN

9th AL

9th AL

STONE

(Open)

(Open)

(Woods)

HARRIS

HARRIS

(Open)

trail

(Woods)

36th MA

45th PA

McGOWAN

the hole in his line but it ran into the much larger 17th Vermont and the 11th New Hampshire. Rather than get annihilated, the Alabamians about faced and raced for the higher ground around the Tapp house. Finding his regiment almost surrounded, Oates stubbornly allowed his men in the 15th Alabama to fire a couple more rounds. The dwindling volume of musketry along his line quickly told him all he needed to know. The regiment had exhausted its ammunition. With the 11th New Hampshire pressing him from the front and with the 6th New Hampshire and the 17th Vermont flowing around his flanks, he yelled for his men to retreat. Those who heard the command ran for their lives. To the right, Bowles knew his small 4th Alabama could not withstand the onslaught. The regiment emptied its rifles and broke to the rear by the right flank.[38]

The 6th New Hampshire overwhelmed parts of the 15th Alabama and E. A. Perry's Florida brigade. The Federals poured over the works screaming "like so many Blackfoot Indians," one of them recalled. Privates Thomas Dickey, Otis Reister, and T. Bradley, all substitutes in Company I, distinguished themselves in the eyes of their comrades when they were among the first men to leap into the Confederate lines. Lieutenant Charles F. Winch (Company K) quickly disarmed a Confederate officer and two other men. In a matter of minutes they captured over 100 enlisted men and several officers. While the victorious Northerners picked their way through the tangle of wounded Confederates they stumbled across a fat prisoner. "Don't kill me! I am wounded—don't kill me!" he pleaded. "Dry up," Private Hiram H. Pool (Company B) snarled at him or he would kill him off then and there. The Rebel shut up and waited to be taken to the rear.[39]

The curses of the 6th New Hampshire bounced off the Southerners' backs. "Halt! Halt! Halt!" they demanded. The Alabamians kept moving. A couple of stray rounds passed overhead. Bowles shot a parting glance over his shoulder at the Federals who swarmed over the works. A lone Federal officer, wearing a linen duster and surrounded by no less than 100 enlisted men, plowed among the wounded Confederates, desperately trying to capture at least one apiece.[40]

To the west, where the 36th Massachusetts breached the Confederate line, a stray soldier from the 1st South Carolina Rifles, hunkered down behind a log and drew a bead on Major William Draper. Without warning, Corporal Herbert A. Kimball (Company A), who was standing near Draper, suddenly lunged forward with his rifle. Swinging the muzzle upward, he knocked the weapon from the Rebel's hand, which discharged it. The rifle ball tore through the brim of Draper's black hat. A minute later, a second rebel bullet plowed into the major's shoulder and knocked him senseless. His men carried him from the field.[41]

Meanwhile, the 6th New Hampshire advanced about one hundred yards without finding any Confederates at all before the colonel halted it.

In all the smoke Pearson refused to listen to his officers when they told him that the regiment had no Federal troops behind it. "No," he stubbornly insisted, "we will not fall back, but go on till the rest of the troops come up to support us." One of his junior officers ran back to the works behind the line and returned with bad news. There were no Federal troops anywhere in sight. The company officers begged the colonel to recall the regiment lest the Confederates surround them at any moment. He relented, "Just as you say, gentlemen. If most of you think it is best to fall back we will do so, but it is a pity to lose the ground we have fought over so well." The New Englanders quickly slipped back into the woods.[42]

Unseen by the 6th New Hampshire, the 11th New Hampshire raced another three hundred fifteen yards south and bolted toward a second line of Confederate works without meeting any serious opposition. White hand-kerchiefs on ramrods bobbed above the headlogs and were semaphored back and forth through the smoke, and the Rebels yelled for the 11th New Hampshire to cease fire. Suspecting a ruse, Colonel Walter Harriman com-manded, "Fix bayonets!" His face blackened from spent powder, with his pistol in one hand and his sword in the other, he stepped to the front center of his line and ordered the regiment to prepare to charge.[43]

Not too far to the south, Colonel William F. Perry reassembled his ex-hausted regiments in the Widow Tapp's field. The day's fighting had cost the Alabamians 50 captured and missing and 238 wounded and killed out of 1,198 engaged.[44] Despite the fury of the last Federal assault, Company C, 4th Alabama, had only one man shot—Private Tom Melton. He was wounded in the foot. More scared than hurt, the panting Southerners hurled themselves to the ground and laughed at Colonel William F. Perry's ques-tionable judgment, "giving Perry full credit for his miscarried coup-de-main," Coles later recollected.[45] Bowles took the time to search out Oates. "You see that fellow over there by that wounded Yankee?" Oates asked as he pointed toward one of his men. "Well, he has just brought him out of the woods on his back so as to get his boots as soon as he dies." Three "huzzahs" rent the air, temporarily distracting the two officers.[46]

Colonel Walter Harriman had sprung upon the second line of Confed-erate works with the 11th New Hampshire only to discover that the 9th Alabama (Perrin's brigade) had disappeared like a burned off mist before the Federals ever reached them. Leaping over the breastworks, the New Englanders advanced a short distance before it dawned upon Harriman that he might have gone too far beyond the rest of the brigade. Calling aside Captain Augustus S. Edgerly (Company C, 6th New Hampshire), an aide-de-camp to Griffin, he said, "Tell the General [Robert B. Potter] that we are driving the enemy before us, but our flanks are exposed. Ask if we shall hold our position until the main line comes up, or shall we push farther? We can do either."[47] The captain disappeared into the smoke-obscured field behind the regiment.

Seconds after he departed, the colonel repeated the same message to Corporal James W. Franklin (Company K). The enlisted man had hardly loped out of sight when Harriman hauled aside Captain Sewell B. Tilton (Company B) and Second Lieutenant Charles E. Frost (Company E) and dispatched them to the rear with the same request. Tilton and Frost quickly parted company. A short distance into the woods behind the regiment Tilton stumbled across Edgerly, who had lost his bearings. The two officers continued rearward but a short distance when the command "Halt!" echoed over their heads from the front. They snapped their heads up and found themselves staring down the rifle muzzles of four Rebels who had taken cover behind an upturned tree root. Tilton immediately turned and ran back toward his regiment. Edgerly wheeled about to do the same when the Rebels cut him down in his tracks.[48]

Tilton reached the regiment seconds before Colonel John M. Stone's and Brigadier General Nathaniel H. Harris' brigades, with the 9th Alabama, counterattacked. Stone's regiments passed around the left front of the New Hampshire regiment, trying to cut it off. At the same time Harris' Mississippians swept past its right flank, heading directly for Bliss' brigade, which had not gotten past the first line of works.

"To the rear, and form a new line to the foe!" Harriman yelled. The Federals scampered over the works and attempted to rally but the Confederates had them bagged. Rifle fire swept through the regiment from two directions before they had time to regroup. "We can hold here," Harriman insisted. "Form in line here." The colonel found himself speaking to the air, his regiment having retreated. Captain Leander Cogswell and Sergeant George F. Edmunds (Company D) ran about fifty feet before glancing back to see if Harriman were with them. The suffocating rifle smoke lifted a little. Bullets were cutting through the air from every direction. In seconds, the battle smoke engulfed their colonel and they kept on running. Another six hundred feet to the north they found the regimental colors and Adjutant Charles R. Morrison. He had about twelve enlisted men with him—all that they could find from their entire regiment.[49]

Harris' Mississippians proved too much for the western end of the Federal line. Unable to sustain the fight, the 36th Massachusetts retreated from the works. Color Corporal Henry Todd (Company B), already suffering from a wounded arm, went down with a bullet in his brain. Corporal Michael Long (Company A) pulled the staff from his dead hands when he too was cut down. Private Gilbert N. Rawson (Company C) caught the staff before the colors touched the ground and led the regiment to the rear.[50]

Behind the Pennsylvanians, Sergeant Ephraim E. Myers (Company K, 45th Pennsylvania) urged his two reluctant men toward the sounds of the battle. As they neared the regiment, the sergeant blurted, without thinking, "I don't know how in such fighting anyone can be saved." Private David S. Edler (Company K) limped up to the sergeant and asked for someone to help him to the rear. "No," Myers said, "you will have to get back yourself. We are needed at the front." While the dejected private hobbled toward the trail, Colonel Simon Griffin, who had lost contact with his brigade, trotted by Myers. Not realizing that he belonged to the First Brigade, the colonel shouted, "Sergeant, get forward there or I'll have those stripes from you." "Colonel," Myers replied, "we have been cut off and are going forward to find our company." Without responding, the colonel disappeared deeper into the forest.

The 45th Pennsylvania, having recovered from its initial contact, rallied in the woods a short distance to the west. Private Samuel Myers (Company K) spotted his brother approaching the company from the rear. He called out, "Eph, get in behind one of these trees. The Johnnies are thick as flies out here." The sergeant dodged behind one close to his brother. Presently, a boy from Company A dropped to his haunches behind a nearby oak and loosed a round. As he turned his back to reload, a Confederate bullet slammed into his skull and he fell forward—dead.[51]

The order carried along the scattered line to charge. Again the Pennsylvanians sprang into the works. The surrounding woods were on fire. Leaves smoldered and flared. The pungent, eye-tearing smoke of burning pines obscured their vision and added a demonic aspect to the fighting. Again the Confederates sent the Federals reeling backward in disorder.[52] Sergeant Ephraim Myers saw Captain John O. Campbell (Company E) drop with a mortal wound. Unable to rescue him or to hear his plaintive calls for assistance, the sergeant watched him beckon in vain to his men to help him.[53] Captain Rees G. Richards (Company G) spied Colonel John I. Curtin (45th Pennsylvania) standing alone off to his right, looking completely forlorn. Richards rushed to Curtin's side. Had the regiment lost the colors? the captain asked. "I do not know," Curtin replied. The captain noticed a Federal flag bobbing through the woods in front of him. Recognizing it as the 45th's, Richards ran up to the color bearer and yanked the staff from his hands. In a gesture borne of desperation the captain sang out, "Rally round the Flag, boys! / Rally once again! / Shouting the battle cry of Freedom." Men close at hand heard him and stopped dead in their tracks. Picking up the refrain, "The Union forever, hurrah, boys, hurrah!", the Pennsylvanians gathered around their intrepid captain and reformed their line.[54] A bullet clipped so close to Sergeant Myers' ear that he involuntarily dodged his head to one side and wrenched his neck. Clasping his head between his hands, he stood there dumbfounded. "Sergeant, are you hurt?" he heard the colonel ask. A faint grin flickered across Myers' face. "No, but I was terribly scared just then."[55] The Pennsylvanians pushed forward a short distance and went prone, determined not to lose any more ground.[56] Curtin assumed command of the brigade, Bliss having succumbed to sunstroke.[57]

While the South Carolinians mercilessly pounded the 45th Pennsylvania, Private William A. Roberts (Company K) was staggering across a small, clear running stream. He quietly bathed his bloodied left arm in the cool water before continuing along the trail. Farther on he came across Hospital Steward James A. Meyers, who tied off his arm. Shortly thereafter, a long stream of wounded wandered into the hospital. Private George Gilbert (Company K)

**Colonel John I. Curtin,
45th Pennsylvania**

When sunstroke debilitated Colonel Zenas Bliss, Curtin assumed the command of the 1st Brigade, Second Division, IX Corps.
Massachusetts Commandery;
MOLLUS, USAMHI

was among them. He had been shot through the neck. The bullet had apparently collapsed his throat. He could not swallow. Roberts cradled him in his lap and tried to give him a drink of water but Gilbert threw his head back and died. Roberts laid his friend down and gathered canteens to get water.[58]

Colonel Walter Harriman (11th New Hampshire) did not capitulate gracefully. When the Confederates demanded his surrender, he defiantly hurled his revolver over their heads and quietly let his sword slip from his hand. The officer commanding the Alabamians requested his sword but Harriman honestly replied that he did not have it. Southern enlisted men thronged the angry Yankee colonel. The Confederate officer explained their fascination with him. He said, "You were a conspicuous figure when you led your men against our works and I ordered them to pick you off, but here you are unharmed." Harriman went to the rear with over 100 Federal prisoners.[59]

Stone's battered regiments replaced the 9th Alabama on the line. He immediately sent his sharpshooters scurrying into the brush fifty yards in front of the brigade. They quickly closed upon the rear of the 6th New Hampshire where they loosed a volley into the Federals' backs and charged. The Federals scattered, leaving a startled Irishman in Company G within the Confederate ranks. Two Rebels nabbed Private Johnnie Hamon and were dragging him to the rear when his Company D rallied and momentarily returned to the fight. The rowdy Irishman, who had attacked the Confederates at Fredericksburg with a field pick, saw them coming. He struggled free of his captors. In the scuffle Hamon snatched one of the Rebels' rifles. Getting the drop on them he cried at their backs, "Halt! Ye divils! Bejazes, ye're my prisoners now!" The jubilant Yankee marched his captors back to his regiment, which had taken cover in the deep ravine paralleling the Confederate works.[60] Despite the capture of over 100 Rebels, Potter's men had lost the field at a cost of 969 officers and men.

**Colonel Walter Harriman,
11th New Hampshire**

Harriman, rather than willingly surrender, threw his pistol and sword away.

Massachusetts Commandery;
MOLLUS, USAMHI

While Stone's skirmishers reoccupied the earthworks north of Tapp's, Harris' men went into line on his left.[61] They kept up a heavy fire which frustrated any Northern attempt to retake the works and angered at least one New Hampshire officer who bitterly resented having to yield the field to the Rebels because their supports failed to come up. Captain Josiah N. Jones (Company F, 6th New Hampshire) threw his revolver on the ground and spat, " This is the meanest thing I have ever seen since the war commenced. If our support had followed us up, we could have captured everything in our front." Tears streaked down his powder-blackened face as he continued, "but, as it is, we have got to fall back, and fight for this same ground again before night." (Major Phineas P. Bixby, who stood nearby, humorously thought to himself how the captain, like

**Major Phineas B. Bixby,
6th New Hampshire**

When Captain Josiah N. Jones (Company F) threw a tantrum because the regiment failed to take the Confederate works, Bixby compared the captain to Alexander the Great, who wept because there were no new worlds to conquer.

Massachusetts Commandery;
MOLLUS, USAMHI

Alexander the Great, was weeping because he had no worlds left to conquer.)[62] To add to the New Englanders' frustrations, the 8th Michigan claimed some of the regiment's captures for itself.[63] The 27th Michigan lay on the forest floor not too far from the Confederate works. Pieces of torn shelter halves draped the brush along the regiment's front. One of Sergeant Charles T. Jeffers' men (Company K) caught sight of them and piped out, "What good towels my wife could make if she had those pieces of tent." Jeffers shrugged it off as one of the fellow's "peculiar" comments.[64]

SOUTH SIDE OF THE BROCK ROAD INTERSECTION

From 3:00 P.M. until around 4:00 P.M., the battlefield fell unusually quiet, like the foreboding silence preceding a violent thunderstorm. Since the rout at noon Hancock's Federals had used the time to strengthen their breastworks along the Brock Road. An exhausted Colonel Robert McAllister propped his back against the eastern side of the second line of log works and tried to scratch a quick letter off to his wife. His favorite horse, Charley, stood nearby, saddled.[65] Seventy yards to the west, Brewster's Excelsior Brigade occupied the left wing of the first line of works.[66] The 20th Indiana, 99th Pennsylvania, 2nd U.S. Sharpshooters, 141st Pennsylvania, and the 124th New York from Ward's brigade held the line to the right, all the way to the crossroads.[67] The three remaining regiments of the brigade reformed behind the second set of works on the eastern side of the road.[68] Lieutenant William H. Rogers' section of 12-pounder Napoleons from Captain Edwin Dow's 6th Maine Artillery, charged with double canister, silently waited in the intersection for something to break loose. The remaining four guns were behind the second line of works on the left of McAllister's brigade, and the 1st New Hampshire Artillery continued the line farther to the south.[69] Crocker's mauled brigade shared the breastworks with them.[70] Eighty yards farther to the east the 21st Massachusetts went prone on the slope of a hill from which the men could see the Brock Road over the top of the second set of works. The rest of Colonel Daniel Leasure's IX Corps brigade huddled down a short distance behind yet another section of earthworks. The 100th Pennsylvania was on the right of the line and the 3rd Maryland on the left.[71]

THE NORTH SIDE OF THE BROCK ROAD INTERSECTION

Immediately north of Rogers' section of guns, Colonel Lewis A. Grant's used-up Vermonters took cover behind the first line of works. Private Wilbur Fisk (Company E, 2nd Vermont), who had seen enough fighting in the last forty-eight hours to last him a lifetime, wrote, "I was tired almost to death, and hungry as a wolf. My patriotism was well nigh used up, and so was I, till I had some refreshments." Barefooted, his foot bruised from having been stepped on by an officer's horse, he limped back into the ranks after

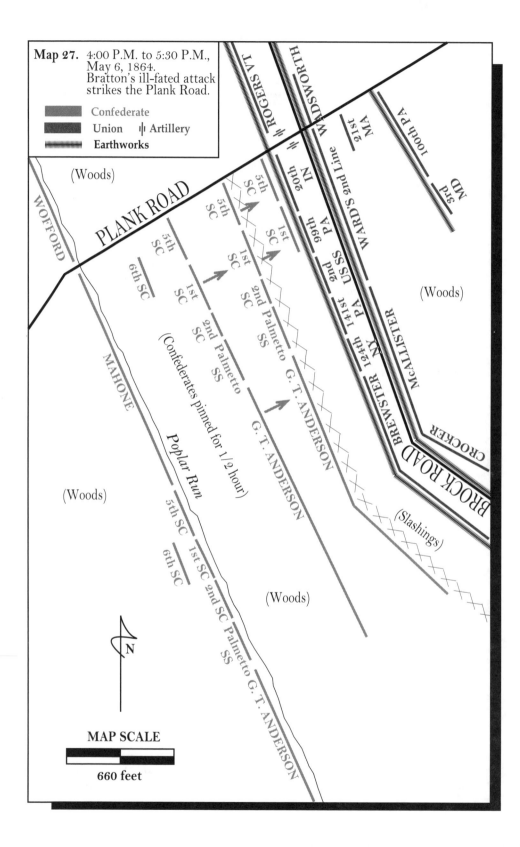

Map 27. 4:00 P.M. to 5:30 P.M., May 6, 1864. Bratton's ill-fated attack strikes the Plank Road.

Confederate

Union ⊩ Artillery

Earthworks

(Woods)

WOFFORD

PLANK ROAD

ROGERS VT

WADSWORTH

21st MA

100th PA

3rd MD

5th SC

5th SC

20th IN

WARD'S 2nd Line

5th SC

1st SC

99th PA

(Woods)

5th SC

1st SC

1st SC

6th SC

1st SC

2nd US SS

141st PA

124th NY

BREWSTER

McALLISTER

2nd Palmetto SS

2nd Palmetto SS

G. T. ANDERSON

CROCKER

(Confederates pinned for 1/2 hour)

MAHONE

Poplar Run

G. T. ANDERSON

BROCK ROAD

(Slashings)

(Woods)

5th SC

1st SC

2nd SC Palmetto G. T. ANDERSON SS

6th SC

(Woods)

N

MAP SCALE

660 feet

having spent a considerable length of time in the woods to the rear.[72] What remained of Wadsworth's exhausted division sat down behind the second row of breastworks north of the Plank Road.[73] Three hundred yards to the east Carroll's bloodied regiments had broken into squads around coffee fires. The men were enjoying their first rations in twenty-four hours.[74] With regiments reduced to companies, and companies to squads, Hancock's once mighty corps seemed to have reached its nadir.

ALONG POPLAR RUN

By 4:00 P.M. Colonel James R. Hagood (1st South Carolina) had become thoroughly miffed with his division commander, Major General Charles W. Field. "After dilly-dallying through the woods for an hour," the nineteen-year-old colonel later griped, "Field's Division was gotten ready and ordered to *feel* the enemy." Wofford's Georgia brigade occupied the northern end of the division, along Wilderness Run, with its right flank on the Plank Road. Mahone's brigade stood in position south of the road with Colonel John Bratton's South Carolinians. Brigadier General George T. Anderson's Georgians completed the formation to the right. Bratton placed the 5th South Carolina on his left with the 1st and 2nd South Carolina, and Palmetto Sharpshooters continuing the front to the south. The 6th South Carolina stayed in the rear as the reserve. At 4:00 P.M., in accordance with extremely vague general orders, Bratton sent his regiments crashing through the shattered woods toward the Brock Road. The original maneuver called for Wofford's brigade to lead the assault with Mahone's, Bratton's, and G. T. Anderson's following in echelons similar to Longstreet's attack upon the Federal left at Gettysburg. Hagood did not like the way the attack unraveled. Colonel Bratton had not given any of the regimental officers specific directions regarding their formations. "I was not told to proceed cautiously as on a reconnaissance and I therefore ordered my men forward with the determination to carry the enemy's position if I could," Hagood later wrote.

Everything went awry from the start. To Bratton's rue, Wofford's and Mahone's regiments did not budge. His brigade and Anderson's struggled across Poplar Run and up the creek bank into the waiting rifles of the Federal skirmishers who had taken positions two hundred yards west of the Brock Road.[75] As they advanced, a South Carolinian snapped off a wild shot, and the 5th South Carolina veered north in an attempt to place its left flank upon the Plank Road.

THE BROCK ROAD INTERSECTION

Three officers from the 1st U.S. Sharpshooters were leaning against a tree west of the Brock Road, watching what was going on in their own lines. Captain William H. Nash stood on the north side of the tree. Captain

Charles A. Stevens covered the south side. First Lieutenant Jean L. Rilliet propped himself against the eastern side. A solitary Confederate round slapped into the west face of the tree with a resounding thud and exited through the other side. The two captains instinctively ducked. The lieutenant remained upright, perfectly still. For a brief, terrible moment the captains, believing the Rebs had killed Rilliet, waited for his corpse to topple over. They asked the remarkably unperturbed lieutenant if he were hit. "If so," he quietly replied, while stepping away from the tree, "I don't feel it."[76]

A flurry of rifle balls was flying overhead while the Confederates drove the Yankee skirmishers through the woods. Bounding across the slashings, they hurled themselves behind the works along the Brock Road.[77] Ward's and Brewster's brigades loosed a tremendous volley into the woods along their front. Tree branches whipped through the air, snapped off by rifle balls. The flash of small arms fire literally illuminated the forest.

About twelve hundred feet farther west, the 5th South Carolina dove to the ground as a body. Their sudden disappearance startled Hagood, who wasted no time in ordering his men to their bellies. The rest of the regiments along the line also went prone. Hagood assumed that some rear echelon officer had countermanded the order to charge. The 1st South Carolina remained on the ground, firing prone. Their colonel did not know what to do.[78]

Ward's and Brewster's Union infantrymen poured devastating volleys into the woods. Anderson's Southerners also hit the dirt, refusing to go deeper into the woods. Within minutes, the Confederates were responding with equal fury. Small trees toppled over at waist and chest height. Bark showered the prone Confederates. Hundreds of leaves fluttered to the forest floor. The Federals were aiming low, punishing the Georgians severely. Captain John G. Webb (Company D, 9th Georgia) watched in horror as the Federals gradually whittled his company down. Private Moser Murray died. Private A. Martin Andrews curled up with a fatal wound in the bowels. Three others left the line wounded. They could not sustain such a beating for much longer.[79]

After half an hour, Colonel Ashbury Coward (5th South Carolina) grabbed the regimental standard from the ensign and stubbornly yelled his men to their feet. Believing that only Yankee bullets and not some order from headquarters had stymied the advance, Colonel James R. Hagood (1st South Carolina) also called for his men to rise up and march toward the enemy.[80] Bent over, as if facing a tornado force wind, the South Carolinians pushed through the bloodied woods toward the Federal works. Coward's 5th South Carolina saw Hagood's men on the move and followed them into the maelstrom. Private Milas Lindsay (Company E, 5th South Carolina) collapsed with bullet wounds in the head and the heel. The line closed up and moved around him.[81]

Ward's first line and Brewster's Excelsior Brigade continued slamming rounds into the smoke-obscured woodline seventy-five yards to their front. The 2nd U.S. Sharpshooters, in the center of Ward's line, armed with their breech-loading Sharps rifles expended a tremendous amount of ammunition on the Carolinians. Sergeant Wyman White (Company F) used primers instead of percussion caps to increase his rate of fire. It seemed to him that his regiment alone stopped the Confederate charge, but a solid wall of felled trees, their interlaced branches facing toward the west, had stalled them, making them stationary targets which were hard to miss.[82] Hagood's and Coward's men clawed over the abatis. The Federals dropped men in every step but the Southerners surged ahead.[83]

Brewster's men saw the Rebels loping toward them, the Rebel yell yipping above the din of musketry. Farther to the right, Ward's four forward regiments temporarily stopped the 5th South Carolina about thirty yards from the works. Lieutenant Colonel Charles Weygant (124th New York) could not believe the stubbornness of the Confederate attack. With each volley, the Yankees were punching holes in the Confederate regiment, yet the veterans continued to feed men into the vacant ranks around their colors.[84]

Ward could not keep still. When the action started, Weygant saw him sitting on a log ten feet behind the regiment. As the fighting dragged on, the general stood up and nervously walked up and down the road. Then he sat down for a few seconds before getting to his feet again to resume his anxious pacing.[85]

Smoke spiraled from the headlogs to the left of the 124th New York where the muzzle flashes from Brewster's brigade had ignited the pine bark in a small section of his works. A stiff, westerly breeze fanned the smoke into sparks. Without any warning the logs burst into flame. The fire rapidly spread south. Brewster's soldiers, having expended fifty rounds of ammunition, could not withstand the incoming Confederate rounds as well as the pine fire which singed their faces. Using the dense pall of smoke for cover, a handful of South Carolinians bolted into the ditch on the western side of the breastworks unobserved by the Federals.

Colonel William R. Brewster, U.S.A.

Brewster's II Corps brigade collapsed twice during the battle on May 6, once from a flanking movement and once from a frontal assault.

Massachusetts Commandery;
MOLLUS, USAMHI

Brewster's regiments wavered, then broke toward the safety of the log works on the eastern side of the road.[86]

Ward did not wait to get captured by the Confederates. He quickstepped to Weygant and, pointing toward the east, told him to pull his New Yorkers back to the second line. The colonel yelled for his men to retreat.[87] But, they stampeded, dragging the 141st Pennsylvania with them. The panicked soldiers swarmed over the second line of works and shattered Ward's three rear regiments, which fled, panic stricken, toward the Plank Road, leaving the right wing of Crocker's brigade up in the air. The Major L. B. Duff, an aide to Birney, watched several of the Confederates and their colors spill into the Brock Road.[88]

The 1st South Carolina exploited the situation and dashed into the ditch along the face of the works. Hagood and his men flattened their bodies against the logs, seeking refuge from the devastating rifle fire from the flanks. Some men from the 5th South Carolina came up on their left and enfiladed the right flank of the 2nd U.S. Sharpshooters.[89] In the excitement, Sergeant Wyman White (Company F, 2nd U.S. Sharpshooters) had no idea what was going on around him. He glanced to the left and discovered that he and a man named Miller from Company H were the only members of the regiment who were still in the line. Where did the boys go? Wyman shouted. The regiment was flanked, Miller coolly answered, and the men had skedaddled to the works behind the regiment. Taking in the situation within seconds, White noticed the Saint Andrews' Cross flapping in the dense smoke, but before he could react, he felt two rounds thunk into him. At the same time Ward raced past him toward the two artillery caissons which were standing near the crossroads. Leaping onto one of the seats, he screamed at the drivers to, "drive like Hell down the plank road to the rear." The artillerymen did not waste any time in obeying the command. The caisson disappeared among the hundreds of demoralized men who swarmed the road. Rather than abandon their pieces, the gunners scurried about the intersection looking for makeshift projectiles with which to pound the Confederates. Before the dust had settled, White took off after Miller for the second line of works.[90]

Farther to the east several little gray rabbits, flushed from cover by the surging troops along the Brock Road, bounded from the brush toward the prone 21st Massachusetts. The New Englanders peered through the smoke-filled woods in front of them and saw what appeared to be Confederate troops moving through the burned over clearing toward the Brock Road. They opened fire toward the commotion.[91] Behind them, at the third line, Colonel Joseph M. Sudsburg commanded the 3rd Maryland to fix bayonets and stop the hundreds of frightened men who were fleeing the Confederates. The Marylanders would not yield to the II Corps troops, who, instead of breaking their formation, flowed around the flanks of the regi-

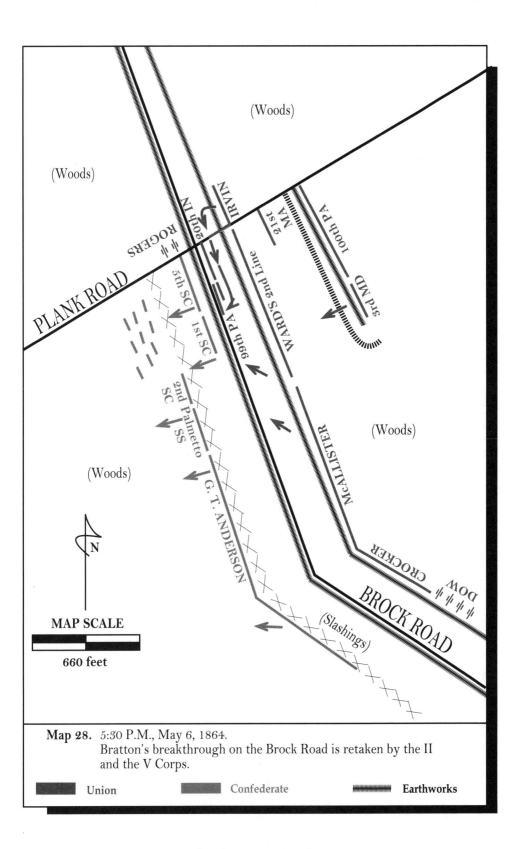

(Woods)

(Woods)

(Woods)

ROGERS

90th IN

IRVIN

21st MA

100th PA

3rd MD

5th SC

1st SC

PLANK ROAD

99th PA

WARD'S 2nd Line

2nd Palmetto
SC
SS

G. T. ANDERSON

McALLISTER

(Woods)

(Woods)

CROCKER

DOW

BROCK ROAD

(Slashings)

N

MAP SCALE

660 feet

Map 28. 5:30 P.M., May 6, 1864.
Bratton's breakthrough on the Brock Road is retaken by the II
and the V Corps.

Union   Confederate   Earthworks

ment and swept away the provost guard behind them.[92] By the time their front cleared, the South Carolinians were retreating to the cover of the Brock Road earthworks.

The 20th Indiana and the 99th Pennsylvania, despite the suffocating, eye-stinging cloud of white pine smoke which engulfed the works to their left, continued to pepper the Confederates from the north.[93] In the meantime the artillerymen from Rogers' section had hauled several boxes of small arms ammunition over to their guns and were stuffing cartridges by the bucketful down the bores of their pieces.[94] Volunteers from the 20th Indiana and the artillerymen shouldered the two guns farther west until they cleared the flank of the infantrymen in the works. Wheeling the pieces to face south, the artillerymen methodically sighted and primed the guns, then loosed their makeshift "canister" into the backs of the South Carolinians, pinning the Confederates along the western face of the front works.

The infantry having raced past their front, the remaining four guns from Dow's 6th Maine, on the left of McAllister's brigade, pounded the South Carolinians with shell and case shot before switching to double canister. Captain Frederick M. Edgell's six guns also joined in the attack. Dow was more concerned about the recruits in his battery than the incoming rifle fire. When using double canister, the Number Five man, who took the round from the limber chest to the gun, was supposed to knock off the powder bag of the second round at the chest before running to the piece. The recruit servicing one of his pieces was breaking the bags off on the left wheel of the gun and allowing them to pile up under the tube. During the height of the engagement, the muzzle flash exploded the stack of bags. The sudden burst of flame disabled the gun, burned all five men who manned it, and set the log earthworks on fire.[95]

The Union troops north of the intersection listened to the intensity of the fighting. Corporal Bradley M. Barnes (Company I, 7th Wisconsin), whose regiment did not leave the woods, timed each blast. The guns averaged two rounds each per minute. It was one of the "sharpest fights" in which he had ever participated.[96]

The suddenness of the attack unstrung an aide on Birney's staff, who, while trying to rally a part of the second line, created a panic. Some of the 17th Maine stayed in line and volleyed into the Rebels.[97] Most fled. The confused mob surged east on the Plank Road, snatching up men from other regiments. An officer ordered Carroll's brigade to its feet. To the amazement of First Lieutenant George Bowen (Company C, 12th New Jersey), the brigade bolted east instead of west.[98] Sergeant Edwin G. Owen (Company I, 141st Pennsylvania) swore the regiments ran at least half of a mile before they could be rallied.[99]

The sight of a Confederate color bearer standing defiantly on top of the headlogs south of the crossroads took Hancock aback. From where he

**The 1st South Carolina places its colors
on the abandoned Federal works along the Brock Road.**

Battles and Leaders, 1:IV, Grant-Lee Edition, 1888

stood in the intersection it became painfully apparent that for the second time in the same day, the Rebels had outflanked his men and had punched a hole through his corps. He wasted no time in dispatching Captain Wilson to the east to ferret out some support. One hundred fifty yards into the woods, he came across Lieutenant Colonel John Irvin (149th Pennsylvania), who commanded what was left of Stone's decimated Pennsylvania brigade and disorganized squads from Rice's brigade. Wilson told Irvin that Hancock wanted to know, "What troops are those?" The colonel, who had managed to gather the colors for the entire brigade in one place, told the captain that his five regiments all belonged to Wadsworth's division of the V Corps. He had 297 rifles and 20 officers at Hancock's disposal.[100]

Wilson commanded the "brigade" to forward at once. With a shout, and completely disregarding unit integrity, the five regiments started falling into column of fours. The front of the strike force took off at the doublequick step without waiting for the men far in the rear to join the formation. Corporal John W. Nesbit (Company D, 149th Pennsylvania), who was in the first rank of four men, heard the ominous clanking of steel on steel as the men fixed bayonets on the run. The makeshift brigade moved by "column left" onto the Brock Road. As the front of the regiments shuffled south, Nesbit looked over his shoulder and saw men still pouring out of the woods and falling into formation behind him.[101]

On the east side of the road a lone infantryman leaped over the second line and gave the frightened Sergeant Wyman White of the 2nd U.S. Sharpshooters a terrible start. "See the sons of bitches," the irate infantryman screamed, "they have got their Rebel rag on that pit. Let's fix bayonets and drive them out." Unsheathing his bayonet he jammed it upon his rifle and screeched, "Come on boys."[102] Squads of soldiers vaulted over the entrenchments and followed after him. Back at the third line of works Captain John Wilson, commanding the 1st U.S. Sharpshooters, leaped on top of a headlog. "Boys," he cried, "I cannot stand this. Forward, left oblique, march!"[103] With Federal infantry rapidly flowing into and toward the Brock Road, the two artillery pieces on the Plank Road and the four guns on McAllister's left ceased fire.[104]

Coward's 5th South Carolina, on Hagood's left, valiantly tried to hold its section of the line against the 20th Indiana and the 99th Pennsylvania.[105] The 1st South Carolina's colors went down a second time. But, a lieutenant snatched them up until Yankee rifle fire cut him down.[106] Hagood did not know what to do. He sadly realized that the rest of his brigade had gotten pinned in the woods. He thought of charging but that would have meant total annihilation. He wanted to send a courier to the rear but he did not believe that anyone could survive the gauntlet of fire. The 5th South Carolina decided the issue for him when it broke to the rear. Seeing his supports stream rearward, Hagood yelled for his regiment to retreat also. "We then fled at the top of our speed while the crash of shot about us, strewing whole trees in our pathway, sounded like the fury of some hell-born passion," he recollected.[107] The rout was too quick for his color bearer and a portion of his regiment who remained along the works.

"On the right, by file into line, march." Professionally, as if on drill, Irvin's Pennsylvanians, having marched between the Confederates and the 21st Massachusetts, right wheeled by pairs back into a regimental front and charged. First Sergeant Patrick DeLacy (Company A, 143rd Pennsylvania), with his pistol drawn, raced ahead of the regiment. Dashing up to the breastworks, he grabbed the Confederate flag staff and shot the color bearer dead. With clubbed muskets and bayonets, the two sides struggled savagely for possession of the line.[108] The Confederates were dying game but they could not withstand the terrific onslaught which was closing in on them. It seemed like every Federal regiment in the area struck the works at the same time and that they had all made that lone Confederate battle flag their objective. First Lieutenant William Ross (Company I), at the head of the 16th Massachusetts, with the regimental colors close behind, claimed to be the first Federal to reach the Confederate position.[109] The 11th New Jersey insisted that its colors reached the works ahead of every other Federal regiment. Bullets slapped into the color guard, one of which hammered Sergeant George W. Lindley (Company K) in the chest. He staggered to the rear, believing he had received a mortal wound only to discover that his sweetheart's

First Sergeant Patrick DeLacy, Company A, 143rd Pennsylvania

DeLacy, shown here with the rank of sergeant major, killed the color bearer of the 1st South Carolina and won the Medal of Honor.

Massachusetts Commandery; MOLLUS, USAMHI

daguerreotype, which he carried in the inside breast pocket of his blouse, had saved his life.[110] Captain Horatio Bell (Company G, 150th Pennsylvania), rifle in hand, stood on top of a headlog and coolly fired into the Rebels at point blank range. Several shots later, a minie ball crashed into his skull and sent him flying backward onto his men.[111]

Still the Rebels stubbornly refused to retreat. Their rifle fire played havoc among the Federal troops which piled into one another along the Brock Road. Color Sergeant J. Madison Tarbell (Company E, 2nd U.S. Sharpshooters) leaped upon the works with the flag in hands, vainly trying to urge his men across when a bullet knocked him into the Brock Road.[112] The Confederates wounded Colonel Robert McAllister slightly when it cut down his favorite horse, Charley. Private David Alpaugh (Company E, 11th New Jersey) dropped to the rear with a buck and ball load in his thigh.[113]

The blood lust was overpowering. The rousing chorus of "Rally Round the Flag, Boys," floated over the 20th Indiana and carried across the road.[114] Singing "On the Road to Boston" Sergeant Wyman White (Company F, 2nd U.S. Sharpshooters), who by this time had worked his way through the mob of soldiers to the breastworks, poked his head over them and saw the Rebel flag on the ground on the other side. Without thinking he placed his hand on the headlog, determined to capture the flag when he heard a bullet snap a bone near him. The man next to him collapsed with a bullet in his forehead. Casting a final glance across the works, he wisely dropped down behind them. No less than 50 Rebels were hugging the ground around the colors. Had he gone after the flag, he would have fallen in the middle of them.[115]

With the troops in front surging toward the Brock Road, Colonel Daniel Leasure decided to commit the 100th Pennsylvania. "Men of the 100th," he yelled, "go up." Captain Joseph F. Carter (Company D), who commanded the right of the 3rd Maryland, watched the Pennsylvanians sweep forward before walking over to Leasure and asking, "Colonel, shall we go too?" "Not yet," Leasure curtly replied.

First Line on the Brock Road

The Federals pleaded with the Confederates to surrender. Realizing they could no longer hold the field, the Rebels scattered, leaving their colors on the charred ground. Major James Glenn (149th Pennsylvania), the only mounted officer with the regiment, leaped his horse over the four-foot-high wall and landed behind them.[116] White decided to make another try for the flag. Before he could get over the works, a lone Confederate on the far side of the clearing tossed aside his equipment and made a dash toward the Federals, who withheld their fire, believing that the man intended to surrender. The second he reached the colors, the Rebel reached down, snatched the end of the staff and raced back to the cover of the woods. The air exploded with a sudden burst of rifle fire, the balls whizzing around the soldier, who miraculously escaped. A Confederate with a broken leg, who had propped himself up on his rifle, died instead, riddled with dozens of bullets. "The man with the flag was a very brave man. No man ever did a braver act," White later wrote.[117] The South Carolinians did not stop running until they reached Poplar Run.

Third Line

Within five minutes, the firing had abated. Colonel Joseph M. Sudsburg, having decided to reinforce the front, ordered, "Third Maryland, go up." The words shot through the Marylanders. They yelled at the 21st Massachusetts in front of them to keep down, because they were going to fire. The New Englanders hugged the ground while the 3rd Maryland volleyed over their heads. Color Sergeant Patrick Moore (Company B) leaped over the headlog and bolted toward the Brock Road. Carter, taking that as a signal, yelled for Company D to follow Moore, and with his men, went over the works. They dragged the rest of the regiment with them. A solitary Rebel bullet struck down a man, severely wounding him. Clearing the second line of works, the Marylanders spilled into the Brock Road where a round killed Captain John Atkinhead (Company A).[118]

The 11th New Jersey and the 26th Pennsylvania crossed the slashings into the woods. Walking over the Confederate dead was unsettling.[119] Behind them, the 124th New York picked up many men who were feigning death to escape capture.[120] Company D, 149th Pennsylvania, spilled over the works as skirmishers and pursued the Confederates a short distance into the woods. Corporal John W. Nesbit stumbled across the corpse of a Confederate officer and decided to take the man's sword until he discovered it had belonged to Colonel Richard P. Roberts of the 140th Pennsylvania, who had died at Gettysburg.[121] He turned the sword over to Second Lieutenant David R. P. Neely (Company I), who promptly received credit for its capture.[122] Private Michael Ansell (Company C, 142nd Pennsylvania) rounded up seven Confederates and brought them in.[123] A lieutenant of the 17th Maine, armed with only a revolver, captured another 18 men.[124]

By 5:30 P.M. it was all over. The 1st and 5th South Carolina regrouped along Poplar Run and counted their losses. Of the 262 officers and men whom Hagood led into the fight he lost 92 killed and wounded and an estimated 80 captured—66 percent. The 5th South Carolina suffered a similar ratio of casualties and had gained nothing.[125] The Federals, having regained their works, were squabbling among themselves over which regiments retreated first and which ones really recovered the lost ground. In the distance a lone sharpshooter continued sniping at the 3rd Maryland from a tree top twenty feet above the works. A few minutes later he killed another Marylander with a head shot. Captain Joseph F. Carter (Company D), having spotted the man, kept the sniper occupied with left oblique fire until he positioned a rifleman to catch the fellow in a cross fire. A single shot dispatched the Reb. The captain watched the Rebel's rifle clatter to the forest floor, followed closely by the killer.[126] Nearby Private James M. Stone (Company K, 21st Massachusetts) witnessed a scene which would haunt him into the next century. A middle-aged soldier was carefully picking among the Union dead until he found a boy—his son. Speaking his son's name, the man took the corpse's hand in his and sat down beside it, crying. Stone, unable to pry his eyes from the fellow, waited for several minutes. Another enlisted man asked the older soldier if he knew the boy. "Yes," the fellow quietly replied, "that is my Charley, that is my cub; but he is silent now, once so full of life and active." Unable to withstand the emotions which inundated him, Stone walked away.[127]

Carter walked over to Sudsburg and asked permission to go into the brush east of the Brock Road to find his hat, which he had lost during the charge, but Hancock stopped him as he stepped into the road. "What brigade is this?" Hancock asked. "Second Brigade, First Division, IX Corps," Carter replied. "Men," Hancock shouted, loud enough for everyone to hear, "you have saved the day." Removing his hat, the general cheered the 3rd Maryland and galloped down the road. Carter retrieved his hat and returned to the works. He asked if he could reconnoiter south on the Brock Road to see if the flank was secure. The colonel sent him at once.[128]

While he was gone, Colonel Samuel Carroll's lost brigade, having been turned about by General Ulysses S. Grant in person, came charging to the front.[129] Ward's brigade followed them into the works, replacing Hoffman's men on picket duty. When the relief party claimed the Confederate colors for themselves, Major Charles M. Cunningham (143rd Pennsylvania) asked Sergeant Patrick DeLacy to have Sergeant Gaines Pritchard (Company D) record the names of every man from the 143rd Pennsylvania who survived the charge. The sergeant recorded 67 enlisted men. The regiment had emerged from the ordeal unscathed.[130] When Carter returned, he found that the 3rd Maryland had been relieved and was behind the second line of works. But by then, Carroll's brigade was already taking the credit for having saved the Union position along the Brock Road.[131]

CONFEDERATE FIELD HOSPITAL NEAR TAPP'S

Brigadier General Micah Jenkins was dying with Major John Cheves Haskell sitting by his side. Unconscious, he continued to cheer his men. In his delirium, he begged them to drive the Federals back to the Rapidan. During the hour which Haskell spent with him, Jenkins raved until exhaustion silenced him. "He was the most remarkable man, full of spirits and enthusiasm and as full of the most resolute courage," his fellow South Carolinian wrote. It was his fearlessness which, Haskell said, killed him and too many good men. The day had been wasted. Despite their successful drives against the Army of the Potomac, the Confederates had gained nothing but time. Grant, Haskell later reflected, "...having reasoned out his problem of wearing out our tens of thousands with his hundreds of thousands...would never hesitate and that killing and disabling one army only brought a fresh one against our worn and half fed men till they were worn to the breaking point."[132]

5:00 P.M.

THE IX CORPS NORTH OF THE TAPP FARM

Grant had no intention of letting the Confederates go so easily. As early as 3:00 P.M. he directed Burnside to pull any regiments he could spare from Christ's brigade, which were still posted in the woods north of Jones' Field, and divert them southeast to support Potter's division. He timed the general assault against Lee's northern flank for later in the afternoon.[133] Christ, taking the 20th Michigan, the 50th Pennsylvania, and the right wing of the 1st Michigan Sharpshooters with him, moved east to support Potter.

Hartranft's regiments reformed in their original alignments to charge the Confederate works again. The 27th Michigan was going to lead the attack, followed by the 2nd Michigan, the 51st Pennsylvania, and the 17th

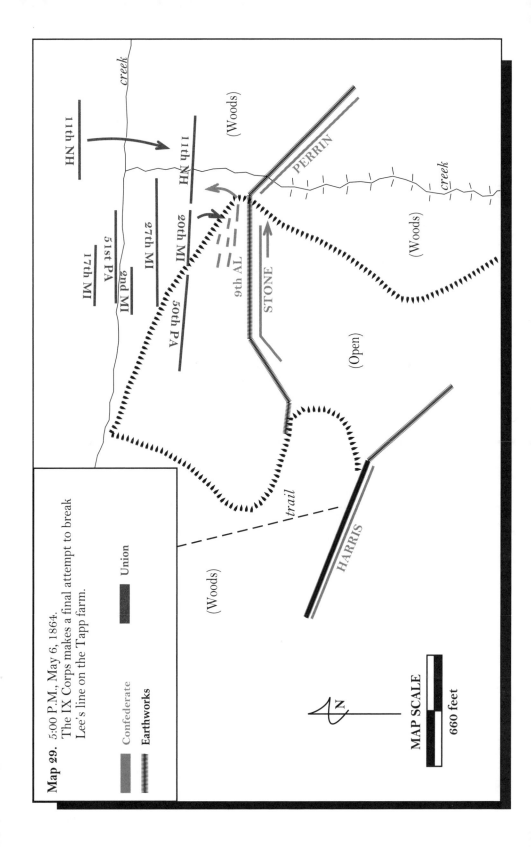

Map 29. 5:00 P.M., May 6, 1864.
The IX Corps makes a final attempt to break
Lee's line on the Tapp farm.

Confederate

Union

Earthworks

MAP SCALE

660 feet

N

(Woods)

PERRIN

creek

(Woods)

STONE

9th AL

(Open)

50th PA

20th MI

27th MI

51st PA

2nd MI

17th MI

11th NH

11th NH

creek

(Woods)

trail

HARRIS

Michigan. The 8th Michigan, having been so badly mauled earlier in the day, was not going to participate in this one. The 109th New York, having shot away all of its ammunition, was also staying out of the fight. At the command all three regiments stepped off. Colonel John M. Stone's North Carolinians and Alabamians poured a devastating fire into them. The 27th Michigan scattered for cover among the trees and hit the dirt. The rest of the brigade reacted just as quickly, the charge dying in its tracks.[134]

Christ's three regiments came onto the field and found Hartranft's men "badly cut up and scattered through the woods," Colonel Byron M. Cutcheon (20th Michigan) later recalled. Christ quickly placed his three regiments into formation. Four companies of the 1st Michigan Sharpshooters deployed behind Hartranft for support. The remaining company moved farther to the left to protect the flank. The 50th Pennsylvania formed the right of his line. Eight companies of the 20th Michigan went into position on the left with the remaining two companies spread out to the front and the left as skirmishers.[135] Not waiting for any instructions, Christ cried out, "Go in and give 'em hell." The 50th Pennsylvania bolted through the woods at a run, taking the 20th Michigan with it. The two regiments disappeared in the low-hanging smoke.

The Michiganders ran headlong into the 9th Alabama, which had not entrenched. The Alabamians gave way, leaving their adjutant and 20 men in the Federals' hands. Flushed with their easy victory, the two regiments pressed forward until the right wing of the Pennsylvanians charged blindly into the works held by Stone's brigade. The Confederates' rifles illuminated the darkening woods with violent flashes. The 20th Michigan attempted a right wheel to flank the Confederate line but instead walked into rifle fire from its own men. The regiment pulled back and went to the ground, leaving the 50th Pennsylvania at the Rebels' mercy. Stone flanked part of his brigade to the right to take the Federals from the rear but Lieutenant Colonel Byron M. Cutcheon (20th Michigan) brought the 11th New Hampshire up to the left of the 20th Michigan, and the Confederates withdrew rather than attempt an assault.

Meanwhile the woods resounded with musketry and screams for several minutes. The Confederates killed or wounded 78 of the 50th Pennsylvania and sent them reeling back upon their supports. Bullets passing through the regiment fell among the Michiganders, wounding six men. The 27th Michigan began fortifying its position. Dragging in felled trees and brush, the men took cover and returned fire. The two teenage musicians from Sergeant Charles T. Jeffers' Company K ran to the rear and returned to the firing line, their stretcher loaded down with packages of cartridges. They coolly trooped the line, handing out ammunition and ignoring the bullets which tore their uniforms. Each time they emptied their stretcher, they picked up a wounded man and carried him to the surgeons. The sergeant admired their selflessness and poise.[136]

The Michiganders kept up a vicious and accurate skirmish fire with Stone's sharpshooters. They pinned First Lieutenant Robert F. Ward (Company B, 42nd Mississippi) behind a sapling on the hill behind the Confederate line, then killed Lieutenant Colonel F. Marion Boone (26th Mississippi) and Second Lieutenant John W. Godfrey (Company B, 42nd Mississippi) to his left. Across the works, he spied Captain Jones C. Donaldson (Company K) poking his head around the side of a very large tree. Every time the captain moved, a Yankee sharpshooter sent a bullet singing by his head. Every now and then the captain would turn around and grin at Ward who was also dodging bullets. Stone was sitting on the ground twenty paces behind Donaldson, calmly holding his horse's reins, apparently unconcerned about the danger he was in. Twice, Ward braved the snipers' bullets to ask the colonel for permission to move Godfrey's body to the rear. He refused both times, saying that there was no use to risk the stretcher bearers' lives. Ward would have to wait until dark to take his friend away. The lieutenant winced at the sun through the trees and wondered if God had ordered it to stand still as He had during the days of Joshua. Godfrey was the last of four friends who had enlisted in the 42nd Mississippi from Greenville, Mississippi. The other three had been killed or disabled at Gettysburg. It broke Ward's heart to see his friend lying in the woods—alone. "Our chief desire was for sudden and thick darkness," Ward later wrote.[137]

Despite the order to not light fires along the IX Corps outposts, a tobacco-addicted Irishman in the 27th Michigan, belonging to Jeffers company, decided he needed a smoke. No one paid any particular attention to the man because he always had his pipe in his mouth. He slept with it. The second he struck the match to light his bowl, a Confederate rifle cracked in the darkness. The soldier yelped, attracting everyone's attention. A quick investigation satisfied them that the Irishman was only wounded, his temerity having cost him a couple of fingers from his left hand and his beloved pipe.[138] The battle frittered away into the pickets taking pot shots at one another. On that part of the field, no one heard any birds chirping.

Colonel John M. Stone, under the cover of darkness, and suffering from a severe wound, finally retired to the hill behind the Confederate works. Lieutenant General A. P. Hill met him there. "Colonel Stone, you have won laurels today. I hope soon to see you a major general," Hill said. Stone, the strain of two days of fighting having taken its toll, fought back the pain welling up within him and stoically replied, "General Hill, I have only done my duty, and if you have any compliments to bestow, give them to these men standing here and their comrades left on the field; they did the fighting, and they deserve the 'laurels.'" The general turned away. Stone remained alone. Turning about, he studied the casualty-littered ground around him and burst into tears.[139]

THE PLANK ROAD

Captain Z. Boylston Adams (Company F, 56th Massachusetts) had been lying along Wilderness Run throughout Bratton's attack against the Brock Road. He busied himself by writing in his diary and pouring water over his shattered knee cap. As the fighting died away, the Federal artillery sent several shells hurtling into the woods after the Confederates. A number of the fragments hissed into the water and splashed Adams without disturbing him too much. Toward dusk he smelled smoke and, glancing toward the eastern crest of the creek bank, he noticed white smoke billowing up along the wood line. He anxiously looked around for some signs of life but there were none—only corpses. He did not want to burn to death. Before long he heard voices echoing along the creek in the dark. He called out and two unarmed Confederates, who had been filling their canteens, helped him to the Plank Road, where they left him behind a small breastwork with a surgeon.

Despite his pain, Adams vividly remembered that a bright, gold haze blanketed the woods. The men moving about on the Plank Road looked like flitting black ghosts. Occasional groans and mumbling broke the eerie silence which had settled over the field.

The surgeon finally came to Adams' assistance. Identifying himself as a former surgeon, he told the Confederate that he needed to be evacuated by an ambulance immediately to a surgical station. His leg was getting hot and painful. He had suffered tremendous blood loss, Adams groaned. "Do you like sardines?" he added without thinking. The question took the Confederate aback. "There is nothing I am more fond of than sardines, and I haven't tasted any since the war," the stunned doctor answered. Adams pulled his poncho off his shoulder and pulled out the can which his friend Hoyt had given him earlier in the day. He handed the sardines to the Rebel. "I'll look out for you," the doctor promised. He immediately sent an enlisted man after a stretcher and personally escorted Adams along the Plank Road until they found an ambulance. Along the way they passed the position formerly held by the 56th Massachusetts. "There goes the captain!" one of his wounded men exclaimed. Adams propped himself up on his elbow. His "boys" were in the ditch which they had defended and in the brush along the road. He recognized John Buckshot who was lying along the road with a shattered thigh. He had never seen such desolation in his life. At one point, the woods looked as if they had been scythed like grass. The small arms fire had literally cut the trees down at the ground.

The surgeon placed him in a two-wheeled ambulance. A short distance down the road the rickety wagon stopped and someone threw a wounded Confederate in beside him. Not too long after that, Adams was awakened out of his stupor by a terrible jolt and a loud crash. The ambulance lurched and collapsed on one side. The other wounded man fell on top of Adams.

For a brief moment he saw the flickering light of a lantern and heard some-one drawl, "Dat ar dog-goned wheel had done come off." He remembered nothing after that. Weakened from his injuries and blood loss, he passed out.[140]

Not too far away, immediately north of the Plank Road, Lieutenant Colonel Charles I. Chandler and his 35-man detachment with the colors of the 57th Massachusetts were still lying in the woods along the front of McGowan's old breastworks. They were tired and scared. For several hours they had lain in the brush watching the Confederates plow through the woods all around them. At one point a stray Rebel stumbled into them but Chandler got the drop on him with his revolver and convinced the fellow to surrender. Late in the afternoon, after the IX Corps suspended its attack against Tapp's farm, a handful of lost soldiers from the 45th Pennsylvania wandered into the frightened huddle of Massachusetts men. Deciding not to stand up and risk capture, the Federals began crawling with their pris-oner in the suspected direction of the Union lines. It took them several hours but they did reach the Brock Road in tact and alive with the colors of the regiment.[141]

CHAPTER SEVEN

"Halt! For God's Sake, boys, rally!"

THE WOODS NORTH OF SAUNDERS FIELD
(2.25 miles northwest of Tapp's)

THE VI CORPS' LINES

Between 10:00 A.M. and 2:00 P.M., the VI Corps troops along the base of the ridge across from Early's division tightened their lines. Brigadier General Truman Seymour recalled the 110th Ohio and placed it on the right of his line. He put the 6th Maryland to its left. The Marylanders went prone on the top of the ridge without entrenching.[1] The 122nd Ohio retired to the left of the Marylanders. Colonel William H. Ball put six companies into the line and placed the remaining four companies in the woods behind the regiment.[2] The 126th Ohio and the 138th Pennsylvania remained in the woods to the west to protect the brigade's right front.[3]

Neill's brigade held the crest to Seymour's left across the Culpeper Mine Road. The 7th Maine and the 49th New York with the 2nd and the 4th New Jersey regiments to their right, remained in the valley as skirmishers.[4] The 43rd and the 77th New York continued the line to the left of the 122nd Ohio. Behind them, the 61st Pennsylvania formed a reserve in the woods and threw up earthworks.[5] One battalion of the 5th Wisconsin linked the 77th New York with the 119th Pennsylvania and the 15th New Jersey.[6]

While the skirmishing in front of the VI Corps continued on and off throughout the morning into the forenoon, Major General John Sedgwick decided to strengthen his right flank by shifting Brigadier General Alexander Shaler's three New York regiments (65th, 67th, and 122nd) toward the north. At 10:00 A.M., the 67th New York deployed into the valley between the lines, relieving the 4th New Jersey. The Jerseymen fell back to the ridge and moved south to rejoin their brigade.[7] Private Edwin Crockett

172

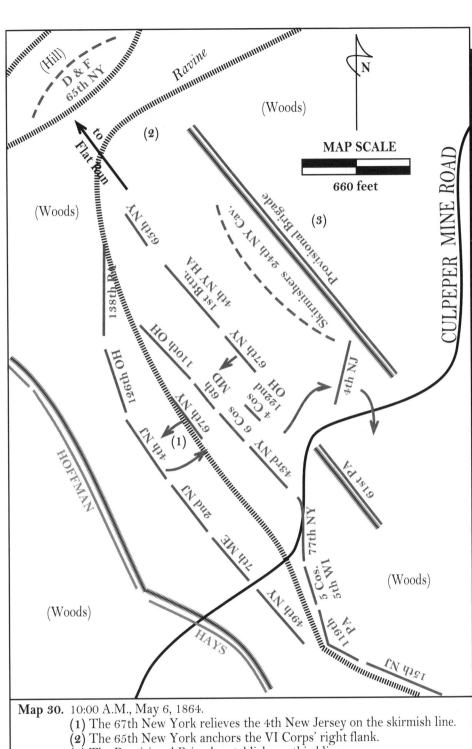

(Hill)

D & F
65th NY

Ravine

(Woods)

N

(2)

to Flat Run

(Woods)

65th NY

138th PA

126th OH

110th OH

67th NY

1st Brig.
4th NY HA

Skirmishers 24th NY Cav.

Provisional Brigade

(3)

MD
6th
4 Cos.

122nd
OH

43rd NY

6 Cos.

4th NJ

4th NJ

(1)

2nd NJ

7th ME

61st PA

77th NY

HOFFMAN

49th NY

5 Cos.

5th WI

119th
PA

15th NJ

HAYS

(Woods)

(Woods)

CULPEPER MINE ROAD

MAP SCALE

660 feet

Map 30. 10:00 A.M., May 6, 1864.
 (**1**) The 67th New York relieves the 4th New Jersey on the skirmish line.
 (**2**) The 65th New York anchors the VI Corps' right flank.
 (**3**) The Provisional Brigade establishes a third line.

Union   Confederate   Earthworks   Ridge

(Company K, 65th New York) saw no less than 2,000 discarded rifles, which Confederate prisoners had been forced to collect, leaning against the large trees along the regiment's rout of march.[8] With enough time, they would be cleaned, loaded, and distributed to the troops on the front lines to provide rapid fire in the event of a frontal assault. Once they reached the deep ravine on the right of the VI Corps, Companies D and F sprayed into the woods along the northern lip of the ravine and formed a tenuous skirmish line.[9]

The 1st Battalion of the 4th New York Heavy Artillery from Colonel Charles H. Tomkins' Artillery Brigade followed them into position. The "Heavies" were artillerymen from the defenses of Washington whom the government had called up as infantry, a demotion of sorts. Artillerymen considered themselves the more intelligent branch of the armed forces because the men were all cross trained to perform each other's functions and they had to be able to read well enough to understand the fuse charts on the inside of the ammunition chests' lids. While they were approaching the rear of the VI Corps, an officer told them they were going to build an artillery embrasure. Private Hiland C. Kirk (Company M) heard a disgruntled veteran grumble, "Well, I'm going to desert to some other branch of the service. We seem to be a Jack of all trades—heavy artillery, light artillery, infantry, and now we are engineers. Next thing we'll be cavalry." A recruit sincerely added, "Never mind, Jack, it is all for the country." The veteran was going to cut loose with a string of profanities in reply when the order came down the line to halt and front, followed by the command to load at will. A minute later, the battalion was moving west by the flank.[10] Along the ridge, about one hundred fifty to two hundred feet to the west, men were entrenching. Burial details had already begun their grisly work—digging trenches and dragging in bodies. The New Yorkers stacked their weapons and began constructing gun lunettes.[11]

By 10:00 A.M., Colonel Elisha G. Marshall's Provisional Brigade, consisting of the 24th New York Cavalry, the 14th New York Heavy Artillery, and the 2nd Pennsylvania Provisional Heavy Artillery, having been deployed as infantry, were marching through the woods to the support of Neill's brigade. They occupied some earthworks on the edge of a cleared section of woods about one hundred eighty-eight yards behind the crest of the ridge, perpendicular to the north side of the Culpeper Mine Road. Quicktempered Second Lieutenant Charles A. Lochbrunner (Company C, 14th New York Heavy Artillery), an undersized officer who was on furlough from the Swiss Army, took his 125 volunteers into the open ground as skirmishers while the remaining two regiments stacked arms and sat down a short distance from the trench. The Jerseymen moved off to the south and rejoined the 3rd and the 10th New Jersey behind the ridge.[12]

GORDON'S BRIGADE

Shortly before noon Brigadier General Robert D. Johnston's North Carolina brigade from Major General Robert E. Rodes' Division was approaching the western edge of the Wilderness. Johnston and his staff, riding in advance of the column, met Lieutenant General Richard S. Ewell near the Culpeper Mine Road-Orange Turnpike intersection. Ewell directed a one-eyed lieutenant to escort Johnston to Early so that he could bring the brigade into line once it arrived. The aide took the general to the cleared fields on the high ground northwest of Flat Run, over one thousand four hundred yards beyond the pike, where he joined Early, Gordon and their staff officers.[13] His brigade arrived around 1:00 P.M. and began entrenching on the left of Gordon's brigade.[14]

HOFFMAN'S BRIGADE

The Federal skirmishers kept the Virginians to the south ducking for the better part of the day. The 49th Virginia lost several men to Yankee bullets when they crawled over the headlogs to loot the knapsacks of the dead and wounded between the lines.[15] A black man in a long-tailed civilian coat wandered into the 31st Virginia looking for a lieutenant in one of Gordon's regiments. A few of the Virginians got into a conversation with the man, hoping to draw Yankee fire. They did not have to wait long before scattered rifle shots sent the fellow running away with the bullets pocking up the dirt at his heels and his coat tails flapping in his wake.[16]

THE VI CORPS' POSITION

At 2:00 P.M., Carter's Virginia battalion, to the left rear of Gordon's brigade, northwest of Flat Run, shelled the VI Corps line to stop the advance of the 122nd New York which had been ordered forward in a bayonet charge from the right of Seymour's line. The New Yorkers crashed into the marshy low land despite the barrage and the deadly musketry from Hoffman's waiting Confederates. Color Corporal Francis Patterson (Company D) was wounded but came off the field. First Lieutenant Martin L. Wilson (Company A) was fatally wounded in the shoulder and Second Lieutenant Charles B. Clark (Company G) went down with a wounded leg. Corporal Isaac H. Merriam (Company I) disappeared in the brush and was given up for dead by First Lieutenant Theodore L. Poole. After losing 57 men in 20 minutes, the regiment retired to the crest and went prone on the right front of the 110th Ohio.[17]

The Confederate artillery traversed the Federal position, raining shells and case shot upon the skirmishers of the 49th New York. It caught Private Christopher G. Funke (Company B) completely off guard. Having stuck his Springfield rifle in the ground by the bayonet, he crawled away from his company to find a safe place to change his shirt. Plopping down behind a huge oak, he removed his knapsack and accouterments and was pulling his shirt over his head when the first round screamed overhead. The sweaty shirt adhered to his body and would not get past his head. Fearing he would be captured partially nude, he frantically tugged and jerked until he had the shirt off and had changed into a cleaner one. With his equipment back on he scrambled back to his company only to discover that he had lost his rifle. After combing the brush for a few minutes, he found a discarded Springfield and decided not to report the incident to anyone.[18]

At 5:00 P.M., part of the 43rd New York (Neill's brigade) and the 67th Pennsylvania (Seymour's brigade) moved down the slope, relieving the 2nd New Jersey, the 7th Maine, and the 67th New York.[19] The 2nd New Jersey went to the rear to rejoin its brigade while the 7th Maine occupied the space vacated by the 43rd New York.[20] The 67th New York tramped north to reunite with its brigade in the ravine on the far end of the VI Corps' line. The 49th New York retired at the same time to the works held by the 61st Pennsylvania, about one hundred yards east of the crest of the hill. The Pennsylvanians moved twenty-five feet farther into the woods and stacked their weapons.[21]

To the right, north of the Culpeper Mine Road, Seymour pulled his brigade to the left. The 6th Maryland was retired from his line with orders to report to Shaler's brigade. He shifted the 126th Ohio about one hundred twenty-five yards to the south with orders to fill the hole in his brigade line and to dig in. The 138th Pennsylvania retired with it.[22] The Marylanders went into line on the right of the 122nd New York, with their left flank on the crest of a deep ravine and their right extending two hundred twenty-nine feet down the slope. The 67th New York extended the line to the right into the bottom of the ravine. The 65th New York held the right of the brigade at right angles to the trenches in the swale. First Lieutenant James Brewer (Company H, 6th Maryland) noticed the New Yorkers to the left entrenching. Colonel John Horn, commanding the Marylanders, having no shovels or picks and under orders not to chop down any trees, could not adequately fortify his position. Nevertheless, his men started digging with bayonets and tin plates because any cover was better than no cover at all.[23] Private Zeno T. Griffin (Company E, 122nd New York) saw a single skirmisher from the 50 to 60 Marylanders on his immediate right lope into the woods and take cover behind a tree when a Rebel sharpshooter shot him through the body. The Marylander collapsed, writhing about in agony and screaming louder than Griffin had ever heard anyone cry. All the while the Confederates were hooting at and swearing at the Federals over the incident.[24] Being busy with a roster for picket duty, Brewer paid no particular attention to the digging until the 122nd New York, having completed its breastworks, sent a detail to him and offered to help the Mary-landers dig in. He thanked them and instructed them to loan his regiment their shovels. Rather than do that, a large number of the New Yorkers, officers and enlisted men alike, helped the Marylanders throw up an ad-equate line of works.[25]

By then a small section of woods north of Saunders Field was in flames. The 15th New Jersey abandoned its attempts to rescue the wounded of both armies, consigning their bodies to the fires, but the stench of the corpses' bloated and bursting bodies, coupled with the gut-wrenching smell of burning flesh, made the regiment's position on the end of the Federal line almost untenable. Chaplain Alanson Haines and a number of men quickly beat the fires out. Among the dead, he found the body of a young Louisiana officer, who had died sword in hand. The preacher clearly saw "C.S.A." stamped on the blade. The fire swept behind the line, blanketing everyone in a ghastly pall of smoke until it eventually burned itself out.[26]

NORTH OF FLAT RUN[27]
GORDON'S BRIGADE

Sometime between 5:00 P.M. and 5:30 P.M., with Early and his aide, Major John W. Daniel, watching the maneuver, Gordon moved his six Geor-gia regiments north across Flat Run, then he flanked them northeast along the creek bottom. Gordon was riding alongside of the 38th Georgia, the next to last regiment in his column, and was talking to the men as they marched. "38th," Fourth Sergeant Francis L. Hudgins (Company K) heard him say, "this is 6th Corps we are going to attack, the same fellows we fought at Maries [sic] Heights; those that we didn't get then, we want now."[28] One half of a mile east of the crossing, the lead regiment in his brigade halted below the line of sight of the two picket companies of the 65th New York which were spread out on the opposite side of the crest.[29] With whis-pered commands the 31st Georgia held the right of the line while the bri-gade deployed over a two thousand one hundred foot front.[30] Gordon was waiting for Johnston's 1,300-man North Carolina Brigade to come up on his left. With Johnston's men covering his left flank and rear, he intended to drive in the Federal right and rear while Hoffman's Virginians demon-strated against the Federals' front. He only hoped there would be enough daylight to execute the maneuver.[31]

6:00 P.M. TO 6:30 P.M.

Gordon's men knew what was expected of them, but none of the sup-porting regiments knew what he intended to do. His brigade skirmishers were forming along the base of the hill along Flat Run several feet in front of the regiments. At the command, they were to advance at the

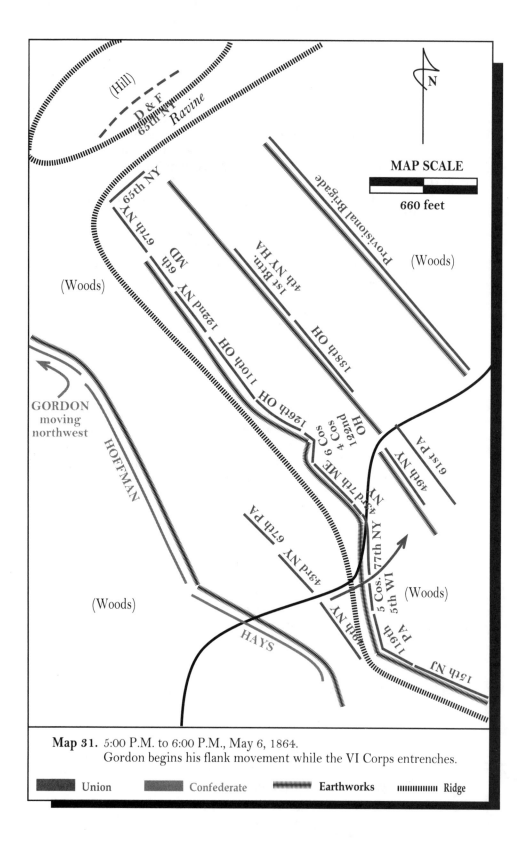

(Hill)

D & F
65th NY
Ravine

65th NY

67th NY

6th MD

1st Btn.
4th NY HA

Provisional Brigade

MAP SCALE

660 feet

(Woods)

138th OH

4th NY HA

(Woods)

122nd OH

110th OH

126th OH

122nd OH
4 Cos

GORDON
moving
northwest

49th NY

61st PA

HOFFMAN

43rd/77th ME
6 Cos

77th NY

49th NY

67th PA

43rd NY

5 Cos.
5th WI

(Woods)

49th NY

119th PA

(Woods)

HAYS

15th NJ

Map 31. 5:00 P.M. to 6:00 P.M., May 6, 1864.
Gordon begins his flank movement while the VI Corps entrenches.

| | Union | | Confederate | | Earthworks | | Ridge |

double quick (one hundred sixty-five steps per minute) up the ridge while the brigade would follow at the quick step (one hundred ten steps per minute), thereby hitting the Federals twice in rapid order. The rear line had explicit orders not to fire until they had passed over the top of the brigade's skirmishers.[32]

As the woods continued to darken, Ewell became more anxious for the attack to start. He began pulling upon his mustache with both hands. The sight of Brigadier General Robert D. Johnston and his huge North Carolina brigade doublequicking toward him immediately caught his attention. "Charge them, General," he shouted to Johnston. "Drive 'em! Charge 'em!"[33] The North Carolinians reached the left of Gordon's line very close to 6:00 P.M. Gordon tersely told Johnston to keep his brigade about fifty yards to the Georgians' left rear and to await further orders from Gordon in person. Johnston, who had no idea of the terrain, the exact position of the Yankee troops and the actual deployment of Gordon's men, quickly brought the 5th, 12th, and the 20th North Carolina into line. The 23rd North Carolina was approaching the rear of the brigade when the fighting began. With no time to think, Johnston told Lieutenant Colonel William S. Davis, commanding the 23rd, to follow the rear of the brigade.[34]

DUSK

NORTHERN END OF THE VI CORPS LINE

With the woods getting so dark, the 4th New York Heavies decided it was time to quit their engineer duties. Their breastworks topped out at two and one half feet, which seemed secure enough. Despite the loss of a few men to stray rounds during the afternoon, the majority of the officers and men felt secure enough to stack their arms, drape their belts and cartridge boxes over the muzzles, and start supper fires. Protected by what they believed were two entrenched lines to the west, they had no reason to feel insecure. The occasional casualties who staggered rearward caused no particular alarm. The company officers sporadically allowed pairs of men and individuals, carrying 10 to 12 canteens, to leave the works and wander down to a fresh water spring which someone had found to the right rear of the regiment. Before long their boiling coffee and frying salt pork was filling the evening air with their tantalizing aromas. Private William D. Robinson (Company C) smirked over the thought that the 122nd New York, on the ridge to their front, was probably drinking water and eating hard crackers and raw pork. Sergeant Major L. J. McVicker left his full haversack and canteen dangling from a dogwood sapling and strolled over the right of the line to watch Major Thomas D. Sears take on the regimental adjutant, First Lieutenant J. Kopper, in a game of euchre.[35]

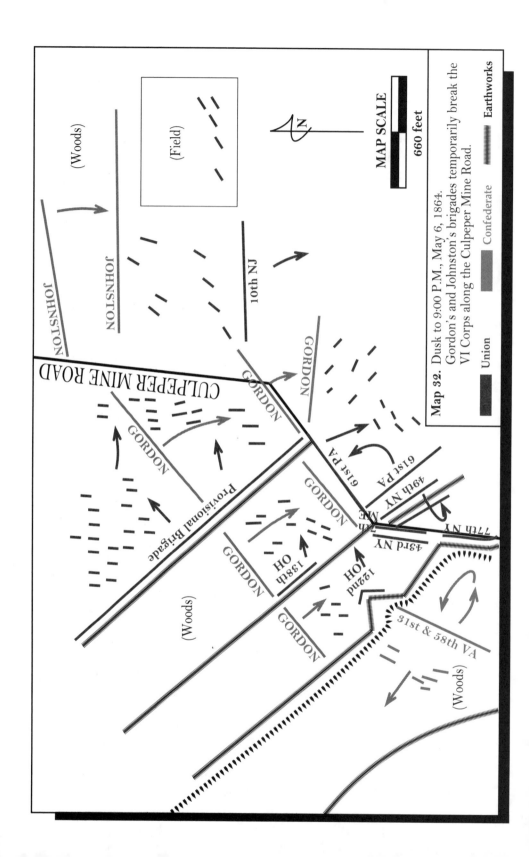

Map 32. Dusk to 9:00 P.M., May 6, 1864. Gordon's and Johnston's brigades temporarily break the VI Corps along the Culpeper Mine Road.

MAP SCALE

660 feet

Union   Confederate   Earthworks

Companies D and F of the 65th New York were relieved by Companies H and K and fell back to the regimental bivouac in the ravine behind the 67th New York.[36] From where he stood near the top of the hill north of the regiment, Private Edwin Crockett (Company K) saw two Rebels skittering through the woods. A couple of the New Yorkers chased after the men who disappeared in the encroaching darkness. The veterans on the skirmish line sensed that something was wrong. As they fell back to the ridge one of Carter's 12-pounders opened fire, the shot whizzing across the ravine behind the two companies.

Simultaneously, minie balls clipped the bark off the trees from the right front.[37] The skirmish line was on its own. The soldiers, loading on the run, darted from tree to tree, stopped in squads to loose rounds into the advancing Georgians.[38] Private Giles Chapman (Company I, 61st Georgia) pitched forward from the Confederate line—dead.[39] A solid shot ricocheted off a tree behind one of the New Yorkers and bounced back toward the Confederates before rolling lazily down into the ravine. One of the recruits from Company K, a tall fellow who stood about 6'3", bolted like a frightened deer. Private Charles Crockett (Company K), Edwin Crockett's brother, yelled at the man to resume his place but the fellow kept on running. Private Edwin Crockett watched him disappear in the woods with blood streaming from a wounded hand.[40] The 31st Georgia completely disregarded the orders not to respond. The skirmishers in front of the regiment, hearing the commands to open fire ring out behind them, hurled themselves to the forest floor seconds before the volley shredded the trees above their heads. As the smoke cleared, they screamed back at the line not to do that again. But, it was too late. Gordon's brigade was already running over the top of them.[41] Private Charles Crockett of the 65th New York limped away from the fighting, mortally wounded.[42]

The 67th New York were passing their picks and shovels across the ravine to the 65th New York when the nerve-chilling Rebel yell echoed through the woods. Colonel John W. Horn (6th Maryland), who was lying in the woods between the regiment and the picket line at the time, trying to fight of a severe headache and nausea, leaped to his feet. What was up? he asked. The sight of Confederates running through the woods behind his regiment and beyond Shaler's flank provided him with the only answer he needed.[43]

The attack caught Shaler, Seymour, and Colonel Benjamin F. Smith (126th Ohio) in the bottom land with the 65th New York. They had just lapped the reins of their horses on the branches overhead when the left wing of Gordon's brigade spilled through the woods behind them. The suddenness of the attack brought the rest of the 65th New York to its feet. The men frantically snatched up their rifles and broke toward the rear, leaving the 67th New York and the 6th Maryland unsupported. Shaler and

Smith immediately mounted up and struggled up the steep slope.[44] The 67th New York fell back toward the crest of the ravine and attempted to make a stand. The 31st and the 61st Georgia each sent a second volley into the confused Federals, cutting down squads of men in their tracks.[45] With rounds snapping the branches off around his head, Smith veered toward the 6th Maryland. Shaler galloped south, looking for troops to assist his men. At the same time Private Edwin Crockett (65th New York) was madly scrambling up the bank on all fours, trying to keep from getting killed when a passing bullet knocked his kepi down over his eyes. Clearing the top of the ravine, he vainly tried to catch up with his company.[46]

Horn, after leaving three officers behind to bring off the skirmishers' line, yelled for the 6th Maryland to retreat.[47] Captain Clifton K. Prentice (Company F) and First Lieutenants Henry J. Hawkins (Company I) and James H. C. Brewer (Company H) frantically managed to call in the skirmishers. In the midst of all the confusion, Brewer found a silver-plated fife and stuffed it into his high-topped boot while telling Prentice he would give it to the regimental fife major, Christopher Roney, when he saw him again. Rifle shots stabbed through the terrifying darkness and shells exploded and flared with hell-like fire above and around the Marylanders. In the valley below them, illuminated by the abandoned coffee fires of their own troops, they could see large blocks of a darker blackness inching along the western side of the 67th New York's abandoned works. They decided to empty their rifles at them before falling back.[48]

Company I, 31st Georgia, on the right of Gordon's brigade, found itself cut off from the rest of the regiment by the Yankee fortifications and unexpectedly walked right into the waiting rifles of Prentice's Marylanders. The first blast sent most of the Georgians diving headfirst onto the opposite side of the breastworks. Private I. Gordon Bradwell, once he recovered from the initial shock, threw himself over the works also only to have the Marylanders drop several friends of his by his side seconds after he rejoined them. While Company I veered southeast with the rest of the regiment and returned fire into the Federals, Bradwell hurled himself back onto the western side of the works. Landing in a heap behind a large oak, he decided to fight his battle from there.[49]

The Marylanders and the 67th New York were buying time with their lives. Every time they halted to fire, the Confederates wounded or killed a number of their men which forced them to yield more ground. During one such stand, the fife fell out of Brewer's boot. He stepped forward and was leaning over to pick it up when a bullet snapped off a small pine tree near his hand before passing between his legs. Prentice yelled at him, in passing to the rear, to pick up the fife, but Brewer ignored him and kept inching back with the line.[50] They eventually uncovered the rear of the 122nd New York on the southern edge of the ravine, leaving the regiment to a swarm of maddened Georgians. The fighting devolved to hand to hand. Colonel Augustus Dwight snatched an enlisted man's rifle by the barrel and, swinging it wildly from side to side, brained a Confederate sergeant with it. A Confederate plunged his bayonet into Corporal Lewis S. Loomis (Company I) as he turned to snap a round along the trench line into the milling Rebels. With their casualties escalating by the second, the New Yorkers began running for their lives south along their own works.[51]

The 110th Ohio, being the next regiment in the line, was surrounded by the stampede. Captain Samuel C. Kerr (Company B, 126th Ohio) estimated that Marylanders and the 122nd New York had bought about fifteen minutes worth of time before the Confederates would swarm around his regiment. The Ohioans attempted to execute a front to rear movement to reverse their front. Instead, the line disintegrated by companies with a domino effect as one company after the other fired, then broke to the rear for safety.[52] Unable to volley for fear of killing their own men, the 126th Ohio abandoned its position.[53] Corporal Francis Cordrey (Company E) began to retreat when he heard a wounded soldier crying piteously for help. He had two broken legs and could not escape. Cordrey dropped his weapon and in the darkness, guided by the man's voice, he darted over to his side. Hoisting the desperately injured man over his back, he ran south toward the Culpeper Mine Road.[54] The rest of Seymour's brigade shattered with the Ohioans.

A little over one hundred twenty-five yards to the east, in the hollow which paralleled the ridge, Private William D. Robinson (Company C, 4th New York Heavy Artillery) noticed the sudden increase in the numbers of wounded who were hobbling by the regiment's defenses. One of the casualties stopped near Robinson and warned the untried troops who were within earshot, "You fellows had better dig out of this; you'll get hell in a minute." He apparently caught Major Thomas D. Sears' attention, because he popped his head over the works and saw squads of wounded men fleeing past his regiment. Calling anyone who could hear to get their weapons and man the works, he told them, "Steady, boys; don't fire till you get the order." Sergeant Major L. J. McVicker was already running toward his haversack and canteen on the opposite end of the line when the first two Confederate shells burst overhead and showered branches down upon the New Yorkers. The man next to Robinson yelped and held out his hand with a finger dangling from a bloodied joint. A volley swept over the top of the works from the right as Georgians swept through the woods behind them. An officer screamed, "Men, get back!" Less than sixty feet from the works McVicker decided to let the Confederates have his goods and never looked back as he took off at a dead run.[55] Nearby, Private Edwin Crockett (Company K, 65th New York), being unable to locate any of his own regiment in the mass of retreating men, threw himself to the ground among the wounded, determined to spend the night.[56]

Of the four companies in the First Battalion, Captain G. L. Morrison's Company M stayed in the works until the last possible moment. By the time it had retreated twenty yards, the Confederates, led by an officer riding a black horse, were leaping over the headlogs. Morrison looked up and to his amazement saw Sedgwick on horseback directly in front of him. The Confederate officer snapped his pistol directly up to Sedgwick's face and ordered, "Surrender, you Yankee bastard." Private William H. Chamberlain (Company M) shot the Rebel from his horse before he had time to fire his pistol. Assistant Surgeon Clinton P. Lawrence, the battalion surgeon, swung into the horse's saddle and took off at a gallop along with the general. A low hanging tree branch knocked Morrison's cap from his head but he kept on running. A short distance away, he stooped to pick up a better cap when a shell burst right beside him. The man who was running by his side shrieked as a fragment tore his arm off and dumped him in a gory heap. Morrison left the wounded man and the several others who were killed in the blast where they were and escaped.[57]

NEILL'S BRIGADE ALONG THE CULPEPER MINE ROAD
(461 yards southeast of the ravine)

The veterans in Neill's brigade were listening apprehensively to the fighting roll toward them.[58] The 7th Maine, on the right of the 43rd New York, turned front to rear on the tenth company and left wheeled until it formed a right angle with the rest of the brigade along the Culpeper Mine Road.[59] The 43rd New York with the 77th New York on its left anchored the brigade line, facing west.[60] The Confederates were firing into the brigade from three directions, all the while demanding that the Federals surrender. The 7th Maine's Major James P. Jones, a Quaker turned warrior, yelled back, "All others may go back, but the 7th Maine never!"[61]

By the time Gordon's men had reached Neill's brigade, the woods and the darkness had completely destroyed his regimental formations. He sent word to Johnston to detach a regiment to support his right flank. Johnston sent Lieutenant Joseph F. Johnston, his assistant adjutant general, to Lieutenant Colonel William S. Davis of the 23rd North Carolina with instructions to assist Gordon.[62] To worsen matters, Hoffman's brigade, in leaving its works to support Gordon, volleyed by the oblique into the backs of the 31st and the 38th Georgia regiments as they surrounded Neill's brigade, and staggered their advance. Gordon, noticing that the two regiments had not kept pace with the center of his brigade, sent Lieutenant Thomas G. Jones over to investigate the matter. When Jones did not return fast enough for his liking, Gordon rode into the regiments. By then, the Georgians were either taking cover or breaking to the rear. He asked them why they had halted. They had taken fire from the flank and the rear the Georgians told him. At that he sent Jones into the woods to the north to get the Virginians to stop their shooting.[63]

Colonel Clement A. Evans (31st Georgia) realized that friendly rounds were pelting the Confederate lines also. Glancing to the west, across the captured Federal works, he saw a solitary muzzle flash stab the darkness. Leaping over the works, he ran over to the man's side. It was Private I. Gordon Bradwell (Company I, 31st Georgia). "Do not fire in that direction," Evans gasped. Those were their own men over there. "Move forward," the colonel commanded.

Staying clear of the Federals' muzzle flashes which were sweeping north along the works, Bradwell worked himself south into the woods. "They were wasting a great deal of ammunition at this time," he recollected, "while the whole force of Confederates was sweeping onward in their rear." After traveling what seemed like a tremendous distance, he spied a small Rebel in a gray uniform taking pot shots at the Federals from behind a tree. Bradwell asked him to what command he belonged. "Hays' Louisiana Brigade," the fellow drawled. Bradwell told him not to shoot to the east because those were Rebels up on the ridge and he might shoot his own men. "They are Federals," the man indignantly replied. Bradwell said he was going to find out for himself and took off at a trot toward the top of the hill with the other man right behind.

Climbing onto the headlogs of the works, they found themselves staring into a huddled, confused mass of men. The two stepped into the mob unobserved and milled around with them until it dawned upon Bradwell that the uniforms were not Confederate and that the men they were with did not speak with Southern dialects. With his friend close by his side, Bradwell whispered the obvious, "They are Federals. Let us run out." With men dropping sporadically around them from incoming rifle fire, they elbowed their way north along the works. Free of the mob, the two Indian-rushed over the next hundred yards until they encountered the 23rd North Carolina who were lying on the ground ready to go to Gordon's assistance. The Tar Heels let the two men pass through their ranks and to safety.[64]

One hundred yards east of Neill's main line, the 49th New York and the 61st Pennsylvania (25 paces to the rear) braced themselves for the inevitable. Private Christopher Funke (Company B, 49th New York) crouched down behind a head log and laid a handful of cartridges on the flat side of another log so he could load more quickly. As the firing drew closer from the west, he snapped off a round over the heads of the line in front and an officer scolded him for firing without orders.

To the northwest, the 122nd Ohio, having come under fire from the front, right flank, rear bolted toward the southeast across Neill's front, heading for his right flank.[65] Alarmed by the tremendous surge of Union troops around his position, Colonel George F. Smith (61st Pennsylvania) called his regiment to its feet and sent it at the double quick by files to the right across their line of retreat. "Shoot them, bayonet them, stop them any way you can," he pleaded. It was no use. The overwhelming numbers of Federal troops who were funneling through the right of the brigade carried away over two thirds of the regiment, including Smith.[66] Twenty-one-year-old Major William Ellis (49th New York) quickly dashed into the frightened ranks of the 250 Pennsylvanians who had remained upon the field with their regimental and state colors and pushed them into a southeasterly running line, diagonal to the 49th New York's right flank.[67]

The attack spread east into the New Jersey Brigade and south toward the right flank of Morris' brigade.[68] It caught the 2nd New Jersey at its coffee fires. The veterans leaped to their feet and fell in across the paths of the retreating soldiers. "Back! Back! You cowards," the Jerseymen shouted at the refugees who were breaking through their ranks. Captain Garrett Brady (Company C) drew his sword and vainly tried slapping frightened soldiers back into the ranks.[69] Sedgwick dismounted, sword in one hand, stood on a log near the Culpeper Mine Road, and screamed, "For God's sake, hold it." First Lieutenant James H. C. Brewer (Company H, 6th Maryland) saw a dejected enlisted man run by the general's side. The general, while swinging his sword over the man's head, cried at him to stop running or he would cut his damned head off. Brewer stepped over to Sedgwick and tried to stem the flow of retreating men. After telling Sedgwick of Seymour's and (erroneously) Shaler's capture, the two retreated.[70] Lieutenant Colonel Charles Wiebecke (2nd New Jersey) was furious. "Second New Jersey," he stormed, "charge bayonets on the cowards!" Having no choice but to let the throng pass to the rear, the Jerseymen waited until their front was cleared when they discovered that the Rebels had apparently disappeared along their front and had swept away the entire right flank of the brigade.[71] Wiebecke ordered the line to fall back but First Lieutenant August Linder and a number of his men from Company E refused to do so without having a "crack" at the Rebs. The handful of stalwarts loosed a few rounds, then retreated into the mob which was heading toward Morris' reforming front.[72]

Colonel Henry O. Ryerson, after watching the Rebels overpower almost an entire company, managed to rally his 10th New Jersey a short distance south of the Culpeper Mine Road near an abandoned farm. He made his men lie down. A sudden burst of musketry pocked up the line along his front and a few of the soldiers jumped to their feet to run. The colonel rose to one knee, shouting for them to return when a minie ball bored through the cloth bugle on the front of his cap and fractured his skull. Captain William H. Snowden (Company D, 10th New Jersey) and Captain Cooke (assistant adjutant general to the brigade) had him carried toward the cabin in the abandoned field.[73]

Many Union soldiers like Private John H. Maguire (Company C, 4th New York Heavy Artillery) were being swept away by the sheer numbers of demoralized soldiers who were stampeding toward the Germanna Plank Road. Some six hundred twenty-five yards east of the regiment's works, he found hundreds of men aimlessly milling about like cattle around the Culpeper Mine Road. Maguire started running north on the wagon trace when a Confederate shell screamed over his head and plowed through the tangle of soldiers in front of him. The sight of body parts and blood splattering in all directions sent him springing off the side of the road where he cleared a six-foot-high thicket without any trouble and kept on running east. He passed a collection point for discarded weapons. They were lying in an orderly stack, one beside the other. About three hundred fourteen yards into the jungle, he came to the abandoned farm yard east of the New Jersey Brigade. The surgeons had already set up a field hospital around the log cabin in the center of the field. A corporal, standing in the trail which ran into the place from the road, was yelling at a startled group of officers to halt and move forward, and, to Maguire's surprise, they obeyed him.

A short distance into the woods Private Phil Fitzsimmons was leading the pack mule for the officers' mess of Company C. With bullets going by its ears, the stubborn animal, laden with camp chairs, tin pans, and kettles, decided to plant itself and move no farther. No amount of beating, pounding, tugging or swearing could get the mule to get off its haunches. Disgusted, the cook let go of the reins at which point the mule bolted away into the night.

JOHNSTON'S BRIGADE

Unable to see fifty yards and guided only by the sounds of the fighting, Johnston led his North Carolinians across the Culpeper Mine Road beyond Sedgwick's right flank. By then, the 23rd North Carolina had returned to the brigade. The North Carolinians went into line along the northern side of the field and swept the area with a volley about the same time that the Federals swarmed into it. Sedgwick, hatless, sword in hand, accompanied by his staff officers, Lieutenant Colonel Thomas Hyde (7th Maine), and Captains Hayden and Arthur McClellan, galloped into the confused mass. Tears streamed down his face into his beard. He screamed, "Halt! For God's sake, boys, rally! Don't disgrace yourselves and your general in this way!" Seeing a young soldier with an artillery guidon nearby, he yelled at him, "Come here, my boy!" The color bearer, with Sergeant Reed L. Brown, Privates William H. Boughton, and George L. Sanders (Company M, 4th New York Heavy Artillery) and several other men advanced about thirty feet to the general's side. Snatching the guidon from the color bearer's hands, Sedgwick jabbed it in the ground. "For God's sake, your country's sake, and my sake," he pleaded, "give them a volley! They will run!" A second burst of Rebel rifle fire flashed across the open ground. They killed one man and wounded the boy and Sedgwick's horse. Boughton and his comrades snapped a few rounds into the shadows and swore they saw a couple of the Confederates hit the ground. The general, while motioning with his sword toward the woods along the northern edge of the field, shouted at his three officers to rally the men behind the field hospital. Muttering, "The damned devils," he raced toward the Culpeper Mine Road.

Hyde, Hayden, and McClellan pushed their horses into the mob behind the log cabin. When the men within earshot heard one of them shout that it was inhuman to abandon the wounded in the cabin to the Rebels, they began falling into formation in the woodline to the south. At the command, the makeshift organization bolted toward the shack only to discover that it was empty. Rather than stay in the open, the line ran toward the low worm fence which crossed the field to the north and opened fire. Brigadier General Alexander Shaler charged into their line and ordered them to halt. Seconds later, a Confederate volley spat smoke and flame from the woods in front of them. On the right of the line, Second Lieutenant James Walker (Company C, 4th New York Heavy Artillery) keeled over—dead. Hayden, who was on foot, collapsed with a bullet through both legs. McClellan went down under a dead horse and the Federal line disintegrated, streaming into the woods to the west and the south. With no one to stand by him, Shaler spurred his horse into the woods, making for the Culpeper Mine Road. Hyde threw himself over his horse's neck, Indian fashion, and escaped in the same direction, determined to find his regiment and his general.[74] The North Carolinians closed in on the farm, capturing about 60 Federals in the surrounding field. They also captured Ryerson (10th New Jersey) and the two captains who had just carried him into the cabin. The Confederate brigade continued pushing south toward the Orange Turnpike, unaware that it had completely turned the VI Corps' right flank.[75]

Farther to the west Major William Ellis, having rallied the 61st Pennsylvania, was reporting back to the 49th New York, when Shaler rode into the Pennsylvanians along the road from the east. Hatless, disheveled, and somewhat frantic, he screamed at them, "For God's sake, men, make a stand on this road; if you think anything of the Army of the Potomac make a stand on this road; if you think anything of your country, for God's sake, make a stand on this road." As he drew nearer, he acted as if he recognized the state colors. "What regiment is this?" he gasped. A number of the men shouted the number at him. "The 61st Pennsylvania," he exclaimed, "why, sergeant, advance with those colors and, Pennsylvanians, don't you desert them." By then the Pennsylvanians noticed the Georgians, who appeared as a solid mass of black floating through the woods, advancing upon them at the doublequick. The regiment stepped forward, halted, and delivered a well aimed volley into them at close range.[76]

The Confederates, many of whom were mixed in with the Federals, were fighting blind like their Union opponents, responding to muzzle blasts in the darkness. While the 61st Pennsylvania stalled part of Gordon's line, his right and left wings became involved in fire fights of their own. The left wing was surging south, beyond the Pennsylvanians' right flank, firing into the Federals as they passed. Second Lieutenant Isaac N. Price (Company A, 61st Pennsylvania), mistaking the troops for Union men, sent Private Frank L. Blair (Company F) and another man to order them to cease fire. Blair did not realize the trouble they were in until the Rebels captured them and shot down the other man after he had surrendered. In the darkness and the chaos, Shaler also rode into their ranks, thinking they were Federals, and was captured. The Confederates forced the humiliated general to dismount and turned his horse over to Gordon, who rode the stallion throughout the rest of the engagement.[77]

Brigadier General Alexander Shaler, U.S.A.

During the chaos of Gordon's flank attack, Shaler accidentally rode into the Confederates and was captured.

Massachusetts Commandery; MOLLUS, USAMHI

Under fire from three directions, Colonel Daniel D. Bidwell (49th New York) ordered his men to leap to the reverse side of their breastworks and return fire. Within minutes, Sedgwick bolted into their ranks and ordered Bidwell to clear a passage through the woods toward the Germanna Plank Road and the VI Corps' right flank. With a cheer, Ellis took Companies B and D over the works into the woods, followed closely by the rest of the regiment.[78] First Lieutenant Charles E. Stevens' orderly sergeant from Company A, 77th New York, took a ball in the body and staggered back to Sedgwick, whom he found standing with an aide in the Culpeper Mine Road. "General," the sergeant said, "I am wounded. Where is the rear?" "Stay right where you are," Sedgwick told him. "I haven't any rear now, but will soon have one."[79]

While the 49th New York was scouring the woods to the west of the third line of works, Private Augustus Wentz (Company A, 14th New York Heavy Artillery) was standing thirty yards behind the line talking with the provost guard who were to keep the three green regiments in Marshall's brigade from running. A prolonged Rebel yell rent through the woods about four hundred yards to the northwest, followed by a staccato of small arms fire from the southwest. The 24th New York Cavalry, without warning, sprang to their feet, snatched their weapons as they ran, and disappeared into the woods to the east. A volley roared from the 14th New York Heavy Artillery before Wentz had time to react and continued to the right of the brigade. The officers shouted at the men, "Stop firing; you are firing into your own people!" Seconds before he reached the works, Wentz saw one of their excited men shoot Private William McFadden (Company A) in the back, killing him instantly. Several others were crippled.[80] One of their rounds which missed the skirmishers struck down Private Christopher Funke of the 49th New York. The bullet, in skirting around the bone in his upper arm and exiting, temporarily paralyzed his left arm and hand. At the same time, Second Lieutenant Julius C. Borcherdt (Company B) got lost in the darkness and was captured by a squad of Confederates who were closing in on the regiment's left flank.

THE WOODS BETWEEN THE LINES
HOFFMAN'S BRIGADE

Colonel John S. Hoffman had attempted to back up Gordon's assault but lost control of his brigade as soon as it left its works. By some fluke, the regiments received orders to advance in two different directions. The left wing was told to guide left and the right wing was told to guide right. In the woods at dusk it would have been very difficult for an ordinary officer to get the brigade properly realigned, Private William W. Smith (Company C, 49th Virginia) observed. But, he concluded, Hoffman was "a very ordinary commander" and therefore completely useless in this particular situation.

Early's assistant adjutant general, Major John W. Daniel, with his pistol drawn, pushed his way into the 58th Virginia near the left of the brigade line. Holstering his weapon, he snatched the colors from the color bearer of the regiment and called out, "Follow me, boys." The Virginians filled the woods with the Rebel yell and struggled after the gallant Daniel.[81]

It took Lieutenant Thomas G. Jones about twenty minutes to find Hoffman floundering in the mud behind the 13th Virginia. He told him to stop his people from shooting into their own ranks, then rode away, expecting the colonel to comply.[82] Hoffman could only control the soldiers he could find but he had no control whatsoever over the 31st and the 58th Virginia. About the time that Jones started back toward Gordon, they were stumbling up hill toward the 77th and the 43rd New York. The Yankee skirmishers darted through the woods in front of the Virginians, Private Jacob Heater (Company D, 31st Virginia) recollected, when a voice not thirty paces away rang out, "Boys, here we are." The Federals stood up behind their works and volleyed. A round struck Daniel in the right thigh and threw him from the saddle. The 31st Virginia shattered and streamed rearward. Second Sergeant Benjamin K. Milam (Company C, 58th Virginia) dropped his musket and snatched the young major by the coat as he fell. Bending over Daniel, he asked if he were dead. No, Daniel gasped, but he was very badly hurt. A stretcher party wasted no time in evacuating him. Judging by the tremendous amount of blood gushing from Daniel's thigh, Milam gave him up for dead. So did Jones, who saw him being carried off. The regiment broke seconds later and headed back toward its works.[83]

The right of the brigade was still struggling through the swampy low ground, unaware of the predicament of its left flank. Every few feet into the knee deep water and mud Captain James Bumgardner, Jr. (Company F, 52nd Virginia) was hearing contradictory commands. "Conflicting orders were repeatedly given, one order was to dress and close to the right, the other order was to dress and close to the left. I heard both orders several times while forcing my way through the swamp," he later wrote.[84] The 13th, 52nd, and 49th Virginia regiments continued to flounder south and southeast.

VI CORPS' POSITION
SOUTH OF THE CULPEPER MINE ROAD

To the southeast, Colonel Emory Upton dispatched the 121st New York and the 95th Pennsylvania by the rear rank into the woods. They proceeded but a short distance before the terrain and the darkness completely destroyed their formations. Upton immediately ordered their recall but managed in retrieving about half of both regiments. A disoriented portion of the Pennsylvanians scared away Lieutenant Julius Borcherdt's captors and rescued him before withdrawing from the fight.[85]

Three hundred yards to the south Captain Richard F. Halsted, aide de camp to Sedgwick, was already pulling the 10th Vermont, 14th New Jersey, and the 106th New York from Morris' right flank to move at right angles across the Confederates' path. Upton threw the remnants of the 95th Pennsylvania and the 121st New York on his right flank and awaited an attack which never developed, Gordon's attack having spent itself. Upton sent two companies of the 95th Pennsylvania to the left to ascertain the condition of the works and Lieutenant Colonel Egbert Olcott (121st New York) rode between the lines to scout the front for himself. A Confederate musket ball struck him in the forehead, knocking him unconscious from the saddle. Corporal Frederick Brice (Company D), seeing him fall, ran into the woods to bring him in when a Confederate infantryman shot him. A Confederate officer demanded Brice surrender his boots. He refused, saying they were from home. A soldier settled the argument by splitting Brice's head open with his rifle barrel. They carried the unconscious Yankee into the woods and left him with one guard.[86]

Colonel Egbert Olcott, 121st New York

As Gordon's attack was dying out in the darkness, Olcott rode between the lines on a private reconnaissance. He was shot in the head and killed.

Massachusetts Commandery; MOLLUS, USAMHI

By 9:00 P.M., the Confederate attack having died with the distance it had covered and the night, the VI Corps began reconsolidating its line. The 61st Pennsylvania occupied the position in front of the trenches formerly held by the 77th New York and the 43rd New York. The 43rd New York stood in the Culpeper Mine Road, facing north with the remnants of the 122nd New York, the 7th Maine, the 77th and the 49th New York finishing the formation to the east.[87] The rest of the corps remained in their respective positions while Johnston's North Carolinians were groping around in the dark behind them. Wheaton's and Eustis' brigades were moving north from the Brock Road intersection toward the Germanna Plank-Orange Turnpike intersection.[88]

Sedgwick was already at the crossroads rounding up artillery support to assist his right flank along the Germanna Plank Road. First Lieutenant Ezra K. Parker's (Company E, 1st Rhode Island Artillery), whose guns were in park near the road when Sedgwick found him, was asked to quickly send a section north to the point where the trail paralleling Caton Run intersected the main road. The lieutenant sent the two guns at a gallop to the crossroads. Shotting the guns with canister, he pointed one north along the main road and the other east along the trail. He told his sergeants to move out along both approaches, halt anyone who was coming in, and force them to rally. Sedgwick bounded into the briar-choked brush next to the guns, trying to get men to reform. He soon came out of the thicket with his thick beaver uniform torn. A number of the soldiers quipped that "Uncle John," as he was known in the VI Corps, would rather face the Rebs than the briars.[89] The 4th New York Heavy Artillery did not stop running on the trail which passed the cabin until they reached the Germanna Plank Road—one mile to the east along Caton Run. The whippoorwills mocked the men with their mournful calls. "Fight you will! Fight you will!" Private William H. Boughton (Company M) heard them sing. Nearby a man in Company C thought he heard someone quip,

"Leap to the rear!" Sedgwick and Parker's two guns were there waiting on them. Sedgwick rode up to Sergeant Asa G. Clark (Company C) and told him to round up as many men as he could find and form a guard in front of the guns. He ordered them to fix bayonets and stop everyone coming into the area. The sergeant and his twelve men amazed Parker. He and Corporal George S. Farwell (Company C) stopped everybody, including officers, and forced them to fall in on regimental front.[90]

IN THE RAVINE
(653 yards north of Neill's brigade)

Private I. Gordon Bradwell (Company I, 31st Georgia) returned to the site of the brigade's initial victory. He found a few of his company gathered around a fire talking with Seymour and Shaler. Private George W. Nichols (Company D, 61st Georgia) was there also. He described Seymour as a tall man who stood about 6'6" and weighed about 150 pounds. Shaler "was a regular cut-short Dutchman about five feet high," and would have weighed about 250 pounds. Seymour was most affable to the Georgians. He told them that the war would be over in short order and that the South would be back in the Union. He was a registered Democrat and his uncle was the current governor of New York. The Confederates liked him immensely. Shaler would not speak to the enlisted man at all. He appeared sullen and moody to Bradwell, who would have stayed longer, but Colonel Clement A. Evans rode up to the group and told him to reform the entire brigade and advance it to the front. The private groused under his breath that he did not see how he was going to do that when he had gotten separated from the command so early in the fight. The fellow next to him agreed to guide him to the men.[91]

IN THE WOODS WEST OF THE VI CORPS' WORKS

Brigadier General John B. Gordon was watching his daring flanking assault dissolve into fitful firefights before his eyes. Frustrated beyond words, his emotions at a fever pitch, he and his courier, William Beasley, leaped their horses over the abandoned Federal works on their right flank and rode into the valley between the lines, looking for Colonel John S. Hoffman and his Virginia brigade. They found the 13th, 49th, and 52nd Virginia in the low swampy ground farther north than their intended line of approach, south of the Culpeper Mine Road.[92] Despite the darkness, Private George Q. Peyton (Company A) recognized Gordon as he rode into the regiment. Hat in hand, with tears coursing down his cheeks into his beard, Gordon begged the Virginians to follow him and recapture the Federals' works.[93] The three regiments staggered forward in terrible disorder. Somewhere in the darkness they lost track of Gordon and Beasley, who had ridden off to another part of the line.[94]

NEILL'S BRIGADE

Private John H. Maguire (Company C, 4th New York Heavy Artillery) was wandering aimlessly through the woods hoping that something would happen to give him an idea of where he was. "Halt! Who goes there?" He froze in place, afraid to answer the challenge from the sentry, whom he could not see. He heard the hammer of a rifle go back to full cock followed by, "Damn you, speak, or I'll put a hole through you." "Friend," Maguire stuttered. A tremendous relief surged over him once he discovered he was among Union men.

Neill's men were not talking. They had no fires lit to expose their position. Around 10:00 P.M. they were listening to the Confederates approaching their position through the woods on the left. The sounds of crunching brush and snapped branches indicated that the Rebels were lost and trying to find the Federal position.[95] Colonel George F. Smith (61st Pennsylvania) made his men lie down and told them to hold their fire.[96]

HOFFMAN'S BRIGADE

Gordon and Beasley, having moved around to the northern side of Neill's line, rode into a cluster of men, who the general believed were Virginians. He could not believe their lax discipline and was going to reprimand them when Beasley leaned over and whispered, "General, these are not our men; they are Federals." "Nonsense," the general shot back as he spurred farther into the milling crowd. Beasley grabbed Gordon's arm and insisted, "I tell you, General, these men are Federals, and we had better get away from here." The courier told the general to see in the starlight how their dark uniforms contrasted with their own. Gordon was beginning to turn his horse around when the Federal officers started shouting for the men to reorganize by regiments. An officer on foot, with his sword drawn, approached the two and politely asked them to identify the brigade to which they belonged. Rather than reply in their deep Georgia accents, they continued to ride away.

"Halt those men!" the Yankee called out. Not waiting to be captured, Gordon threw himself on the right side of his horse, Indian fashion, and yelled, "Follow me, Beasley!" Spurring their horses into a gallop, they knocked a handful of Federals down and disappeared into the woods.[97]

While Gordon and Beasley were escaping to the north, Hoffman's disjointed regiments blindly floundered through the woods. The 49th Virginia was in front, followed by the 52nd Virginia, then the 13th Virginia. None of them were visible to one another. None of the regiments were in an organized formation. They had fragmented into squads. Company D, 49th Virginia, emerged from the swamp in the bottom land and started up the slight hill in their front without saying a word. Only the tramp of their feet on the

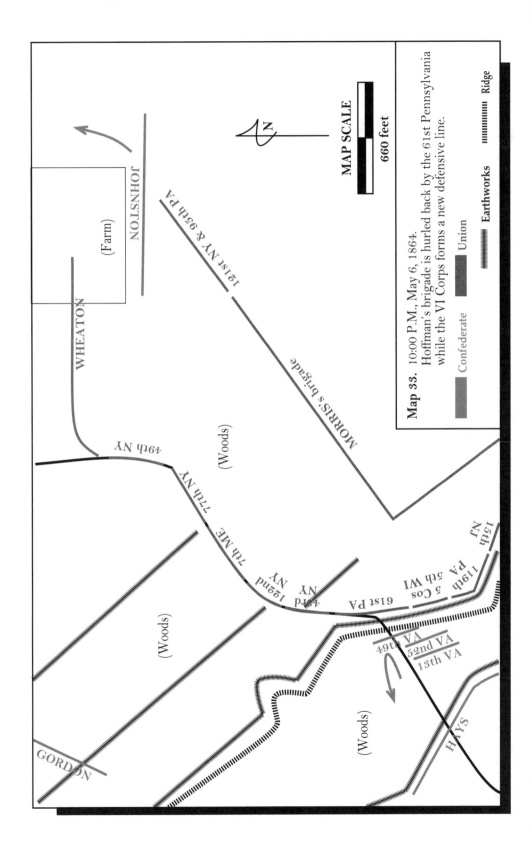

Map 33. 10:00 P.M., May 6, 1864. Hoffman's brigade is hurled back by the 61st Pennsylvania while the VI Corps forms a new defensive line.

MAP SCALE

660 feet

Confederate

Union

Earthworks

Ridge

JOHNSTON

(Farm)

WHEATON

121st NY & 95th PA

MORRIS's brigade

N

49th NY

77th ME

7th ME

122nd NY

43rd NY

5th WI

61st PA

5 Cos

119th PA

15th NJ

49th VA

52nd VA

13th VA

HAYS

GORDON

(Woods)

(Woods)

(Woods)

(Woods)

forest floor seemed to make any sound. First Lieutenant Robert D. Funkhouser, with Sergeant William Leach by his side, believed they saw a line of men lying down in the woods a short distance to their front. Believing them to be their own troops, they made straight for them.[98] The 61st Pennsylvania allowed the Confederates to close to within ten feet before Colonel George F. Smith shouted, "Fire!" The Pennsylvanians rose as a man and volleyed point blank into Company D. Funkhouser caught a muzzle blast alongside the head which nearly knocked his eye out. He and the entire front line went down in a heap. Before he could recover, the Federals were running over the top of them, rushing toward the lower ground.[99]

The reports of the volley from the south sent Private I. Gordon Bradwell (Company I, 31st Georgia) and his 200 men from Gordon's Georgia brigade to the ground. They had advanced as far as they were going to go.[100] Private William W. Smith's section of men from Company C, 49th Virginia, a short distance northwest of the Pennsylvanians, believing there could not be more than a dozen Federals in that area, returned fire. In the meantime, the 13th Virginia loosed rounds into the backs of the 52nd Virginia and wounded a couple of men. Rather than continue forward, those Virginians ignored their officers' commands and turned back toward the swamp. The 13th Virginia, guided by the muzzle flashes in the dark, slowly maneuvered into line and silently started forward toward the prone Company D.

The Pennsylvanians fell back over the wounded and stunned Virginians to their works and waited for the expected charge. Twenty minutes later, they heard the sounds of a larger body of men moving toward them through the woods. Hoffman rode his horse right up to the works and asked "What regiment is this?" "The 61st Pennsylvania," came the reply. The Federals called at him to give up as he attempted to wheel the horse about. "I didn't volunteer to surrender," he shouted back. They cut down his horse in a flurry of riflery. The colonel leaped out of the saddle, and ran for cover while the 13th Virginia gave a Rebel yell and charged into the works. The Pennsylvanians retreated a short distance, rallied, and fired again into the headlogs. By then, the Federal troops on both flanks were pouring an enfilade into the Virginians. Company A, 13th Virginia, lost three men in quick order. Private Christian J. Miller was mortally wounded. Private Oliver Towles Terrill received a broken leg and David C. Mallory had a little finger shot off. The Rebels deserted the line as quickly as they had occupied it. Behind them, with their officers calling out, "Don't fire; it's Gordon's men," the squad from Company C of the 49th Virginia dove for cover behind a log, hoping to wait out the battle.[101] There were no major engagements after that flare up at 10:20 P.M. Both sides had pretty well fought themselves out. All that remained was for the routed troops to get themselves organized and for the prisoner detachments to bring in their captives.

DESERTED FIELD NEAR THE CULPEPER MINE ROAD

Lieutenant Colonels Thomas W. Hyde (7th Maine) and Jacob F. Kent, of Sedgwick's staff, were trooping the new corps line along Caton Run, posting sentries and reorganizing troops.[102] Wheaton's and Eustis' brigades were moving into the gap on Neill's right flank by the time First Lieutenant James H. C. Brewer (Company H, 6th Maryland) wandered into the abandoned field which the North Carolinians had cleared not too long before. Colonel John W. Horn, noticing him approach in the darkness, yelled at him to make a stand. Brewer turned about in the field and saw a color sergeant, with his colors unfurled, standing not too far away. The lieutenant dashed over to the soldier and, recognizing the flag as that of the 102nd Pennsylvania, grabbed for the staff, but the colorbearer pulled them back and curtly asked him what he wanted. To make a stand around the colors, Brewer replied, at which the sergeant jammed the staff in the ground and exclaimed, "By God! I'll rally with you." Within minutes, several hundred stragglers were assembling around the two men, and a forward movement was ordered.[103]

Not too far south of the field, Brigadier General Robert Johnston was listening to the severe rifle fire emanating from the woods behind him. He decided to pull his brigade back to the ravine. As he neared the Culpeper Mine Road, he heard officers shouting commands and could see what appeared to be a large body of troops moving into line across his front. Riding up to the column, Johnston asked them to identify themselves. The response—139th Pennsylvania, First Brigade, Second Division, VI Corps—took him aback. Returning as quietly as he could to his North Carolinians, he redirected the column farther east and marched around Wheaton's flank, undetected.[104]

Private F. L. Blair (Company F, 61st Pennsylvania) was being escorted to the rear by three very young Confederates when they crossed the path of First Lieutenant August Linder (Company E, 2nd New Jersey) and his Rebel prisoner. The lieutenant's prisoner, catching sight of Blair and his captors called out, "Say, boys, this Yank wants to take me prisoner, but I'll be damned if I go." To Blair's utter amazement, Linder threw his pistol and sword to the ground and surrendered. Dejected, they headed toward the Confederate lines.[105] The woods belonged to the dead, the wounded, and the looters.[106] Having been robbed of his hat, boots, and coat, Corporal Frederick Brice (Company D, 121st New York) decided to die game. While walking in a single file behind one guard and two other prisoners, he abruptly struck the guard behind him and ran into the brush.[107]

Brigadier General Robert D. Johnston and his men, with nominal losses, returned to the ravine along Flat Run glad to have gotten away with their lives. At the same time he was bitterly disappointed. In his official report of the action he noted:

"General Gordon did not have time to give me the necessary information in regard to the movement and the character of the ground. If proper information had been given me I could have accomplished a great deal more and believe that the result of the action would have been far greater and more disastrous to the enemy."[108]

The two Confederate brigades had torn a tremendous hole almost half a mile wide and half a mile deep in the Northern right flank. They scattered and demoralized 17 regiments, forced Meade to send 9 battle-wearied regiments on a four-mile countermarch to reinforce one of the finest corps in the army, captured 600 men, including two generals, and inflicted a large number of casualties. Neill's, Shaler's, and Seymour's brigades lost heavily in officers. Shaler counted 7 dead, 27 wounded, and 15 missing among his regimental officers. In the two days of fighting, the two other brigades tallied 14 officers dead, 47 wounded, and 10 missing.[109] Despite Gordon's later unproved assertions that Ewell at Early's behest had delayed the attack so long that Lee had to personally intervene, he had inflicted a tremendous amount of damage upon the VI Corps under conditions which would have made almost any officer, but John Brown Gordon, flinch.

CHAPTER EIGHT

"I'd never believe that [the Federals] had such men as that in their army."

MAY 7, 1864 – MIDNIGHT TO DAWN

THE DISPOSITION OF THE OPPOSING ARMIES

The fighting of the previous two days had left both armies battered and disorganized with the Northerners being more disoriented and unsettled than the Confederates. Gordon's flanking attack had virtually uprooted the VI Corps from the Culpeper Mine Road. Sedgwick peeled back Morris', Upton's, and Russell's brigades shortly after midnight and sent them south to the Orange Turnpike. Morris' men stayed behind while the rest of the troops marched east to the Germanna Plank Road, where they turned north for another one thousand one hundred thirty-two yards. They began entrenching along a seven hundred fifty-four yard front northeast of the road.

Neill's brigade, on the left of the corps, went into position on the south side of Caton's Run, facing north, nine hundred forty-three yards east of Saunders Field. Morris' brigade connected with the brigade's left flank, facing west at right angles to the line. Eustis and Wheaton put their brigades in on Neill's right.[1] The V Corps occupied the works which it had constructed on May 5 in a line that stretched one and one third miles to the south. The IX Corps abandoned its position north of Tapp's and had withdrawn to an east to west line six hundred sixty yards north of and parallel to the Plank Road. The II Corps, with Grant's detached VI Corps brigade, occupied the Brock Road line from the Germanna Plank Road to Trigg's—a three and two tenths mile front.

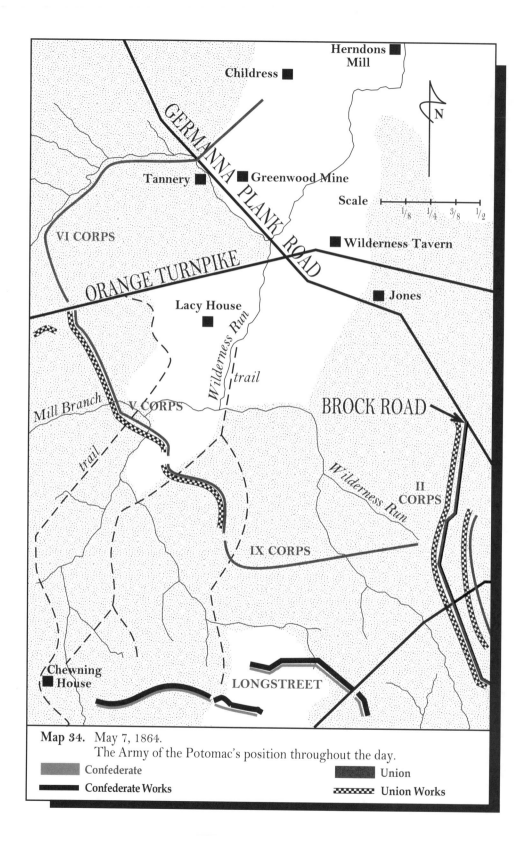

Herndons
Mill

Childress

GERMANNA PLANK ROAD

Tannery   Greenwood Mine

N

Scale   1/8   1/4   3/8   1/2

VI CORPS

Wilderness Tavern

ORANGE TURNPIKE

Jones

Lacy House

Wilderness Run

trail

Mill Branch   V CORPS

BROCK ROAD

trail

Wilderness Run

II CORPS

IX CORPS

Chewning
House

LONGSTREET

Map 34. May 7, 1864.
The Army of the Potomac's position throughout the day.

Confederate   Union

Confederate Works   ▨▨▨▨ Union Works

Lee's line had not changed since the afternoon of May 5, with the exception of Gordon's and Johnston's brigades which occupied the ravine on the north end of the former VI Corps line. Ewell's Corps stretched from the woods north of Saunders Field south to Higgerson's. A. P. Hill's battered corps continued the line from Higgerson's to the Plank Road and Longstreet's men finished the line to the south along Poplar Run. The two days of tenacious fighting had cost Lee over 8,500 casualties and Grant over 17,300 officers and men.[2] Neither side had gained anything and had seemingly fought each other to a standstill.

5:30 A.M.

THE ORANGE TURNPIKE
(943 yards east of Saunders Field)

Shortly after dawn Confederate skirmishers pushed into the woods south and east of Saunders Field to "feel out" the V Corps' positions south of the Orange Turnpike. North of the road, they encountered the 87th Pennsylvania and 100 men from 151st New York.[3] South of the road, they ran into pickets from the 22nd Massachusetts. The Federal officers wisely instructed their men to retire to draw the Rebels into their new line of works across the road.[4]

Brigadier General William H. Morris' brigade, Colonel J. Howard Kitching's 6th and 15th New York Heavies and Colonel Jacob Sweitzer's brigade were waiting for them behind a newly constructed line of works nine hundred forty-three yards east of Saunders Field. They had no less than 12 field pieces, loaded with double canister, run into the works.[5] Rifle fire pattered the head logs long before the Confederates reached the slashings in front of the waiting troops.

In the clearing on the north side of the road, a lone sentry from the 10th Vermont stepped out from behind the large tree near the middle of the field into the path of a Confederate rifle ball. He died instantly. Lieutenant Colonel William W. Henry asked his men, "Who will volunteer to go and take that man's place?" A terrible silence fell over the regiment. A few moments later, a private from Company A quietly stepped forward. He was a devout Christian, whom many of the men ridiculed because he prayed aloud and often. Rifle in hand, he crawled over the works and walked in silence into the open ground. Halfway between the regiment and the tree, he kneeled in the grass, laid his weapon down, lifted his eyes to the sky and prayed loud and earnestly. No one remembered what he said but to Captain George E. Davis (Company D) it seemed like the Rebels had ceased fire. His prayer finished, the soldier walked up to the tree and spent the day there, unscathed.[6]

The Confederate push swerved south of the road, away from the open ground and ran pell-mell into the waiting Federal guns. According to Private Robert G. Carter (Company H, 22nd Massachusetts), the gunners "cut them [the Confederates] down like grass." Captain Edwin C. Bennett (Company C, 22nd Massachusetts) summarized the forlorn hope with an officer's more clinical eye when he wrote, "An attack...was repulsed, with heavy loss inflicted by our artillery, for which a good position had been found for the first time in this campaign."[7]

HOFFMAN'S BRIGADE

The Federals continued shelling the woods north of the road. A number of the rounds fell among the sleeping soldiers of Colonel John S. Hoffman's Virginia brigade. The concussions from the exploding shells brought Private George Peyton (Company A, 13th Virginia) to his feet with a start. It seemed as if the entire VI Corps had crept up to the works and were firing point blank in their faces. Leaping to his feet, he took off at a run with the men around him and would have kept on going had not Colonel James B. Terrill, brandishing his huge cavalry saber, "persuaded" him to return to the line. Peyton wedged his way in between Private Wesley C. "Old Man" Carter (Company H) and Private Waller L. Holladay (Company A). A bullet, fired from behind, smashed into the lockplate of Carter's rifle, destroying it. In a fit of rage, he left the line to scrounge up a discarded weapon. The firing ceased by the time he returned.[8]

Hoffman immediately sent his brigade into the charred woods between the opposing lines. "I imagined I could see bayonets and caps and almost clouds of smoke along the line," Private Jacob Heater (Company D, 31st Virginia) recollected. His entire body went numb. Several times during the advance he put his hand on top of his head to see if his cap was still there. He concluded that his hair must have been standing straight up.[9] The morning's fright had cost the 13th Virginia 8 men, Lieutenant Wilson S. Newman (Company A) and the regimental colors, all of whom had scattered during the incident. The ground between the opposing lines was littered with the debris of the previous day's battle. Knapsacks, canteens, haversack, and rifles lay everywhere along with the Federal dead and wounded.[10]

SOUTH OF THE ORANGE TURNPIKE

The Confederates left the woods to their sharpshooters who were perched in the trees overlooking the Yankee works. Brigadier General Charles Griffin, who had lost his patience in front of Grant the afternoon before, was in no mood to needlessly sacrifice his men to them. He ordered Brigadier General Joseph Bartlett to advance his seven regiments into the woods and sweep the noisome Confederates from the area. Bartlett's 2,420 rifles fell in behind Kitching's and Sweitzer's men. Bartlett mounted the works and waved the division flag as the signal to move out. With a cheer, the veterans leaped over the headlogs and pushed through the woods, raking the tree tops with rifle balls as they advanced. A couple of Confederates fell through the tree branches and struck the ground with resounding thuds. Others were seen leaping from tree branch to tree branch trying to escape. The foray lasted several minutes and the regiments returned to their works content. They were not pestered by skirmishers for the rest of the day.[11]

NEAR THE TRAIL TO THE RAILROAD CUT
(629 yards west of McGowan's works)

The morning began in an annoying way for the seriously wounded Captain Z. Boylston Adams (Company F, 56th Massachusetts). Having spent a dreamless night, totally unconscious, he awoke with the eerie sensation of something trickling over his face. Running his hand over his eyes he was taken aback to find it covered with blood. A panic seized him. He quickly surveyed his surroundings. He was lying under a poncho supported by four uprights. Around him he saw legs protruding from white aprons standing about him. Twisting his head to one side, his eyes latched onto an amputated leg lying next to his face. The sight gave him a start. He cried out in alarm. One of the pairs of legs stepped back. They belonged to a Confederate orderly, who bent over to see who caused the noise. "Hulloa!" the attendant exclaimed, a smile spreading across his face. "How did you come there?" The stewards quickly dragged Adams from under their operating table and placed in a drier place. Finding out that he was a doctor, they asked the captain what he thought should be done. They told him he was in Perrin's brigade hospital, then left him alone while they tended to their own casualties.[12]

12:00 P.M.

THE PLANK ROAD – BROCK ROAD INTERSECTION
(1.8 miles southeast of the Wilderness Tavern)

Colonel Lewis A. Grant's Vermont Brigade was still in the works immediately north of the Plank Road, paralleling the Brock Road. Two days of severe fighting had left the five veteran regiments shells of their former selves. Of the 2,890 officers and men he had taken into action, only 1,621 remained uninjured. Nevertheless, at noon, in compliance with orders from Major General David Birney for a general reconnaissance of the Confederate lines, he dispatched a thin skirmish line under Major Richard B. Crandall of the 6th Vermont to silence the Confederate pickets along Wilderness Run. Private Wilbur Fisk (Company D, 2nd Vermont) did not like the as-

signment. The small picket line came so close to their Confederate counter-
parts that they could distinctly hear them talking as they retired before the
Vermonters toward Wilderness Run.[13]

While the Vermonters crunched through the blasted woods north of
the road, Colonel John Crocker's brigade from Birney's division advanced
on the south side. Crocker told the 1st U.S. Sharpshooters, who were leading the attack, to capture a Confederate "jackass battery" farther west along
the Plank Road.[14] The Sharpshooters also drew provost duty for about 20
skulkers whom the cavalry had rounded up during the two previous days.
The "cowards" were put in front of Captain Rudolf Aschmann's Company
A with the understanding that if they showed any signs of wavering, the
Sharpshooters were to cut them down where they stood. Crocker deployed
the regiment in column of fours in the road.[15]

The rest of the brigade fell in below the road in close column by division. A division consisted of a two-company front rather than a ten-com-
pany front. Closed column meant that rather than have a line ten companies long and two ranks deep, the regiment formed a moving box two
companies wide and ten ranks deep. The formation made it impossible for
the brigade to respond correctly to any attack.[16]

The 17th Maine under the command of Captain John Perry (Company
D) led the column. Private John Haley (Company I), speaking for a great
many of the men, described Perry as "a very earnest man, and as ignorant
as he is earnest." Knowing nothing about tactics or the manual in which
they were written, he was prone to invent commands and to threaten his
men with punishments which defied logic. During one tirade he ordered a
man to be court-martialed, shot, then tied to a tree if he refused to comply
with the captain's request. Haley never understood why being tied to a
tree would disturb a man who had already been shot. That morning, Perry
had dragged the regiment through every briar patch and mud hole he could
find before posting the men in the middle of a swamp. Haley was not in
the mood to follow the captain much farther.[17]

The 2nd U.S. Sharpshooters (Ward's brigade) were told to send a detachment out with the column. When the officers called out the detail, Private Charles Fox, a recruit in Company F, told First Sergeant Wyman S.
White he did not feel able to go. White, who was trying to clean the lead
from his rifle's bore, volunteered to go in his place. The company officers
gave him permission to replace Fox. White never said why he decided to
go. All he said was that it was Fox's first campaign.[18]

Birney and his staff officers fell in behind the 1st U.S. Sharpshooters
and the reconnaissance began. A very short distance down the Plank Road,
the column halted. The 1st U.S. Sharpshooters with the skulkers to the left
front deployed in battle formation across the road, their right wing over-
lapping the front of the Vermonters. They were not prepared for the ghastly

sights which greeted them along the line of march. Long lines of corpses were stretched out in battle formation beyond the slashings in front of the works. Beyond that spot the bodies lay in clusters and heaps. Delirious, wounded men were mingled among the dead, pleading for water to quench their thirst.[19] The column came under fire long before it covered the four hundred fifty-five yards between the Brock Road and Wilderness Run and Poplar Run.[20]

At the edge of the slashings, Birney and his officers rode by the huddled body of a dead Confederate. The second they passed him, the corpse sprang to life and snapped off a round at the general's back. The bullet missed Birney. The veterans of the 17th Maine mercilessly dispatched the Rebel and left his riddled body along the roadside.[21]

At the same time, the right wing of the 1st U.S. Sharpshooters and the Vermonters were approaching the base of the small hill in front of which Hays had been shot two days before. The Vermonters halted to let Company I of the Berdans assume their position along the crest. A round killed Private George R. Merrill right in front of Private Wilbur Fisk (Company E, 2nd Vermont) which alerted everyone to the presence of snipers.[22] The Berdans ran for their lives, leaving the field to the New Englanders. "Forward," Crandall ordered. A number of the veterans flinched. Fisk was too proud to show how scared he was. "I wouldn't act the coward," he recollected. Private Lyndon George (Company E) turned about and cried out, "Come on, boys." Grasping his weapon tighter, Fisk decided to die like a man and, with the rest of the skirmishers, followed his comrade toward the crest of the hill where they immediately came under small arms fire. The Federals returned fire and forced the Confederates to retire toward Wilderness Run.[23]

The left wing of the 1st U.S. Sharpshooters and Crocker's brigade, having temporarily lost contact with the Rebels, shoved through the smoldering, shattered woods and crossed Wilderness and Poplar Runs. Only the dead and the hopelessly wounded greeted them. Along the banks of the creeks they saw lines of corpses, lying in formation. In other areas lay piles of bodies. Wounded men pleaded for water from the sharpshooters who could not stop to help them. Their plight deeply grieved Aschmann, who could not leave his men to tend to their needs.[24]

Glancing over the road toward the right front, Haley (17th Maine) noticed several blankets hanging over some low tree branches in the distance. Without warning, the blankets were pushed aside from behind. The approaching Federals found themselves staring down the muzzles of a Confederate battery. At the same time, a line of infantry rose up from behind their works. The woods flamed and roared with artillery fire and a volley.[25] Canister crashed through the trees, catching the 1st U.S. Sharpshooters at point-blank range. A corporal in Company A died instantly. Five others were wounded. Within seconds, the Berdans lost 18 officers and men. They slowly retired very slowly, leaving Sergeant Frank H. Cobb (Company C), whose right side was crushed, to die from his wounds.[26]

The rest of Birney's column was unraveling. The Vermonters on the north side of the road, following Crandall's example, left the field, but at a much slower pace. "He got safely back long before we did," Fisk later noted.[27] South of the road, the 17th Maine's fleet footed Captain John Perry (Company D), with his coat tails flapping out behind him, raced madly through the woods repeatedly screaming "Halt!" without personally setting the example. The 17th Maine peeled toward the rear, exposing the next regiment in line.[28] One by one each regiment retreated in turn.

The 3rd Michigan, at the rear of the column, fell into regimental front and charged. A stretcher party struggled through its ranks. The wounded man, whom they were carrying, caught a glimpse of the regimental colors and began singing, "Rally Round the Flag, Boys." A passing soldier chimed in with the chorus and it spread through the ranks like an electrical current. The regiment surged forward up to the same works which they had attacked the day before. A hand to hand fight ensued. Captain Andrew Nickerson (Company K) died from a bayonet thrust. There were too many Rebels. The regiment could not sustain the fight and began to retreat. Color Sergeant Daniel G. Grotty turned about to bring off the regimental flag when he tripped and was thrown down. No less than a dozen rounds zipped over him as he hit the ground face first. Within seconds he was on his feet and running with the rest of the color guard for the Brock Road. The Confederates pursued the fleeing Federals almost to the slashings. A couple blasts of canister stopped them cold. They fell back to Poplar Run.[29]

The Berdans formed a skirmish line beyond the cleared field of fire. The 5th Michigan, which escaped the fighting unscathed, moved into the rear of the sharpshooters to round up Confederate stragglers. Sergeant Harrison Caril (Company C), First Sergeant John Collin, and Private John Casey, who had hurt his hand during the round-up, stopped by a large tree to bind up Casey's wound. They noticed a commotion behind a small clump of trees and ordered whoever was behind them to come out. Two Rebels stepped into the open, the larger of whom called out, "We'uns quit, Yank. Take us in; we'uns got enough." They were escorting the two prisoners to the rear when one of them turned to Collins and exclaimed, "Hell, man, we saw you'uns at Chancellorsville. We thought hell had broke loose there and nicknamed you'uns the `Bloody Devils from Michigan'."[30] Flushed with their relatively bloodless foray, the three returned to their lines. The fighting along the Brock Road was over.

On the north side of the road, Crandall and his skirmishers came across a cache of discarded weapons which the Confederates had collected during the night. He sent word of his discovery back to Colonel Lewis A. Grant, who in turn dispatched a wagon to the front to collect the weapons.[31] Before the wagons could come out to pick them up, the 1st U.S. Sharpshooters had gotten into them. The pickets of both sides were soon amusing themselves by shooting the ramrods from the discarded weapons at each other. Laughter and mirthful shouts echoed above the moans of the wounded while the skirmishers dodged the ramrods, listening for the peculiar hissing they made while in flight. Around 2:00 P.M., Hancock sent the 124th New York into the woods south of the road to pick up rifles and muskets. The regiment collected about 1,500 weapons in less than an hour.[32]

Meanwhile rescue parties scrounged the woods looking for wounded men. Sergeant Frank H. Cobb (Company C, 1st U.S. Sharpshooters) was lying behind the Confederate works in terrible agony when he discovered that they belonged to the 11th Alabama. Attracting the attention of one of the men, he asked him to find Private W. H. Sanders (Company C). The two had met while on picket along the Rappahannock River in May 1863, where, contrary to orders, they swapped tobacco and sugar across the river. At that time, Sanders and three of his comrades made a pact with Cobb that, should any of them be found wounded in the other's lines, they would take care of each other. Sanders and his three friends came to Cobb's aid. The sight of their friend touched them deeply. They tenderly carried him to a field hospital where the surgeon, at their insistence, tended to Cobb immediately. The four Rebels tearfully left Cobb in the hospital and returned to their regiment, convinced that they would never see each other again.[33]

THE DISPOSITION OF THE FEDERAL CAVALRY

Brigadier General David McMurtrie Gregg's division was at Piney Branch Church, about two and one half miles northeast of Todd's Tavern on the Catharpin Road. His regiments spent the morning listening to the rumbling thunder of artillery in the distance.[34] He sent the 10th New York Cavalry from Colonel J. Irvin Gregg's brigade on a mounted reconnaissance toward the Tavern shortly after the morning fog burned away, but otherwise did nothing.[35] From the church his troopers could deploy south toward Spotsylvania Court House or west toward the Tavern, depending upon the necessities of the tactical situation. Brigadier General Alfred T. A. Torbert's division was at the Catharine Furnaces, on the Catharine Furnace Road, approximately four miles northeast of the Tavern. His men were there to protect the Army of the Potomac's wagon trains on the road from Chancellorsville.[36]

The day began on a dour note for Private Thomas Carr (Company F), the regimental artist of the 6th New York Cavalry. Shortly after "Boots and Saddles" was sounded that morning, he rode over to Sergeant Alonzo Foster (Company F) and said, "If we get under fire today I shall be killed."

Foster brushed Carr's gloomy premonition aside with a jest. Carr rode away only to return some time later. "There is my wife's name and address," he said emphatically as he handed Foster a card. "If I am killed today write her and tell her how I fell and the circumstances of my death." The look in Carr's faced convinced Foster of his sincerity. He unsuccessfully tried to reassure Carr that the premonition meant nothing, that it had no bearing upon his future.[37]

Colonel Alfred Gibb's Reserve Brigade was bivouacked at Aldrich's, nearly 5 miles northeast of Todd's Tavern on the Catharpin Road. Grant had pulled back his cavalry to protect his rear and flanks from any possible surprise attack and in so doing had left the crossroads at Todd's Tavern open to Confederate occupation. "The fear of being flanked was an ever present terror to the army of the Potomac," Major James H. Kidd (6th Michigan Cavalry) wrote years later, "and the apparition which appeared to McDowell at Manassas, to Pope at the second Bull Run, to Hooker at Chancellorsville, flitted over the Wilderness also, and was the principal reason why that campaign was not successful."[38] Kidd blamed Meade for the poor deployment of the cavalry while overlooking the fact that Grant did not have to follow Meade's suggestions. In any event, the cavalry's present location effectively blinded the Army of the Potomac.

DISPOSITION OF THE CONFEDERATE CAVALRY

Brigadier General Lunsford L. Lomax's three Virginia regiments (5th, 6th, and 15th) were picketed north and east of Todd's Tavern, covering the Brock and Catharpin Roads.[39] Brigadier General Williams C. Wickham's four Virginia regiments (1st, 2nd, 3rd, and 4th) were three miles away on the Brock Road near its intersection with Piney Branch Road. They were in their saddles by daylight.[40] Brigadier General Thomas L. Rosser's Virginians had spent the night at Shady Grove Church on the Catharpin Road, over three miles southwest of Todd's Tavern.[41] Brigadier Generals James B. Gordon's North Carolina Brigade (W. H. F. Lee's Division) and Pierce M. B. Young's Georgia and Mississippi regiments (Hampton's Division) were on their way to join Stuart's men. They left Milford Station, fourteen miles southeast of Massaponax Church, that morning.[42]

DAYLIGHT

SHADY GROVE CHURCH
(3.5 miles southwest of Todd's Tavern)

Before daylight, Stuart went on a reconnaissance along the Catharpin Road and the trail to the previous day's cavalry field. Colonel Walter H. Stevens, Chief Engineer of the Army of Northern Virginia, Lieutenant Theodore Garnett, other members of his staff, and several couriers accompa-

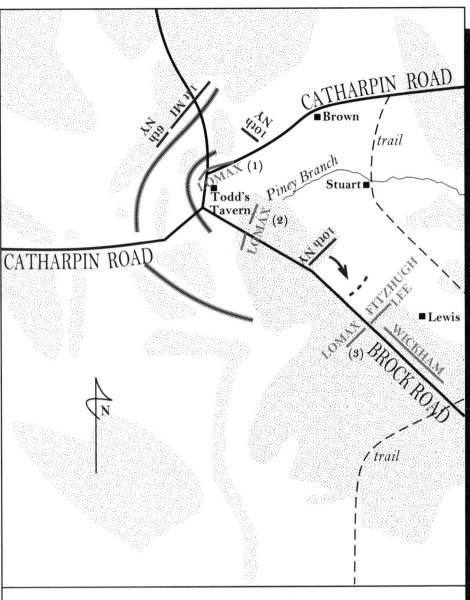

CATHARPIN ROAD

Brown ■

6th NY

1st NY

10th NY

trail

LOMAX (1)

Piney Branch

Stuart ■

Todd's Tavern ■

LOMAX (2)

CATHARPIN ROAD

10th NY

Lewis ■

FITZHUGH LEE

LOMAX (3)

WICKHAM

BROCK ROAD

N

trail

Map 35. The cavalry fighting along the Brock Road, May 7, 1864.
8:00 A.M. to 9:00 A.M.

(1) Devin and Custer corner Lomax at Todd's Tavern, while the 10th New York closes in from the right.

(2) At 9:00 A.M. the 10th New York pushes Lomax out of Todd's Tavern.

(3) From 9:00 A.M. to 2:00 P.M., the 10th New York becomes involved in a prolonged skirmish.

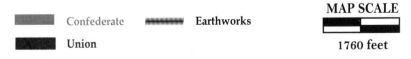

Confederate   Earthworks

Union

MAP SCALE

1760 feet

nied him. Garnett and the rest of the officers did not want to return to the field south of Trigg's, but they knew better than to share their feelings with the general. Stuart and his entourage rode beyond Rowe's into the hollow on the edge of Trigg's field. They spent over an hour within several hundred yards of Miles' II Corps brigade without seeing any pickets or any activity whatsoever. Impressed with the absence of any Federal troops in that quarter, the Confederates returned to Shady Grove Church to enjoy the morning in relative quiet.[43] Stuart felt very secure in his position. The 11th Virginia picketed the Wilderness between the church and railroad cut across the White Hall plantation. The rest of Rosser's brigade remained with him.[44]

THE LEWIS HOUSE
(1.1 miles southeast of Todd's Tavern
and .2 miles northeast of the Brock Road)

With Lomax securing Todd's Tavern, Major General Fitzhugh Lee and his staff spent the morning at Old Man Lewis' house.[45] At first light, he had Wickham's brigade mounted and in the Brock Road. Wickham raced his regiments all over the countryside in the intense heat without giving the rank and file any idea of what was going on. To Private Alexander Hunter (Company H, 4th Virginia), a former infantryman, the troopers were riding around like drunken sailors. The tremendous amount of dust which they churned up clung to their sweat-soaked uniforms and wet skin. Breathing became harder with each passing hour. With the Federals so close, it seemed ludicrous to be dashing about from pillar to post in search of nothing.[46]

8:00 A.M. TO 9:00 A.M.

While the Confederate cavalry were marking time, uncertain of the Federals' intentions, Torbert's division left the Furnaces with Devin's brigade ahead of Custer's. Very shortly after the head of the column turned south from the Furnace Road onto the Brock Road it ran headlong into skirmishers from Lomax's brigade. Devin sent part of the 6th New York charging down the road toward the dismounted Rebels, who had taken cover behind some barricades north of the Tavern. Shots rang out. A few New Yorkers spilled into the road. The cavalrymen unexpectedly wheeled about, heading back toward their brigade.[47] Devin dismounted the rest of the regiment, sending them into the woods on the south side of the road to flank the Rebels and to protect his own flank. By then, Custer became aware of the skirmishing. He responded by sending the 1st Michigan (his saber regiment) into the woods on both sides of the road.[48] Lieutenant Colonel Peter Stagg (1st Michigan) ordered Captain Brevoort to lead his squadron on a mounted reconnaissance down the road. Brevoort's men clattered into a flurry of small arms fire. The Virginians wounded four troopers and sent them back upon their own supports. Another squadron dismounted in the woods on the right of the regiment. Before too long a third squadron plugged the gap between the second squadron and the left flank of the 6th New York.[49]

9:00 A.M. TO 2:00 P.M.

By 9:00 A.M., the 1st Michigan and the 6th New York, having been unable to secure the Brock Road by frontal assault, were closing in on the western side of the tavern.[50] The 10th New York Cavalry (Gregg's brigade) had finally reached the vicinity by the Catharpin Road and was applying pressure to Lomax's right flank.[51] The dismounted 6th Virginia put up a stubborn resistance until 10:00 A.M. Retiring into the pine forest on both sides of the Brock Road, immediately south of the Tavern, the Rebels began fighting from tree to tree.[52] Private Samuel Rucker, Sr. (Company F) saw a minie ball strike the man, who was lying next to him, across the top of his head, killing him instantly. Orders traveled along the line to pull back. Rucker left the dead man upon the field.[53] Private Joseph Donohoe (Company K) was shot through both lungs but managed to get away. The Federals cut down an unusually large number of the Virginians' officers. They mortally wounded Lieutenant William Fuller (Company E), Captain Charles H. Ball (Company K) and Private Virgil Weaver (Company H). They seriously wounded Captain Alfred B. Carter (Company F).[54] The New Yorkers cautiously pursued them across the open ground until the Confederates reached the edge of a second set of pine woods and the remaining two regiments of their brigade.

They had taken cover behind a line of hastily assembled barricades. The Virginians opened fire upon the New Yorkers, forcing them to withdraw a respectable distance and dismount.[55] For four hours, the dismounted Confederate cavalry held their own in a very desultory but costly skirmish. The Federals killed another officer—Colonel G. R. Collins (15th Virginia), a highly respected Pennsylvanian who had married into a Virginia family. The immaculately dressed, fair haired Collins always showed up on the field with a clean, white collar and a new uniform. Private Luther W. Hopkins (Company A, 6th Virginia Cavalry), when reflecting upon the brave officer's death, lamented, "death loves a shining mark."[56]

12:00 NOON TO 4:00 P.M.

The intense morning heat left an indelible impression upon Private Alexander Hunter of the "Black Horse Troop" (Company H, 4th Virginia Cavalry). After spending the morning marching and counter marching between Spotsylvania Court House and the flanks of Lee's division, Wickham's brigade halted around noon to eat. With the hot sun beating down upon their dust-caked heads, the troopers knocked the dirt off their

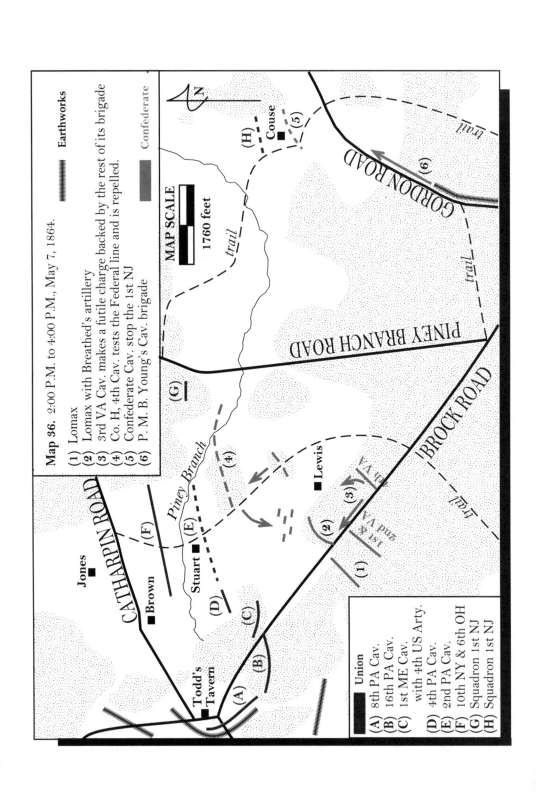

Map 36. 2:00 P.M. to 4:00 P.M., May 7, 1864.

(1) Lomax
(2) Lomax with Breathed's artillery
(3) 3rd VA Cav. makes a futile charge backed by the rest of its brigade
(4) Co. H, 4th Cav. tests the Federal line and is repelled.
(5) Confederate Cav. stop the 1st NJ
(6) P. M. B. Young's Cav. brigade

Earthworks

Confederate

MAP SCALE

1760 feet

N

Couse

(H)

(5)

GORDON ROAD

(6)

trail

trail

trail

PINEY BRANCH ROAD

trail

BROCK ROAD

trail

(G)

Piney Branch

(4)

(E)

(F)

Stuart

(D)

Brown

CATHARPIN ROAD

Jones

Todd's Tavern

(A)

(B)

(C)

(1)

(2)

(3)

1st & 2nd VA

3rd VA

Lewis

Union

(A) 8th PA Cav.
(B) 16th PA Cav.
(C) 1st ME Cav. with 4th US Arty.
(D) 4th PA Cav.
(E) 2nd PA Cav.
(F) 10th NY & 6th OH
(G) Squadron 1st NJ
(H) Squadron 1st NJ

haversacks and ate their raw, fatty meat and hard crackers without dismounting. The bugler sounded and the column moved out toward the front. The brigade spent some time in a ravine, supporting a section of Major James Breathed's horse artillery battalion.[57] Shortly after 1:00 P.M., the cavalrymen were pulled back to the Brock Road.

All around him, Hunter heard his comrades repeatedly ask the rhetorical question, "Where are we going?" Hunter did not know nor did he really care. Covered with throat-clogging dust, drenched in sweat, he sat on his horse with his leg thrown over the pommel, fanning himself with his hat and wishing he could find some fresh, cold, well water. It was so hot that the horses could not keep their heads up. "...they were like the tall grass in the fields, wilting beneath the rays of the sun," he recollected. From their position, the troopers could hear none of the fighting to the north. Hunter believed that all of them would have traded a year of their lives for cold water.

Around 2:00 P.M., Colonel Robert Randolph (4th Virginia) called out, "Fourth, attention! Prepare to dismount! Number four, hold horses! Dismount!" The Numbers 1, 2, and 3 men slid to the ground. Leaving their sabers and revolvers hanging from the pommels of their saddles, the troopers handed their reins to the horse holders. Unsnapping their carbines from their cross belts, they spread into a skirmish formation and disappeared into the woods on the north side of the road. The Virginians were uncomfortable as infantry, a large number of them having never fought on foot before. With officers as unfamiliar with dismounted fighting as their men, the formation became "all curves."[58]

While Wickham's men were feeling their way through the woods, Gregg's Federal brigade was creating an extended line from Todd's Tavern toward the Piney Branch Church Road. The 16th Pennsylvania Cavalry went into line in the woods southwest of the tavern, below the Brock Road. On the opposite side of the road one wing of the 1st Maine Cavalry moved onto the firing line while the other half remained in the rear as support. Part of the 4th Pennsylvania and the 2nd Pennsylvania extended the line farther to the left. The 8th Pennsylvania maneuvered into the woods on the right of the 16th Pennsylvania due west of the Tavern.[59] The 16th Pennsylvania and the 1st Maine began tearing down fence rails along the road to construct breastworks inside the woodline. While the New Englanders were hauling their rails from the roadside, Chaplain Edward P. Tobie heard someone call from across the road, "What regiment is that?" "First Maine," yelled a fellow who was loaded down with rails. "Bully for you! This is the Sixteenth Pennsylvania." Turning toward his own men, the Pennsylvanian shouted, "We are all right, boys, the First Maine is on our left."[60]

It was 3:00 P.M. when Colonel J. Irvin Gregg rode into the open ground between the two lines to the skirmishers of the 10th New York, and urged them to remain firm. While Captain John D. Myrick's mounted detachment (Company K) from the 1st Maine advanced down the road in column, the New Yorkers fell back five hundred fifty-seven yards to the brigade.[61] Lomax's brigade used the temporary lull to retire through the pines toward Spotsylvania Court House, just as Wickham's Virginians had reached the crossroads one and one half of a mile below the Tavern. Colonel Thomas H. Owen (3rd Virginia) placed Captain John Chappell's squadron across the road. The rest of the regiment with the 1st and 2nd Virginia came up through the woods north of the road while the 4th Virginia was moving at the oblique along the trail which branched northeast from the crossroads.[62]

Owen sent Private Ned R. Ragland (Company C) forward with instructions for Lomax to hold his ground because help was on its way. Drawing his saber, he set off at a trot, feeling relatively secure. There was not a Yankee in sight. A short distance from the front lines, Myrick's New Englanders emerged from the cover of the pines, surrounding him. In the dark shadows of the trees, one of them asked Ragland to identify his regiment. When he answered "the Third," the Yankee pointed his revolver at him. "I am your prisoner," Ragland said as he surrendered his sword. He quickly asked the Federals to take him to the rear. The entire brigade was behind him, he nervously blurted, and he did not want to accidentally die at their hands.[63] Myrick's troopers heard the unnerving Rebel yell echoing up the road. It came from Chappell's squadron which was careening down the road. The Federals momentarily turned their backs upon Ragland to deliver a scattered carbine volley at the Confederates. Rifle shots rang down the Brock Road. A bullet snapped off Owen's index finger on his left hand and another cut his horse down.[64] His troopers stampeded around him, intent upon driving the Federals back. Without wasting any time, the Federals wheeled about in the road and spurred toward their brigade. In the confusion, Ragland bolted into the woods. A branch knocked his hat from his head, but he did not stop to pick it up. He was making tracks for safer ground.[65]

The 3rd Virginia got as far as the northwestern edge of the woods at the point where the Brock Road passed through a narrow defile. A section from Lieutenant Rufus King, Jr.'s, Company A, 4th U.S. Artillery and one wing of the 1st Maine were waiting for the Rebels on the opposite side of the clearing. The Virginians were trying to maneuver through the road cut when the Yankee gunners, who had waited for the Mainers to clear their line of fire, emptied two rounds of canister into them. The unexpected blasts threw the Confederates into terrible confusion. Despite the strenuous efforts of their officers, the cavalrymen milled about in the ravine. To First

Lieutenant Noble D. Preston (Regimental Commissary, 10th New York) they resembled a mob more than a military organization.[66] Having lost their cohesiveness, they retreated deeper into the woods, well beyond Gregg's range.

Major James Breathed brought two guns under First Lieutenant Edwin L. Halsey (Hart's South Carolina Battery) right into Lomax's works to stall a possible counterattack.[67] King's guns got their range before the Confederates could open fire. Two well placed rounds disabled one gun and killed four enlisted men and their officer.[68] More rounds followed in quick succession. The artillerymen hurriedly withdrew their pieces. A shell burst between Lomax's flank regiment and the 4th Virginia, which was shuffling through the woods, heading for the Federal left flank. The uneasy troopers involuntarily ducked "as nervous as old women," Hunter of the 4th Virginia recalled.

Breaking from the cover of the woods below the Lewis farm, the 4th Virginia immediately came under small arms fire from the skirmishers of the 2nd Pennsylvania. King's artillerymen opened upon them with shell as well, which unnerved a number of the soldiers and sent them scrambling for safer ground. With the Rebel yell resounding above the noise of battle, the Virginians surged into the fields around the house (Fitzhugh Lee's headquarters) and drove the Pennsylvanians toward a small belt of woods five hundred eighty-seven yards north of the main house.[69] The 10th New York quickly shifted to the left of the brigade to reinforce the 2nd Pennsylvania.[70]

While the rest of the 4th Virginia hurled itself to the ground, the Black Horse Troop continued along the trail which led directly through the Pennsylvanians' new position. Being comprised of former infantrymen, the troop maintained its unit integrity and outran the two solid shot which the Federal artillerymen sent after them. "If I cannot ride a horse," Hunter overheard one of the dismounted troopers gasp as he raced for cover, "I can at least hide behind a tree, and in one way or another see this fight." The veterans reached the stand of woods amid a steady patter of carbine fire which showered them with twigs and spattered them with tree bark. Without orders, they went prone to regroup and ponder their next move.[71]

Along the Brock Road, the serious skirmishing seemed to be over. Sniper fire clipped across the field between the lines. During the lull, a private in Company L, 1st Maine, decided to enliven the action. Raising his kepi above the works on a stick, he taunted the Rebels to pick it off. Very shortly thereafter, the Confederates snapped a couple of rounds at the kepi and missed. He derisively hooted at them for their bad marksmanship, whereupon a Confederate poked his hat over his works. The Mainer fired at the hat and missed. The Rebel chided him for it. Chaplain Tobie watched the two men taunt each other several times by exchanging shots to no avail. The two became too involved in the game to quit it. During the last exchange the

Yankee inadvertently stood up at the wrong time. The Confederate's bullet struck him in the shoulder and knocked him onto his back. His friends and the Rebels laughed uncontrollably at his stupidity. Too embarrassed to go to the rear, he remained on the skirmish line until the regiment retired to the tavern after dark.[72]

Quartermaster Sergeant Samuel Cormany (16th Pennsylvania) experienced a similar fate. Rather than tend to his dismounted men as a file closer, he took part in the sharpshooting. "A Johny got my range," he wrote in his diary. He saw the Confederate's carbine flare and puff and saw the ball strike the ground some distance in front of him, whereupon a "buddy" told him to watch out for that Reb. Cormany told his friend, "You fond and peck him." A few minutes later a bullet ricocheted off a pine knot in front of Cormany's face. The flattened ball struck him above the right eye and knocked him out. As he fell upon his face he heard someone exclaim, "Cormany's shot." Second Lieutenant George Brooks (Company B) rolled him onto his back. He threw water into Cormany's face, to revive him. "I was in bad shape," the adjutant recalled with typical understatement. Nevertheless, he refused to leave the field, insisting to be left behind the line near his men.[73]

On the left of the Northern line, the 2nd Pennsylvania blasted the woods along the Black Horse troop's front which sent the Virginians scurrying for cover. Fighting from tree to tree, with the Federals no more than fifty yards away, the Confederates valiantly attempted to hold their own. In their first volley, they dropped a Yankee officer and his horse. Both sides peppered the trees with a tremendous volume of carbine rounds but inflicted relatively few casualties on each other.[74] Within a few minutes, a Yankee captain carelessly galloped down the trail right into the Black Horse Troop. Realizing his error in judgment seconds before the Confederates noticed him he wheeled his horse about, threw himself low over the horse's neck, dug his spurs into the horse's flanks, and raced for the safety of his own lines. "Shoot him! Shoot him!" echoed above the fusillade of bullets which snapped off the branches about his head. Private Alexander Hunter stepped into the road directly in front of the captain and leveled his carbine at his head. The second Hunter squeezed the trigger, the horse unexpectedly flinched under the impact of another incoming round. As the smoke cleared, he saw the dauntless officer bounding his horse through the woods with his arm dangling limply by his side.

After fifteen minutes of severe fighting, Second Lieutenant Marshall K. James sprang to his feet and ordered the Black Horse Troop to charge. The Pennsylvanians yielding under the renewed pressure, slowly abandoned their skirmish line. The Virginians herded them northeast through the marshy low ground bordering Piney Branch and across the creek into the woods west of the Piney Branch Church Road. Private John R. "Dick"

Martin and the intrepid Hunter were the first men to cross to the north-eastern side of the trail. They were after booty. The dead Yankee officer and his horse immediately caught their attention. Hunter snatched the full haversack from the pommel of the dead man's saddle and threw it around his neck. Martin loosened the man's fine saddle and jerked it off the horse, naively believing he could safely bring it off the field while skirmishing. Nearby lay the officer, a captain—dead—his throat ripped open by a bullet.[75]

Brigadier General Henry E. Davies' brigade was coming onto the field from the vicinity of Piney Branch Church. Captain John Hobensack (Company F, 1st New Jersey Cavalry) took the 1st Battalion forward to establish vidette outposts far in advance of the general line. First Lieutenant John Kinsley (Company F), in response to the firing, immediately sent 20 dismounted troopers forward. Hobensack went with them to personally observe the fighting. Instead of a heavy skirmish line, he found himself facing the well organized Black Horse Troop. Pulling back his right flank, Hobensack directed his men to take a wooded hill on his left flank. The Rebels anticipated his move. The opposing skirmish lines dashed east, heading for the high ground from opposite sides. They fired wildly as they ran. The New Jersey troopers reached the hill first. Facing south and southeast, they volleyed into the Virginians who were struggling through the bog along Piney Branch.

While the right of the line was engaged with Hobensack's skirmishers, Hunter bellied up to a fence rail on the north side of the woods with Martin and his saddle close behind. Edging up to the Virginia worm fence, they peered over the bottom rail, totally unprepared for what they saw approaching them.[76] The dismounted 6th Ohio Cavalry was advancing to the support of the Jerseymen through the open ground west of the hill. Connecting with the 10th New York they made a combined force of about 882 men which covered about a half mile front in a single rank.[77] The Ohioans lost 10 men wounded in quick order.[78] Davies dismounted two battalions from the 1st Pennsylvania and rushed them forward to support the Westerners and the 1st New Jersey.[79] Martin threw the saddle onto the forest floor and with Hunter raced back to their company which was about seventy-five yards to the right rear. The disorganized volley which followed them killed two men and wounded three more. There were thousands of Federals out there, Hunter blurted to Captain Alexander D. Payne, and they had better make tracks. Payne, who had served with the company since the war began, was dumbfounded. Having never fought dismounted, he did not know what to do. When Martin informed James of their predicament, the lieutenant bellowed the order to withdraw.

The Virginians did not run. Every few feet, individual soldiers turned and shot back at the Federals whose well ordered "huzzahs" resounded across the field. The Rebels, who responded with their shrill "yipping," joked with each other . They behaved admirably. It was eighteen-year-old Private Harold "Harry" Alston's first action. He was standing behind a hickory sapling capping his weapon when a bullet ripped through his sleeve and split the tree trunk in half. Lie down, Private James "Ker" Sowers yelled at him. The young Englishman, ignoring both the Yankee bullets and Sowers, coolly returned fire as if nothing had happened. Turning to Hunter, Sowers blew threw his teeth, "If all Englishmen fight like that boy, no wonder they have never been conquered." Before Hunter could reply, the Ohioans reached the northern edge of the woods. The Confederates increased their rate of fire. The Federals were so close they could clearly see the yellow piping on their shell jackets. Another "huzzah" tore through the woods, followed by a volley.

"Good-by, Black Horse!" Private Joseph F. Boteler cried out as he turned and ran. "O, that I had wings!" Dick Martin chimed in as he too turned on his heels and raced for the Brock Road. The Black Horse, to a man, burst from the woods into the large open field northeast of the Lewis farm. They were heading for the large farm house and its outbuildings in the middle of the field. Hunter and Alston were with the squad which made for the spring near the house. Scooping up a kepi full of water, Hunter took a couple of gulps as he ran. Alston threw himself on his stomach to lap up the water. Glancing over his shoulder as he ran, Hunter saw Alston gain his feet too late to escape. In an instant he saw the Englishman throw his hands into the air and surrender to the Federals who were swarming around him. Ignoring the Federals' shouts for him to surrender, Hunter continued running a zigzag course for the woods. Far to the right, he heard a rattling volley. It was the rest of the brigade, providing cover support for the Black Horse Troop. He dashed for the fence row on the northern edge of the woods. Hurling himself over the top rail, he collapsed on the ground, heaving for air and glad to be alive. The sporadic firing ceased for several minutes. While regaining his composure, Hunter noticed that the brigade had torn down the fence and piled up the rails to make low breastworks.[80]

Meanwhile the 3rd Battalion from the 1st New Jersey remained in the rear along the high ground northwest of the Piney Branch Church Road. The 2nd Battalion came forward and relieved the 1st Battalion on the wooded hill. Hobensack, however, did not pull his men back. They remained on the knoll when the 2nd Battalion with the 6th Ohio drove the Confederates into the open low ground on the southwest side of the road.

Some time between 3:00 and 4:00 P.M., while the brigade relieved the pressure along the left flank, Captain Walter R. Robbins (Company G) took his squadron (Companies G and L) from the 3rd Battalion and a section of artillery at a charge down the country lane which led to the Couse farm, intent upon providing cover fire. The guns swung into position in the woods north of the house. Company L stayed behind with the guns in support while Robbins took Company G at a gallop toward the farm.[81]

Catherine Couse, who had been trapped in the main house since the fighting began on May 5, was too frightened to venture beyond a front window. What she saw from there convinced her that the war was too terrible to bear. All morning long Confederate cavalry videttes had spent the day idly lounging about the farm lane as if no battle were going on nearby. A dense, eye-stinging pall of smoke, created by the hundreds of fires in the Wilderness, blanketed the woods and fields. Without warning, a lone Confederate ran in among the other troopers, shouting an alarm. The cavalrymen swung into their saddles. In the distance, Couse spotted the head of Robbins' squadron galloping directly toward her home. The Rebels broke into a gallop near the end of the lane amidst a flurry of small arms fire which swept across the nearby field. Robbins' men pursued them as far as the orchard near the house. Nearing the spring, a few of them dismounted and threw down the fence between them and the house.[82] The Confederate cavalry rallied on the south side of the farm and countercharged, forcing Robbins and his troopers to take cover in an abandoned farm building. From there he drove the Rebels back to their side of the farm. At the same time the Confederate horse artillery lobbed a couple of rounds toward the Yankee guns opposite them. A shell whizzed into the rear rank of Company L. It burrowed itself into the ground under the hind legs of one of the mounts. Sergeant William L. Stout and his men remained motionless as if nothing had happened.[83]

Catherine Couse, while watching the fighting, anxiously continued a letter to friends of hers which she had started two days earlier. "Oh, God," she scratched in her letter, "human beings killing each other. This wicked war. Will it ever come to an end?"[84] Within the hour, Robbins' troopers withdrew toward their brigade along Piney Branch taking a few prisoners with them.

4:00 P.M. TO 5:00 P.M.

The 6th Pennsylvania Cavalry suddenly appeared on the Brock Road, leading Colonel Alfred Gibbs' Reserve Brigade. The Pennsylvanians were deploying by battalions to probe the Confederate lines. Captain Charles L. Leiper's battalion went into line in the clearing on the north side of the road, opposite Wickham's brigade. Captain E. M. Carpenter's four companies remained mounted in the road behind them as support. Captain Joseph H. Clark's battalion was dismounted in the woods on the south side. As soon as the Federals came under fire from the Confederates, Leiper's squadrons pushed forward, but ran into very stubborn resistance.[85]

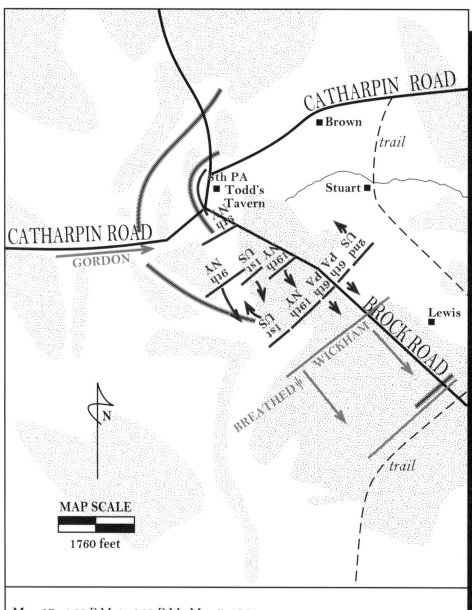

Map 37. 4:00 P.M. to 5:00 P.M., May 7, 1864.
Under severe pressure, Wickham's brigade is forced to retire to breastworks along the Brock Road. A brief lull settles over the field. Gordon moves in on Todd's Tavern from the west.

Confederate   Earthworks   Artillery

Union

The fighting was fierce. Major James Starr (6th Pennsylvania), riding his wounded horse up to the Confederate works, was shot in the face by a pistol ball which severed his tongue. Unable to speak, he wheeled his horse about and left the field. The command of the regiment devolved upon Leiper.[86] The Pennsylvanians were hitting the Confederates equally hard. Company C of the 2nd Virginia took a terrible beating. Private "Lil" Johnson glanced over the works and caught a round in the forehead. Another bullet spat between the rails and killed Private Creed Hubbard. Privates R. H. Peck, Charles Price, and Newton Shaver were kneeling side by side when a ball thudded into Shaver's chest. He collapsed onto his back without saying a word. Peck immediately ran his hand over Shaver's heart but could not feel any blood. They brought him to his senses by pouring water over his face. The moment he came around, a courier galloped up to the line and was shot dead.[87]

Meanwhile the 1st New York Dragoons (19th New York Cavalry) dismounted in the Brock Road seven hundred thirty-three yards north of Todd's Tavern. The troopers doublequicked south toward 6th Pennsylvania. Screaming as loud as they could, they loaded and fired as they ran, never thinking that their own men were in their line of fire.[88] The New Yorkers bolted into the woods south of the road to assist Clark's four companies while Carpenter's battalion charged into the open field on the left of Leiper's men.[89] Bolstered by the additional troopers on the line, Companies H and I from the 1st Dragoons and Clark's Pennsylvanians rushed through the pine forest for the crest of a small hill occupied by Chappell's squadron on the Confederates' left flank.[90]

The New Yorkers, gaining the high ground ahead of the Pennsylvanians, suddenly found themselves surrounded by portions of the 3rd Virginia which had filled the gap between the two Yankee regiments. Acting adjutant, Lieutenant William Kirk, Regimental Commissary of the 6th Pennsylvania was shot off his horse close to the Rebel lines. Carpenter and First Lieutenant Edward Hazel (Company F), in attempting to rescue Kirk, were captured. Company E, besides having two men killed and five wounded, also lost its captain, whom the Rebels captured. Private Clement Hoffman (Company E) later informed his mother that it was the heaviest casualties the company had suffered during the entire war to date.[91] The Confederates punched a temporary hole in the Pennsylvanians' line. Stripping Kirk of his boots and robbing him of his valuables, they pulled back when Leiper shoved more Pennsylvanians into the gap.[92] Small parties of troopers in Wickham's line began drifting to the rear.[93] The 6th Pennsylvania's guidon bearer from Company I was shot dead, but a wounded trooper snatched the standard before it touched the ground.[94] The 1st U.S. Cavalry went into line on the right of the 1st New York Dragoons. The 2nd U.S. Cavalry maneuvered into the field on the other side of the road and joined in the fray.[95]

The help arrived too late to assist either the New Yorkers or the Pennsylvanians. The Rebels had already captured over 30 enlisted men and officers.[96] In a matter of minutes the Confederates wounded 6 of the 1st U.S.' 18 officers, among them Captain Edwin Vose Sumner, Jr. In all the regiment lost 45 men, 8 of whom were killed.

On the opposite side of the road, the 2nd U.S. ran into lighter opposition and had a confrontation of an unexpected nature. Captain Charles M. Leoser was directing his skirmishers across the small farm in the middle of the open ground between the two lines when the old lady who lived on the property came to the front door of the small house with a bucket in her hand. Would the captain, she asked, fetch her a bucket of water from the well in the yard. Her tone of voice took the captain aback. Without any regard for the literal rain of lead which whistled about the place, she acted as if the captain would not be hurt by braving a few extra rounds. Leoser told her as politely as the circumstances allowed that he was somewhat occupied at the moment but he would get her the water if she could wait until he had finished his present task. The woman wheeled about and with a curse hurled the bucket at a black man who was crouching in the kitchen while the captain returned to his men.[97]

Devin's brigade was hurrying south in response to the rifle fire. The continuous, sharp cracks of carbines rolled louder and louder across the regiment's right flank, telling the veterans that the Rebels were gaining ground south of the tavern. The dense pine woods stopped Devin's men cold.[98]

The 6th New York dismounted. The regiment broke into sections of four men each. The Numbers 1, 2, and 3 men in each section strapped their sabers to their saddles, handed the reins to the remaining Number 4 man, and dismounted. Private Thomas Carr (Company F), a Number 2 man, fell in next to Sergeant Alonzo Foster (Company F). Union cavalrymen were falling back through the pines along their front with the dismounted 3rd Virginia not too far behind. The order rippled along the line to advance. A carbine shot cracked very close to Foster. Private Harry Sharpe (Company F) immediately snapped his weapon to his shoulder and loosed a round. He dropped the Rebel who had shot at him. Before the smoke settled he and Foster saw Carr lying on the ground with a bullet through his heart. As the cavalry men pushed the Confederates back, Sharpe stopped by the man he had hit. The gray-haired Rebel was in a great deal of pain. Defiant to the end he told Sharpe he was ready to die since he had killed a Yankee.[99]

Brigade Surgeon Augustus P. Clarke (U.S.A.) was riding toward the tavern from the front lines when he came across a wounded trooper who was staggering toward the rear with a bullet wound in his right foot. The man loudly insisted that the doctor dismount and tend his wound but

Clarke told him he had better keep going because he was too close to the battle lines. He knew a large column of Confederate cavalry was very close by. The trooper complained more loudly about his wound. The surgeon decided, against his better judgment, to dismount to apply a temporary dressing to the man's wound. An unexpected burst of rifle fire swept across the road, knocking the man down with a shattered right arm. Clarke knew on sight that the rear line surgeons would have to amputate it.[100]

Wickham's Virginians were retreating. The courier who had been killed behind the 2nd Virginia was carrying an order in his hand to withdraw. The troopers did not lose any time in executing the movement. Both ends of the 2nd Virginia's works had caught fire from their muzzle flashes.[101] Thick, suffocating smoke blanketed the woods, obscuring everyone's vision and making it impossible to stay on the line. Men broke to the rear by squads. Panic spread throughout the regiments. The men of the 4th Virginia, on the right of the line, saw shadows darting through the trees about them. Someone screamed, "We are flanked! The Federals are in our rear!" The Virginians scattered, each man for himself in a race to the rear.[102] In the 2nd Virginia, Peck and Price waited until the last minute to evacuate their wounded friend, Shaver. Price took the wounded man's rifle. While Peck was pulling Shaver to his feet by the arm, a minie ball thunked into it. Peck dragged his injured friend with him, leaving his two dead comrades to the Federals and the flames.[103] The rout became general. The Federals moved forward to find themselves in possession of burned fence rails and the Confederate dead.

Meanwhile, the 9th New York dismounted and crashed through the woods toward the right flank of the 1st New York Dragoons. The 1st U.S. Cavalry saw them coming and retired from the field. When they peeled back, the 2nd U.S. on the north side of the road also abandoned their position. The Confederates rolled some artillery into position on the edge of the woods across from the New Yorkers and opened fire. Canister swept the open fields, forcing the Federals to the ground.[104] Again, the firing quieted down.

5:00 P.M. TO 7:00 P.M.

THE CATHARPIN ROAD
(.6 miles west of Todd's Tavern)

Shortly before sundown, Stuart received his much needed reinforcements at Shady Grove. Brigadier General James B. Gordon's North Carolina cavalry brigade arrived from Milford, Virginia and was sent into action along the Catharpin Road. Gordon had one wing of the 1st North Carolina and the 2nd and 5th regiments with him. Stuart sent his aide, Garnett, and one courier, Private Charles D. Lowndes (Company E, 4th

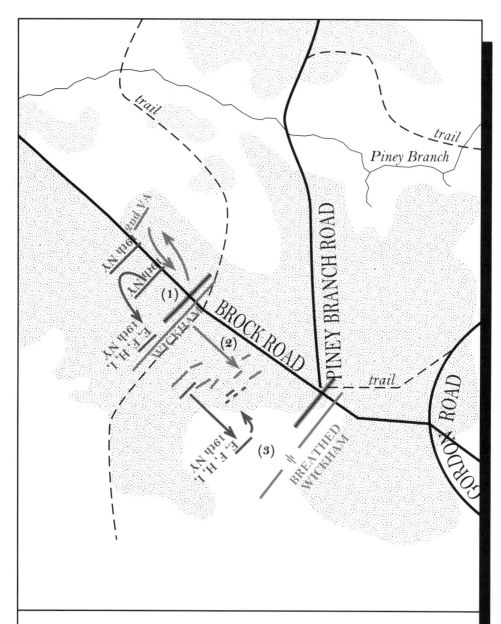

trail

trail

Piney Branch

PINEY BRANCH ROAD

2nd VA

9th NY

9th NY

E, F, H, I,
19th NY

WICKHAM

BROCK ROAD

(1)

(2)

trail

GORDON ROAD

E, F, H, I,
19th NY

(3)

BREATHED
WICKHAM

Map 38. Dark, May 7, 1864.
(1) The 19th New York is repelled by the 2nd Virginia.
(2) Companies E, F, H, I, 19th New York attack Wickham
    and break his line.
(3) Wickham with Breathed repel the four companies of the
    19th New York.

N

MAP SCALE

1760 feet

 Confederate ‖‖‖‖‖‖‖‖ **Earthworks**

 Union

Virginia), out from his headquarters to ascertain the condition of his flank. The two arrived just a Gordon was dismounting the 5th North Carolina to probe the Yankee picket outposts. Stuart's two men rode forward with the North Carolinians.

Passing the open fields over which Rosser's men had fought the day before, the skirmishers entered a small belt of woods which crossed the road six hundred seventy-five yards west of the tavern. Without warning, a party of men broke from cover in front of the Carolinians. Shots rang out in the darkening woods, accompanied with shouts of alarm, and followed by an embarrassing silence when the Confederates realized that they had exchanged rounds with one of their own scouting parties. While the startled cavalrymen were reorganizing their line and calming their nerves, Garnett and Lowndes rode alone through the woods to the next small belt of trees one hundred seventeen yards away. They were heading toward a heavy barricade which the Federals had constructed across their path. Upon nearing the works, the two Confederates saw two Yankee cavalrymen slowly ride their horses into the open and proceed down the road toward the tavern. Riding up to the obstruction, Garnett and Lowndes dismounted at the works and were peeking through the apertures when two loud reports jolted them. Two artillery projectiles skimmed over the headlogs, arched over the heads of the North Carolinians, who were quietly riding their mounts toward the barricade, and exploded harmlessly in the road behind them. The column immediately shifted to the north side of the road and dismounted. The horse holders went to the rear, while Gordon rode into the regiment and ordered the men to attack the Yankee works. Gardner and Lowndes left the North Carolinians with a positive report for Stuart. As they trotted away, they heard the staccato of carbine fire rise in to a steady crescendo.[105] They were taking on Gregg's 8th Pennsylvania Cavalry who were dismounted behind a small line of works two hundred ninety-three yards west of the tavern.

The Couse Farm
(1.0 miles south of the Catharpin Road)

As Gordon's men pressed back the 8th Pennsylvania, Brigadier General Pierce M. B. Young and his five Georgia and Mississippi cavalry regiments were relieving Fitzhugh Lee's right flank. His dismounted troopers, hollering as they advanced to the northern edge of Couse's field, sent volley after volley into the darkening shadows. The fact that she was now surrounded by her own army, did not offer Catherine Couse any comfort. "I feel so weak & generally miserable," she wrote to her friends, "I can scarcely sit up most of the time. Oh! the poor wounded dead and dying soldiers." While Confederate supply wagons creaked across the farm, she became acutely aware of the suffering which the war had brought to her once tranquil home.[106]

THE BROCK ROAD
(1.25 miles southeast of Todd's Tavern)

Privates R. H. Peck (Company C, 2nd Virginia) never looked back until he dragged the wounded Newt Shaver into the works which Lomax's men had thrown up during the previous evening. Shoving Shaver over the headlogs, Peck dropped to the ground next to his friend. As they lay there, catching their breath, he asked Shaver why the first ball, which struck him in the breast, had not killed him. The Bible which his mother gave him stopped the round, Shaver panted. The unbelieving Peck reached inside the wounded man's blouse and pulled the Bible from his inside pocket. Noticing the bullet

**Brigadier General
Pierce M. B. Young, C.S.A.**

Young's Confederate cavalry brigade secured Fitzhugh Lee's right flank near the Couse farm late in the day on May 7.

Massachusetts Commandery;
MOLLUS, USAMHI

hole through the cover, he paged through the scriptures until he found the bullet imbedded near the middle of the book. Peck returned the Bible to his friend, then assisted him to an ambulance behind the line.[107] Nearby, Private Alexander Hunter of the Black Horse Troop, 4th Virginia Cavalry, lay in the woods with his comrades, grateful for the respite from the fighting. Ever observant of the minutiae of the soldier's existence, he distinctly recollected his comrades' powder-stained faces. The troopers who owned the Richmond version of the Sharpe's carbine were in particularly sorry shape. Those poorly made copies of that Northern long arm simultaneously spit fire from the muzzle and the breeches, scorching the soldiers' faces and singing their facial hair. Its recoil rivaled that of the Harper's Ferry rifled musket, which also "killed at both ends."

A short distance away, Lieutenant Colonel Robert L. Randolph, commanding the 4th Virginia, and his aides sat comfortably on their horses with their right legs lazily balancing across the pommels. Wickham posted no pickets. It seemed as if they had outrun the Federals.[108]

The Federals, however, were not going to give the Confederates any respite. Around 7:00 P.M. the 1st New York Dragoons headed southeast along the Brock Road to probe any weakness in the Confederate line. With it growing dark and ominous around them, they cautiously sallied about one fourth of a mile into the woods on both sides of the road and got as far as Lomax's barricades before the 2nd Virginia Cavalry, acting as Wickham's rearguard, saw them and struck back.[109] Peck could hear the New Yorkers' battle line crashing through the woods but noticed that only their sharpshooters ventured close enough to the works for the Virginians to see them. Sporadic sniper fire pinged into the logs without taking effect. After waiting several minutes for something to happen, Colonel Thomas Munford (2nd Virginia) ordered his own sharpshooters to flush the Federals away from their front. With Lieutenant Edward Brugh in the lead, Company C leaped over the headlogs and began dodging from tree to tree amidst an increased volume of fire. Peck raced up to a large tree just as a Yankee popped out from behind it and shot Brugh through the lungs. Peck darted around the opposite side, trying to take the soldier from the rear but the fellow had already ducked behind another tree. With Lieutenant Hayth assuming command, the Confederates pushed the Yankee skirmishers back toward the far edge of the woods where the fighting had begun earlier that day.

By then Peck was in the front line when the command to halt reached him. Nearby, with his bullet-cracked head between two shrubs, lay a dead Yankee officer. Judging by the quality of his uniform, Peck assumed he was wealthy enough to be robbed. He slipped over to the corpse and began rifling his pockets for money. Finding none, he settled for the officer's fine silver watch. As he pulled the watch from the dead man's vest, a private from Company K came up. "I am going to take his boots, he'll never need them again," he said. While pulling one of them off, the "dead" Yankee unexpectedly kicked the Rebel in the behind and send him sprawling head over heels into the brush. Peck suddenly discovered that the line had pulled back without them.[110]

Companies E, F, H, and I from the 1st Dragoons were rushing through the woods toward them.[111] The two Rebels did not stand on orders to leave. They took off at a run with the Federals' bullets splintering the tree bark around them. Peck clenched the watch tightly in his hand, ready to throw it away in a moment should the Federals collar him. He did not want to get caught alive with captured Federal property in his possession. Racing for their lives, the Virginians beat the New Yorkers to the protection of their works. Throwing himself on the ground next to Captain James Breckinridge he heard, "The boys thought you were either killed or captured as you didn't get back with them." He was not dead Peck reassured him while showing him the captured watch. Breckinridge inspected it and offered to trade it for his own gold one. The silver watch had belonged to Colonel E. L. Sindler of the 1st Virginia Cavalry, the captain said. Colonel Thomas Munford, who was standing nearby, overheard him and added that he had known the deceased Sindler well. They had gone to West Point together.

Peck agreed to the swap, then settled down for what hopefully would be a peaceful evening.[112]

The New Yorkers, however, did not abandon the pursuit. They took Wickham's brigade entirely by surprise. In the darkness of the woods, their carbine fire sounded like a volley of five thousand muskets to Private Alexander Hunter (Company H, 4th Virginia). Rounds cut the twigs off around their heads, slapped into the logs of the earthworks, and struck down unsuspecting soldiers. Private Kerfoot Sowers (Company H, 4th Virginia) and others died instantly. The Virginians panicked and broke from the works. One hundred yards into the pines, their officers bullied them back into line and led them back to the barricades. By then the Federals were spilling over them. The woods rang with small arms fire. Smoke hung in the trees, making it difficult to clearly identify targets. "Every tree and sapling was marked by the flying lead, and a steady stream of wounded were going back," Hunter recalled. The fighting waxed hotter. The men on both sides stopped cheering and yelling, the work having become too exhausting to engage in such nonsense. The Federals doggedly pushed the Virginians back a mile to a small line of works northwest of Alsop's Gate.[113] A section of guns from Major James Breathed's battalion was waiting for the Federals behind an earthwork in an open field west of the Brock Road. The lieutenant in charge of the field pieces patiently waited for the cavalrymen to take cover on his side of the works before hurling two solid shot at the New Yorkers who were still in the woods to the north. During the retreat, Hunter had strayed too far to the left. Glancing to the south, he noticed a line of cavalry approaching the battery from behind. Through the thick dust, he could not identify their uniforms but he strongly suspected they were Federals. Running over to the lieutenant in command of the section, he shouted at him to watch his rear. He had better save the guns, Hunter warned him. "Not by a damn sight!" the lieutenant shot back.[114] The lieutenant did not have to worry about the cavalry to his rear. Whoever they were, they did not threaten his position. He was more concerned with the four companies of the 1st New York Dragoons who, despite his artillery fire, did not immediately relinquish the field.

The New Yorkers were taking a terrific pounding. A bullet shattered Private Josiah Flint's carbine stock. Grabbing the weapon by the barrel he charged ahead with Company I. Within half an hour, the Confederates had inflicted over 24 casualties upon them. Company I left three men behind. The Rebels riddled Corporal Emerson Rude beyond description. They literally shot him to pieces. Flint and his comrade, Private Hirman J. Woodward, were overwhelmed and captured. Private Jared Ainsworth's (Company E) good friend, Sergeant Robert Ware, had his jaw shot away. (They both perished in Andersonville Prison.)[115] Private Marcus Prentiss headed for the rear with a fatal wound through both lungs. Captain Russell Britton

(Company H) perished in the brawl.[116] Unable to sustain the fight any longer, they started retiring toward Todd's Tavern.

Hunter saw two of them break into the open not forty yards away from him. Drawing a bead upon one of them, he squeezed off a round. One of the Federals, dropping his rifle, clasped his shattered left arm, and limped back into the woods. The other New Yorker snapped a round in Hunter's direction. The bullet slapped through Hunter's hat brim. A second later, he drew a bead upon the fellow and jerked the trigger only to hear the cap snap. In the excitement, he had forgotten to reload his carbine. The Yankee dropped to his knee. Hunter turned aside to throw a cartridge into his carbine's empty breech when he saw a muzzle flash and felt something strike him in the body. He threw himself to the ground. The Yankee's next bullet ripped the sole off Hunter's boot. He flattened himself out further to play dead when another Confederate ran to his side to assist him. Brown dust flew from the Rebel's collar where the Yankee's bullet struck him. Grasping his neck, the man ran from the field, howling. From the corner of his eye, Hunter watched the New Yorker disappear into the forest.

Feeling secure for the moment, Hunter sat upright and unbuttoned his tunic. No blood. His arms, his head, and his chest were not hurt. He had no idea where he had been hit until he attempted to stand. Unable to sustain his weight, he dropped onto his behind. Two bullet holes in his trousers above his left knee—one an entry and the other an exit—told him all he needed to know. He suddenly became aware of the blood running down to his ankle. It was hot and sticky. He stopped the bleeding with a makeshift tourniquet made from his handkerchief, then wiggled his toes to see if they still worked. Then he sat alone in the dark, grumbling to himself about the high cost of war. He had paid $250.00 for those boots.[117] In seven hours of fighting both cavalry forces lost an estimated 250 men apiece over a little over one and one half miles of road.[118] The Confederates still held the Brock Road and the Court House. The Federals had regained Todd's Tavern, the key to their own left flank.

AFTER DARK

Under the cover of darkness both armies began shifting south toward Spotsylvania Court House. Lee's army would get there first, mostly because of the delaying actions of his cavalry that day. The infantrymen on both sides had little to record of the night marches other than that they were irksome and exhausting.

Lee's army had changed, had been transformed. He did not know it but the men did. They knew this was no longer a war which would be fought by conventional rules of warfare. Grant was not going to back off after being bloodied. He was going to come back for more. He was going to rip the throat out of the Army of Northern Virginia and destroy the Army of the Potomac to do it. They were facing the end of their dreams of independence. They knew it but they could not say it. They felt it.

That feeling manifested itself in a callous sense of humor. That night, as the Army of Northern Virginia moved south through the woods, a series of ten cheers rippled through the ranks from the right of the army to the left. They swept through the ranks like a succession of waves breaking along a shore where, as one wave broke and ebbed, another crashed upon the top of it. The sound of the cheer reaching a crescendo when it swept over the 1st South Carolina, then fading in the distance, thrilled Sergeant Berry Benson (Company H) to his soul. But then it was followed by a more cynical message. The message, "Grant's wounded! Grant's wounded!" traveled along the human chain until it passed through the South Carolinians. The regiment behind them changed it to "Grant's dead! Grant's dead!" Soon after, from the right of the army came, "Grant's wife's got a baby! Grant's wife got a baby!", followed by a ripple of laughter as it passed through the regiment. Then came, "It's a nigger one! It's a nigger one!" Benson and many of his friends would not repeat that line. "...only a few men took it up," he wrote, "and it was held in such disgrace that I don't think it got far beyond us before dying out. I felt so ashamed of the men who had participated in that jeer, and I think they felt ashamed afterwards themselves."[119] It was the humor of those who knew their days were numbered.

Captain Z. Boylston Adams (Company F, 56th Massachusetts) noted the change in another way. After lying until the afternoon without receiving any medical attention, Surgeons Miner and Gaston (Mahone's brigade) finally tended to his wound. Before they put him under with chloroform, he distinctly recalled how they reeked of whiskey. He awoke on the ground in a fly tent with the fibula of his wounded leg five inches shorter than it had been before. To his right lay another officer on a stretcher. The star on the shoulder boards of the man's blue coat told Adams the fellow was a brigadier general. Propping himself on his elbow, Adams stared into the other man's face. He was James S. Wadsworth.

The captain opened the general's eyelids. They were getting glassy, fixed in place. Adams took his pulse. It was steady, but the general's breathing was labored, occasionally punctuated by a deep sigh. Wadsworth's mouth drooped on the left side. He could not move his right arm, indicative of brain injury on the left side. Adams inspected the entry wound. The ball had penetrated the skull from the back, near the crown just to the left center. Wadsworth's left hand, which lay upon his chest, every now and then twitched. He clasped a piece of paper with his name on it.

Throughout the day, the two officers lay unattended. All day long Confederate troops marched past the tent, heading southeast toward the distant sounds of the fighting at Todd's Tavern. Every once in a while a soldier would stop by and pull the note from the general's hand to read it, at which point Wadsworth would frown and sweep his hand across his buttoned coat until the paper was placed back in his hand.

Toward the end of the day, a young, drunken Confederate staff officer and his friends wandered into the tent. The "gentleman" swore at Adams when he was told that Wadsworth was in the tent. Calling the captain a liar, he vehemently added that all the Federals' officers were raving brigands, abolitionists, and foreign mercenaries. Adams, having had about all of the abuse he could handle, argued the point with the Confederate. When the captain said he was from Massachusetts, the fellow exploded into a louder rage, blubbering that he would conduct the roll call of his slaves upon Bunker Hill one day. Adams shouted a nasty reply in the Rebel's face. Within seconds, the captain found himself staring down the muzzle of a service revolver. Had his friends not grabbed the weapon from his hand and jerked him from the tent, the officer would have murdered Adams. The war had finally come to that. The rules of "civilized warfare" no longer applied.[120]

Grant's grand flanking movement to beat the Confederates to Spotsylvania Court House had failed. His offensive in the Wilderness had failed. Three days of fighting had cost him over 17,000 effectives, double the estimated Confederate casualties and he had gained no real tactical advantage. Unlike his predecessors, however, Grant was not retreating. He would continue to probe the Army of Northern Virginia until he could penetrate its weakest link.

The armies would never be the same after that day. The Army of the Potomac, despite its severe casualties, still had men to feed into the front lines. It was just a matter of time. The war of attrition had begun. The Confederates, like the deceased Jenkins, knew that their days were numbered. A number of their enlisted men said it best. As they gazed at the dying Wadsworth, they marveled at the man's quiet, tenacious struggle to stay alive. Time and again, Adams heard individual soldiers exclaim, "I'd never believe that [the Federals] had such men as that in their army."[121] The Federals would not quit until it was over.

# APPENDIX

ORDER OF BATTLE[1]

THE UNION ARMY: Lieut. Gen. Ulysses S. Grant
THE ARMY OF THE POTOMAC: Maj. Gen. George G. Meade
Provost Guard: Brig. Gen. Marsena Patrick

	Present[2]
1st Mass. Cav., Cos. C & D	109
3rd Pa. Cav.	337
80th N.Y. (20th Militia)	417
68th Pa.	265
114th Pa.	240
Total	1,368

Volunteer Engineer Brigade

	Present	Killed	Wounded	Missing	Total
50th N.Y.	1,400		1		1

II ARMY CORPS: Maj. Gen. Winfield Scott Hancock
Escort: 1st Vt. Cav., Co. M
First Division: Brig. Gen. Francis C. Barlow
1st Brigade: Col. Nelson A. Miles

	Present	Killed[3]	Wounded	Missing	Total
26th Mich.	423		7		7
61st N.Y.	280		3		3
81st Pa.	228				
140th Pa.	478	3	10		13
183rd Pa.	586				
Total	1,995	3	20		23

Second Brigade: Col. Thomas A. Smyth

	Present	Killed	Wounded	Missing	Total
28th Mass.	380	15	86	14	115
63rd N.Y.	286	9	78	8	95
69th N.Y.	371	7	37	8	52
88th N.Y.	260	10	38	4	52
116th Pa.	379	6	24	4	34
Total	1,676	47	263	38	348

Third Brigade: Col. Paul Frank

	Present	Killed	Wounded	Missing	Total
39th N.Y.	540	14	99	23	136
52nd N.Y.	364		4		4
57th N.Y.	206	7	50	1	58
111th N.Y.	435	42	119	17	178
125th N.Y.	305	6	17	5	28
126th N.Y.	191	5	62	9	76
Total	2,041	74	351	55	480

Fourth Brigade: Col. John R. Brooke

	Present	Killed	Wounded	Missing	Total
2nd Del.	213				
64th N.Y.	217		8		8
66th N.Y.	260	1	6	4	11
53rd Pa.	532	1	3		4
145th Pa.	445			1	1
148th Pa.	688	1			1
Total	2,355	3	17	5	25
Div. Total	8,667	127	653	98	878

Second Division: Brig. Gen. John Gibbon
Provost Guard: 2nd Co., Minn. Sharpshooters
First Brigade: Brig. Gen. Alexander S. Webb

	Present	Killed	Wounded	Missing	Total
19th Me.	458	22	130	6	158
15th Mass.	269	4	16	3	23
19th Mass.	221	3	13	3	19
20th Mass.	443	23	108	9	140
7th Mich.	293	8	43	9	60
42nd N.Y.	301		8	15	23
59th N.Y.	160	2	8	4	14
82nd N.Y.	284	4	13	12	29
Total	2,429	66	339	61	466

Second Brigade: Brig. Gen. Joshua T. Owen

	Present	Killed	Wounded	Missing	Total
152nd N.Y.	360	9	37	5	51
69th Pa.	172	3	11	5	19
71st Pa.	338	1	35	8	44
72nd Pa.	330	4	40	13	57
106th Pa.	216	10	43	5	58
Total	1,416	27	166	36	229

Third Brigade: Col. Samuel S. Carroll

	Present	Killed	Wounded	Missing	Total
14th Conn.	414	9	67	13	89
1st Del.	319	6	89	4	99
14th Ind.	261	6	22	6	34
12th N.J.	419	12	62	5	79
10th N.Y.	298	17	60	18	95
108th N.Y.	221	5	43	4	52
4th Ohio	351	11	32	3	46
8th Ohio	224	3	16	3	22
7th W. Va.	346	2	38	3	43
Total	2,853	71	429	59	559
Div. Total	6,698	164	934	156	1,254

Third Division: Maj. Gen. David B. Birney
First Brigade: Brig. Gen. J. H. Hobart Ward

	Present	Killed	Wounded	Missing	Total
20th Ind.	502	19	102	3	124
3rd Me.	462	15	74	39	128
40th N.Y.	632	20	156	37	213
86th N.Y.	337	2	49	8	59
124th N.Y.	342	1	55	2	58
99th Pa.	265	11	45	1	57
110th Pa.	293	9	38	7	54
141st Pa.	324	6	72	4	82
2nd U.S.S.S.	292	16	49	11	76
Total	3,449	99	640	112	851

Second Brigade: Brig. Gen. Alexander Hays (Killed, May 5)
                  Col. John S. Crocker

	Present	Killed	Wounded	Missing	Total
4th Me.	368	32	136	3	171
17th Me.	507	22	155	15	192
3rd Mich.	376	22	62	19	103

Second Brigade: Brig. Gen. Alexander Hays (Killed, May 5)
            Col. John S. Crocker (Cont.)

	Present	Killed	Wounded	Missing	Total
5th Mich.	362	16	79	2	97
93rd N.Y.	509	42	213	5	260
57th Pa.	375	22	128	3	153
63rd Pa.	526	32	146	13	191
105th Pa.	372	38	116	6	160
1st U.S.S.S.	292	14	39	8	61
Total	3,687	240	1,074	74	1,388
Div. Total	7,136	339	1,714	186	2,239

Fourth Division: Brig. Gen. Gershom Mott
First Brigade: Col. Robert McAllister

	Present	Killed	Wounded	Missing	Total
1st Mass.	430	2	12	5	19
16th Mass.	325	6	30	3	39
5th N.J.	274	6	54	4	64
6th N.J.	219	8	28	1	37
7th N.J.	257	1	13	5	19
8th N.J.	220	6	114	4	124
11th N.J.	245		22		22
26th Pa.	401	3	27	2	32
115th Pa.	140	2	8	2	12
Total	2,511	34	308	26	368

Second Brigade: Col. William R. Brewster

	Present	Killed	Wounded	Missing	Total
11th Mass.	419	9	54	12	75
70th N.Y.	280	4	18	5	27
71st N.Y.	246		5	4	9
72nd N.Y.	320	2	16	9	27
73rd N.Y.	338	6	54	6	66
74th N.Y.	210	1	16	7	24
120th N.Y.	272	5	48	8	61
84th Pa.	403	5	42	1	48
Total	2,488	32	253	52	337
Div. Total	4,999	66	561	78	705

Artillery Brigade: Col. John C. Tidball
  55 guns   **Present:** 1,601

	Killed	Wounded	Missing	Total
F, 6th Me. Lgt.		8		8
F, 1st Pa. Lgt.	1	2		3

10th Mass. Lgt.   1st N.H. Lgt.   G, 1st N.Y. Lgt.   3rd Bttn.,   4th N.Y. Hvy.   F, 1st Pa. Lgt.   A, 1st R.I. Lgt.   B, 1st R.I. Lgt.   K, 4th U.S.   C & I, 5th U.S. *(No casualties.)*

	Present	Killed	Wounded	Missing	Total
Corps Total	26,900	696	3,861	518	5,075

V ARMY CORPS: Maj. Gen. Gouverneur K. Warren
Provost Guard: 12th N.Y. Bttn.
First Division: Brig. Gen. Charles Griffin
First Brigade: Brig. Gen. Romeyn Ayres

	Present	Killed	Wounded	Missing	Total
140th N.Y.	627	23	118	114	255
146th N.Y.	589	20	67	225	312
91st Pa.	401		9	2	11
155th Pa.	488	7	42	6	55
2nd U.S.	173		1		1
11th U.S.	277	11	35	19	65
12th U.S.	394	15	51	44	110
14th U.S.	448	4	79	35	118
17th U.S.	242	1	7		8
Total	3,639	81	409	445	935

Second Brigade: Col. Jacob B. Sweitzer

	Present	Killed	Wounded	Missing	Total
9th Mass.	514	26	108	3	137
22nd Mass.	327	5	34	3	42
32nd Mass.	401		16	3	19
4th Mich.	272	5	33	4	42
62nd Pa.	640	8	47	6	61
Total	2,154	44	238	19	301

Third Brigade: Brig. Gen. Joseph J. Bartlett

	Present	Killed	Wounded	Missing	Total
20th Me.	427	13	82	16	111
18th Mass.	358	8	27	29	64
1st Mich.	242	5	47	12	64
16th Mich.	423	3	37		40
44th N.Y.	420	4	62	1	67
83rd Pa.	644	15	61	24	100
118th Pa.	538	2	38	25	65
Total	3,052	50	354	107	511
Div. Total	8,845	175	1,001	571	1,747

Second Division: Brig. Gen. John C. Robinson
First Brigade: Col. Samuel H. Leonard (May 5)
              Col. Peter Lyle (assigned, May 6)

	Present	Killed	Wounded	Missing	Total
16th Me.	476		19	21	40
13th Mass.	264		10	1	11
39th Mass.	516	5	12		17
104th N.Y.	204		2		2
Total	1,460	5	43	22	70

Second Brigade: Brig. Gen. Henry Baxter (wounded, May 6)
               Col. Richard Coulter (May 6)

	Present	Killed	Wounded	Missing	Total
12th Mass.	354	14	48	8	70
83rd N.Y.	541	18	82	15	115
97th N.Y.	412	15	71	13	99
11th Pa.	512	6	136	13	155
88th Pa.	268		1		1
90th Pa.	340	5	73	16	94
Total	2,427	58	411	65	534

Third Brigade: Col. Andrew W. Denison

	Present	Killed	Wounded	Missing	Total
1st Md.	325	5	11	9	25
4th Md.	284	5	8	5	18
7th Md.	557	7	52	22	81
8th Md.	281	5	48	9	62
Total	1,447	22	119	45	186
Div. Total	5,334	85	573	132	790

Third Division: Brig. Gen. Samuel Crawford
First Brigade: Col. William McCandless

Reserves	Present	Killed	Wounded	Missing	Total
1st Pa.	374			1	1
2nd Pa.	242	1	3	6	10
6th Pa.	313	5	25	5	35
7th Pa.	370			303	303
11th Pa.	371	4	37	58	99
13th Pa.	328	3	31	3	37
Total	1,998	13	96	376	485

Third Brigade: Col. Joseph W. Fisher

Reserves	Present	Killed	Wounded	Missing	Total
5th Pa.	382	4	10	2	16
8th Pa.	347	5	40	2	47
10th Pa.	463	3	15	4	22
12th Pa.	329		3		3
Total	1,521	12	68	8	88
Div. Total	3,519	25	164	384	573

Fourth Division: Brig. Gen. James S. Wadsworth (mortally wounded and captured, May 6)
        Brig. Gen. Lysander Cutler (May 6)
First Brigade: Brig. Gen. Lysander Cutler (May 6)
        Col. William W. Robinson (May 6)

	Present	Killed	Wounded	Missing	Total
7th Ind.	510	16	92	54	162
19th Ind.	320	14	78	11	103
24th Mich.	320	14	48	42	104
1st N.Y. S.S.	157	1	27	7	35
2nd Wis.	237	6	16	18	40
6th Wis.	361	8	40	15	63
7th Wis.	504	27	155	35	217
Total	2,409	86	456	182	724

Second Brigade: Brig. Gen. James C. Rice

	Present	Killed	Wounded	Missing	Total
76th N.Y.	551	27	69	186	282
84th N.Y.	404	1		2	3
95th N.Y.	437	18	64	92	174
147th N.Y.	511	15	97	59	171
56th Pa.	257	10	22	10	42
Total	2,160	71	252	349	672

Third Brigade: Col. Roy Stone (disabled, May 6)
        Col. Edward S. Bragg (May 6)

	Present	Killed	Wounded	Missing	Total
121st Pa.	227	1	19	9	29
142nd Pa.	317	3	36	16	55
143rd Pa.	746	23	136	61	220
149th Pa.	695	11	109	95	215
150th Pa.	325	7	61	24	92
Total	2,310	45	361	205	611
Div. Total	6,879	202	1,069	736	2,007

Artillery Brigade: Col. Charles S. Wainwright
  36 guns   **Present:** 1,415

	Killed	Wounded	Missing	Total
D, 1st N.Y. Lgt.		5	3	8
2nd Bttn., 4th N.Y. Hvy.		2		2
B, 1st Pa. Lgt.		1		1
Total		8	3	11

C, Mass. Lgt.   E, Mass. Lgt.   E & L, 1st N.Y. Lgt.   H, 1st N.Y. Lgt.   B, 4th U.S.
D, 5th U.S. *(No Casualties.)*

	Present	Killed	Wounded	Missing	Total
Corps Total	25,992	487	2,815	1,826	5,128

VI ARMY CORPS: Maj. Gen. John Sedgwick
Escort: Co. A, 8th Pa. Cav.
First Division: Brig. Gen. Horatio G. Wright
First Brigade: Col. Henry W. Brown

	Present	Killed	Wounded	Missing	Total
1st N.J.	490	17	106	39	162
2nd N.J.	421	5	18	23	46
3rd N.J.	342		7	1	8
4th N.J.	452	8	73	15	96
10th N.J.	711	3	16	19	38
15th N.J.	500	3	9	2	14
Total	2,464	36	229	99	364

Second Brigade: Col. Emory Upton

	Present	Killed	Wounded	Missing	Total
5th Me.	294		3		3
121st N.Y.	503	15	37	21	73
95th Pa.	490	9	13	3	25
96th Pa.	407	1	7	2	10
Total	1,694	25	60	26	111

Third Brigade: Brig. Gen. David A. Russell

	Present	Killed	Wounded	Missing	Total
6th Me.	318		2		2
49th Pa.	693	3	35	5	43
119th Pa.	520	12	74		86
5th Wis.	524	4	121	10	135
Total	2,055	19	232	15	266

Fourth Brigade: Brig. Gen. Alexander Shaler (captured, May 6)
            Col. Nelson Cross

	Present	Killed	Wounded	Missing	Total
65th N.Y.	283	8	28	21	57
67th N.Y.	334	11	62	20	93
122nd N.Y.	427	9	70	40	119
Total	1,044	28	160	81	269
Div. Total	7,257	108	681	221	1,010

Second Division: Brig. George W. Getty (wounded, May 6)
              Brig. Gen. Frank Wheaton (May 6)
              Brig. Gen. Thomas H. Neill (May 7)
First Brigade: Brig. Gen. Frank Wheaton

	Present	Killed	Wounded	Missing	Total
62nd N.Y.	122	14	58		72
93rd Pa.	299	15	114		129
98th Pa.	481	11	65		76
102nd Pa.	236	21	132		153
139th Pa.	567	33	157	5	195
Total	1,705	94	526	5	625

Second Brigade: Col. Lewis A. Grant

	Present	Killed	Wounded	Missing	Total
2nd Vt.	719	49	285	14	348
3rd Vt.	609	38	167	6	211
4th Vt.	570	41	223	4	268
5th Vt.	520	33	187	26	246
6th Vt.	472	34	155	7	196
Total	2,890	195	1,017	57	1,269

Third Brigade: Brig. Gen. Thomas H. Neill (promoted, May 7)
             Col. Daniel D. Bidwell (May 7)

	Present	Killed	Wounded	Missing	Total
7th Me.	472	24	80	13	117
43rd N.Y.	444	21	106	71	198
49th N.Y.	434	29	54	6	89
77th N.Y.	453	11	44	9	64
61st Pa.	664	20	113	18	151
Total	2,467	105	397	117	619

Fourth Brigade: Brig. Gen. Henry L. Eustis

	Present	Killed	Wounded	Missing	Total
7th Mass.	401	13	103	4	120
10th Mass.	443	21	105	2	128
37th Mass.	609	30	101	6	137
2nd R.I.	511	12	66	5	83
Total	1,964	76	375	17	468
Div. Total	9,026	470	2,315	196	2,981

Third Division: Brig. Gen. James B. Ricketts
First Brigade: Brig. Gen. William H. Morris

	Present	Killed	Wounded	Missing	Total
14th N.J.	556	1	4		5
106th N.Y.	564	4	6	1	11
151st N.Y.	418	3	14	4	21
87th Pa.	429		19	4	23
10th Vt.	629	2	10		12
Total	2,596	10	53	9	72

Second Brigade: Brig. Gen. Truman Seymour (captured, May 6)
              Col. Benjamin F. Smith (May 6)

	Present	Killed	Wounded	Missing	Total
6th Md.	405	24	112	34	170
110th Oh.	581	17	106	25	148
122nd Oh.	522	18	110	48	176
126th Oh.	527	22	125	62	209
67th Pa.	214	7	39	19	65
138th Pa.	553	21	97	32	150
Total	2,802	109	589	220	918
Div. Total	5,398	119	642	229	990

Artillery Brigade: Col. Charles H. Tompkins
   50 guns   **Present:** 1,525

	Killed	Wounded	Missing	Total
1st Bttn., 4th N.Y. Hvy.	2	14	6	22

D, Me. Lgt.   A, Mass. Lgt.   1st Btty., N.Y. Lgt.   3rd Btty., N.Y. Lgt.   C, 1st R.I. Lgt.
E, 1st R.I. Lgt.   G, 1st R.I. Lgt.   M, 5th U.S. *(No casualties.)*

	Present	Killed	Wounded	Missing	Total
Corps Total	23,206	699	3,652	652	5,003

IX ARMY CORPS: Maj. Gen. Ambrose E. Burnside
Present: 269
Provost Guard: 8th U.S. Infantry
First Division: Brig. Gen. Thomas G. Stevenson
First Brigade: Col. Sumner Carruth (sunstruck, May 6)
　　　　　　　Col. Jacob P. Gould (May 6)

	Present	Killed	Wounded	Missing	Total
35th Mass.	2,53[4]				
56th Mass.	609	8	54	11	73
57th Mass.	559	57	158	30	245
59th Mass.[5]	550	10	35	10	55
4th U.S.	293	5	19	10	34
10th U.S.	200	8	51	5	64
Total	5,254	88	317	66	471

Second Brigade: Col. Daniel Leasure

	Present	Killed	Wounded	Missing	Total
3rd Md.[6]	227	3	9	12	24
21st Mass.	270	2	7	7	16
100th Pa.	650	1	28	8	37
Total	1,147	6	44	27	77
Div. Total	6,411+	94	361	93	548

Second Division: Brig. Gen. Robert B. Potter
First Brigade: Col. Zenas R. Bliss (sunstruck, May 6)
　　　　　　　Col. John I. Curtin (May 6)

	Present	Killed	Wounded	Missing	Total
36th Mass.	496	12	61		73
58th Mass.		6	32	7	45
51st N.Y.	373	20	54	5	79
45th Pa.[7]	701	17	119	7	143
48th Pa.	790	3	10		13
7th R.I.	281		1		1
Total	2,641+	58	277	19	354

Second Brigade: Col. Simon Griffin

	Present	Killed	Wounded	Missing	Total
31st Me.	540	5	24	2	31
32nd Me.[8]	349				
6th N.H.	434	1	32	14	47
9th N.H.	596				
11th N.H.	449	2	43	11	56
17th Vt.	443	8	63	3	74

Second Brigade: Col. Simon Griffin (Cont.)

	Present	Killed	Wounded	Missing	Total
Total	2,811	16	162	30	208
Div. Total	5,452	74	439	49	562

Third Division: *Brig. Gen. Orlando B. Willcox*
First Brigade: *Col. John F. Hartranft*

	Present	Killed	Wounded	Missing	Total
2nd Mich.	301	6	32		38
8th Mich.	517	11	80	14	105
17th Mich.	413	5	37		42
27th Mich.	838	12	60	6	78
109th N.Y.	878	11	64	1	76
51st Pa.	633	9	58	1	68
Total	3,580	54	331	22	407

Second Brigade: Col. Benjamin C. Christ

	Present	Killed	Wounded	Missing	Total
1st Mich. S.S.	682	4	23	2	29
20th Mich.	419		6	1	7
79th N.Y.[9]	273				
60th Oh.	583		2	3	5
50th Pa.	610	12	59		71
Total	2,567	16	90	6	112
Div. Total	6,147	70	421	28	519

Fourth Division: *Brig. Gen. Edward Ferrero*
(All of the infantry regiments were African-American. No casualties. Not engaged.)

First Brigade: *Col. Joshua K. Sigfried*

	Present
27th U.S.	439
30th U.S.	676
39th U.S.	656
43rd U.S.	433
Total	2,204

Second Brigade: Col. Henry G. Thomas

	Present
30th Conn.	207
19th U.S.	543
23rd U.S.[10]	521
Total	1,271
Div. Total	3,475+

Fourth Division Cavalry:

	Present	Killed	Wounded	Missing	Total
3rd N.J.	852			6	6
22nd N.Y.[11]		1		4	5
2nd Oh.	621	1		1	2
13th Pa.[12]	522				
Total	2,517+		2	11	13

Corps Artillery: Two companies to each division. (No casualties.)
  35 guns   **Present: 1,241**
First Division: B, Me Lgt   14th Btty., Mass. Lgt
Second Division: 11th Btty., Mass. Lgt.   19th Btty., N.Y. Lgt.
Third Division: G, Me. Lgt.   34th Btty., N.Y. Lgt.
Fourth Division: D, Pa. Lgt.   3rd Vt.

	Present	Killed	Wounded	Missing	Total
Corps Total	27,184+	238	1,223	181	1,642

Reserve Artillery:[13]
  27th Btty., N.Y. Lgt   D, 1st R.I. Lgt.   H, 1st R.I. Lgt.   E, 2nd U.S.   G, 3rd U.S.
  L & M, 3rd U.S. *(No casualties.)*
Provisional Brigade:[14] Col. Elisha G. Marshall
  (Served as infantry.)

	Present	Killed	Wounded	Missing
24th N.Y. Cav.[15]	997			
14th N.Y. Hvy.	1,272	1	7	8
2nd Pa. Prov. Hvy.	1,062		1	1
Total	3,331	1	8	9

CAVALRY CORPS: *Maj. Gen. Philip H. Sheridan*
Escort: 6th U.S.
First Division: Brig. Gen. Alfred T. A. Torbert (sick, May 7)
            Brig. Gen. Wesley Merritt (May 7)
First Brigade: Brig. Gen. George A. Custer

	Present	Killed	Wounded	Missing	Total
1st Mich.	714	3	21		24
5th Mich.	655	3	13		16
6th Mich.	381	3	13	4	20
7th Mich.	414		1	1	2
Total	2,164	9	48	5	62

Second Brigade: Col. Thomas C. Devin

	Present	Killed	Wounded	Missing	Total
4th N.Y.[16]	375				
6th N.Y.	436	1	11	1	13
9th N.Y.	469	5	20	3	28
17th Pa.	648	1	13		14
Total	1,928	7	44	4	55

Reserve Brigade: Brig. Gen. Wesley Merritt (promoted, May 7)
Col. Alfred Gibbs (May 7)

	Present	Killed	Wounded	Missing	Total
19th N.Y.[17]	599	20	36	35	91
6th Pa.	398	3	28	3	34
1st U.S.	467	8	34	3	45
2nd U.S.	343	2	21	2	25
5th U.S.	240	1	2		3
Total	2,047	34	121	43	198
Div. Total	6,139+	50	213	52	315

Second Division: Brig. Gen. David McM. Gregg
First Brigade: Brig. Gen. Henry E. Davies, Jr.

	Present	Killed	Wounded	Missing	Total
1st Mass.	556	3	24	14	41
1st N.J.	853	7	41	10	58
6th Oh.	712		10	1	11
1st Pa.	455		5		5
Total:	2,576	10	80	25	115

Second Brigade: Col. J. Irvin Gregg

	Present	Killed	Wounded	Missing	Total
1st Me.	415	1	4		5
10th N.Y.	515	1	8	1	10
2nd Pa.	518	6	13	1	20
4th Pa.	195	1			1
8th Pa.	247		5	1	6
16th Pa.	472		4		4
Total	2,362	9	34	3	46
Div. Total	4,938	19	114	28	161

Third Division: Brig. Gen. James H. Wilson

Escort:	Present	Killed	Wounded	Missing	Total
8th Ill.	97	1	3	3	7

First Brigade: Col. Timothy M. Bryan, Jr. (acting commander)
        Col. John B. McIntosh (with the 5th N.Y.)

	Present	Killed	Wounded	Missing	Total
1st Conn.	603		7	37	44
2nd N.Y.	317	3	12	15	30
5th N.Y.	481	16	21	13	50
18th Pa.	337		11	30	41
Total	1,738	19	51	95	165

Second Brigade: Col. Charles H. Chapman

	Present	Killed	Wounded	Missing	Total
3rd Ind.	327		3	4	7
8th N.Y.	478	1		3	4
1st Vt.	516	5	30	11	46
Total	1,321	6	33	18	57
Div. Total	3,059	25	84	113	222

First Brigade Horse Artillery: Capt. James M. Robertson
Present: 926

	Killed	Wounded	Missing	Total
6th Btty., N.Y. Lgt.	2	1		3
C & E, 4th U.S.		2		2
Total	2	3		5

B & L, 2nd U.S.   D, 2nd U.S.   M, 2nd U.S.   A, 4th U.S. (No casualties.)

Cav. Corps

	Present	Killed	Wounded	Missing	Total
Total	15,159	97	417	196	710

Artillery: Brig. Gen. Henry J. Hunt
Artillery Reserve: Col. Henry S. Burton
First Brigade: Col. Howard J. Kitching

	Present	Killed	Wounded	Missing	Total
6th N.Y. Hvy.	1,046		2	10	12
15th N.Y. Hvy.	1,458	4	32	8	44
Total	2,504	4	34	18	56

Second Brigade: Maj. John A. Tompkins
    E, Me. Lgt.   A, 1st N.J. Lgt.   B, 1st N.J. Lgt.   5th Btty., N.Y. Lgt.
    12th Btty., N.Y. Lgt.   B, 1st N.Y. Lgt.   (No casualties.)

Third Brigade: Maj. Robert H. Fitzhugh
(Not engaged.)
    9th Btty., Mass. Lgt.   C, 1st N.Y. Lgt.   11th Btty., N.Y. Lgt.   15th Btty., N.Y. Lgt.
    H, 1st Oh. Lgt.   E, 5th U.S.

Horse Artillery
Second Brigade: *Capt. Dunbar R. Ransom*
(Not engaged.)
    E & G, 1st U.S.   H & I, 1st U.S.   K, 1st U.S.   A, 2nd U.S.   G, 2nd U.S.
    C, F & K, 3rd U.S.

	Present[18]	Killed	Wounded	Missing	Total
II Corps	31,269	696	3,862	518	5,076
V Corps	25,992	487	2,815	1,826	5,128
VI Corps	23,206	699	3,652	652	5,003
IX Corps	27,184+	238	1,231	181	1,651
Cavalry	15,159	97	417	196	710
Artillery	2,504	4	34	18	56
Total	125,314	2,221	12,011	3,391	17,624
OR Total	118,000	2,246	12,037	3,383	17,666

THE CONFEDERATE ARMY
ARMY OF NORTHERN VIRGINIA: General ROBERT E. LEE
FIRST ARMY CORPS: Lt. Gen. James Longstreet (wounded, May 6)
                             Maj. Gen. Richard H. Anderson (May 6)
Present: 10,000[19]
Kershaw's Division: *Brig. Gen. Joseph B. Kershaw*
Kershaw's Brigade:

	Killed	Wounded	Missing	Total
2nd S.C.[20]	13	37	1	51
3rd S.C.[21]	14	49		63
7th S.C.	15	51		66
8th S.C.[22]	4	17	7	28
15th S.C.	8	63		71
3rd Bttn.	5	22		27
Total	59	239	8	306

Humphreys Brigade: *Brig. Gen. Benjamin G. Humphreys*
    13th Miss.   17th Miss.   18th Miss.[23]

	Killed	Wounded	Missing	Total
21st Miss.[24]	27	85	1	113

Wofford's Brigade: *Brig. Gen. William T. Wofford*

	Killed	Wounded	Missing	Total
16th Ga.[25]	21	54		75
18th Ga.	13	38		51
24th Ga.	17	90		107
Cobb's Leg.	8	41	5	54

Wofford's Brigade: Brig. Gen. William T. Wofford (Cont.)

	Killed	Wounded	Missing	Total
Phillips' Leg.	11	34		45
3rd Bttn.	2	32		34
Total	72	289	5	366

Bryan's Brigade: Brig. Gen. Goode Bryan

	Killed	Wounded	Missing	Total
10th Ga.[26]	5	39		44
50th Ga.[27]				
51st Ga.	4[28]	32		36
53rd Ga.	5	39		44
Total	14	110		124
Div. Total	172	723	14	909

Field's Division: Maj. Gen. Charles W. Field
Jenkins' Brigade: Brig. Gen. Micah Jenkins (killed, May 6)

	Present	Killed	Wounded	Missing	Total
1st S.C.[29]	261[30]	13	87		100
2nd S.C. Rifles[31]	300	25	100	5	130
5th S.C.[32]		13	81	20	114
6th S.C.[33]		7	40		47
Palmetto S.S.[34]		5	66	1	72
Total		63	374	26	463

Anderson's Brigade: Brig. Gen. George T. Anderson

	Present	Killed	Wounded	Missing	Total
7th Ga.		2	11	2	15
8th Ga.	500[35]	7[36]	42	17	66
9th Ga.[37]		3	11	1	15
11th Ga.		2	9	1	12
59th Ga.	300	4	1	2	7
Total	800+	18	74	23	115

Law's Brigade: Brig. Gen. McIver Law (under arrest, May 6)
            Col. William F. Perry (May 6)

	Present	Killed	Wounded	Missing	Total
4th Ala.	203	13	49	7	69
15th Ala.	298	5	26	13	44
44th Ala.	280	6	36	5	47
47th Ala.	242	16	49	17	82
48th Ala.	171	5	13	8	26
Total	1,194	45	173	50	268

Gregg's Brigade: Brig. Gen. John Gregg

	Present[38]	Killed	Wounded	Missing	Total
3rd Ark.	155	15	55	13	83
1st Tex.	248	26	89	6	121
4th Tex.	207	26	95	3	124
5th Tex.	180	18	92	2	112
Total	790	85	331	24	440

Benning's Brigade: Brig. Gen. Henry L. Benning

	Present	Killed	Wounded	Missing	Total
2nd Ga.[39]		15[40]	53	2	70
15th Ga.		5	41	5	51
17th Ga.	225	20	105		125
20th Ga.		16	70	3	89
Total	750	56	269	10	335

Artillery: Brig. Gen. E. Porter Alexander
Huger's Battalion: Lt. Col. Frank Huger
  Fickling's Va. Btty. Moody's La. Btty. Parker's Va. Btty. J. D. Smith's Va. Btty.
  Taylor's Va. Btty. Woolfolk's Va. Btty.
Haskell's Battalion: Maj. John C. Haskell
  Flanner's N.C. Btty. Garden's S.C. Btty. Lamkin's Va. Btty. Ramsay's N.C. Btty.
Cabell's Battalion: Col. Henry C. Cabell
  Callaway's Ga. Btty. McCarthy's Va. Btty. Carlton's Ga. Btty. Manly's N.C. Btty.

	Present	Killed	Wounded	Missing	Total
1st Corps	10,000	354	1,513	123	2,090

SECOND ARMY CORPS: Lt. Gen. Richard S. Ewell
Early's Division: Maj. Gen. Jubal Early
Hays' Brigade: Brig. Gen. Harry T. Hays
Present: 1,000[41]   **Casualties:** 250[42]
  5th La. 6th La. 7th La. 8th La. 9th La.

Pegram's Brigade: Brig. Gen. John Hoffman (wounded, May 5)
Present: 1,500

	Killed	Wounded	Missing	Total
13th Va.[43]	15	18		33
31st Va.	14	76	11	101
49th Va.[44]	2	14		16
52nd Va.				
58th Va.[45]	5	42		47
Total	24+	152+	11+	187+

Gordon's Brigade: Brig. Gen. John B. Gordon
Present: 2,300

	Killed	Wounded	Missing	Total
13th Ga.[46]	8	53		61
26th Ga.				
31st Ga.[47]	12	72		84
38th Ga.				
60th Ga.				
61st Ga.				
Total	20+	125+		145+

	Present	Killed	Wounded	Missing	Total
Div. Total	6,000	44+	277+	11+	582+

Johnson's Division: Maj. Gen. Edward Johnson
Stonewall Brigade: Brig. Gen. James A. Walker
Present: 1,200

	Killed	Wounded	Missing	Total
2nd Va.				
4th Va.[48]	5	45		50
5th Va.[49]	11	42	5	58
27th Va.				
33rd Va.				
Total	16+	87+	5+	108+

Steuart's Brigade: Brig. Gen. George H. Steuart
Present: 1,425[50]

	Present	Killed	Wounded	Missing	Total
1st N.C.[51]	350	2	9	21	32
3rd N.C.[52]	348				
10th Va.[53]	250	5	33		38
23rd Va.[54]	250	4	26		30
37th Va.	300				
Total	1,425	11+	68+	21+	100+

Jones' Brigade: Brig. Gen. John M. Jones (killed, May 5)
Present: 2,100

	Killed	Wounded	Missing	Total
21st Va.	4	40		44
25th Va.[55]	7	4	114	125
42nd Va.				
44th Va.[56]	6	32	146	184
48th Va.[57]				88
50th Va.				
Total	17+	76+	260+	444+

Stafford's Brigade: Brig. Gen. Leroy Stafford (killed, May 5)
Present: 900

	Killed	Wounded	Missing	Total
1st La.[58]	10	18	47	75
2nd La.	17	29	64	110
10th La.[59]	5	18	8	31
14th La.	6	28	63	97
15th La.	6	16	63	85
Total	44	109	245	398

	Present	Killed	Wounded	Missing	Total
Div. Total	5,625	88+	340+	531+	1,050+

Rodes' Division: Maj. Gen. Robert E. Rodes
Daniel's Brigade: Brig. Gen. Junius Daniel
Present: 1,550
32nd N.C.   43rd N.C.   2nd. N.C. Bttn. *(Casualties are not reported.)*

	Killed	Wounded	Missing	Total
45th N.C.[60]	11	63		74
53rd N.C.[61]	2+	5+	4+	11
Total	13+	68+	4+	85+

Ramseur's Brigade: Brig. Gen. Stephen D. Ramseur
Present: 1,400

	Killed	Wounded	Missing	Total
2nd N.C.[62]	1	15	6	22
4th N.C.	4	14	3	21
14th N.C.	3	52	11	66
30th N.C.				
Total	8+	81+	20+	109+

Doles' Brigade: Brig. Gen. George Doles
Present: 1,250

	Killed	Wounded	Missing	Total
4th Ga.[63]	45	39	3	87
12th Ga.	24	17	5	46
44th Ga.	16	19		35
Total	85	75	8	168

Battle's Brigade: Brig. Gen. Cullen A. Battle
Present: 1,250

	Killed	Wounded	Missing	Total
3rd Ala.[64]	22	60	1	83

Battle's Brigade: Brig. Gen. Cullen A. Battle (Cont.)

	Killed	Wounded	Missing	Total
5th Ala.				
6th Ala.[65]	28	83	37	148
12th Ala.[66]		1+		1+
26th Ala.				
61st Ala.				
Total	50+	144+	38+	232+

Johnston's Brigade: Brig. Gen. Robert D. Johnston
Present: 1,300
5th N.C.   12th N.C.   20th N.C.   23rd N.C.   *(Casualties not reported.)*

	Present	Killed	Wounded	Missing	Total
Div. Total	6,750	156+	367+	70+	593+
2nd Corps	18,375	288+	985+	612+	2,226+

Artillery: Brig. Gen. Armistead L. Long
(Casualties are not stated.)
Hardaway's Battalion: Col. J. T. Brown (Brown commanded three of the artillery battalions in the division.)
   Graham's Va. Btty. C. B. Griffin's Va. Btty. Jones' Va. Btty. B. H. Smith's Va. Btty.
Nelson's Battalion: Col. J. T. Brown
   Kirkpatrick's Va. Btty.   Massie's Va. Btty.   Milledge's Ga. Btty.
Braxton's Battalion: Col. J. T. Brown
   Carpenter's Va. Btty.   Cooper's Va. Btty.   Hardwick's Va. Btty.
Cutshaw's Battalion: Col. Thomas H. Carter
   Carrington's Va. Btty.   A. W. Garber's Va. Btty   Tanner's Va. Btty.
Page's Battalion: Col. Thomas H. Carter
   W. P. Carter's Va. Btty.   Fry's Va. Btty.   Page's Va. Btty.   Reese's Ala. Btty.

THIRD ARMY CORPS: Lt. Gen. Ambrose P. Hill
Anderson's Division: Maj. Gen. Richard H. Anderson
Perrin's Brigade: Brig. Gen. Abner Perrin
Present: 1,400

	Killed[67]	Wounded	Missing	Total
8th Ala.		46		46
9th Ala.[68]	4	25	17	46
10th Ala.[69]	21	89	12	122
11th Ala.	13	37	2	52
14th Ala.	8	58		66
Total	46	255	31	332

Mahone's Brigade: Brig. Gen. William Mahone
Present: 1,550
6th Va.   16th Va.   41st Va.   61st Va.   *(Casualties not reported.)*

	Killed	Wounded	Missing	Total
12th Va.[70]	6	40	1	47
Brig.[71]	14	86	6	106
Total	20	86	7	153

Harris' Brigade: Brig. Gen. Nathaniel Harris
Present: 1,500

	Killed	Wounded	Missing	Total
12th Miss.[72]	13	33	13	59
16th Miss.	36	84	31	151
19th Miss.	22	55	45	122
48th Miss.	9	29	33	71
Total	80	201	122	403

Wright's Brigade: Brig. Gen. Ambrose R. Wright
Present: 1,500
3rd Ga.   22nd Ga.   48th Ga.   2nd. Ga. Bttn.   *(Casualties are not stated.)*

Perry's Brigade: Brig. Gen. E. A. Perry
Present: 500
2nd Fla.   5th Fla.   *(Casualties are not reported.)*

	Present	Killed	Wounded	Missing	Total
8th Fla.	140[73]	10	30	5	45
Brig. Total	10+	30+	5+	235+[74]	74
Div. Total	6,450	156+	612+	152+	826+

Heth's Division: Maj. Gen. Henry Heth
Davis' Brigade: Col. John M. Stone
Present: 1,200
26th Miss. *(Casualties not reported.)*

	Killed	Wounded	Missing	Total
2nd Miss.[75]	16	101	3	120
11th Miss.	12	53	7	72
42nd Miss.				10+ [76]
55th N.C.[77]	43	119	13	175
Total	71+	273+	23+	377+

Cooke's Brigade: Col. William MacRae
Present: 1,753[78]

	Killed	Wounded	Missing	Total
15th N.C.[79]	9	121	2	132
27th N.C.[80]	17	172		189

Cooke's Brigade: Col. William MacRae (Cont.)

	Killed	Wounded	Missing	Total
46th N.C.[81]	39	251		290
48th N.C.	8	125		133
Total	73	669	2	744

Kirkland's Brigade: Brig. Gen. William W. Kirkland
Present: 1,800
11th N.C.   26th N.C.   44th N.C.   52nd N.C.   *(Casualties are not reported.)*

	Killed	Wounded	Missing	Total
47th N.C.[82]	6	93	5	104
Total	6+	93+	5+	104+

Walker's Brigade: Brig. Gen. Henry H. Walker
Present: 1,500

	Killed	Wounded	Missing	Total
40th Va.[83]	3	25	16	44
47th Va.[84]	4	23	7	34
55th Va.[85]	2	17	31	50
22nd Va. Bttn.[86]	1	25	9	35
13th Ala.[87]	4	50	54	108
1st Tenn.	11	28	25	64
7th Tenn.	8	18	12	38
14th Tenn.	6	18	30	54
Total	39	204	184	427

	Present	Killed	Wounded	Missing	Total
Div. Total	6,253	189+	1,239+	214+	1,652+

Wilcox's Division: Maj. Gen. Cadmus Wilcox
Lane's Brigade: Brig. Gen. James H. Lane
Present: 1,400

	Killed	Wounded	Missing	Total
7th N.C.[88]	3	65	38	106
18th N.C.	7	36	14	57
28th N.C.	14	57	17	88
33rd N.C.	18	55	38	111
37th N.C.	1	16	36	53
Total	43	229	143	415

Scales' Brigade: Brig. Gen. Alfred M. Scales
Present: 1,750
16th N.C.   22nd N.C.   34th N.C.   38th N.C.   *(Casualties are not reported.)*

	Killed	Wounded	Missing	Total
13th N.C.[89]	5	24	17	46
Total	5+	24+	17+	46+

McGowan's Brigade: Brig. Gen. Samuel McGowan
Present: 1,300

	Killed[90]	Wounded	Missing	Total
1st S.C.	16	114	7	137
12th S.C.	16	64	22	102
13th S.C.	5	53	5	63
14th S.C.	6	71	8	85
Orr's Rifles	12	81	1	94
Total	55	383	43	481

Thomas' Brigade: Brig. Gen. Edward L. Thomas
Present: 1,400
14th Ga.   35th Ga.   *(Casualties are not recorded.)*

	Killed	Wounded	Missing	Total
45th Ga.[91]	6	94	1	101
49th Ga.[92]	24	73	29	126
Total	30+	167+	30+	227+

	Present	Killed	Wounded	Missing	Total
Div. Total	5,850	133+	803+	233+	1,169+
3rd Corps	18,553	478+	2,654+	599+	3,647+

Artillery: Col. R. Lindsay Walker
Poague's Battalion: Col. William T. Poague
  Richard's Miss. Btty.   Utterback's Va. Btty.   Williams' N.C. Btty.   Wyatt's Va. Btty.
McIntosh's Battalion: Lt. Col. D. G. McIntosh
  Clutter's Va. Btty.   Donald's Va. Btty.   Hurt's Ala. Btty.   Price's Va. Btty.
Pegram's Battalion: Lt. Col. W. J. Pegram
  Brander's Va. Btty.   Cayce's Va. Btty.   Ellett's Va. Btty.   Marye's Va. Btty.
  Zimmerman's S.C. Btty.
Cutts' Battalion: Col. A. S. Cutts
  Patterson's Ga. Btty.   Ross' Ga. Btty.   Wingfield's Ga. Btty.
Richardson's Battalion: Lt. Col. Charles Richardson
  Grandy's Va. Btty.   Landry's La. Btty.   Moore's Va. Btty.   Penick's Va. Btty.

CAVALRY CORPS: Maj. Gen. J. E. B. (Jeb) Stuart
Hampton's Division: Maj. Gen. Wade Hampton
Young's Brigade: Brig. Gen. Pierce M. B. Young
    7th Ga.   20th Ga. Bttn.   Cobb's Ga. Legion   Phillips Ga. Legion
    Jeff Davis Miss. Legion

Rosser's Brigade: Brig. Gen. Thomas L. Rosser

	Present	Killed	Wounded	Missing	Total
7th Va.[93]		4	39		43
11th Va.[94]	300	16	84	3	103
12th Va.[95]		5	29	1	35
35th Va. Bttn.		7	20		27
Total	1,000	32	172	4	208
Div. Total					

Fitzhugh Lee's Division: Maj. Gen. Fitzhugh Lee
Lomax's Brigade: Brig. Gen. Lunsford L. Lomax

	Present	Killed	Wounded	Missing	Total
5th Va.					
6th Va.		1[96]			1
15th Va.	200[97]				
Total		2+	22		24+

Wickham's Brigade: Brig. Gen. Williams C. Wickham

	Present	Killed	Wounded	Missing	Total
1st Va.		1	2		3
2nd Va.[98]		13	52	5	70
3rd Va.[99]	524[100]	4	13		17
4th Va.[101]		3	21		24
Total		21	88	5	114
Div. Total					250[102]

W. H. F. Lee's Division: Maj. Gen. W. H. F. Lee
Chambliss' Brigade: Brig. Gen. John R. Chambliss, Jr.
    9th Va.   10th Va.   13th Va.   *(Not engaged.)*
Gordon's Brigade: Brig. Gen. James B. Gordon
    1st N.C.   2nd N.C.

	Killed	Wounded	Missing	Total
5th N.C.[103]				18

Horse Artillery: Maj. Roger P. Chew
Breathed's Battalion: Maj. James Breathed
   Hart's S.C. Btty.   Johnston's Va. Btty.   McGregor's Va. Btty.   Shoemaker's Va. Btty.
   Thomson's Va. Btty.

	Present	Killed[104]	Wounded	Missing	Total
1st Corps	10,000	354	1,513	123	2,090
2nd Corps	18,375	288	985	612	2,226
3rd Corps	18,553	478	2,654	599	3,647
Cavalry	8,727	55	282	9	612
Artillery	4,854				
Total	60,509	1,175	5,434	1,343	8,575[105]

NDNOTES

Chapter One

1 Letter, William W. Smith to John W. Daniel, October 24, 1904, Special Collections Department, William R. Perkins Library, Duke University, Durham, N.C., 1.

2 Samuel Buck, "Recollections of an Old Confed," Samuel Buck Papers, ca. 1890, Special Collections Department, William R. Perkins Library, Duke University, Durham, N.C., 94–96.

3 McHenry Howard, *Recollections of a Maryland Confederate Soldier and Staff Officer Under Johnston, Jackson and Lee* James I. Robertson, (ed.) (Dayton: Morningside Bookshop, 1975), 277.

Francis L. Hudgins, "38th Georgia Regiment in the Wilderness," Confederate Veteran Papers, Battles 1861–1932, n.d., Box 1, Special Collections Dept., William R. Perkins Library, Duke University, Durham, N.C., 5.

4 Francis L. Hudgins, "38th Georgia Regiment in the Wilderness," Confederate Veteran Papers, Battles 1861–1932, n.d., Box 1, Special Collections Dept., William R. Perkins Library, Duke University, Durham, N.C., 6.

5 Jones did not know the name of the artillery officer in the area but Mr. Lowell Reidenbaugh in his history of the 33rd Virginia said that Michael Garber's section of artillery was placed on the right of the Confederate line. The NPS maps, however, indicate that the two guns on the left came from Carter's Battalion. Statements from the 49th New York record casualties resulting from a 10-pounder bolt, which indicate that one of the guns was a 10-pounder Parrott. Carter's had a 10-pounder in his battalion.

Letters, Thomas G. Jones to John W. Daniel, July 3, 1904, 7, and June 20, 1904, 2, Special Collections Department, William R. Perkins Library, Duke University, Durham, N.C. Lowell Reidenbaugh, *33rd Virginia Infantry* (Lynchburg: H. E. Howard, Inc., 1987), 83. Daniel Davidson Bidwell, (comp.), *History of the Forty-Ninth New York Volunteers* (Albany: J. B. Lyon Co., 1916), 46.

6 Robert N. Scott, (comp.), *The Official Records of the War of the Rebellion* XXXVI, part 1 (Washington, D.C.: U.S. Government Printing Office, 1887), 722. Report of Brig. Gen. William H. Morris, 1st Brig., 3rd Div., VI Corps.

7 Payne said that the brigade turned at right angles before the afternoon attack which does not make any sense because the Northern position was secure to the north. He then said that during Gordon's flank attack at 6:00 P.M. the brigade faced north in two lines. Thompson, the captain of Company F, 10th Vermont, said that the 10th Vermont and the 106th New York turned north during the flank attack. They were the only regiments in the brigade which changed direction which indicates that the brigade had been on a single front prior to that time.

J. Payne, "The Wilderness, The Turning of the Right Flank, May 6, 1864," *The National Tribune*, July 18, 1889, 3. J. S. Thompson, "Turning the Right Flank, May 6, 1864," *The National Tribune*, August 1, 1889, 3. (*OR*, XXXVI, part 1, 722) Report of Brig. Gen. William H. Morris, 1st Brig., 3rd Div., VI Corps.

8 Alanson A. Haines, *History of the Fifteenth Regiment New Jersey Volunteers* (New York: Jenkins & Thomas, Printers, 1883), 147.

9 A. T. Brewer, *History Sixty-first Regiment Pennsylvania Volunteers 1861–1865* (1911), 83. James Bumgardner, "Pegram's Brigade, Early's Division," *Richmond Dispatch*, October 8, 1905, Manuscript Dept., Alderman Library, University of Virginia.

10 C. G. Funke, "In the Wilderness. A New York Comrade Gives His Experience of Fighting in the Woods and Brush," *The National Tribune*, July 14, 1892, 4.

11 (Brewer 1911, 82–83)

12 (*OR*, XXXVI, part 1, 732, 745 and 751. Reports of Col. Warren J. Keifer, 110th Ohio; Col. William H. Ball, 122nd Ohio, and Col. Matthew R. McClennan, 138th Pa.

13 Grayson M. Eichelberger, 6th Maryland Infantry Regiment, Memoirs written in October 1912, CW Misc. Coll., USAMHI, 18.

14 Sunup was recorded at 4:52 A.M. Buck said he left the picket line about one half an hour before sunrise and that he had just started his coffee fire when the firing broke out on the skirmish line. That would place the approximate time of the attack at 4:30. Lieutenant Julius Borcherdt of the 49th New York timed the opening engagement at 4:00 A.M., but that does not agree with most of the Confederate and Federal accounts which place it about daylight. Samuel Buck, "Recollections of an Old Confed," Samuel Buck Papers, ca. 1890, Special Collections Department, William R. Perkins Library, Duke University, Durham, N.C., 96. Z. T. Griffin, "The Wilderness, The Turning of the Right Flank May 6, 1864," *The National Tribune*, August 15, 1889, 3.

15 Laura Virginia Hale and Stanley S. Phillips, *History of the Forty-Ninth Virginia Infantry C.S.A. "Extra Billy Smith's Boys"* (Lynchburg: H. E. Howard, Inc., 1981), 106–107.

16 Samuel Buck, "Recollections of an Old Confed," Samuel Buck Papers, ca. 1890, William R. Perkins Library, Duke University, Durham, N.C., 96.

17 For the sake of conformity I substituted "and" for the "&" and wrote "company" without the capital "C".
(Hale and Phillips 1981, 107)

18 (Ibid., 107)

19 (Haines 1883, 147)

20 (*OR*, XXXVI, part 1, 747–748) Report of Lt. Col. Aaron W. Ebright, 126th Ohio.

21 (Ibid., 666) Report of Col. Emory Upton, 2nd Brig., 1st Div., VI Corps.

22 Z. T. Griffin, "The Wilderness, The Turning of the Right Flank May 6, 1864," *The National Tribune*, August 15, 1889, 3.

23 Berry G. Benson, "Reminiscences of Berry Greenwood Benson, C.S.A.," Vol. 1, Berry G. Benson Miscellaneous Writings, Southern Historical Collection, Library of the University of North Carolina, Chapel Hill, 256.

24 When studying the maps in the *OR* atlas and the map in Morris Schaff's *The Battle of the Wilderness*, McGowan's position becomes quite evident. Schaff's map shows the domelike bulge on the Plank Road, east of Tapp's within 200 yards of the tip of a small branch of the Wilderness Run. One fourth of a mile to the rear of the bulge is a second line of broken works behind which is a small stream, then the Tapp farm and Lee's headquarters.
J. F. J. Caldwell, 1st North Carolina, erred when he said the batteries were 200 yards behind the line. That would have placed the guns well forward with a woods on their immediate front blocking their line of sight.

25 Diary, May 5 and 6, 1864, George W. Hall, 14th Ga. Vols. (Georgia Room, University of Georgia).

26 William Thomas Poague, *Gunner With Stonewall*, Monroe F. Cockrell, (ed.) (Jackson, Tenn.: McCowat-Mercer Press, Inc., 1957), 88–89.

27 Thomas Alfred Martin Memoir, 38th North Carolina, Wilmer D. Martin Collection, 10.

28 Walter Clark, (ed.), *Histories of the Several Regiments and Battalions From North Carolina in the Great War* Vol. IV (Raleigh: E. M. Uzzell Printer and Binder, 1901), 191.
    Account of Lieutenant George H. Mills, Company G, 16th North Carolina.

29 (Ibid., 676)

30 From Lane's description it is evident that the 7th North Carolina and the 28th North Carolina were not in the front line during the Federal attack on May 6. He also makes it clear that the 33rd North Carolina held the angle of his line that morning.
    J. H. Lane, "History of Lane's North Carolina Brigade", SHSP, IX, 1881, 126–127.

31 Captain Robert Monteith, "Battle of the Wilderness, And Death of General Wadsworth," *War Papers Read Before the Commandery of the State of Wisconsin Military Order of the Loyal Legion of the United States* Vol. I. (Milwaukee: Burdick, Armitage & Allen, 1891), 413 and 415.

32 Thomas Francis Galwey, *The Valiant Hours*, Wilbur S. Nye, (ed.) (Harrisburg: Stackpole, 1961), 197. Franklin Sawyer, *A Military History of the 8th Regiment Ohio Vol. Inf'y.*, George A. Groot, (ed.) (Cleveland: Fairbanks and Co., 1881), 162.

33 Charles D. Page, *History of the Fourteenth Regiment, Connecticut Vol. Infantry* (Meriden: Horton Printing Co., 1906), 235.

34 (Ibid., 241)

35 Based upon the 4th Ohio's relatively light casualties, it seems rather apparent that the regiment was near the brigade's third line. The other two lines suffered heavier losses per regiment than the 14th Indiana, 8th Ohio, 4th Ohio and 7th West Virginia, which indicates their more severe engagement during the fighting.
    William Kepler, *History of the Three Months' and Three Years Service From April 16th, 1861, to June 22nd, 1864, of the Fourth Regiment Ohio Volunteer Infantry in the War for the Union* (Cleveland: Leader Printing Co., 1886), 164.

36 Charles W. Cowtan, *Services of the Tenth New York volunteers (National Zouaves) in the War of the Rebellion* (New York: Charles H. Ludwig), 248.
    (Galwey 1961, 197)

37 William P. Seville, *History of the First Regiment, Delaware Volunteers* (Longstreet House, 1986), 106. (Cowtan 1882, 248)

38 These position are based upon known troop placements from the previous day and upon the order in which they entered the fighting on May 6 along the Brock Road. Owen went into the fight before Webb. Neither one had contact with the other throughout the day.

39 (OR, XXXVI, 677, 682, 698, 710–711, 714)

40 Emil and Ruth Rosenblatt, (eds.), *Hard Marching Every Day, The Civil War Letters of Private Wilbur Fisk, 1861–1865* (Lawrence, Kan.: University Press of Kansas, 1992), 216.

41 L. A. Grant, "In the Wilderness," *The National Tribune*, February 2, 1897, 1.

42 (OR, XXXVI, part 1, 708) Report of Col. Lewis A. Grant, Vermont Brigade.

43 James L. Bowen, *History of the Thirty-Seventh Regiment Mass. Volunteers in the Civil War of 1861–1865* (Holyhoke, Mass.: Clark W. Bryan & Co., 1884), 277.

44 Russell C. White, (ed.), *The Civil War Diary of Wyman S. White, First Sergeant of Company F, 2nd United States Sharpshooter Regiment, 1861–1865* (Baltimore: Butternut and Blue, 1991), 362.

45 Ashbury F. Haynes, "How Haynes Won His Medal of Honor," *The National Tribune*, October 21, 1926, 3.

46 "Troop Movement Map—The Wilderness, May 6, 1864, Daybreak—6:30 A.M.," United States Department of the Interior, National Park Service, Division of Design and Construction, Eastern Office, 1962.
    Hereafter cited as NPS Map.
    The 141st Pennsylvania kept its right on the Plank Road and not on the left of Crocker's brigade as indicated in the Park Service maps. It seems that Ward's brigade shifted behind Crocker's men.
    David Craft, *History of the One Hundred Forty-First Regiment, Pennsylvania Volunteers, 1862–1865* (Towanda, Pa.: Reporter-Journal Printing Co., 1885), 180.

47 C. A. Stevens, *Berdan's United States Sharpshooters in the Army of the Potomac 1861–1865* (Dayton, Ohio: Morningside Bookshop, 1984), 403 and 407.

48 (Ibid., 403)

49 (White 1991, 362)

50 The position of the 124th New York is implied by the left turn maneuver which that regiment later made. Had there been Federal troops to its left, the 124th New York would not have faced fire in that direction.

(*OR*, XXXVI, part 1, 477) Report of Lt. Col. Casper W. Tyler, 141st Pa.

51 (*OR*, XXXVI, part 1, 473) Report of Capt. Madison M. Cannon, 40th N.Y.

52 (Ibid., 488) Report of Col. Robert McAllister, 1st Brig., 4th Div., II Corps.

53 I arrived at this figure based upon the estimated troop strengths from the Army of the Potomac's Returns for April 1864, casualty tabulations, and approximate brigade frontages as described in this text.

54 Returns of the II Corps, Army of the Potomac, April 1864, Box 9, RG OAG Volunteer Organizations, Civil War, NA.

55 (Page 1906, 235)

56 A. P. Smith, *History of the Seventy-Sixth New York Volunteers* (Cortland: 1867), 291.

57 NPS Maps, "Dawn–6:30 A.M."

In a footnote, Lysander Cutler said the division moved onto the field in four lines. Dawes' illustration of the troop positions with the II Corps on the right of the V Corps is erroneous. Rufus R. Dawes, *Service With the Sixth Wisconsin Volunteers* (Dayton, Ohio: Morningside Bookshop, 1984), 262. (Curtis 1891, 235)

58 (Dawes 1984, 262)

59 (Cowtan 1882, 248)

60 (Galwey 1961, 197)

(Page 1906, 235)

61 Owen T. Wright, (Sgt., D Co., 14th IN), "Liked Gen. Grant's Story. One Who Was There Tells How He Was Taken in by the Johnnies," *The National Tribune*, February 25, 1897, 3.

62 (Seville 1986, 107)

63 (Page 1906, 235)

(Seville 1986, 107)

64 (Craft 1885, 179)

65 Sessions, who served in Company I, 1st Sharpshooters, said his regiment was formed in regimental front in Hays' second line.

N. Sessions, "In the Wilderness. The Part Taken by Berdan's 1st U. S. Sharpshooters," *New York Tribune*, February 2, 1891, 3.

Caril said that Ward's brigade came to Crocker's rescue, which implies that Ward's brigade was behind them during the frontal assault against Thomas, Confederate brigade.

Harrison Caril, "Campaigning With Grant Through Virginia," *The National Tribune*, April 9, 1925, 5.

C. A. Stevens of the 1st U.S. Sharpshooters said the Berdans were in a clearing ahead of the rest of the division. This also supports the idea that Crocker's men had worked their way into the front of the column.

(Stevens 1984, 403)

66 Grant said that the commands shifted to the south side of the road when the V Corps came onto the field. This rings more true than Wheaton's report who apparently confused Wadsworth Division of the V Corps with Stevenson's division of the IX Corps.

(*OR*, XXXVI, part 1, 698) Report of Col. Lewis A. Grant, Vermont Brigade, 2nd Div., VI Corps.

67 Bowen's description of the troop formation and the distance he says the regiment was from the Confederates indicate that the brigade did not cross the eastern branch of Poplar Run until Longstreet's counterattack later that day.

(Bowen 1884, 278)

68 (*OR*, XXXVI, part 1, 488) Report of Col. Robert McAllister, 1st Brig., 4th Div., II Corps. NPS Map, "Dawn to 6:30 A.M."

69 Benson recorded the captain's name as Dunlap. He was W. S. Dunlop, who authored *Lee's Sharpshooters*.

Berry G. Benson, "Reminiscences of Berry Greenwood Benson, C.S.A.," Vol. 1, Berry G. Benson Miscellaneous Writings, Southern Historical Collection, Library of the University of North Carolina, Chapel Hill, 257.

70 Private Hall indicated that the brigade was connected with McGowan at the Plank Road. He said the regiments formed a "V" with the troops on the left of the pike and that the regiment was hit on the flank, front, and rear and that the right of the line lost a great many captured. There were no other Confederate troops on Thomas' right flank but Scales was in line to his right rear. The length of Thomas' line (approximately 1,400 feet) would have been slightly overlapped by Ward's first line (1,420 feet).
Entry, May 6, 1864, Diary of George W. Hall, 14th Georgia Volunteers, Georgia Room, University of Georgia.

71 Charles H. Weygant, *History of the One Hundred Twenty-Fourth Regiment, N.Y.S.V.* (Newburgh: Journal Printing House, 1877), 290.

72 (Ibid., 291)

73 Entry May 6, 1864, Diary of George W. Hall, 14th Georgia Volunteers, Georgia Room, University of Georgia.

74 Letter, May 8, 1864, from Francis Solomon Johnson, Jr. to Emily Hutchings, Special Collections, University of Georgia.

75 James Longstreet, *From Manassas to Appomattox* (Da Capo Press: New York, 1992), 557–559. J. B. Polley, *A Soldier's Letter to Charming Nellie* (Gaithersburg: Butternut Press, 1984), 231.

76 Major General Charles W. Field, "Campaign of 1864 and 1865," SHSP, XIV, 1886, 543.

77 (Field, SHSP, XIV, 1886, 543) William F. Perry, "Reminiscences of the Campaign of 1864 in Virginia," SHSP, VII, 1879, 49–51. P. D. Bowles, "Annals of the War, Battle of the Wilderness, The Fourth Alabama Regiment in the Slaughter Pen on May 6, 1864," *Philadelphia Weekly Times*, Saturday, October 4, 1884.

78 "John Cheves Haskell Memoirs, 1861–65," Special Collections Department, William R. Perkins Library, Duke University, Durham, N.C., 42.

79 According to Kershaw his brigade had nearly reached the front when Wilcox's division broke. This indicates that Longstreet had reached the front before Lee knew he had, because Lee dispatched a courier after Longstreet after McGowan's South Carolinians retreated to Tapp's.
Joseph B. Kershaw, "Operations of Kershaw's Division," SHSP, VI, 1878, 81.

80 J. H. Lane, "History of Lane's North Carolina Brigade," SHSP, IX, 1881, 126–127.

81 (Clark 1901, II:569) Account of Major J. A. Weston, 33rd North Carolina.

82 Thomas Alfred Martin, Memoir, 11.

83 The Federal reports indicate that Rice's right regiments were flanked and had to face front to rear on the left companies to silence the Confederate pressure. Had the brigade continued due west and those regiments had performed that maneuver, they would have fired into their own men. If, however, they had presented their flank to Poague's artillery and McGowan's sharpshooters, they could have responded in that manner and not hit their front line. Scales' North Carolinians and Thomas' men said they were hit from the east, south and north.

84 Joseph B. Kershaw, "Operations of Kershaw's Division," SHSP, VI, 1878, 80.

85 C. R. Dudley, "What I Know About the Wilderness," Confederate Veteran Papers, Special Collections Department, William R. Perkins Library, Duke University, Durham, N.C., 3–4.

86 (Poague 1957, 88–89)

87 N. Sessions, "In the Wilderness. The Past Taken by Berdan's 1st U.S. Sharpshooters," *The National Tribune*, February 5, 1891, 3.

88 Samuel Dunham, "Death of General Hays," *The National Tribune*, November 12, 1885, 3.

89 N. Sessions, "In the Wilderness. The Past Taken by Berdan's 1st U.S. Sharpshooters," *The National Tribune*, February 5, 1891, 3.

90 Harrison Caril, "Campaigning With Grant Through Virginia," *The National Tribune*, April 9, 1925, 5.

91 May 6, Diary of George W. Hall, 14th Georgia Volunteers, Georgia Room, University of Georgia.

92 (Clark 1901, I:675) Account of Lieutenant R. S. Williams, Company I, 13th North Carolina.

93 (Ibid.) Account of Lieutenant R. S. Williams, Company I, 13th North Carolina.

94 Thomas Alfred Martin, Memoir, 11.

95 Orderly Sergeant Harrison Caril (Company C, 5th Michigan) said that after Ward's brigade came to their rescue that they pursued the Confederates as far as the second line of works. He said the brigade retreated some distance when the reinforced Confederates attacked them.

 Harrison Caril, "Campaigning With Grant Through Virginia," *The National Tribune*, April 9, 1925, 5.

96 (Craft 1885, 180)

97 Thomas Alfred Martin, Memoir, 11.

98 U.S. Dept. of the Army, *The Medal of Honor of the United States* (Washington, D.C.: U.S. Government Printing Office, 1948), 152. George W. Kilmer, "With Grant in the Wilderness," *The National Tribune*, July 17, 1924, 7. (Craft 1885, 180-181)

99 Thomas Alfred Martin, Memoir, 11. (Craft 1885, 180–181)

100 George W. Kilmer, "With Grant in the Wilderness," *The National Tribune*, July 17, 1924, 7. (Craft 1885, 185)

101 (Clark 1901, I:675) Account of Lieutenant Rowland S. Williams, Company I, 13th North Carolina.

102 (Clark 1901, IV:191) Account of Lieutenant George H. Mills, Company G, 16th North Carolina.

103 (Clark 1901, II:569) Account of Major J. A. Weston, 33rd North Carolina).

104 The citation reads, "Capture of the flag of the 31st North Carolina (C.S.A.) in a personal encounter." The 31st North Carolina was not at the Wilderness. Kemp captured the colors of the 33rd North Carolina. (U.S. Department of the Army 1948, 152) Notes and sketches from the research of Howard Michael Madaus, Cody, Wyoming.

105 (Clark 1901, IV:191) Account of Lieutenant George H. Mills, Company G, 16th North Carolina.

106 Alfred Proffitt, Letter to R. L. Proffitt, May 8, 1864, Alfred Proffitt Papers, Southern Historical Collection, University of North Carolina, Chapel Hill, N.C.

107 (Clark 1901, II:48) Account of Adjutant William H. McLaurin, 18th North Carolina.

108 (Ibid.)

109 Berry G. Benson, "Reminiscences of Berry Greenwood Benson, C.S.A.," Mss, Vol. 1, Berry G. Benson miscellaneous writings, Southern Historical Collection, UNC, Chapel Hill, 257–258.

110 (Ibid.)

111 Lieutenant Caldwell insisted that the brigade did not run in a panic but retired intact. The testimony from Wyman White (2nd U.S. Sharpshooters) and Berry Benson does not corroborate this. White's description of the incident dovetails well with Caldwell's account of the 12th South Carolina being flanked.

 J. F. J. Caldwell, *The History of a Brigade of south Carolinians Known First as "Gregg's:" and Subsequently as "McGowan's Brigade"* (Marietta: Continental Book Co., 1951), 132, 133. (White 1991, 362)

112 Caldwell reported that Orr's Rifles had one man captured at the Wilderness. The Union soldiers reported they captured the entire Confederate skirmish line.

 (Caldwell 1951, 136) (A. P. Smith 1988, 291)

113 Samuel P. Bates, *History of Pennsylvania Volunteers 1861–5* Vol. II (Harrisburg: S. Singerly, Printers, 1869), 222.

114 Too many II Corps units in the vicinity of Tapp's and the position held by Scales insist that there were no Federal troops north of the Plank Road when they arrived there. That implies that Rice could not have advanced as far as those works. Otherwise his presence would have been recorded. A four hundred yard radius taken from that spur of Tapp's, which sits on top of a table of land northeast of McGowan's position, would place the Confederate gun in that area of Tapp's farm.

 F. M. Norton, "That Tangle in the Wilderness," *The National Tribune*, June 26, 1913, 7.

CHAPTER TWO

1   Funke mistakenly thought that Sergeant John Leveck was killed instead of Weissmantel. (Bidwell 1916, 45), C. G. Funke, "In the Wilderness. A New York Comrade Gives His Experience of Fighting in the Woods and Brush," *The National Tribune*, July 14, 1892,. 4. Z. T. Griffin, "The Wilderness, The Turning of the Right Flank May 6, 1864," *The National Tribune*, August 15, 1889, 3.

2   (Brewer 1911, 83)

3   Seymour stated that his brigade attacked at 7:00 A.M. Colonel John Horn of the 6th Maryland and Lieutenant Colonel Aaron W. Ebright of the 126th Ohio reported the attack at around 9:00 A.M. Sergeant Grayson M. Eichelberger (6th Maryland) said the firing became very heavy around 7:00 A.M. He was shot about that time. Haines of the 15th New Jersey said the regiment moved to the attack an hour after sunrise. Borcherdt of the 49th New York gave the time as sometime after 6:30 A.M. First Lieutenant Robert W. Funkhouser said the Federals advanced against him around 8:00 A.M. and Captain James Bumgardner, Jr. of the 52nd Virginia placed the time at sometime between daylight and sunrise. Captain Oliver W. Holmes, Jr. on the VI Corps staff placed the time precisely at 7:40 A.M.
The dilemma centers around the time of the attack and it hinges on the distinction between daylight and sunrise. Daylight occurred at 4:52 A.M. Sunrise occurred when the men could first see the sun through the trees. Believing that Holmes, Seymour and Eichelberger, and Borcherdt had the correct times is more feasible than 9:00 A.M. or later. Nearly all of the participants said the fighting occurred very early in the day as opposed to the forenoon.
(OR, XXXVI, part 1, 729, 737, 748) Reports of Brig. Gen. Truman Seymour, Col. John Horn, and Lt. Col. Aaron W. Ebright (Haines 1883, 147). Z. T. Griffin, "The Wilderness, The Turning of the Right Flank May 6, 1864," *The National Tribune*, August 15, 1889, 3. Mar De Wolfe Howe, *Touched With Fire: Civil War Letters and Diary of Oliver Wendell Holmes, Jr., 1861–1864* (Cambridge: Harvard University Press, 1946), 106.

4   James Bumgardner, Jr., "Hoffman's Brigade, Early's Division," Richmond *Dispatch*, October 8, 1905, Manuscript Dept., University of Virginia.

5   Samuel Buck, "Recollections of an Old Confed," Samuel Buck Papers, ca. 1890, Special Collections Dept., William R. Perkins Library, Duke University, Durham, N.C., 96.

6   Jacob Heater, "Battle of the Wilderness," *Confederate Veteran*, XIV, 1906, 263.

7   James Bumgardner, Jr., "Hoffman's Brigade, Early's Division," Richmond *Dispatch*, October 8, 1905, Manuscript Dept., University of Virginia.

8   Samuel Buck, "Recollections of an Old Confed," Samuel Buck Papers, ca. 1890, Special Collections Dept., William R. Perkins Library, Duke University, Durham, N.C., 96.

9   (OR, XXXVI, part 1, 748) Report of Lt. Col. Aaron W. Ebright, 126th Ohio.

10 Francis Cordrey, "The Wilderness. What a Private Saw and Felt in That Horrible Place," *The National Tribune*, June 21, 1994, 3. Samuel C. Kerr, "The Wilderness, Turning the Right Flank on May 6," *The National Tribune*, July 11, 1889, 3.

11 Jacob Heater, "Battle of the Wilderness," *Confederate Veteran*, XIV, 1906, 263.

12 James Bumgardner, Jr., "Hoffman's Brigade, Early's Division," Richmond *Dispatch*, October 8, 1905, Manuscript Dept., University of Virginia.

13 (Hale and Phillips 1981, 107)

14 Samuel Buck, "Recollections of an Old Confed," Samuel Buck Papers, ca. 1890, Special Collections Dept., William R. Perkins Library, Duke University, Durham, N.C., 97–98.

15 (OR, XXXVI, part 1, 744, 751) Reports of Lt. Col. Otho H. Binkley, 122nd Ohio and Col. Matthew R. McClennan, 138th Pa.

16 (OR, XXXVI, part 1, 737) Report of Col. John W. Horn, 6th Md.

17 Grayson M. Eichelberger, 6th Maryland Infantry Regiment, Memoirs written in October 1912, CW Misc. Coll., Manuscripts Dept., USAMHI, 18.

18 Edwin Crockett, "First Time Under Fire. Moving Into the Awful Hell of the Wilderness," *The National Tribune*, May 5, 1904, 3. William E. S. Whitman and Charles H. True, *Maine in the War for the Union: A History of the Part Borne by Maine troops* (Lewiston: Nelson Dingley,

Jr. & Co., 1865), 186. George T. Stevens, *Three Years in the VI Corps* (Albany: S. R. Gray, 1866), 310.

19 Z. T. Griffin, "The Wilderness, The Turning of the Right Flank May 6, 1864," *The National Tribune*, August 15, 1889, 3. C. G. Funke, "In the Wilderness. A New York Comrade Gives His Experience of Fighting in the Woods and Brush," *The National Tribune*, July 14, 1892, 4.

20 Z. T. Griffin, "The Wilderness, The Turning of the Right Flank May 6, 1864," *The National Tribune*. August 15, 1889,3. C. G. Funke, "In the Wilderness. A New York Comrade Gives His Experience of Fighting in the Woods and Brush," *The National Tribune*, July 14, 1892, 4.

21 (Whitman and True 1865, 186)

22 (Westbrook 1898, 188)

23 (Westbrook 1898, 188) (Howe 1946, 106) Diary, May 6, 1864, Alfred Thompson, Jay Luvaas Coll., USAMHI.

24 (Haines 1883, 148)

25 Berry G. Benson, "Reminiscences of Berry Greenwood Benson, C.S.A.," Vol. 1, Berry G. Benson Miscellaneous Writings, Southern Historical Collection, UNC, Chapel Hill, N.C., 258. Edward Porter Alexander, *Military Memoirs of a Confederate* (Charles Scribner's Sons: New York, 1907, 503. (Caldwell 1951, 133) Gary G. Gallagher, (ed.), *Fighting for the Confederacy, The Personal recollections of General Edward Porter Alexander* (University of North Carolina: Chapel Hill, N.C., 1989), 357.

26 Colonel C. S. Venable, "The Campaign from the Wilderness to Petersburg," SHSP, XIV, 1886, 525.

27 (Gallagher 1989, 357)

28 Report of Henry Heth, Spring 1864 to October 1864, mss., ANV, Leaders, Vol. 178, FSNBP. Charles Jones, "Historical Sketch," *Our Living and Our Dead*, April 15, 1874, 3. Special thanks to Mr. Bryce Suderow for making these sources available to me.

29 (Ibid.)

30 (Polley 1976, 230–231)

31 Polley indicates that the 4th and the 5th Texas crossed to the south side of the Plank Road and the 3rd Arkansas and the 1st Texas, which were on line with them, did not but remained north of the road.
    (Polley 1976, 232) E. J. "Dock" Parrent, "General Lee to the Rear," *Confederate Veteran*, III, 1895, 14.

32 C. R. Dudley, "What I Know About the Wilderness," Confederate Veteran Papers, Special Collections Department, William R. Perkins Library, Duke University, Durham, N.C., 4.

33 Berry G. Benson, "Reminiscences of Berry Greenwood Benson, C.S.A.," Vol. 1, Berry G. Benson Miscellaneous Writings, Southern Historical Collection, UNC, Chapel Hill, N.C., 258. (Alexander 1907, 503) (Caldwell 1951, 133)

34 C. R. Dudley, "What I Know About the Wilderness," Confederate Veteran Papers, Special Collections Department, William R. Perkins Library, Duke University, Durham, N.C., 4.

35 Berry G. Benson, "Reminiscences of Berry Greenwood Benson, C.S.A.," Vol. 1, Berry G. Benson Miscellaneous Writings, Southern Historical Collection, UNC, Chapel Hill, N.C., 258. (Alexander 1907, 503) (Caldwell 1951, 133)

36 Byron M. Cutcheon, *The Story of the Twentieth Michigan Infantry* (Lansing: Robert Smith Printing Co., 1904), 107.

37 Amos Hadley, (ed.), *History of the Sixth New Hampshire Regiment in the War for the Union* (Concord: Republican Press Assoc., 1891), 226–227.

38 (*OR*, XXXVI, part 1, 934) Report of Maj. William B. Reynolds, 17th Vt.

39 (Hadley 1891, 217–218) Peter S. Carmichael, *Lee's Young Artillerist* (Charlottesville: University Press of Virginia, 1995), 116-117.

40 Berry G. Benson, "Reminiscences of Berry Greenwood Benson, C.S.A.," Mss., Vol. 1, Berry G. Benson Miscellaneous Writings, Southern Historical Collection, University of North Carolina, Chapel Hill, N.C., 259.

41 (*OR*, XXXVI, part 1, 934) Report of Maj. William B. Reynolds, 17th Vt. (Caldwell 1951, 134–135) Berry G. Benson, "Reminiscences of Berry Greenwood Benson, C.S.A.," Mss., Vol. 1,

Berry G. Benson Miscellaneous Writings, Southern Historical Collection, University of North Carolina, Chapel Hill, N.C., 259.

42 Berry G. Benson, "Reminiscences of Berry Greenwood Benson, C.S.A.," Mss., Vol. 1, Berry G. Benson Miscellaneous Writings, Southern Historical Collection, University of North Carolina, Chapel Hill, N.C., 259.

43 (Caldwell 1951, 134) (Hadley 1891, 217, 227) Berry G. Benson, "Reminiscences of Berry Greenwood Benson, C.S.A.," Mss., Vol. 1, Berry G. Benson Miscellaneous Writings, Southern Historical Collection, University of North Carolina, Chapel Hill, N.C., 258–259.

44 Benson said there was a halt and some delay before he returned to the brigade with the sharpshooters. By saying he returned to the place where the action started he had to have been on the approach trail from the southeast onto Chewning's farm. Caldwell said that the brigade followed the skirmishers in and then retired two hundred yards to build works that would have placed them in the line opposite the house on its east side. He said they were on a ridge and retired about 100–200 yards and put up works. This fits the description given by the men in Bliss' brigade. Caldwell leaves the impression that the fighting lasted several minutes.
(Caldwell 1951, 134–135)

45 (OR, XXXVI, part 1, 966–967) Report of Lt. Col. Byron M. Cutcheon, 20th Mich. (Cutcheon 1904, 106–107)

46 (Ibid., 107)

47 (Ibid., 106)

48 D. Augustus Dickert, History of Kershaw's Brigade (Dayton: Morningside Bookshop, 1976), 345.

49 On the topographical map from the NPS an earthwork shows up across the Plank Road at this point. The IX put up those works around 8:00–11:00 A.M. They were on the flank of Wheaton's brigade. L. A. Grant had to have passed beyond Wheaton at this point because when Benning's brigade struck the Federals after the collapse of Gregg's Texas Brigade, Grant said that his right flank was hit and that Wheaton had to advance to his assist.
L. A. Grant, "In the Wilderness," The National Tribune, February 4, 1897, 1.

50 Selden Connor, "In the Wilderness," War Papers Read Before the Commandery of the State of Maine, Military Order of the Loyal Legion of the United States Vol. IV. (Wilmington, N.C.: Broadfoot Publishing Co., 1992), 218.

51 Henry Roback, (comp.), The Veteran Volunteers of Herkimer and Ostego Counties in the War of the Rebellion: Being a History of the 152nd N. Y. V. (Little Falls, N.Y.: L. C. Childs & Son, 1888), 69.

52 (Connor 1992, 218)

53 Selden Connor said his regiment waited an hour or two after the jump off which would have placed the time of advance at 6–7:00 A.M. Galwey places the attack at 7:00 A.M. John D. Smith, historian of the 19th Maine, erred when he said the regiment was engaged while under Owen about 8:30 A.M. He said that when the regiment was picked up by Webb that the IX Corps was just coming onto the field. That would place the regiment's second advance at 8:00 A.M. The regiment was engaged before the Texas Brigade came onto the field.

54 (OR, XXXVI, part 1, 488 and 493) Report of Col. Robert McAllister, 1st Brig., 4th Div., II Corps.

55 (Cowtan 1882, 248)

56 (Page 1906, 241)

57 (Ibid., 236)

58 (Galwey 1961, 197)

59 (Ibid.)

60 (Ibid.)

61 (Ibid.)

62 J. J. Walley, "In the Wilderness. Another Account of the Fight at the Angle," The National Tribune, December 18, 1890, 4.

63 (Roback 1888, 69)

64 (Connor 1992, 218)

65 Mac Wyckoff, *A History of the 2nd South Carolina Infantry: 1861–65.* (Fredericksburg: Sgt. Kirkland's Museum and Historical Society, Inc., 1994), 115.

66 (Roback 1888, 71)

67 J. J. Walley, "In the Wilderness. Another Account of the Fight at the Angle," *The National Tribune,* December 18, 1890, 4.
(Connor 1992, 218–219) (Dickert 1976, 348)

68 Goode Bryan, "Report of General Goode Bryan," SHSP, VI, 1878, 83.

69 C. R. Dudley, "What I Know About the Wilderness," Confederate Veteran Papers, Special Collections Department, William R. Perkins Library, Duke University, Durham, N.C., 4.

70 In his unfootnoted regimental Calvin Collier refers to a sergeant in Company G, 3rd Arkansas who, while standing in formation, turned Lee's reins while Lee was riding in front of the regiment. The 1st sergeant would have been the closest noncommissioned officer to Lee. That man had to have been 1st Sgt. Robert White. Venable said that a sergeant stepped out and took the reins of Lee's horse. Collier asserts that Lee then moved over to the right of the brigade line and repeated the same incident with the 4th Texas which would coincide with Polley's and Gee's accounts.
Harold B. Simpson, *Hood's Texas Brigade: Lee's Grenadier Guard* (Dallas: Alcor Publishing Co., 1983), 396. Harold B. Simpson, *Hood's Texas Brigade: A Compendium* (Hillsboro: Hill Junior College Press, 1977), 295. Calvin L. Collier, *"They'll Do to Tie To," The Story of the Third Regiment, Arkansas Infantry C.S.A.* (Little Rock: Pioneer Press, 1959), 175.

71 Robert Campbell, "Texans Always Move Them!" , *The Blue and the Gray,* Henry Steele Commager, ed. (New York: Bobbs-Merrill, 1950), 983.

72 Joseph B. Polley did not state how Lee sounded, but considering his recent confrontation with McGowan and his unsettled demeanor during Heth's and Wilcox's rout, it is safe to say that Lee was trying to use his personality to keep the Texans true to their purpose. Had he had full faith in his presence and the Texans he would not have had to have said what he did.
J. B. Polley, "Texas in the Battle of the Wilderness," *Confederate Veteran,* V, 1897, 290.
Leonard Grace Gee, "The Texan Who Held Gen. R. E. Lee's Horse," *Confederate Veteran,* XII, 1904, 478.

73 (Commager 1950, 984)

74 Letter, October 21, 1877, Charles S. Venable to General James Longstreet, Southern Historical Collection, University of North Carolina, Chapel Hill, N.C. James A. Graham, Letter to his mother, May 9, 1864, James A. Graham Papers 1861–1901, Special Collections Department, Duke University, Durham, N.C. (Clark 1901, II:446) Account of Captain James A. Graham, Company G, 27th North Carolina.

75 In his account Parrent apparently confused the 5th Texas with the 1st Texas. In the first mention of the incident, he places the 4th Texas on the right of the 1st Texas and then he said Lee came up on the left of the 1st Texas, which according to Collier, he did. Polley asserted that Lee was near the 5th Texas when the incident occurred. Collier also supports this.
Charles S. Venable, "The Scene in the Wilderness," SHSP, Vol. 8, 1880, 109. (This is a reiteration of the same material in Venable's 1877 letter to Longstreet.) J. B. Polley, "Texas in the Battle of the Wilderness," *Confederate Veteran,* V, 1897, 290. "Hood's Texas Brigade," *Confederate Veteran,* XI, 1903, 393. Leonard Grace Gee, "The Texan Who Held General R. E. Lee's Horse," *Confederate Veteran,* XII, 1904, 478. Letter, October 21, 1877, Charles S. Venable to James Longstreet, Southern Historical Collection, University of North Carolina, Chapel Hill, N.C. (Commager, 1950, 984) E. J. "Dock" Parrent, "General Lee to the Rear," *Confederate Veteran,* III, 1895, 14.

76 W. Gart Johnson, "Barksdale-Humphreys Mississippi Brigade," *Confederate Veteran,* I, 1893, 207.

77 (Dickert 1976, 350)

78 (Connor 1992, 219)

79 (*OR*, XXXVI, part 1, 437) Report of Brig. Gen. Alexander Webb, 1st Brig., 1st Div., II Corps.
80 This is based upon descriptions of troop dispositions given by witnesses later in the day.
81 (Smith 1909, 137 and 142)
82 Webb said that his brigade front was only a "few hundred yards" long, and not the 730 yards it would have covered had it been deployed in a single battle line. The 19th Maine (158 casualties) and the 20th Massachusetts (140 casualties) were definitely in the front line. The 7th Michigan (60 casualties) was probably in the front line as well. The frontage of these four regiments was approximately 360 yards. The second line would have been about 40 yards longer. Casualty returns, particularly in the Wilderness, are good indicators of front line troops because the first lines tended to suffer heavier losses than the ones further back.
83 Charles H. Myerhoff, "The Wilderness. The Charge of Carroll's Celebrated Brigade," *The National Tribune*, October 30, 1890, 4. (Sawyer 1881, 162)
84 Letter, October 21, 1877, Charles S. Venable to James Longstreet, Southern Historical Collection, University of North Carolina, Chapel Hill, N.C.
85 (Polley 1984, 234)
86 F. M. Norton's (76th New York) testimony indicated that the 56th Pennsylvania and the 76th New York had resumed their places on the right of Rice's brigade line. This would have left the original skirmishers along the brigade's front.
    F. M. Norton, "That Tangle of the Wilderness," *The National Tribune*, June 26, 1913, 7. J. B. Polley, "Texas in the Battle of the Wilderness," *Confederate Veteran*, V, 1897, 290.
87 J. B. Polley, "Texas in the Battle of the Wilderness," *Confederate Veteran*, V, 1897, 290. F. M. Norton, "That Tangle at the Wilderness," *The National Tribune*, June 26, 1913, 7.
88 (White 1991, 362)
89 (Simpson 1983, 402–404)
90 (Polley 1984, 233–234)
91 (Simpson 1983, 402–404)
92 (Polley 1976, 232)
93 Collier said that the regiment lost about 65 percent of its men and had about 90 men present for duty. Simpson arrived at the figures which I quoted here.
    (Collier 1959, 176–178)
94 (Connor 1992, 220)
95 (Polley 1984, 235–236)
96 Charles H. Myerhoff, 14th IN, "The Wilderness. The Charge of Carroll's Celebrated Brigade," *The National Tribune*, October 23, 1890, 4. (Polley 1976, 232)
97 Flanigan, a member of the 15th Georgia, recorded that many of the men who laughed were dead within ten minutes. Benning's brigade lost 208 wounded and 10 killed. In his letter to Sallie, Captain Edgeworth Bird (Company E, 15th Georgia) named four of the ten who died. Two of them, Joseph Hines and Thomas Culver (both from Company K, 15th Georgia), perished in the fighting.
    W. A. Flanagan, "Account of How Some Flags Were Captured," *Confederate Veteran*. Vol. XIII, 1905, 250. John Rozier, (ed.), *The Granite Farm Letters, The Civil War Correspondence of Edgeworth and Sallie Bird* (Athens: The University of Georgia Press, 1988), 164.
98 (Sawyer 1881, 162)
99 (Rozier 1988, 164)
100 William F. Perry, "Reminiscences of the Campaign of 1864 in Virginia," *Southern Historical Society Papers*. Vol. VII, No. 2, February, 1879, 52.
101 Coles noted that Lee was "very much perturbed over his misfortune."
    William C. Oates, *The War Between the Union and the Confederacy*. (Morningside Bookshop: Dayton, OH, 1974), 344–345. R. T. Coles, "History of the Fourth Regiment Ala. Vol. Infantry," Regimental History File, Alabama Department of Archives and History, Montgomery, Ala., Chapter 18, 10.
102 (Oates 1974, 343)

103 Coles said that when the brigade joined the skirmishers the Federals' fire became very brisk and was very close to their line.
    R. T. Coles, "History of the 4th Alabama Volunteer Infantry," Alabama Department of Archives and History, Chapter 18, 11.

104 (Galwey 1961, 197)

105 Coles' account dovetails beautifully with the fragmented Federal accounts. His memoirs were based upon Bowles' account.
    R. T. Coles, "History of the Fourth Alabama Volunteer Infantry," Alabama Department of Archives and History, Ch. 18, 11. (Oates 1974, 345)

106 William F. Perry, "Reminiscences of the Campaign of 1864 in Virginia," *SHSP*, Vol. VII, #2, Feb. 1879, 55.

107 (Ibid.)

108 Oates' and Perry's accounts assert that the New York regiments fled from the field in the wildest disorder in less than five minutes. Jordan implies that the time was much longer and the diary entry for May 6 from Corporal W. J. Dailey, Company M, 6th New York Heavy Artillery, mentions no rout. His diary gives no intimation of a hurried flight from the field as has been traditionally maintained. I am inclined to think that no rout did occur but that the New Yorkers withdrew from the fighting rather than try to outflank the Confederates.
    (Oates 1974, 346) William F. Perry, "Reminiscences of the Campaign of 1864 in Virginia," SHSP, Vol. VII, #2, Feb. 1879, 54.
    William C. Jordan, *Some Events and Incidents During the Civil War.* (Paragon Press: Montgomery AL, 1909), 74–76. Diary of Corporal W. J. Dailey, Company M, 6th Regiment New York State Heavy Artillery, Jan. 2, 1864–May 30, 1864, CWTI Collection, USAMHI.

109 The 14th Indiana lost 6 killed, 22 wounded and 6 missing for a total of 34 casualties. Again this is indicative of minor action in the Wilderness.
    (*OR*, XXXVI, part 1, 121)

110 (Sawyer 1881, 163)

111 Nancy B. Baxter, *Hoosier Farm Boy in Lincoln's Army: The Civil War Letters of Pvt. John R. McClure* (privately printed, 1971), 60.

112 Owen T. Wright, "Liked Gen. Grant's Story. One Who Was There Tells How He Was Taken in by the Johnnies," *The National Tribune*, February 25, 1897, 3.

113 (Galwey 1961, 199)

114 (Ibid., 200)

115 (Jordan 1909, 75)

116 F. M. Norton, "In That Tangle at the Wilderness," *The National Tribune*, June 26, 1913, 7.

117 (A. P. Smith 1867, 291)

118 Chamberlin said the break occurred sometime between 9:00 A.M. and 10:00 A.M. It happened closer to 9:00 A.M. What matters is that this assault is skipped over in many of the regimental accounts.
    Thomas Chamberlin, *History of the One Hundred and Fiftieth Regiment Pennsylvania Volunteers, Second Regiment, Bucktail Brigade* (Philadelphia: F. McManus, Jr. & Co., 1905), 211.
    (Bates 1:261) John D. Vautier, *History of the 88th Pennsylvania Volunteers in the War for the Union, 1861–1865* (Philadelphia: J. B. Lippincott, 1894), 174. Benjamin F. Cook, *History of the Twelfth Massachusetts Volunteers (Webster Regiment)* (Boston: Twelfth [Webster] Regiment Association, 1882), 128.

119 O. B. Curtis, *History of the Twenty-Fourth Michigan of the Iron Brigade* (Detroit: Winn & Hammond, 1891), 235.

120 Frank M. Mixon, *Reminiscences of a Private* (J. J. Fox: Camden, S.C.), 67.

121 W. Gart Johnson, "Barksdale-Humphreys Mississippi Brigade," *Confederate Veteran*, I, July 1893, 207. W. Gart Johnson, "Truth of History," *Confederate Veteran*, IV, 1896, 15.

122 James R. Hagood, "Memoirs of the First South Carolina Regiment of Volunteer Infantry in the Confederate war for Independence from April 12, 1861 to April 10, 1865," The South Carolinia Library, University of South Carolina, Columbia, 141.

123 The regimental historian placed the time that the regiment retired to get ammunition at 8:00 A.M.

   (*OR*, XXXVI, part 1, 477) Report of Lt. Col. Casper W. Tyler, 141st Pa. (Craft 1885, 182)

124 Ashbury F. Haynes, "How Haynes Won His Medal of Honor," *The National Tribune*, October 21, 1926, 3.

125 George B. Russell, "From the Wilderness to Andersonville," *The National Tribune*, October 22, 1925, 3.

126 Ashbury F. Haynes, "How Haynes Won His Medal of Honor," *The National Tribune*, October 21, 1926, 3.

127 (Cowtan 1882, 250–258)

128 Diary, May 6, 1864, First Lieutenant George A. Bowen, Company C, 12th New Jersey.

129 (Page 1906, 236)

130 (Ibid., 242)

131 (Seville 1987, 107)

132 (Page 1906, 236)

133 L. A. Grant, "In the Wilderness," *The National Tribune*, February 4, 1897, 1. Harrison Caril, "Campaigning with Grant Through Virginia," *The National Tribune*, April 9, 1925, 5.

134 Lewis A. Grant, "In the Wilderness," *The National Tribune*, February 4, 1897, 1.

135 Ashbury F. Haynes, "How Haynes Won His Medal of Honor," *The National Tribune*, October 21, 1926, 3.

136 (*OR*, XXXVI, part 1, 682)

137 The Confederates broke the following Federal brigades: Crocker's, Webb's, Owen, and Carroll's, and scattered parts of Ward's, Stone's, Rice's, and Cutler's.

138 (Chamberlin 1905, 216)

139 George B. Russell, "From the Wilderness to Andersonville," *The National Tribune*, October 22, 1925, 3.

140 (Page 1906, 107)

141 (*OR*, XXXVI, part 1, 473, 487) Reports of Capt. Madison M. Cannon, 40th N.Y. and Col. Robert McAllister, 1st Brig., 4th Div., II Corps.

CHAPTER THREE

1 Letter, Thomas G. Jones to John W. Daniel, July 3, 1904, John W. Daniel Papers, 1849–1904, Special Collections Dept., William R. Perkins Library, Duke University, Durham, N.C., 1. I. G. Bradwell, 'Gordon's Ga. Brigade in the Wilderness," *Confederate Veteran*, XVI, 1908, 640.

2 Jones was not certain of the time. He thought it was around 8:00 A.M. He said that he left no more than an hour and a half after Gordon started his reconnaissance and that Gordon went on the scout after the first heavy volleys had subsided. The heavy volleys were between Seymour and Hoffman and ended at 9:00 A.M. which means that Jones started out to find Early or Ewell around 9:30 A.M. and not 8:00 A.M.

   Letter, Thomas G. Jones to John W. Daniel, July 3, 1904, John W. Daniel Papers, 1849–1904, Special Collections Dept., William R. Perkins Library, Duke University, Durham, N.C., 4–5.

3 (Ibid., 6)

4 R. T. Coles, "History of Fourth Regiment Alabama Volunteer Infantry," Alabama Department of Archives and History, Montgomery, Chapter 18, 12.

5 R. T. Coles, "History of the Fourth Regiment Alabama Volunteer Infantry," Alabama Department of Archives and History, Montgomery, Chapter 18, 12–13. William F. Perry, "Reminiscences of the Campaign of 1864 in Virginia," SHSP, Vol. VII, #2, Feb. 1879, 56.

6 R. T. Coles, "History of the Fourth Regiment Alabama Volunteer Infantry," Alabama Department of Archives and History, Montgomery, Chapter 18, 12–13. William F. Perry, "Reminiscences of the Campaign of 1864 in Virginia," SHSP, Vol. VII, #2, Feb. 1879, 56.

7 William F. Perry, "Reminiscences of the Campaign of 1864 in Virginia," SHSP, Vol. VII, #2, Feb. 1879, 54.

8 R. T. Coles, "History of the Fourth Regiment Alabama Volunteer Infantry," Alabama Department of Archives and History, Montgomery, Chapter 18, 12–13. William F. Perry, "Reminiscences of the Campaign of 1864 in Virginia," SHSP, Vol. VII, #2, Feb. 1879, 56. (Chamberlin 1905, 215–216)

9 (Bowen 1884, 278–279)

10 (Bowen 1884, 279–280)

11 Adams, Z. Boylston, "In the Wilderness," *Civil War Papers Read Before the Commandery of Massachusetts, Military Order of the Loyal Legion of the United States* Vol. II (Boston: 1900), 376. Nelson V. Hutchinson, *History of the Seventh Massachusetts Volunteer Infantry in the War of the Rebellion of the Southern States 1861–1865* (Taunton, Mass.: Regimental Association, 1900), 178.

12 Stephen M. Weld placed the 56th Massachusetts in the third line and he heard of the wounding of Colonel Bartlett (57th Massachusetts) before his colonel was hit. The historian of the 35th Massachusetts was not in the battle. His order of battle is probably in error.
    Stephen M. Weld, *Civil War Diary and Letters of Stephen Minot Weld 1861–1865* (Boston: Massachusetts Historical Society, 1979), 286. Committee of the Regimental Association, *History of the Thirty-Fifth Regiment Massachusetts Volunteers, 1862–1865.* (Boston: Mills, Knight and Co., 1884), 226.

13 (Adams 1900, 376) (Hutchinson 1890, 178)

14 (Weld 1979, 286)

15 (Adams 1900, 376) John Anderson, *The Fifty-Seventh Regiment of Massachusetts Volunteers in the War of the Rebellion* (Boston: E. B. Stillings & Co., 1896), 37.

16 (*35th Mass. Vols.* 1884, 226)

17 (Adams 1900, 376)

18 The account of Lieutenant Colonel Stephen Weld indicates that there was a creek behind the regiment after it advanced for the final time.
    (Adams 1900, 375–377)

19 James R. Hagood, "Memoirs of the first South Carolina Regiment," South Carolinia Library, University of South Carolina, Columbia, 142. (Alexander 1989, 359)

20 (Mixon 1910, 67–68)

21 "Wounded at the Wilderness, A Question Settled," The Atlanta *Journal*, February 23, 1901.

22 A. J. McBride, "From the Chuckee to the Wilderness," The Atlanta *Journal*, June 29, 1901.

23 (Weygant 1877, 291)

24 (Ibid., 493) Report of Lt. Col. John Schoonover, 11th N.J.

25 (Ibid., 488) Report of Col. Robert McAllister, 1st Brig., 4th Div., II Corps.

26 (Ibid., 499) Report of Capt. Thomas C. Thompson, 7th N.J.

27 Brewster's report of the fighting is nearly useless. Sergeant Henri LeFevre Brown (Company B, 72nd New York) implied that the brigade was in two lines when he states that the 73rd New York, later in the day, came up on the 72nd's left to provide fire support.
    Henri LeFevre Brown, *History of the Third Regiment Excelsior Brigade 72nd New York Volunteer Infantry 1861–1865* (privately printed, 1902), 126.

28 (OR, XXXVI, part 1, 488–489) Report of Col. Robert McAllister, 1st Brig., 4th Div., II Corps.

29 (Ibid., 473) Report of Capt. Madison W. Cannon, 40th N.Y.

30 McAllister said that other troops were under fire on his left (south) and rear (east) during Longstreet's counterattack. Those other troops were not Frank's which had already left the field. They had to have been Brewster's troops.
    (Ibid., 489) Report of Col. Robert McAllister, 1st Brig., 4th Div., II Corps.

31 (Brown 1902, 123, 126)

32 (Simons 1888, 200–202)

33 W. S. Dunlop, *Lee's Sharpshooters* (Dayton: Morningside Bookshop, 1988), 378.

34 The action described by Wallace of the 2nd South Carolina indicates that the regiment was put in line on the right of the 6th South Carolina to fill a gap. They caught the Yankees at a range of forty yards and after a well aimed volley, they drove the Federals from the field.

This describes pretty much what McAllister said happened to Frank's brigade. (Dickert 1976, 348)

35 M. McDonald, "March and Battle," *The National Tribune*, April 2, 1896, 3.

36 The 111th New York suffered the largest number of casualties in the brigade. It lost 42 killed and 119 wounded in the two days of fighting. (Dickert 1976, 348) (OR, XXXVI, part 1, 120)

37 (OR, XXXVI, part 1, 489) Report of Col. Robert McAllister, 1st Brig., 4th Div., II Corps.

38 (Dunlop 1988, 378)

39 (Simons 1888, 200 and 202) (Dunlop 1988, 379)

40 (Simons 1888, 200 and 202)

41 (OR, XXXVI, part 1, 489) Report of Col. Robert McAllister, 1st Brig., 4th Div., II Corps.

42 "Report of General James Longstreet," SHSP, Vol. VI, 1878, 79.

43 "Wofford's Georgia Brigade," Atlanta, *Southern Confederacy*, June 15, 1864.

44 (Alexander 1989, 359) Letter, James M. Goggin to James Longstreet, August 10, 1887, Longstreet Papers, Southern Historical Collection, Library of the University of North Carolina at Chapel Hill.

45 George S. Bernard, *War Talks of Confederate Veterans* (Petersburg: Fenn & Owen, 1892), 90.

46 James R. Hagood, "Memoirs of the First South Carolina Regiment," The South Carolinia Library, University of South Carolina, Columbia, 143.

47 (Mixon 1910, 68)

48 "Wofford's Georgia Brigade," Atlanta *Southern Confederacy*, June 15, 1864.

49 James Eldred Phillips Memoir, James Eldrid Phillips Papers, Virginia Historical Society, Richmond, Virginia.

50 (Bernard 1892, 94 and 104)

51 (OR, XXXVI, part 1, 489) Report of Col. Robert McAllister, 1st Brig., 4th Div., II Corps.

52 (Bowen 1884, 279–280)

53 (Oates 1974, 347)

54 (Chamberlin 1905, 216) R. T. Coles, "History of the Fourth Alabama Volunteer Infantry," Alabama Department of Archives and History, Montgomery, Chapter 18, 13.

55 R. T. Coles, "History of the Fourth regiment Alabama Volunteer Infantry," Alabama Department of Archives and History, Montgomery, Chapter 18, 13–14. P. D. Bowles, "Annals of the War," *Philadelphia Weekly Times*, Saturday, October 4, 1884.

56 C. H. Banes in his "History of the Philadelphia Brigade," describes a large mass of Federals crossing the Plank Road when Webb met with Wadsworth. Frank's brigade was the only Federal brigade which quit the field prior to the slight lull that McAllister, Weygant, and Chamberlin mention. Webb's own account in *Battles and Leaders* is somewhat suspect also, as pointed out by Selden Connor in his article for MOLLUS, Maine (IV, 1915) who corrected errors made in reference to Connor in that same volume. Connor attributes the memory error to the severe head wound which Webb received at Spotsylvania. Robert U. Johnson and Clarence C. Buel, (eds.), *Battles and Leaders of the Civil War* Vol. IV (Castle: Secaucus, N.J.), 160.

57 Coles' description of an officer jumping an obstruction in the road and being brought down coincides exactly with Webb's account of the event as related by men in the 20th Massachusetts to him. Webb, however, insists that Wadsworth was killed leading the 20th Massachusetts into action. He was, but not at this time. Earl M. Rogers, one of Wadsworth's A.D.C.s, said that Wadsworth had just lost his second horse and then pushed a regiment forward. The historian of the 20th Massachusetts said that there had to have been a lull to get the 20th Massachusetts to move into an exposed position. It could be implied that the New Englanders did refuse to follow Wadsworth at first but then did go in once the action calmed down a bit. Robert Monteith, his other A.D.C., said that the general was killed after a lull in the battle after the Confederates had turned his right flank. P. D. Bowles of the 4th Alabama did not see Wadsworth go down. One of his men said he shot a Yankee officer off his horse in the road, and later that night Wadsworth was found near that spot.

Zebulon B. Adams, surgeon turned soldier, said the ball struck Wadsworth in the back of the head near the top and had lodged in the left side of his brain. He attested later that the general's horse had been shot from under him at the time or that the general had been leaning forward to escape a volley. Evidence indicates that he was shot around 11:30 A.M. by the 8th Alabama whose men were on the hillside which would account for the wound being in the top of his head.

R. T. Coles, "History of the Fourth Regiment Alabama Volunteer Infantry," Alabama Department of Archives and History, Chapter 18, 14. (*B & L.* IV:160) (Monteith 1891, 413) Earl M. Rogers, "How Wadsworth Fell," *The National Tribune*, December 24, 1885, 1. P. D. Bowles, "Annals of the War," *Philadelphia Weekly Times*, Saturday, October 4, 1884. (Adams, 1900, 391)

58 Diary, May 6, 1864, Corporal W. J. Dailey, Co. M, 6th Regiment New York State Heavy Artillery, January 2, 1864–May 30, 1864, Manuscript Department, USAMHI.

59 (Oates 1974, 347) William F. Perry, "Reminiscences of the Campaign of 1864 in Virginia," SHSP, Vol. VII, #2, Feb. 1879, 54.

60 William F. Perry, "Reminiscences of the Campaign of 1864 in Virginia," SHSP, Vol. VII, #2, Feb. 1879, 56. P. D. Bowles, "Annals of the War," *Philadelphia Weekly Times*, Saturday, October 4, 1884.

61 William F. Perry, "Reminiscences of the Campaign of 1864 in Virginia," SHSP, Vol. VII, #2, Feb. 1879, 57.

62 (Weygant 1877, 291–292)

63 (Ibid.)

64 (Ibid.)

65 (Page 1906, 238)

66 The 141st Pennsylvania was the only regiment in Ward's brigade which had come from the First Division of the Third Corps following its destruction at Gettysburg. The red diamond was the corps badge for the First Division, III Corps.
   (Ibid.) (*OR*, XXXVI, part 1, 477) Report of Lt. Col. Casper W. Tyler, 141st Pa. George W. Kilmer, "With Grant in the Wilderness," *The National Tribune*, July 17, 1924, 7.

67 There is no eyewitness to Wadsworth being unhorsed other than the accounts of the 4th Alabama. Again, it is the author's belief that the 4th Alabama did not kill Wadsworth. All the Federal accounts indicate that he died during the height of Longstreet's counterattack. The account of Perrin's Alabama brigade, which replaced William F. Perry's men on the Plank Road, clearly indicates that it was tied in with Longstreet's attack, which the 4th Alabama did not take part in. Schaff in *The Battle of the Wilderness* does say that Wadsworth was unhorsed in the road after trying to get the 20th Massachusetts to leave its works.

68 (Adams 1900, 377)

69 (Chamberlin 1905, 216)

70 (Adams 1900, 377)

71 (Monteith 1891, 415)

72 W. F. Perry, "Reminiscences of the Campaign of 1864 in Virginia," SHSP, Vol. VII, #2, Feb. 1879, 57.

73 *The Alabama Historical Quarterly*, Vol. XXXIX, Alabama State Department of Archives and History, 133.

74 S. W. Vance, "Heroes of the Eighth Alabama Infantry," *Confederate Veteran*, Vol. VII, 1899, 492.

75 (Bernard 1892, 98)

76 (Brown 1902, 126)

77 (*OR*, XXXVI, part 1, 489) Report of Col. Robert McAllister, 1st Brig., 4th Div., II Corps.

78 McAllister had to have already turned his line back, otherwise the Virginians would have struck him from the front. Brewster's men advanced against the Confederates, then collapsed into McAllister's formation.

79 (Bernard 1892, 98–99)

80 (OR, XXXVI, part 1, 489) Report of Col. Robert McAllister, 1st Brig., 4th Div., II Corps.

81 John F. Sale Diary, John F. Sale Papers, Virginia State Library, Richmond, Virginia.

82 (Bernard 1892, 93, 96, 104–106)

83 There was not enough room for all three brigades to be on the same line as traditionally shown. Anderson, according to the Atlanta Southern Confederacy of June 15, 1864, did not suffer many casualties because he came up behind the Union rear. Had it done that it would have come under fire from the Federal works along the Brock Road. That did not happen. Anderson had to have been behind Wofford.

CHAPTER FOUR

1   Entry, May 6, 1864, Diary of Col. William R. Carter, Confederate Miscellaneous Vol., Chatham Hall, Fredericksburg and Spotsylvania National Battlefield Park. "The Second Virginia Cavalry in the Late fights," The Sentinel, May 21, 1864, col. 3, 1. (OR, XXXVI, part 1, 867) Itinerary of the 8th Pennsylvania Cavalry.

2   Henry R. Pyne, Ride to War, The History of the First New Jersey Cavalry, Earl Schenk Miers, (ed.) (New Brunswick: Rutgers University Press, 1961), 190. Entry, May 6, 1864, Diary Jan. 1–Dec. 29, 1864, Henry P. Turner, 1st Mass. Cav., Civil War Miscellaneous Collection, Tuffman-Walker, USAMHI.

3   Entry, May 6, 1864, Diary Jan. 1–Dec. 29, 1864, Henry P. Turner, 1st Mass. Cav., Civil War Miscellaneous Collection, Tuffman-Walker, USAMHI.

4   Alexander Hunter, Johnny Reb and Billy Yank (New York: The Neale Publishing Co., 1905), 534.

5   (OR, XXXVI, part 1, 867) Itinerary of the 8th Pennsylvania Cavalry.

6   (Hunter 1905, 534)

7   Woodford B. Hackley, The Little Fork Rangers (Richmond: The Dietz Printing Co., 1927), 89.

8   Ms. Couse said that a rough Federal raiding party robbed them of their fowl and corn despite their protests. Catherine Couse could see troops moving on the Court House road and could hear firing near Alsop's. The historian of the 1st Maine said that the regiment got lost and was cut off behind the Confederate lines where it came under sharp fire. Ms. Couse wrote that the Confederates were on one side of the farm and the Yankees were on the other. Ressler said the 1st Maine took part in a carbine charge, which more than likely occurred on the Couse farm.

   Edward P. Tobie, History of the First Maine Cavalry, 1861–1865 (Boston: Emery and Hughes, 1887), 251. Letter May 4–20, 1864, Catherine Couse to Mr. and Mrs. H., from Laurel Hill, Va., Special Collections Department, Alderman Library, University of Virginia. Entry, May 6, 1864, Capt. Isaac H. Ressler, Co. L, 16th Pa. Cav., Diary 1862–1865, Civil War times Illustrated Collection, R - Res, USAMHI. Historical Overlay and Topographical Overlay of Spotsylvania Battlefield, NPS, Chatham Hall, Fredericksburg, Va.

9   (Tobie 1887, 251–252) Entry, May 6, 1864, Capt. Isaac H. Ressler, Co. L, 16th Pa. Cav., Diary 1862–1865, Civil War times Illustrated Collection, R - Res, USAMHI.

10 (OR, XXXVI, part 1, 857) Report of Brig. Gen. Henry E. Davies, Jr., 1st Brig., 2nd Div., Cav. Corps.

11 The 2nd and the 8th Pennsylvania both had three men wounded.
    "Nominal Casualties for the First Division, Cavalry Corps, from May 4th to June 20th, 1864," RG 27, Box 28, National Archives, Washington, D.C.

12 R. H. Peck, Reminiscences of a Confederate Soldier of Company C, 2nd VA. Cavalry (1911), 44. Entry, May 6, 1864, Diary of Col. William R. Carter, Confederate Miscellaneous Vol., Chatham Hall, Fredericksburg and Spotsylvania National Battlefield Park.

13 Entry, May 6, 1864, Diary of Col. William R. Carter, Confederate Miscellaneous Vol., Chatham Hall, Fredericksburg and Spotsylvania National Battlefield Park.

14 (Hunter 1905, 535)

15 Custer and Stagg said the brigade left its bivouac at 2:00 A.M. Alger said his regiment left the bivouac at 3:00 A.M., which would have placed it one hour behind the 7th Michigan.

The 1st and the 6th Michigan were engaged first, then the 5th and the 7th Michigan. The 1st was at the end of the brigade column and was turned north after reaching Todd's Tavern. Custer merely turned his regiments about in place to advance.

(*OR*, XXVI, part 1, 816, 826, 827) Reports of Brig. Gen. George A. Custer, 1st Brig., 1st Div. Cav. Corps; Lt. Col. Peter Stagg, 1st Mich. Cav., and Col. Russell A. Alger, 5th Mich.

16 Stagg said that the regiment was engaged at 8:30 A.M. I believe his time is in error. Allowing one hour for each regiment to arrive at Todd's Tavern, the sequence would be as follows: the 7th Michigan (394 men)—7:00 A.M.; the 5th Michigan (633 men)—8:00 A.M., the 6th Michigan (361 men)—9:00 A.M. and the 1st Michigan (687 men)—10:00 A.M. Stagg's said he was engaged at 8:30 A.M. Supposing he erred on the time by two hours he would have been engaged at 10:30 A.M. which would coincide with the time established by Lieutenant Colonel Theodore Garnett on Stuart's staff. The Catharine Furnace Road is narrow. If his regiments were marching in a column of two it would have stretched almost 3 miles. His brigade averaged 1.128 miles per hour that day. It would have taken almost 3.4 hours for all of his troopers to have reached Todd's Tavern.

(Ibid., 826) Theodore Garnett Memoirs, Alderman Library, Special Collections Department, University of Virginia.

17 Writing in 1908, Colonel J. H. Kidd (6th Michigan) recollected that they passed the 6th Vermont in the predawn hours along the Catharine Furnace road. This is not likely. Stagg said that his regiment relieved the Vermonters after daylight.

(*OR*, XXXVI, part 1, 826) Report of Lieutenant Colonel Peter Stagg, 1st Mich. Cav. J. H. Kidd, *Personal Recollections of a Cavalryman With Custer's Michigan Cavalry Brigade in the Civil War* (Ionia, Mich.: Sentinel Printing Co., 1908), 265.

18 (Kidd 1908, 264–266)

19 The location of this field was established by Mr. G. B. Catlett of Spotsylvania, Virginia on August 15, 1994. The Rowe farm belongs to his wife's family. He showed the property line to Mr. Bryce Suderow and me and described the dimensions of the field in which the fighting took place.

Report of John J. Shoemaker, Stuart Horse Artillery, September 1, 1864, Preston Library, VMI Archives, Lexington, Va. Report of Major James Breathed, September 14, 1864, Halsey Papers #2447, Southern Historical Collection, University of North Carolina, Chapel Hill, N.C. Bryce Suderow, "Todd's Tavern, Va., May 5–8, 1864, Sheridan Vs. Stuart: The Opening Round," unpublished monograph, 8.

20 The field appears in the lower right side of the map in *Battles and Leaders*, IV:120. Myers in *The Commanches* said the battalion crossed a stream and came upon a fork in the road. The map shows a stream and a fork in the road at this location. Mr. Catlett showed me the old road bed where it branches from the Jackson trail .7 miles south of the Trigg farm. He said the road marked the boundary of the field. The map in Schaff's Wilderness book shows the road cutting to the northeast in a line indicative of a meandering creek bed. Mr. Catlett showed us where the creek entered the southwest corner of the field and said it drained into the lower creek between Trigg's and the cavalry field. The ravine in the field runs southwest to northeast and nearly bisects the field as described in Kidd's *Recollections of a Cavalryman*. Kidd said the brigade faced in a westerly direction as opposed to a due west direction with the stream running past the brigade's right rear. To be positioned in that manner the brigade had to have faced southwest. The ground was swampy.

(Kidd 1908, 266) Frank M. Myers, *The Commanches: A History of White's Battalion, Virginia Cavalry* (Marietta, Ga.: Continental Book Co., 1956), 264–265.

21 (Kidd 1908, 265–266)

22 Both Myers in *The Commanches* and McDonald in the *Laurel Brigade* say that the brigade was on the road at daylight. Garnett, being Stuart's aide, is the more reliable of the sources. Myers' book predates McDonald's and it looks like McDonald borrowed his information from Myers.

Theodore Garnett Memoirs, Special Collections Department, Alderman Library, University of Virginia.

23 Wood mistakenly said his regiment was protecting Thomson's Battery. Chew's Report dated November 19, 1864, said that Johnston was left behind. Neese from Thomson's Battery describes the battery's role in the fight that day. It could not have been left behind.
    Entry, May 6, 1864, Diary of Private James F. Wood, Company F, 7th Virginian Cavalry, Virginia State Archives. R. P. Chew, Report, HQ, Horse Artillery, Army of Northern Virginia, November 19, 1864, VMI Archives, Preston Library, VMI. George M. Neese, *Three Years in the Confederate Horse Artillery* (Dayton: Morningside, 1983), 261.
24 (Myers 1956, 263–264) William N. McDonald, *A History of the Laurel Brigade*, Bushrod C. Washington, (ed.) (Kate S. McDonald, 1907), 234.
25 Theodore Garnett Memoirs, Special Collections Department, Alderman Library, University of Virginia.
26 (Myers 1956, 264–265)
27 Letter, May 6, 1864, James D. Rowe, Michigan Historical Collections, Bentley Historical Library, University of Michigan.
28 (Myers 1956, 265, 272)
29 (Kidd 1908, 265–266)
30 (Myers 1956, 266)
31 (Ibid., 266, 272)
32 (Ibid., 266)
33 Memoirs, McDonald Papers, Southern Historical Collection, Special Collections Department, University of North Carolina, Chapel Hill, N.C., 102–103.
34 (Kidd 1908, 268)
35 Memoirs, McDonald Papers, Southern Historical Collection, Special Collections Department, University of North Carolina, Chapel Hill, N.C., 103.
36 William S. Ball, "Reminiscences," Virginia Historical Society, Richmond, Va., 33.
37 (Kidd 1908, 269)
38 Memoirs, McDonald Papers, Southern Historical Collection, Special Collections Department, University of North Carolina, Chapel Hill, N.C., 103.
39 Elijah V. White, Letter, *Confederate Veteran*, Vol. IX, 1901, 167.
40 The 7th Virginia Cavalry, contrary to William McDonald's and Myers' accounts was not engaged in this action. Nor were any of Fitz Lee's cavalry as stated in Steere. Colonel Russell A. Alger said that his regiment fought Rosser's brigade and a portion of Jones' Confederate cavalry. He was right. The 11th Virginia and the 35th Virginia Battalion had belonged to Jones' brigade at Gettysburg in 1863. The Michiganders were taking on only three Confederate cavalry regiments, a force well under 1,000 men strong.
    (McDonald 1907, 235) (Myers 1956, 266) (*OR*, XXXVI, part 1, 827) Report of Col. Russell A. Alger, 5th Mich. Cav.
41 Diary of W. H. Arehart, *The Rockingham Recorder*, II, #3, October, 1959, 151.
42 (McDonald 1907, 235) (Myers 1956, 266)
43 Captain Isaac Plumb, Co. C, 61st N.Y. Vol. Inf., "Recollection of Life and Service Compiled from Letters," Civil War Miscellaneous Collection, Pepper—Oost, Manuscript Department, USAMHI.
44 Memoirs, McDonald Papers, Southern Historical Collection, Special Collections Department, University of North Carolina, Chapel Hill, N.C., 103.
45 (Kidd 1908, 269)
46 (*OR*, XXXVI, part 1, 372) Report of Maj. Nathan Church, 26th Mich.
47 Newton Kirk, "Reminiscences," Newton Thorne Kirk Papers, #1397, Archives and Historical Collections, Bentley Historical Library, University of Michigan, Central Campus, Ann Arbor, Mich.
48 (Kidd 1908, 269)
49 "Diary of W. H. Arehart," *The Rockingham Recorder*, II, #3, October, 1959, 151.
50 Edward A. Green, "The War of the Confederacy," Eleanor S. Brockenbrough Library, Museum of the Confederacy, Richmond, Va.

51 Newel Cheney, *History of the Ninth Regiment, New York Volunteer Cavalry* (Poland Center, N.Y.: 1901), 157. (*OR,* XXXVI, part 1, 833) Report of Col. Thomas C. Devin, 2nd Brig., 1st Div., Cav. Corps.

52 McDonald, who was severely wounded that day, did not see the entire action. The accounts indicate that Thomson's and Shoemaker's Batteries participated in the fighting and not just one gun.
(McDonald 1907, 235) Edward A. Green, "The War of the Confederacy," Museum of the Confederacy, Richmond, Va. Report of John J. Shoemaker, Stuart Horse Artillery, VMI Archives, Preston Library, VMI, Lexington, Va. Report of P. P. Pendleton, Stuart Horse Artillery, November 19, 1864, VMI Archives, Preston Library, VMI, Lexington, Va.

53 Theodore Garnett Memoirs, Special Collections Department, Alderman Library, University of Virginia.

54 (Neese 1983, 261)

55 (Myers 1956, 266)

56 Asa B. Isham, "Through the Wilderness to Richmond," *Sketches of War History 1861–1865 Papers Read Before the Ohio Commandery of the Military Order of the Loyal Legion of the United States 1883–1886,* Vol. 1 (Cincinnati: Robert Clarke & Co., 1888), 202–203. See also an article by the same title and author in *The National Tribune,* June 5, 1902, 7.

57 (McDonald 1907, 236)

58 (Kidd 1908, 270)

59 (Pyne 1961, 190) Lilian Rea, (ed.), *War Record and Personal Experiences of Walter Raleigh Robbins From April 22, 1861, to August 4, 1865* (n.d.), 80–81.

60 (Kidd 1908, 270)

61 McGuire was the only captain in the 11th Virginia who was wounded that day.
Memoirs, McDonald Papers, Southern Historical Collection, Special Collections Department, University of North Carolina, Chapel Hill, N.C., 103.

62 Report of Captain John J. Shoemaker, Stuart's Horse Artillery, September 1, 1864, VMI Archives, Preston Library, VMI, Lexington, Va.

63 (Neese 1983, 261)

64 Theodore Garnett Memoirs, Special Collections Department, Alderman Library, University of Virginia.

65 (McDonald 1907, 236–237) (Myers 1956, 267)

66 Letter, F. M. Myers to his Parents, May 15, 1864, courtesy of Bryce Suderow.

67 Theodore Garnett Memoirs, Special Collections Department, Alderman Library, University of Virginia.

68 (Myers 1956, 267–268)

69 (Rea, 81)

70 Report of Capt. P. P. Pendleton, Horse Artillery, November 19, 1864, VMI Archives, Preston Library, VMI, Lexington, Va.

71 (Kidd 1908, 270–271) (*OR,* XXXVI, part 1, 816) Report of Brig. Gen. George A. Custer, 1st Brig., 1st Div., Cav. Corps.

72 Rosser lost 120 men on May 6. Shoemaker's battery lost 10 men, with the other two batteries escaping without any casualties. Custer's Michigan regiments lost 64 men. The 1st had 3 killed, 23 wounded; the 5th—3 killed, 15 wounded; and the 6th—5 killed, 11 wounded, 4 missing.
"Nominal Casualties for the First Division, Cavalry Corps, from May 4th to June 20th, 1864," RG 27, Box 12, National Archives, Washington, D.C. (Neese 1983, 261) (Myers 1956, 271) Bryce Suderow, "casualties in the Confederate Cavalry Corps, May 5–June 4, 1864," Monograph.

73 (Myers 1956, 272–273) (Kidd 1908, 270–271)

74 Rosser had 1,000 effectives on May 5, 1864, and lost 186 men that day, leaving him with 814 effectives. On May 6, the 35th Battalion had about 150 men. The 11th Virginia had about 300 officers and men, leaving about 364 effectives between the 7th and the 12th Virginia. Dividing that number by 2 leaves approximately 182 men in both regiments. (The 7th was not

engaged on May 6). The 35th Battalion lost 18 men on May 6. The 11th Virginia lost 103 men and the 12th Virginia lost at least 4 officers and men in Company H.

(Myers 1956, 263, 395–399) "Diary of W. H. Arehart," *The Rockingham Recorder*, II, #3, October, 1959, 151. Entry, May 6, 1864, Jasper Hawse Diary, Microfilm, Alderman Library, University of Virginia.

CHAPTER FIVE

1 George A. Bruce, *The Twentieth Regiment of Massachusetts Volunteer Infantry 1861–1865.* (Boston: Houghton, Mifflin & Co., 1906), 353–354.

2 Warren Wilkinson, in *Mother May You Never See the Sights I Have Seen*, recorded that the regiment which the 57th passed probably were the U.S. Regulars, particularly since the regiment came under fire within ten feet of the Confederate works. There were no other troops in front of the regiment at that time.
Warren Wilkinson, *Mother, May You Never See the Sights I Have Seen* (New York: Quill, 1990), 73.

3 (Anderson 1896, 39, 51, 53, 69) (Wilkinson 1990, 70)

4 (Weld 1979, 287)

5 (Adams 1900, 377) (Weld 1979, 287)

6 (*OR*, XXXVI, part 1, 473) Report of Capt. Madison M. Cannon, 40th N.Y.

7 (Rosenblatt 1992, 216–217)

8 (Weygant 1877, 292–293)

9 (Ibid., 293)

10 (Page 1906, 238)

11 (Ibid., 238, 242)

12 (Ibid., 241)

13 (Ibid., 241, 243)

14 (Ibid.)

15 (Ibid., 243)

16 (Ibid., 238, 241)

17 (Monteith 1891, 415)

18 Earl M. Rogers, "How Wadsworth Fell," *The National Tribune*, December 14, 1885, 1.

19 *The Alabama Historical Quarterly*, Vol. XXXIX, Alabama State Department of Archives and History, 134.

20 Earl M. Rogers, "How Wadsworth Fell, *The National Tribune*, December 24, 1885, 1.

21 S. W. Vance, "Heroes of the Eighth Alabama," *Confederate Veteran*, Vol. VII, 1899, 494–495.

22 Earl M. Rogers, "How Wadsworth Fell," *The National Tribune*, December 24, 1885, 1.

23 (Bruce 1906, 354)

24 (Mixon 1910, 68–69)

25 (Bruce 1906, 354)

26 (Anderson 1896, 36)

27 (Anderson 1896, 60) (Wilkinson 1990, 79)

28 (Anderson 1896, 38–39)

29 (Chamberlin 1905, 217)

30 (Mixon 1910, 69–70)

31 (Chamberlin 1905, 217)

32 (Connor 1915, 219)

33 (Smith 1909, 138)

34 (Connor 1915, 219)

35 (Smith 1909, 138)

36 According to George Bernard the charge completely disorganized the brigade formation. The 12th Virginia crossed the road at some breastworks near the eastern branch of Wilderness Run, the position which the 56th Massachusetts had just vacated. The 12th Virginia did

not meet with heavy opposition during the assault. Wofford's men pursued the 56th Massachusetts.

(Adams 1900, 381) The Atlanta *Southern Confederacy*, June 15, 1864. (Bernard 1892, 94)

37 The Atlanta *Southern Confederacy*, June 15, 1864. Letter, May 7, 1864, John G. Webb, 9th Georgia, Lewis Leigh Collection, Manuscript Department, USAMHI.

38 (Adams 1900, 378) (Weld 1979, 286)

39 (Anderson 1896, 55)

40 (Adams 1900, 378) (Weld 1979, 286)

41 (Adams 1900, 378–380) (Weld 1979, 286)

42 (Weygant 1877, 293–294)

43 Captain Charles W. Baldwin, Company G, Cobb's Legion, Infantry, Civil War Miscellany, Personal Papers, Drawer 283, Box 17, Georgia Archives, 17–18.

44 John Eldred Phillips Memoir, James Eldred Phillips Papers, Virginia Historical Society, Richmond, Va.

45 (Bernard 1892, 88, 94)

46 (Adams 1900, 378–380) (Weld 1979, 286)

47 (Adams 1900, 378–380) (Weld 1979, 286)

48 (Bernard 1892, 92, 105)

49 (Adams 1900, 378–382) (Weld 1979, 286)

50 (Adams 1900, 378–382) (Weld 1979, 286)

51 (Galwey 1961, 200)

52 (Ibid.)

53 O. G. Daniels, "At the Crossroads, The Charge Made by Carroll's Brigade," *The National Tribune*, December 4, 1890, 4.

54 Charles H. Myerhoff, "The Wilderness, The Charge of Carroll's Celebrated Brigade," *The National Tribune*, October 23, 1890, 4.

55 (Galwey 1961, 200)

56 (Page 1906, 241)

57 (Seville 1986, 107) Charles H. Myerhoff, "The Wilderness, The Charge of Carroll's Celebrated Brigade," *The National Tribune*, October 23, 1890, 4.

58 Diary, May 6, 1864, First Lieutenant George A. Bowen, Co. C, 12th N.J.

59 (Page 1906, 238, 241, 281)

60 O. G. Daniels, "At the Crossroads, The Charge Made by Carroll's Brigade," *The National Tribune*, December 4, 1890, 4.

61 (Ibid.)

62 Myerhoff said the troops next to the 20th Indiana broke. That had to have been the 40th New York of its own brigade. (Ibid.) Charles H. Myerhoff, "In the Wilderness. One of Carroll's Brigade Takes Comrade Carter to Account," *The National Tribune*, December 3, 1891, 4. (*OR*, XXXVI, part 1, 514) Report of Capt. Edwin Dow, 6th Me. Btty.

63 (Page 1906, 238, 241, 281) Charles H. Myerhoff, "The Wilderness, The Charge of Carroll's Celebrated Brigade," *The National Tribune*, October 23, 1890, 4.

64 (Galwey 1961, 200)

65 (Ibid.) Charles H. Myerhoff, "The Wilderness, The Charge of Carroll's Celebrated Brigade," *The National Tribune*, October 23, 1890, 4. O. G. Daniels, "At the Crossroads, The Charge Made by Carroll's Brigade," *The National Tribune*, December 4, 1890, 4.

66 (Cowtan 1882, 253)

67 (Weygant 1877, 295)

68 John Cheves Haskell Memoirs, Manuscript Department, William R. Perkins Library, Duke University, Durham, N.C., 43.

69 (Weygant 1877, 295)

70 John Cheves Haskell Memoirs, Manuscript Department, William R. Perkins Library, Duke University, Durham, N.C., 43.

71 John D. McDonnell, *Recollections of the Civil War*, Winthrop College Archives and Special Collections Department, 8.

72 John Cheves Haskell Memoirs, Manuscript Department, William R. Perkins Library, Duke University, Durham, N.C., 43.

73 (Bernard 1892, 104)

74 (Ibid., 100, 106)

75 (Longstreet 1992, 564)

76 (Bernard 1892, 100)

77 Francis W. Dawson, *Reminiscences of Confederate Service 1861–1865*, Bell I. Wiley, (ed.). (Baton Rouge: Louisiana State University Press, 1980), 115. (Longstreet 1990, 563)

78 (Bernard 1892, 100)

79 (Ibid., 106) Diary entry, May 7, 1864, George S. Bernard Papers, Alderman Library, University of Virginia, Charlottesville, Va.

80 James Eldred Phillips Memoir, James Eldred Phillips Papers, Virginia Historical Society.

81 (Bernard 1892, 92)

82 (Dawson 1980, 115)

83 (Bernard 1892, 90)

84 The Richmond *Daily Dispatch*, May 18, 1864.

85 Longstreet wrote, "At the moment that Jenkins fell I received a severe shock from a minie ball passing through my throat and right shoulder," which would lead one to think that the bullet came in from the north and exited through his right shoulder. Sorrel said the impact lifted the general straight up and down. The newspaper account confirms that Longstreet was hit from the front and from lower ground. The ball, fired from lower ground, would have lifted him up and down as Sorrel described.
(Longstreet 1990, 564) (Bernard 1892, 102) (Dawson 1980, 115) G. Moxley Sorrel, *Recollections of a Confederate Staff Officer* (Jackson, Tenn.: McCowat-Mercer Press, 1958), 233-234.

86 (Bernard 1892, 102) John Daniel McDonnell, "Recollections of the Civil War," Winthrop College Archives and Special Collections Department, 8.

87 Jeffry D. Wert, *General James Longstreet, The Confederacy's Most Controversial Soldier–A Biography*. (New York: Simon & Schuster, 1993), 387.

88 (Longstreet 1992, 567) A. J. McBride, "From the Chuckee to the Wilderness," The Atlanta *Journal*, June 29, 1901.

89 (Dawson 1980, 115)

90 John Cheves Haskell Memoirs, Manuscript Department, William R. Perkins Library, Duke University, Durham, N.C., 44. (Bernard 1892, 106)

91 John Daniel McDonnell, "Recollections of the Civil War," Winthrop College Archives and Special Collections Department, 8.

92 (Bernard 1892, 95, 105)

93 (Ibid., 92)

94 (Adams 1900, 382–383)

95 Westwood A. Todd, Reminiscences, Vol. I, part 2, Westwood A. Todd Papers, Southern Historical Collection, University of North Carolina, Chapel Hill, N.C., 193.

96 (Mixon 1910, 71)

97 Spencer Glascow Welch, *A Confederate Surgeon's Letters to His Wife* (Continental Book Co.: Marietta, Ga., 1954), 95.

98 (Bernard 1892, 106) (Longstreet 1992, 566–567)

99 Robert Stiles, *Four Years Under Marse Robert* (N.Y.: The Neale Publishing Co., 1903), 247.

100 (Dawson 1980, 117)

CHAPTER SIX

1 (Longstreet 1992, 567) John Cheves Haskell, "Memoirs," John C. Haskell Memoirs, 1861–65, Manuscript Dept., William R. Perkins Library, Duke University, Durham, N.C., 44.

2 May 6, 1864, Diary, 1st Lt. George A. Bowen, Co. C, 12th New Jersey.

3 Lieutenant Ira Goodrich (21st Massachusetts) said the brigade advanced on brigade front. Walcott mentions only the 21st Massachusetts and the 100th Pennsylvania being on line with the 21st on the left. Mr. Gavin places the 3rd Maryland on the right of the brigade line yet within 100 yards of the Brock Road. The 21st had 209 men and the 100th Pennsylvania had 629 men. If they maintained their brigade formation as Walcott asserted, the front would have occupied about 800 feet. There was no room for the 3rd Maryland unless it was behind the two of them. Captain Joseph F. Carter (Company D, 3rd Maryland) said that the regiment kept in sight of the works during the entire movement, which is something the 21st Massachusetts, being over 600 feet from the Brock Road, could not have done. There is no account of the 3rd Maryland being on the extreme right of the formation. Had it been there, the 21st Massachusetts would have ended up on the western side of Poplar Run behind the Confederates. That did not happen. The brigade covered the ground between the Brock Road and Poplar Run.
Charles F. Walcott, *History of the 21st Massachusetts Volunteers in the War for the Preservation of the Union, 1861–1865* (Boston, 1882), 316. William G. Gavin, *The 100th Pennsylvania Volunteers, The Roundhead Regiment* (Dayton: Morningside, 1989), 388. Ira B. Goodrich, "In the Wilderness, The Controversy Between Carroll's and Leasure's Brigades," *The National Tribune*, January 1, 1894, 1. Joseph F. Carter, "Leasure's Brigade, Another Account of the Fight at the Salient Angle," *The National Tribune*, September 25, 1890, 3.

4 (Walcott 1882, 317–318)

5 (Gavin 1989, 388–389)

6 (Walcott 1882, 317–318)

7 (Steere 1960, 414, map)

8 (Oates 1974, 349) William F. Perry, "Reminiscences of the Campaign of 1864 in Virginia,"*SHSP*, VII, # 2, Feb. 1879, 60.

9 P. D. Bowles, "Annals of the War," *Philadelphia Weekly Times*, Saturday, October 4, 1884.

10 (Caldwell 1951, 134)

11 The Mississippi brigade was held in reserve and supported Perrin and Perry late in the afternoon, around 3:00 P.M. This position is contrary to the maps in Steere and the National Park Service Maps. None of Heth's regimental historians, except Major W. S. Dunlop from Stone's brigade record having been engaged after the initial rout that morning but all said they were placed upon the extreme left which would have placed them in the vicinity of Higgerson's or Chewning's places. Stone was isolated from all Confederate troops according to Dunlop. Steere places the troops too far forward to fit the descriptions from McGowan's brigade and places Harris on the left near Higgerson's. The NPS maps place Thomas' and Lane's brigades on the right of McGowan near Chewning's where they would have been engaged when the Federals attacked the farm in the afternoon. They were not engaged. They probably were farther to the left.
Austin C. Dobbins, *Grandfather's Journal, Company B, Sixteenth Mississippi Infantry Volunteers, Harris' Brigade, Mahone's Division, Hill's Corps, A. N. V.* (Dayton: Morningside Books, 1988), 191.

12 (Dunlop 1988, 380–381)

13 This is based upon the map on p. 159, Volume IV, *Battles and Leaders of the Civil War*. It is interesting to note that the caption reads, "Relative Positions in the Wilderness, May 6." To date, I have not found enough primary evidence to exactly pinpoint the specific brigade locations of any of Heth's or Wilcox's brigades, except McGowan's, following the morning defeat.

14 Leander W. Cogswell, *A History of the Eleventh New Hampshire Regiment Volunteer Infantry in the Rebellion War, 1861–1865* (Concord: Republican Press Assoc., 1891), 341.

15 (Cutcheon 1904, 106)

16 (Cogswell 1891, 340) (Hadley 1891, 220–221) C. T. Jeffers, "What the IX Corps Did," The *National Tribune*, July 2, 1896, 1.

17 Henry S. Burrage, *History of the Thirty-Sixth Regiment Massachusetts Volunteers, 1862–1865* (Boston: Press of Rockwell and Churchill, 1884), 152. Ephraim E. Myers, "Trials and Travels of the 45th Pennsylvania," *The National Tribune*, December 10, 1925, 3.

18 William F. Perry did not tell the same story as either R. T. Coles or William C. Oates. His version of the incident implied that Robert E. Lee ordered him to face east rather than north which contradicted Oates, who said that Perry wanted him and E. A. Perry to "feel for the enemy" and R. T. Coles who stated that after the action with the IX Corps, the men laughed at W. F. Perry's half-baked attack in echelon.
    William F. Perry, "Reminiscences of the Campaign of 1864 in Virginia," SHSP, VII, #2, Feb. 1879, 60–61.

19 R. T. Coles, "History of Fourth Regiment Alabama Volunteer Infantry," Alabama Department of Archives and History, Montgomery, Chapter 18, 18–19.

20 (Oates 1974, 349–350)

21 C. T. Jeffers, "What the IX Corps Did," *The National Tribune*, July 2, 1896, 1.

22 Henry S. Burrage, *History of the Thirty-Sixth Regiment Massachusetts Volunteers, 1862–1865* (Boston: Press of Rockwell and Churchill, 1884), 152. Ephraim E. Myers, "Trials and Travels of the 45th Pennsylvania," *The National Tribune*, December 10, 1925, 3.

23 Allen D. Albert, (ed.), *History of the Forty-Fifth Regiment Pennsylvania Veteran Volunteer Infantry 1861–1865* (Williamsport, Pa.: Grit Publishing Co., 1912), 114–115.

24 Ephraim E. Myers, "Trials and Travels of the 45th Pennsylvania," *The National Tribune*, December 10, 1925, 3.
    (Albert 1912, 114)

25 C. T. Jeffers, "What the IX Corps Did," *The National Tribune*, July 2, 1896, 1.

26 (Oates 1974, 350)

27 (Burrage 1884, 152)

28 (Oates 1974, 350) (Albert 1912, 121)

29 The 27th Michigan charged the Floridians and was repulsed. The 109th New York, which suffered the next heaviest casualties and was a larger regiment, probably followed next. The 51st Pennsylvania, numbering 200 fewer men, came next and the 8th Michigan (488 men) came last.
    C. T. Jeffers, "What the IX Corps Did," *The National Tribune*, July 2, 1896, 1. Edward C. Marsh, "In the Wilderness. In the Hottest of the Fight at Spotsylvania, and wounded at Bethesda Church," *The National Tribune*, July 10, 1913, 7.

30 Edward C. Marsh, "In the Wilderness," *The National Tribune*, July 10, 1913, 7.

31 (OR, XXXVI, part 1, 948) Report of Col. John F. Hartranft, 1st Brig., 3rd Div., IX Corps.

32 Marsh said the regiment lost its colonel, four officers and thirty-six men in the charge. The ORs credited the regiment with 105 casualties. Hartranft said the regiment lost its colonel inside the Confederate works. The evidence does not indicate this. Oates was overrun once not twice which would have had to had happened had the 8th Michigan actually broken the line.
    Edward C. Marsh, "In the Wilderness," *The National Tribune*, July 10, 1913, 7.

33 (Albert 1912, 121)

34 (Burrage 1884, 154)

35 (Hadley 1891, 220–221) (Cogswell 1891, 356)

36 (Cogswell 1891, 341 and 345)

37 P. D. Bowles, "Annals of the War,... Battle of the Wilderness," *Philadelphia Weekly Times*, Saturday, October 4, 1884, 5.

38 R. T. Coles, "History of Fourth Regiment Alabama Volunteer Infantry," Alabama Department of Archives and History, Montgomery, Chapter 18, 20.

39 (Hadley 1891, 222, 228, 229)

40 (Oates, 1974, 350) P. D. Bowles, "Annals of the War...Battle of the Wilderness," *Philadelphia Weekly Times*, October 4, 1884, 5–6. R. T. Coles, "History of Fourth Regiment Alabama Volunteer Infantry," Alabama Department of Archives and History, Montgomery, Chapter 18, 19.

41 (Burrage 1884, 154)

42 (Hadley 1891, 222)

43 (Cogswell 1891, 341 and 348) P. D. Bowles, "Annals of the War...Battle of the Wilderness," *Philadelphia Weekly Times*, October 4, 1884, 6.

44 Morris Penney, manuscript copy of Law's casualties at the Wilderness. P. D. Bowles, "Annals of the War...Battle of the Wilderness," *Philadelphia Weekly Times*, October 4, 1884, 6.

45 R. T. Coles, "History of Fourth Regiment Alabama Volunteer Infantry," Alabama Department of Archives and History, Montgomery, Chapter 18, 20.

46 P. D. Bowles, "Annals of the War...Battle of the Wilderness," *Philadelphia Weekly Times*, October 4, 1884, 6.

47 (Cogswell 1891, 341 and 348)

48 (Ibid., 341, 353)

49 (Cogswell 1891, 342, 343, 345, 348, 353) (Dunlop 1988, 380–381) (Dobbins 1988, 191)

50 (Burrage 1884, 154)

51 Ephraim E. Myers, "Trials and Travels of the 45th Pennsylvania," *The National Tribune*, December 17, 1925, 3.

52 (Albert 1912, 121)

53 Ephraim E. Myers, "Trials and Travels of the 45th Pennsylvania," *The National Tribune*, December 17, 1925, 3.

54 (Albert 1912, 121–122)

55 Ephraim E. Myers, "Trials and Travels of the 45th Pennsylvania," *The National Tribune*, December 17, 1925, 3.

56 (Albert 1912, 121–122)

57 (*OR*, XXXVI, part 1, 131)

58 Roberts said he had to walk at least a mile to the dressing station. In his dazed state, he probably erred as to the distance. The rout of the brigade would not have affected a station that far to the rear.
(Albert 1912, 115)

59 The regimental historian said the 11th New Hampshire had forty-two officers and men captured compared to the eleven reported in the *Official Records*. Franklin L. Riley (Company B, 16th Mississippi) claimed that Harris' men captured about 100–150 Northerners.
(Cogswell 1891, 345) (Dobbins 1988, 191)

60 (Hadley 1891, 228)

61 (Dobbins 1988, 191) (Dunlop 1988, 381)

62 (Hadley 1891, 123)

63 (Ibid., 223)

64 C. T. Jeffers, "What the IX Corps Did," *The National Tribune*, July 2, 1896, 1.

65 (Robertson, 415)

66 (Marbaker 1898, 163) (Brown 1902, 127)

67 N. Sessions, "In the Wilderness," *The National Tribune*, February 9, 1891, 3. (Weygant, 1877, 296) Charles H. Myerhoff, "The Wilderness," *The National Tribune*, October 23, 1890, 4. (Scott 1993, 97) (Craft 1885, 184)

68 George W. Kilmer, "With Grant in the Wilderness," *The National Tribune*, July 17, 1894, 7.

69 Kate M. Scott, *History of the One Hundred and Fifth Regiment of Pennsylvania Volunteers* (Baltimore: Butternut and Blue, 1993), 97. J. E. Rhodes, "The Wilderness Campaign," March 24, 1910, 7. (Marbaker 1898, 163) (*OR*, XXXVI, part 1, 514) Report of Capt. Edwin B. Dow, 6th Me. Arty.

70 F. E. Doak, "The Wilderness," *The National Tribune*, January 29, 1891, 3.

71 Ira B. Goodrich, "Helped Save the Day," *The National Tribune*, April 30, 1890, 3. William Gilfillan Gavin, *Infantryman Pettit* (Shippensburg: White Mane, 1990), 145. James Madison Stone, *Personal Recollections of the Civil War* (Boston, 1918), 160. Joseph M. Sudsburg, "In the Wilderness. The Colonel of the 3rd Maryland Takes a Hand in the Controversy," *The National Tribune*, January 15, 1891, 4.

72 (Rosenblatt 1994, 217)

73 Letter from A. McC. Bush to General J. W. Hoffman, September 21, 1872. Letter from John A. Black to General J. W. Hoffman, October 23, 1872, Winfield S. Hancock Papers 1863–85, Special Collections Department, William R. Perkins Library, Duke University, Durham, N.C.

74 (Cowtan 1882, 253–254) (Seville 1986, 107) Entry May 6, 1864, Diary, 1st Lt. George A. Bowen, Co. C, 12th New Jersey.
   Joseph F. Carter, "In the Wilderness. The Troops at the Crossroads Saved by the Wall of Fire," *The National Tribune*, April 7, 1892, 4.

75 James R. Hagood, "Memoirs of the First South Carolina Regiment of Volunteer Infantry in the Confederate War for Independence from April 12, 1861 to April 10, 1865," The South Carolinia Library, University of South Carolina, Columbia, S.C., 145–146.

76 (Stevens 1984, 408)

77 (White 1991, 229) George W. Kilmer, "With Grant in the Wilderness," *The National Tribune*, July 17, 1924, 7.

78 James R. Hagood, "Memoirs of the First South Carolina Regiment of Volunteer Infantry in the Confederate War for Independence from April 12, 1861 to April 10, 1865," The South Carolinia Library, University of South Carolina, 1928, 145–146.

79 Letter, May 7, 1864, from John G. Webb to Mr. A. B. Webb, Lewis Leigh Coll., Manuscripts Dept., USAMHI.

80 James R. Hagood, "Memoirs of the First South Carolina Regiment of Volunteer Infantry in the Confederate War for Independence from April 12, 1861 to April 10, 1865," The South Carolinia Library, University of South Carolina, 1928, 147.

81 John D. McDonnell, *Recollections of the Civil War*, Special Collections Dept., Winthrop College Archives, 8.

82 (White 1991, 229)

83 James R. Hagood, "Memoirs of the First South Carolina Regiment of Volunteer Infantry in the Confederate War for Independence from April 12, 1861 to April 10, 1865," The South Carolinia Library, University of South Carolina, 1928, 145–147.
   John D. McDonnell, *Recollections of the Civil War*, Special Collections Dept., Winthrop College Archives, 8. B. M. Barnes, "The Wilderness, Another Account of What Took Place at the Plank Road," *The National Tribune*, August 6, 1891, 3.

84 (Weygant 1877, 296)

85 (Ibid., 297)

86 (Craft 1885, 183) (Brown 1902, 127) (Scott 1993, 97)
   James R. Hagood, "Memoirs of the First South Carolina Regiment of Volunteer Infantry in the Confederate War for Independence from April 12, 1861 to April 10, 1865," The South Carolinia Library, University of South Carolina, 1928, 147.

87 (Weygant 1877, 297)

88 (Scott 1993, 97) (Craft 1885, 184)

89 James R. Hagood, "Memoirs of the First South Carolina Regiment of Volunteer Infantry in the Confederate War for Independence from April 12, 1861 to April 10, 1865," The South Carolinia Library, University of South Carolina, 1928, 145–146.

90 (White 1991, 230–232) (Craft 1885, 183)

91 (Stone 1918, 161)

92 Joseph M. Sudsburg, "In the Wilderness. The Colonel of the 3rd Maryland Takes a Hand in the Controversy," *The National Tribune*, January 15, 1891, 4. Joseph F. Carter, "Leasure's Brigade, Another Account of the Fight at the Salient Angle," *The National Tribune*, September 25, 1890, 3.

93 N. E. Miller, "The Wilderness. What the 20th Indiana Did at the Junction of the Brock and Plank Roads," *The National Tribune*, January 21, 1892, 4. (Scott 1993, 97)

94 (Craft 1885, 183)

95 Edgell's battery fired 190 rounds at the South Carolinians, averaging 31 rounds per gun. At a rate of two shots per minute, the suggested rate of fire for a heavily engaged piece, it would have taken fifteen and one half minutes to expend that amount of ammunition. Dow's guns fired at that rate and therefore shot about 190 rounds also. No infantry crossed the

gunners' line of sight, therefore the Federal troops did not rally as quickly as they implied in their writings.
J. E. Rhodes, "The Wilderness Campaign," *The National Tribune*, March 24, 1910, 7. (*OR*, XXXVI, part 1, 514 and 519) Reports of Capts. Edwin P. Dow and Frederick M. Edgell.

96 (Craft 1885, 183) B. M. Barnes, "The Wilderness. Another Account of What Took Place at the Plank Road," *The National Tribune*, August 6, 1891, 3.

97 (Silliker 1985, 146)

98 For 28 years the veterans of Rice's and Leasure's brigades argued with the men of Carroll's brigade over who actually saved the works along the Plank Road. On September 21, 1872, Gen. J. W. Hoffman received the following note from A. McC. Bush, an officer on Hoffman's staff:
"I remember distinctly hearing Gen'l Rice say that Gen'l Hancock voluntarily promised to see that full credit should be given the 5th Corps, and especially our brigade or that part of it under your immediate command in the movement. This, however, was not fulfilled, the press reports never alluding to the opportune support given [to] the 2nd Corps on the 5th."
Letters, from A. McC. Bush to J. W. Hoffman, September 21, 1872, and L. Curtis to J. W. Hoffman, May 31, 1866, Winfield S. Hancock Papers, 1863–1885, Special Collections Dept., William R. Perkins Library, Duke University, Durham, N.C. See also: Joseph F. Carter, "In the Wilderness. The Troops at the Crossroads Saved by the Wall of Fire," *The National Tribune*, April 7, 1892, 4. D. J. Dickson, *The National Tribune*, March 12, 1891, 3. Avery Harris, "Personal Reminiscences of the Author from August 1862 to June 1865, War of the Rebellion," Avery Harris Papers, Manuscripts Dept., USAMHI, 168. Diary, May 6, 1864, 1st Lt. George A. Bowen (Co. C, 12th N.J.).

99 (Craft 1885, 184)

100 Letter, Nov. 9, 1872, from John Irvin to J. W. Hoffman, Winfield S. Hancock Papers, 1861–1885, Special Collections Dept., William R. Perkins Library, Duke University, Durham, N.C.

101 J. W. Nesbit, "Cross Roads in the Wilderness," *The National Tribune*, March 22, 1917, 7.

102 (White 1991, 230)

103 N. Sessions, "In the Wilderness, The Part Taken by the 1st S.S. Sharpshooters," *The National Tribune*, February 5, 1891, 3.

104 W. F. Beyer and O. F. Keydel, (ed.), *Deeds of Valor*, I. (Stamford, Conn.: Longmeadow Press, 1992), 321. Avery Harris, "Personal Reminiscences of the Author from August 1862 to June 1865, War of the Rebellion," Avery Harris Papers, Manuscripts Dept., USAMHI, 168.

105 James R. Hagood, "Memoirs of the First South Carolina Regiment of Volunteer Infantry in the Confederate War for Independence from April 12, 1861 to April 10, 1865," The South Carolinia Library, University of South Carolina, 1928, 148.

106 (White 1991, 230)

107 James R. Hagood, "Memoirs of the First South Carolina Regiment of Volunteer Infantry in the Confederate War for Independence from April 12, 1861 to April 10, 1865," The South Carolinia Library, University of South Carolina, 1928, 148.

108 (Beyer and Keydel 1992, 321) Avery Harris, "Personal Reminiscences of the Author from August 1862 to June 1865, War of the Rebellion," Avery Harris Papers, Manuscripts Dept., USAMHI, 168.

109 William H. Wheeler, "War Record and Reminiscences," W. H. Wheeler Papers, Special Collections Dept., William F. Perkins Library, Duke University, Durham, N.C., 13.

110 (Marbaker 1898, 164–165)

111 (Chamberlin 1895, 189)

112 (Stevens 1984, 407)

113 (Marbaker 1898, 165) (Robertson, 416)

114 Charles H. Myerhoff, "The Wilderness, the Charge of Carroll's Celebrated Brigade," *The National Tribune*, October 23, 1890, 4.

115 (White 1991, 230)

116 J. W. Nesbit, "Cross Roads in the Wilderness," *The National Tribune*, March 22, 1917, 7.

117 (White 1991, 231)
118 Joseph M. Sudsburg, "In the Wilderness. The Colonel of the 3rd Maryland Takes a Hand in the Controversy," *The National Tribune*, January 15, 1891, 4. Joseph F. Carter, "Leasure's Brigade, Another Account of the Fight at the Salient Angle," *The National Tribune*, September 25, 1890, 3.
119 (Marbaker 1898, 166)
120 (Weygant 1877, 299)
121 J. W. Nesbit, "Crossroads in the Wilderness. The Bitter Fighting There May 6, 1864," *The National Tribune*, March 22, 1917, 7.
122 Letter from Col. John Irwin to Gen. J. W. Hoffman, Nov. 9, 1872, Winfield S. Hancock Papers, 1863–1885, Special Collections Dept., William R. Perkins Library, Duke University, Durham, N.C.
123 Letter, Henry G. Elder to J. W. Hoffman, September 27, 1862, Winfield S. Hancock Papers, 1863–1885, Special Collections Dept., William R. Perkins Library, Duke University, Durham, N.C.
124 (Silliker 1985, 147)
125 James R. Hagood, "Memoirs of the First South Carolina Regiment of Volunteer Infantry in the Confederate War for Independence from April 12, 1861 to April 10, 1865," The South Carolinia Library, University of South Carolina, 1928, 148. *SHSP*, XIII, 1885, 435. Report of Col. J. R. Hagood, 1st S.C.
126 J. F. Carter, "In the Wilderness, The Controversy Between Carroll's and Leasure's Brigades," *The National Tribune*, January 1, 1891, 4.
127 (Stone 1918, 161)
128 Joseph M. Sudsburg, "In the Wilderness. The Colonel of the 3rd Maryland Takes a Hand in the Controversy," *The National Tribune*, January 15, 1891, 4. Joseph F. Carter, "Leasure's Brigade, Another Account of the Fight at the Salient Angle," *The National Tribune*, September 25, 1890, 3.
129 Diary, May 6, 1864, 1st Lt. George A. Bowen (Co. C, 12th N.J.)
130 Avery Harris, "Personal Reminiscences of the Author from August 1862 to June 1865, War of the Rebellion," Avery Harris Papers, Manuscripts Dept., USAMHI, 168. Letters from John Irwin to J. W. Hoffman, Nov. 9, 1872, and Henry G. Elder to J. W. Hoffman, September 27, 1872, Winfield S. Hancock Papers, 1863–1885, Special Collections Dept., William R. Perkins Library, Duke University, Durham, N.C.
131 Hancock sent Sudsburg a personal letter the next day which thanked the colonel and his regiment for saving the guns along the Brock Road.
Joseph M. Sudsburg, "In the Wilderness. The Colonel of the 3rd Maryland Takes a Hand in the Controversy," *The National Tribune*, January 15, 1891, 4. Joseph F. Carter, "Leasure's Brigade, Another Account of the Fight at the Salient Angle," *The National Tribune*, September 25, 1890, 3.
132 John Cheves Haskell, "Memoirs," John C. Haskell Memoirs, 1861–65, Manuscript Dept., William R. Perkins Library, Duke University, Durham, N.C., 44–45.
133 (Cutcheon 1904, 107) (Lane 1905, 168)
134 C. T. Jeffers, "What the IX Corps Did," *The National Tribune*, July 2, 1896, 1. (*OR*, XXXVI, part 1, 953, 957, and 961) Reports of Col. William Humphrey, 2nd Mich.; Col. Constant Luce, 17th Mich., and Capt. Edwin Evans, 109th N.Y.
135 (*OR*, XXXVI, part 1, 966) Report of Lt. Col. Byron M. Cutcheon, 20th Mich.
136 The *OR*s listed the 50th Pennsylvania with 12 killed and 59 wounded for a total of 71 casualties.
(Cutcheon 1904, 107) (*OR*, XXXVI, part 1, 133) C. T. Jeffers, "What the IX Corps Did," *The National Tribune*, July 2, 1896, 1. (*OR*, XXXVI, part 1, 966–967) Report of Lt. Col. Byron M. Cutcheon, 20th Mich.
137 (Dunlop 1988, 381–382)
138 C. T. Jeffers, "What the Gallant IX Corps Did," *The National Tribune*, July 9, 1896, 1.

139 *Confederate Veteran*, IX, 1901, 165.
140 (Adams 1900, 385–388)
141 (Anderson 1896, 39)

CHAPTER SEVEN

1 (*OR*, XXXVI, part 1, 736, 742) Reports of Col. John W. Horn, 6th Md. and Lt. Col. Otho H. Binkley, 110th Ohio.
2 (Ibid., 745) Report of Col. William H. Ball, 122nd Ohio.
3 (Ibid., 748, 751) Reports of Lt. Col. A. W. Ebright, 126th Ohio and Col. Matthew R. McClennan, 138th Pa.
4 I believe that the 2nd New Jersey was on the right of the 49th New York, because the evening before the 4th New Jersey had been on the 49th's right. The author of the article in the *Grand Army Scout* said that the 2nd New Jersey was relieved on the picket line by two regiments from the 2nd and the 3rd division, which would have been part of the 43rd New York regiments and the 67th Pennsylvania.
(Bidwell 1916, 44) "An Incident in the Battle of the Wilderness," *Grand Army Scout and Soldiers' Mail*, January 12, 1884, 2.
5 (Whitman and True 1865, 186) (Lewiston: Nelson Dingley Jr. & Co., Publishers, 1865), 186. A. L. Syphers, "In the Wilderness, Was the Right Flank Turned May 6?" *The National Tribune*, June 13, 1889, 3. Christopher G. Funke, "In the Wilderness. A New York Comrade Gives His Experience of Fighting in the Woods and Brush," *The National Tribune*, July 14, 1892, 4. J. P. Beech, "Gallantry of the 4th New Jersey in the Wilderness. The Break in the lines of the VI Corps," *Grand Army Scout and Soldiers' Mail*, October 25, 1884, 1.
6 This formation is based upon the map in *Nowhere to Run*, Map 27.
7 Captain William J. Haverly, Company D, 65th New York, mistakenly stated that the 67th New York was with the wagon train. The regiment relieved the 4th New Jersey on the picket line and later in the day lost 93 men in the fighting.
William J. Haverly, "The Wilderness, Turning the Right Flank, May 6, 1864," *The National Tribune*, October 3, 1889.
J. P. Beech, "Gallantry of the 4th New Jersey in the Wilderness. The Break in the Lines of the VI Corps," *Grand Army Scout and Soldiers' Mail*, October 25, 1884, 1. (*OR*, XXXVI, part 1, 136)
8 Edwin Crockett, "First time Under Fire. Moving Into the Awful Hell of the Wilderness," *The National Tribune*, May 5, 1904, 3.
9 Edwin Crockett, "Turning the Right Flank, May 6, 1864," *The National Tribune*, October 10, 1889, 3. William J. Haverly, "The Wilderness, Turning the Right Flank, May 6, 1864," *The National Tribune*, October 3, 1889, 3.
10 "In the Wilderness," *The National Tribune*, September 12, 1889, 1.
11 (Ibid.)
12 Funke (pronounced "funky") mistakenly believed that the 49th New York occupied trenches constructed by the 14th New York Heavies. The 14th New York occupied a set of works behind the 49th New York. The map in Schaff's *The Battle of the Wilderness* shows there were three lines of works in the VI Corps area. The first line followed the crest of the ridge running northeast from Saunders Field. Schaff also put a second line of works (125.5 yards to the east) which paralleled the first from below the Culpeper Mine Road to the far right of the line. This set of works does not appear on any other map which I have seen to date. The third line on Schaff's map parallels the other two at a distance of 188.6 yards from the second line. The 49th New York was hit in the front by fire from the 14th New York Heavy Artillery while moving east.
Christopher G. Funke, "In the Wilderness. A New York Comrade Gives His Experience of Fighting in the Woods and Brush," *The National Tribune*, July 14, 1892, 4. A. Wentz, "Closing Days of the War," *The National Tribune*, January 28, 1904, 3. J. P. Beech, "Gallantry of the 4th New Jersey in the Wilderness. The Break in the lines of the VI Corps," *Grand Army Scout and Soldiers' Mail*, October 25, 1884, 1.

13 Note, undated from Robert Johnston to John W. Daniel, John Warwick Daniel, Papers, 1905–1910, Special Collections Department, William R. Perkins Library, Duke University, Durham, N.C.

14 Report of Robert D. Johnston, January 1865, John Warwick Daniel, Papers, 1849–1904, Special Collections Department, William R. Perkins Library, Duke University, Durham, N.C.

15 (Hale and Phillips 1981, 108)

16 Jacob Heater, "Battle of the Wilderness," *Confederate Veteran*, XIV, 1906, 263.

17 The *ORs* and most of the contemporary accounts establish the time of the attack at 2:00 P.M. as opposed to a couple of participants who said the attack occurred two hours later.
    David B. Swinfin, (ed.), *Ruggles' Regiment: The 122nd New York Volunteers in the American Civil War* (Hanover: University Press of New England, 1982), 35. (*OR*, XXXVI, part 1, 742) Report of Lt. Col. Otho H. Binkley, 110th Ohio.

18 Christopher G. Funke, "In the Wilderness. A New York Comrade Gives His Experience of Fighting in the Woods and Brush," *The National Tribune*, July 14, 1892, 4.

19 Stevens said that part of the 43rd New York held the line with the 77th New York. The remaining regiments of the brigade can be accounted for except for part of the 43rd New York. The author of the *Grand Army Scout* said the 2nd New Jersey was relieved by part two regiments from the 2nd and the 3rd Divisions of the VI Corps. The 43rd New York belonged to the 2nd Division and was in the immediate vicinity. The 67th Pennsylvania, which belonged to the 3rd Division, is the only regiment in Seymour's brigade which is not mentioned in the *ORs*. It was attached to the 138th Pennsylvania and consisted of men who had not reenlisted in 1863. All of the other regiments were either in the line or behind the works cooking when the assault occurred. The 67th lost 65 men in the Wilderness, the lowest number in the brigade, and was the only regiment from that division which could have gone into the valley to relieve the 2nd New Jersey.
    George T. Stevens, *Three Years in the VI Corps* (Albany: S. R. Gray, 1866), 311. "An Incident in the Battle of the Wilderness," *Grand Army Scout and Soldiers' Mail*, January 12, 1884, 2. (Whitman and True 1865, 187)

20 (Whitman and True 1865, 186)

21 Z. T. Griffin, "The Wilderness, The Turning of the Right Flank May 6, 1864," *The National Tribune*, August 15, 1889, 3. Christopher G. Funke, "In the Wilderness. A New York Comrade Gives His Experience of Fighting in the Woods and Brush," *The National Tribune*, July 14, 1892, 4.

22 Samuel C. Kerr, "The Wilderness, Turning the Right Flank on May 6," *The National Tribune*, July 11, 1889, 3. (*OR*, XXXVI, part 1, 751) Report of Col. Matthew R. McClennan, 138th Pa.

23 Brewer said that the 67th New York had entrenched. This was clarified by Horn's report in the *ORs*. I placed the 6th Maryland on the southern side of the ravine for several reasons. Brewer said the Marylanders passed the tools to the regiment to the right "over the ravine" which implied that the 6th Maryland was at a narrow spot where the men could literally do that. My research indicates that the 122nd Ohio (approximately 300 men), the 110th Ohio (454 men), the 126th Ohio (389 men), and the 122nd New York (240 men) would have covered a front of about 1,383 feet. Their line began at the end of Neill's brigade on the Culpeper Mine Road. Depending on which map one uses—the one in IV, *Battles and Leaders* or the NPS pamphlet, "Gordon's Flank Attack Trail," the distance from the road to where the Park Service says that the Federal works end varies from 1,385.6 feet (*B&L*) to 1384.5 feet. With that in mind, the 6th Maryland's trench has to be the one which the NPS shows as a Confederate one. It extends from the crest of the ravine into the valley for 519.6 feet (*B&L*) to 639 feet (NPS) at which point a break occurs in the works and is labeled "U" on one side and "C" on the other, which indicates that both sides used the works. The small, detached piece is quite possibly a Confederate addition to the Union works. That same little piece of trench also shows up on Morris Schaff's map in the frontispiece of *The Battle of the Wilderness* (Boston: Houghton, Mifflin, 1910). The 6th Maryland had 229 men in it and the 67th New York had 320 for a total of 529 feet which means that those regiments were entrenched and the troops to the right, the 65th New York, were not.

James H. C. Brewer, "The Wilderness," *The National Tribune*, June 14, 1888, 3. (*OR*, XXXVI, part 1, 736–737) Report of John W. Horn, 6th Md. Edwin Crockett, "First Time Under Fire. Moving Into the Awful Hell of the Wilderness," *The National Tribune*, May 5, 1904, 3.

24 Z. T. Griffin, "The Wilderness, The Turning of the Right Flank May 6, 1864," *The National Tribune*, August 15, 1889, 3.

25 James H. C. Brewer, "The Wilderness," *The National Tribune*, June 14, 1888, 3. (*OR*, XXXVI, part 1, 736–737) Report of John W. Horn, 6th Md.

26 (Haines 1883, 148)

27 NPS, Map "May 6, 1864 5 PM–DARK"

28 Francis L. Hudgins, "38th Ga. regiment at the Wilderness," *Confederate Veteran* Papers, Battles, 1861–1932 & n.d., Box 1, Special Collections Department, William R. Perkins Library, Duke University, Durham, N.C., 7.

29 Thomas G. Jones to John W. Daniel, Letter, February 29, 1904, Special Collections Department, William R. Perkins Library, Duke University, Durham, N.C.

30 I. G. Bradwell, "Gordon's GA. Brigade in the Wilderness," *Confederate Veteran*, XVI, 1908, 641.

31 There is a great deal of controversy as to when Gordon received the order to attack and who issued that order. In his recollections, Gordon said that Lee personally gave the command to attack. I. Gordon Bradwell, an enlisted man with the 31st Georgia, said he saw Lee riding near the left of the brigade prior to the assault.

I. G. Bradwell, "Gordon's Ga. Brigade in the Wilderness," *Confederate Veteran*, XVI, 1908, 641. John B. Gordon, *Reminiscences of the Civil War* (Dayton: Morningside, 1985), 248.

32 I. G. Bradwell, "Gordon's Ga. Brigade in the Wilderness," *Confederate Veteran*, XVI, 1908, 641.

33 "Notes to Governor Johnston," John Warwick Daniel Papers, Papers 1905–1910, Special Collections Department, William R. Perkins Library, Duke University, Durham, N.C.

34 Report, Johnston's Brigade, John Warwick Daniel Papers, 1849–1904, Special Collections Department, William R. Perkins Library, Duke University, Durham, N.C.

35 "In the Wilderness, Chapter XII of Lt. Kirk's History of the 4th H.Y.H.A.," *The National Tribune*, September 19, 1889, 1.

36 William J. Haverly, "The Wilderness, Turning the Right Flank, May 6, 1864," *The National Tribune*, October 3, 1889, 3.

37 Edwin Crockett, "Turning the Right Flank, May 6, 1864," *The National Tribune*, October 10, 1889, 3. Edwin Crockett, "First Time Under Fire. Moving Into the Awful Hell of the Wilderness," *The National Tribune*, May 5, 1904, 3.

38 Edwin Crockett, "First Time Under Fire. Moving Into the Awful Hell of the Wilderness," *The National Tribune*, May 5, 1904, 3.

39 George W. Nichols, *A Soldier's Story of His Regiment (61st Georgia)* (Kennesaw: Continental Book Company, 1961), 148.

40 Edwin Crockett, "First Time Under Fire. Moving Into the Awful Hell of the Wilderness," *The National Tribune*, May 5, 1904, 3.

41 I. G. Bradwell, "Gordon's Ga. Brigade in the Wilderness," *Confederate Veteran*, XVI, 1908, 641. I. G. Bradwell, "Second Day's Battle of the Wilderness, May 6, 1864," *Confederate Veteran*, XXVIII, 1920, 20–21.

42 Edwin Crockett, "First Time Under Fire. Moving Into the Awful Hell of the Wilderness," *The National Tribune*, May 5, 1904, 3.

43 James H. C. Brewer, "The Wilderness," *The National Tribune*, June 14, 1888, 3.

44 (Ibid.)

45 The 65th New York lost 57 officers and men, 21 of whom were captured. The 67th New York lost 93 officers and men, 20 of whom were captured. The 122nd New York, which made a stand, lost 119 soldiers, 40 of whom were missing. The 31st Georgia came under a considerable amount of fire in the vicinity of the works. It had to have come from more than the skirmishers of the 6th Maryland.

(*OR*, XXXVI, part 1, 126) I. G. Bradwell, "Gordon's Ga. Brigade in the Wilderness," *Confederate Veteran*, XVI, 1908, 641. I. G. Bradwell, "Second Day's Battle of the Wilderness, May 6, 1864," *Confederate Veteran*, XXVIII, 1920, 21.

46 James H. C. Brewer, "The Wilderness," *The National Tribune*, June 14, 1888, 3. William J. Haverly, "The Wilderness, Turning the Right Flank, May 6, 1864," *The National Tribune*, October 3, 1889, 3. Edwin Crockett, "First Time Under Fire. Moving Into the Awful Hell of the Wilderness," *The National Tribune*, May 5, 1904, 3.

47 (*OR*, XXXVI, part 1, 737) Report of John W. Horn, 6th Maryland.

48 James H. C. Brewer, "The Wilderness," *The National Tribune*, June 14, 1888, 3.

49 I. G. Bradwell, "Gordon's Ga. Brigade in the Wilderness," *Confederate Veteran*, XVI, 1908, 641. I. G. Bradwell, "Second Day's Battle of the Wilderness, May 6, 1864," *Confederate Veteran*, XXVIII, 1920, 21.

50 James H. C. Brewer, "The Wilderness," *The National Tribune*, June 14, 1888, 3.

51 The regiment never recovered the body of Loomis who was left in the works when the regiment retreated. The only other corporal who died from his wounds after the battle was Hiram Wicks of Company G. Bayonet *wounds* were so rare that had he been wounded with one it would have been noted. Loomis, in all likelihood was the bayoneted man. When people generally talk of bayonet wounds it is in reference to men who survived them and not the fatalities.
Zenas T. Griffin, "The Wilderness, The Turning of the Right Flank, May 6, 1864," *The National Tribune*, August 15, 1889, 3. (Swinfin 1982, 127, 143)

52 (*OR*, XXXVI, part 1, 748) Report of Lt. Col. Aaron W. Ebright, 126th Ohio.

53 Thomas S. Berry, "In the Wilderness; Second Brigade, Second Division, VI Corps, May 6, 1864," *The National Tribune*, October 17, 1889, 5. (*OR*, XXXVI, part 1, 742) Report of Lt. Col. Otho H. Binkley, 110th Ohio.

54 Francis Cordrey, "The Wilderness. What a Private Saw and Felt in That Horrible Place," *The National Tribune*, June 21, 1994, 3.

55 "In the Wilderness, Chapter XII of Lt. Kirk's History of the 4th H.Y.H.A.," *The National Tribune*, September 19, 1889, 1.

56 Edwin Crockett, "Turning the Right Flank, May 6, 1864," *The National Tribune*, October 10, 1889, 3.

57 "In the Wilderness, Chapter XII of Lt. Kirk's History of the 4th H.Y.H.A.," *The National Tribune*, September 19, 1889, 1.

58 (Whitman and True 1865, 187)

59 Thomas W. Hyde, *Following the Greek Cross Or, Memories of the Sixth Army Corps* (Boston: Houghton, Mifflin & Co., 1894), 187. Samuel C. Kerr, "The Wilderness, Turning the Right Flank on May 6," *The National Tribune*, July 11, 1889, 3.

60 C. E. Stevens, "Not a Fighting Regt.," *The National Tribune*, October 8, 1908, 7.

61 (Whitman and True 1865, 187)

62 Report of Robert Johnston, January 1865, Special Collections Department, William R. Perkins Library, Duke University, Durham, N.C.

63 Letter, Thomas G. Jones to John Warwick Daniel, July 3, 1904, John Warwick Daniel Papers, 1849–1904, Special Collections Department, William R. Perkins Library, Duke University, Durham, N.C., 8.

64 I. G. Bradwell, "Second Day's Battle of the Wilderness, May 6, 1864," *Confederate Veteran*, XXVIII, 1920, 21.

65 (*OR*, XXXVI, part 1, 745–746) Report of Colonel William H. Ball, 122nd Ohio.

66 (Brewer 1911, 85)

67 Christopher G. Funke, "In the Wilderness. A New York Comrade Gives His Experience of Fighting in the Woods and Brush," *The National Tribune*, July 14, 1892, 4.

68 The skirmishers from the 2nd New Jersey were on the same line as those of Morris' brigade. E. C. Hall, "In the Wilderness, Incident of That Battle Connected With the VI Corps," *Grand Army Scout and Soldiers' Mail*, January 26, 1884, 2.

69 Edmund English, "More About That Incident in the Battle of the Wilderness," *Grand Army Scout and Soldiers' Mail*, February 9, 1884, 2.

70 James H. C. Brewer, "The Wilderness," *The National Tribune*, June 14, 1888, 3.

71 J. P. Beech, "Gallantry of the 4th New Jersey in the Wilderness. The Break in the Lines of the VI Corps," *Grand Army Scout and Soldiers' Scout*, October 25, 1884, 1. (Baquet 1910, 117)

72 "An Incident in the Battle of the Wilderness," *Grand Army Scout and Soldiers' Mail*, January 12, 1884, 2.

73 (Haines 1883, 149)

74 Hyde did not mention who the frightened brigadier general was, but Shaler was the only free roaming one in the area. He later showed up on the Culpeper Mine Road, approaching the 61st Pennsylvania from the east. In his report Johnston said he crossed the "Germania Ford Road" when he actually described the Culpeper Mine Road.
"In the Wilderness, Ch. XII, Lt. Kirk's History of the 4th New York Heavy Artillery," *The National Tribune*, September 19, 1889, 1. (Hyde 1894, 186–187) Report of Robert Johnston, January 1865, Special Collections Department, William R. Perkins Library, Duke University, Durham, N.C.

75 Letter, Thomas G. Jones to J. W. Daniel, June 20, 1904, John Warwick Daniel Papers, 1849–1904, Special Collections Department, William R. Perkins Library, Duke University, Durham, N.C. Report of Robert Johnston, January 1865, Special Collections Department, William R. Perkins Library, Duke University, Durham, N.C.

76 (Brewer 1911, 85)

77 (Brewer 1911, 85), F. L. Blair, "That 'Incident' in the Wilderness," *Grand Army Scout and Soldiers' Mail*, February 9, 1884, 2. (Gordon 1985, 265)

78 Christopher G. Funke, "In the Wilderness. A New York Comrade Gives His Experience of Fighting in the Woods and Brush," *The National Tribune*, July 14, 1892, 4.

79 C. E. Stevens, "Not a Fighting Regiment," *The National Tribune*, October 8, 1908, 7.

80 Augustus Wentz, "The Wilderness. A Heavy Artilleryman's Story of the Big Battle," *The National Tribune*, July 30, 1891, 3.

81 Letter, William W. Smith to John W. Daniel, October 24, 1904, John Warwick Daniel Papers, 1849–1904, Special Collections Department, William R. Perkins Library, Duke University, Durham, N.C., 2. Letter, B. K. Milam to John W. Daniel, December 4, 1904, John W. Daniel Papers, Acc. # 158, 5383, Box 24, A & E, Special Collections Department, Alderman Library, University of Virginia, Charlottesville, Va.

82 Letter, Thomas G. Jones to John Warwick Daniel, July 3, 1904, John Warwick Daniel Papers, 1849–1904, Special Collections Department, William R. Perkins Library, Duke University, Durham, N.C., 8.

83 Letter, B. K. Milam to John W. Daniel, December 4, 1904, John W. Daniel Papers, Acc. # 158, 5383, Box 24, A & E, Special Collections Department, Alderman Library, University of Virginia, Charlottesville, Va. Jacob Heater, "Battle of the Wilderness," *Confederate Veteran*, XIV, 1904, 263.

84 James Bumgardner, Jr., "Pegram's Brigade, Early's Division," *Richmond Times Dispatch*, October 8, 1905, Special Collections Department, Alderman Library, University of Virginia, Charlottesville, Va.

85 Christopher G. Funke, "In the Wilderness. A New York Comrade Gives His Experience of Fighting in the Woods and Brush," *The National Tribune*, July 14, 1892, 4. Zenas T. Griffin, "The Wilderness, The Turning of the Right Flank, May 6, 1864," *The National Tribune*, August 15, 1889, 3. (*OR*, XXXVI, part 1, 666) Report of Colonel Emory Upton.

86 (*OR*, XXXVI, part 1, 666 and 723) Reports of Colonel Emory Upton and Brig. Gen. William H. Morris. J. S. Thompson, "Turning the Right Flank, May 6, 1864," *The National Tribune*, August 1, 1889, 3. Frederick S. Brice, "Split His Head Open," *The National Tribune*, May 30, 1918, 8.

87 (Stevens 1866, 317)

88 Wheaton said his men were at the intersection of the Germanna Plank Road and the Orange Turnpike. Eyewitness reports placed him in the vicinity of the abandoned field, five hours

before he said his men filled the gap on the right of Neill's brigade.

NPS Map, 5:00 PM to Dark. (*OR*, XXXVI, part 1, 682) Report of Brig. Gen. Frank Wheaton.

89 E. K. Parker, "In the Wilderness; The Turning of the Right Flank, May 6, 1864," *The National Tribune*, November 14, 1889, 3.

90 "In the Wilderness, Chapter XII, Lt. Kirk's History of the 4th New York Heavy Artillery," *The National Tribune*, September 19, 1889, 1. E. K. Parker, "In the Wilderness; The Turning of the Right Flank, May 6, 1864," *The National Tribune*, November 14, 1889, 3.

91 I. Gordon Bradwell, "Gordon's Ga. Brigade in the Wilderness," *Confederate Veteran*, XVI, 1908, 641–642. I. Gordon Bradwell, "Second Day's Battle of the Wilderness, May 6, 1864," *Confederate Veteran*, XXVIII, 1920, 20. (Nichols 1961, 149)

92 This position is based upon various individual accounts. The attacks described by the men of the three Virginia regiments coincide almost exactly with the records of the 61st Pennsylvania and the 4th New York Heavy Artillery. For that attack to have taken place, the regiments had to have gotten south of the Culpeper Mine Road.

93 George Quintus Peyton, "A Civil War record for 1864–1865," 1906, Fredericksburg and Spotsylvania National Battlefield Park, Chatham Hall, Fredericksburg, Va., 22.

94 Gordon's account of the incident is that he had sent a force of unspecified size to deploy as pickets across his front and that he became impatient when their commanding officer did not report back to him as quickly as he desired it. Gordon decided to ride to the front and superintend the force's deployment. There is no reason to doubt that Gordon and Beasley did lead a force into action but in light of Jones' account concerning Gordon's retreating right flank, I tend to doubt that Gordon was deploying a skirmish force. The reports from Pegram's brigade tend to say otherwise.

(Gordon 1985, 263–264)

95 "In the Wilderness, Ch. XII, Lt. Kirk's History of the 4th New York Heavy Artillery," *The National Tribune*, September 19, 1889, 1.

96 (Brewer 1911, 86)

97 (Gordon 1895, 265–266) Francis L. Hudgins, "38th Ga. Regiment at the Wilderness," *Confederate Veteran* Papers, Battles 1861–1932 & n.d., Box 1, Special Collections Department, William R. Perkins Library, Duke University, 9.

98 (Hale and Phillips 1981, 109)

99 (Ibid.)

100 I. Gordon Bradwell, "Second Day's Battle of the Wilderness, May 6, 1864," *Confederate Veteran*, XXVIII, 1920, 21.

101 Letter, William W. Smith to John W. Daniel, October 24, 1904, John Warwick Daniel Papers, 1849–1904, Special Collections Department, William R. Perkins Library, Duke University, Durham, N.C., 2. (Brewer 1911, 86) James Bumgardner, Jr., "Pegram's Brigade, Early's Division," *Richmond Dispatch*, October 8, 1905, Special Collections Department, Alderman Library, University of Virginia, Charlottesville, Va. George Quintus Peyton, "A Civil War Record for 1864–1865," Fredericksburg and Spotsylvania National Battlefield Parks, Chatham Hall, Fredericksburg, Va., 22.

102 (Hyde 1894, 188)

103 James H. C. Brewer, "The Wilderness," *The National Tribune*, June 14, 1888, 3.

104 Johnston incorrectly remembered the regiment as the 137th Pennsylvania.

Report of Robert Johnston, January 1865, Special Collections Department, William R. Perkins Library, Duke University, Durham. N.C.

105 Linder did not identify himself by name. He did sign the piece with Lieutenant Company E, 2nd New Jersey. He was the first lieutenant of the company at the time and would have stayed with his men when the line fell back. The New Jersey rosters do not list men when they were captured, but the officer who wrote the article for the *Grand Army Scout* was captured with a prisoner. They were near the 61st Pennsylvania.

"An Incident in the Battle of the Wilderness," *Grand Army Scout and Soldiers' Mail*, January 12, 1884, 2. F. L. Blair, "That 'Incident' in the Wilderness," *Grand Army Scout and Soldiers' Mail*, January 26, 1884, 2.

46 (Hunter 1905, 536)

47 (*OR*, XXXVI, part 1, 833) Report of Col. Thomas C. Devin, 2nd Brig., 1st Div., Cav. Corps, commanding.

48 (Ibid., 817-818) Report of Brig. Gen. George A. Custer, 1st Brig., 1st Div., Cav. Corps.

49 (Ibid., 826) Lt. Col. Peter Stagg, 1st Mich. Cav. (Kidd 1908, 278)

50 (*OR*, XXXVI, part 1, 833) Report of Col. Thomas C. Devin, 2nd Brig., 1st Div. Cav. Corps, commanding.

51 Entry, May 7, 1864, Diary of Col. William R. Carter, 3rd Virginia Cavalry, Confederate Miscellaneous vol. 18, Fredericksburg and Spotsylvania National Battlefield Parks.

52 (Hopkins 1914, 153)

53 Samuel Burns Rucker, Sr., "Recollections of My War Record During the Confederacy," January 5, 1930, Civil War Misc. Coll., Rid-SA, Manuscript Department, USAMHI, 2.

54 Michael P. Musick, *6th Virginia Cavalry* (Lynchburg: H. E. Howard, Inc., 1990) 1st ed., 56.

55 (Preston 1892, 171–172)

56 Fitzhugh Lee wrote the following about Collins: "He was a graduate of West Point—an officer of northern extraction, but of high scientific attainments, spotless integrity and great courage: he was justly esteemed one of the rising officers of our Army, & his death was universally lamented."
(Hopkins 1914, 152–153) "Report of Major General Fitzhugh Lee of the operations of His Cavalry Division, A. N. V. from May 4th 1864 To September 19th 1864, (both inclusive), Eleanor S. Brockenbrough Library, Museum of the Confederacy, Richmond, Va. Major, A.A.G., J. D. Ferguson, "Memoranda of the Itinerary and Operations of Major General Fitz Lee's Cavalry Division of the Army of Northern Virginia from May 4th 1864 to October 15th 1864, inclusive," Thomas T. Munford Papers, Special Collections Department, William R. Perkins Library, Duke University, Durham, N.C., 1.

57 To date, I have not been able to ascertain the exact location of that section of artillery except that the Federal batteries were about 600 yards away.

58 (Hunter 1905, 535–538)

59 Edward P. Tobie, *History of the First Maine Cavalry, 1861-1865.* (Boston: Press of Emery & Hughes, 1887), 252. Captain Isaac Ressler, Co. L, 16th Pa. Cav., Diary 1862–1865, CWTI Coll., R-Res., Manuscript Department, USAMHI. (Mohr 1982, 420–421)

60 (Tobie 1887, 252–253)

61 (Preston 1892, 171–172)

62 There is no concrete evidence that the brigade deployed exactly as described here. What is known is that there was a Confederate mounted unit in the road. Major J. D. Ferguson, Fitzhugh Lee's A.A.G., merely cites the gallantry of the 1st Virginia. Colonel William Carter of the 3rd Virginia noted that "several regiments: of the brigade were dismounted without referring to his own regiment, which implies that it remained mounted. One squadron of the 3rd Virginia was placed in line with the balance of the brigade in the woods on the right, dismounted. Colonel Owen of the 3rd led the mounted squadron on the left of the road. Alexander Hunter of the 4th Virginia clearly stated that his regiment was dismounted. R. H. Peck of the 2nd Virginia also states that his regiment fought dismounted behind works.
(Peck 1911) (Hunter 1905, 537–538) Major, A.A.G., J. D. Ferguson, "Memoranda of the Itinerary and Operations of Major General Fitz Lee's Cavalry Division of the Army of Northern Virginia from May 4th 1864 to October 15th 1864, inclusive," Thomas T. Munford Papers, Special Collections Department, William R. Perkins Library, Duke University, Durham, N.C., 1. Entry, May 5 and 7, 1864, Diary of Col. William R. Carter, Confederate Misc., Vol. 18, Chatham Hall, Fredericksburg and Spotsylvania National Battlefield Parks.

63 Ragland, who wrote his reminiscences in 1928 said it was after sundown when he was ambushed. The road was narrow and the pines tall which made the road darker than usual. As the years passed, he remembered the event as occurring after sundown. Lieutenant Colonel William R. Carter of the 3rd Virginia did not write his diary entry in a chronological sequence. The first six lines in the typed transcript give a synopsis of the day's action. The rest of the entry, when carefully scrutinized, describes the action in detail and ends with the

regiment behind the second set of barricades. Carter said that Owen was wounded while leading the squadron on the left of the road. It happened during the day and not at night as Ragland said it did. Cavalry charges were not made in the woods after sundown.

Ned Ragland, "Reminiscences," *Confederate Veteran* Papers, Reminiscences 1861–1932, Box C, Special Collections Department, Duke University, Durham, N.C., 2. Entry, May 7, 1864, Diary of Col. William R. Carter, Confederate Misc., Vol. 18, Chatham Hall, Fredericksburg and Spotsylvania National Battlefield Parks.

64 Ned Ragland, "Reminiscences," *Confederate Veteran* Papers, Reminiscences 1861–1932, Box C, Special Collections Department, Duke University, Durham, N.C., 2. Entry, May 7, 1864, Diary of Col. William R. Carter, Confederate Misc., Vol. 18, Chatham Hall, Fredericksburg and Spotsylvania National Battlefield Parks.

65 Ned Ragland, "Reminiscences," *Confederate Veteran* Papers, Reminiscences 1861–1932, Box C, Special Collections Department, Duke University, Durham, N.C., 2.

66 (Ibid., 420)

67 According to James Breathed, Johnston's battery was engaged on the 7th and lost only horses in the fighting. Halsey's section from Hart's Battery was also engaged but no mention was made of his losses. In all likelihood, the casualties which the Federals saw were among Halsey's men.

Report of Operations, Headquarters, Horse artillery, September 14, 1864, Halsey Papers #2447, Southern Historical Collection, University of North Carolina, Chapel Hill, N.C. Report of Headquarters, Horse Artillery, November 19, 1864, Bryce Suderow Papers.

68 (Mohr 1982, 421)

69 (Hunter 1905, 538)

70 (Mohr 1982, 421)

71 The NPS map shows two small woods east and north of Lewis'. The first is 440 feet east of the house and is bisected by the trail from the Brock Road. The second is north of the Lewis house but is east of the trail. Based upon Hunter's description, the woods had to have overlapped the trail at this point.

(Hunter 1905, 538)

72 (Tobie 1887, 253–254)

73 (Mohr 1982, 420)

74 The 2nd Pennsylvania was the only regiment in Gregg's brigade which reported an officer killed and the 10th New York was the only one in the brigade which had an officer wounded.

(*OR*, XXXVI, part 1, 129) (Hunter 1905, 539)

75 (Ibid., 541)

76 (Ibid., 540)

77 (Ibid. 541) Return of April 30, 1864, RG 94, "Return, Army of the Potomac, 1864," Box 126, Consolidated Morning Report of the Cavalry Corps, NA. Henry R. Pyne, *Ride to War, The History of the First New Jersey Cavalry*, Earl Schenck Miers, (ed.) (New Brunswick: Rutgers University Press, 1961), 192-193.

78 (*OR*, XXXVI, part 1, 129)

79 William Penn Lloyd, *History of the First Regiment Pennsylvania Reserve Cavalry* (Philadelphia: King and Baird, Printers, 1864), 91.

80 (Hunter 1905, 541–542)

81 (Pyne 1961, 192–193)

82 Letter, Katherine Crouse to Mr. and Mrs. H., from Laurel Hill, Va., Manuscript Department, Alderman Library, University of Virginia, Mss 10441.

83 (Pyne 1961, 192–193)

84 Letter, Katherine Crouse to Mr. and Mrs. H., from Laurel Hill, Va., Manuscript Department, Alderman Library, University of Virginia, Mss 10441.

85 (Gracey 1868, 235)

86 (Ibid., 235)

87 (Peck 1911, 44)

88 J. R. Bowen, *Regimental History of the First New York Dragoons* (J. R. Bowen, 1900), 143.

89 (Gracey 1868, 235–236)

90 Richard J. Del Vecchio, *With the First New York Dragoons: From the Letters of Jared L. Ainsworth* (1971), 76. Entry, May 5 and 7, 1864, Diary of Col. William R. Carter, Confederate Misc., Vol. 18, Chatham Hall, Fredericksburg and Spotsylvania National Battlefield Parks.

91 Letter, May 17, 1864, Clement Hoffman to his mother, Clement Hoffman, 6th Pa. Cav. Regt., HQ, VI Corps and Left Grand Division and Army of the Potomac; Ambulance Park, Dept. of Army, 17th U.S. Inf. Regt., Letters to his mother, Feb. 12, 1863–July 14, 1867, Harrisburg, CWRT, FLE-L, Manuscript Dept., USAMHI. (Gracey 1868, 235)

92 (Gracey 1868, 235–236)

93 (Hunter 1905, 542)

94 (Del Vecchio 1976, 76)

95 E. R. Hagemann, (ed.), *Fighting Rebels and Redskins: Experiences in Army Life of Colonel George B. Sanford 1861-1892* (Norman: University of Oklahoma Press), 228. Theodore F. Rodenbough, (comp.), *From Everglade to Cain With the Second Dragoons (Second United States Cavalry)* (New York: D. Van Nostrand, 1875), 304–305.

96 (Del Vecchio 1971, 76–77.)

97 The 2nd U.S. had to have been on the northeast side of the Brock Road because there was only one small farm in the field in that area and none in the woods to the south. Newel Cheney, historian of the 9th New York Cavalry, placed the U.S. Regulars on both sides of the road.
    Newel Cheney, *History of the Ninth Regiment, New York Volunteer Cavalry, War of 1861 to 1865* (New York: Martin Merz & Son, 1901), 158. (Hagemann, 228) (Rodenbough 1875, 304–305)

98 (Foster 1892, 53)

99 (Foster 1892, 54)

100 Augustus P. Clarke, "A Cavalry Surgeon's Experiences in the Battle of the Wilderness," *The United Service*, II, February 1894, not paginated.

101 (Peck 1911, 45) "The Second Virginia Cavalry in the Late Fights," *The Sentinel*, May 21, 1864, 1:col. 1.

102 (Hunter 1905, 543)

103 (Peck 1911, 45)

104 (Cheney 1901, 158)

105 "Barringer's N.C. Brigade of Cavalry," *The Daily Confederate*, February 22, 1865. Theodore Garnett Memoirs, Manuscript Department, Alderman Library, University of Va., Charlottesville, Va.

106 Letter, Catherine Couse to Mr. and Mrs. H., from Laurel Hill, Va., Manuscript Department, Alderman Library, University of Virginia, Mss 10441.

107 (Peck 1911, 45)

108 Hunter's description of the 4th's position during the retreat is a little confusing. What is apparent is that the regiment was in line some distance to the front of Breathed's guns and was forced to retire to a barricade and the support of Breathed's guns. I believe he described the retreat from Lomax's old line to Wickham's line above Alsop's Gate.
    (Hunter 1905, 543–544)

109 (Del Vecchio 1971, 77)

110 (Peck 1911, 45)

111 (Del Vecchio 1971, 77)

112 (Peck 1911, 45)

113 (Hunter 1905, 544) (Bowen 1900, 144)

114 (Hunter 1905, 545)

115 (Bowen 1900, 143 and 144)

116 (Del Vecchio 1971, 77)

117 (Hunter 1905, 545–546)

118 "The Fight Near Spotsylvania Court House Between Fitzhugh Lee and the Enemy," *Daily Richmond Examiner*, May 11, 1864, 1, col.4.
119 Berry G. Benson, "Reminiscences of Berry Greenwood Benson, C.S.A.," Berry G. Benson Misc. Writings, Typed mss., Vol. 1, Southern Historical Collection, U.N.C., Chapel Hill, 266.
120 (Adams 1888, 390–391)
121 (Ibid., 391)

APPENDIX

1 The Order of Battle is taken from *Battles and Leaders of the Civil War*, Vol. IV.
2 All of the troop strengths for the Army of the Potomac are from RG 94, OAG, Volunteer Organizations, Civil War Returns, Second Corps, April, 1864, Boxes 9, 19, 22, 24, and 126, NA.
3 All casualty returns for the Army of the Potomac are from *OR*, XXXVI, part 1, 119-133.
4 Not engaged.
5 Regimental strengths for the 59th Mass., 4th and 10th U.S. are based upon returns for May 1864 plus casualties incurred during that month.
6 Regimental strength is based upon returns for May 1864 plus casualties incurred during that month.
7 The regimental strength of the 58th Massachusetts was not in RG 94. The 7th Rhode Island was detached as a train guard.
8 The 32nd Maine and the 9th New Hampshire were cleaning up a train accident and did not take part in the battle.
9 Not present.
10 Regimental strength is based upon returns for May 1864 plus casualties incurred during that month.
11 The regimental strengths for the 22nd N.Y. and the 13th Pa. were not in RG 94.
12 Regimental strength is based upon returns for May 1864 plus casualties incurred during that month.
13 Troop strengths were not listed in RG 94.
14 Troop strengths were not listed in RG 94.
15 Brigade strength is based upon returns for May 1864 plus casualties incurred during that month.
16 This regiment was serving as a train guard.
17 Brigade strength is based upon returns for May 1864 plus casualties incurred during that month.
18 These numbers do not include staff casualties.
19 (Longstreet 1992, 553)
20 (Wyckoff 1994, 117)
21 The brigade casualties are from a letter dated May 7, 1864, in the Columbia *Daily South Carolinian*, May 25, 1864, 2: col. 2-5.
22 *Charleston Mercury*, June 9, 1864, 1: col. 2.
23 The casualties for these regiments were not found in the newspapers.
24 *Richmond Enquirer*, June 14, 1864, 2: col. 3.
25 *Daily Intelligencer*, June 4, 1864, 1: col. 3–5.
26 The casualties for the 10th and the 53rd Ga. are from:
   The Savannah *Republican*, May 21, 1864, 1: col. 3–4.
27 Casualties were not listed in the newspapers.
28 Letter from Col. E. Ball, June 9, 1864, in the *Macon Daily Telegraph*, June 21, 1864, 2: col. 2.
29 Letter dated May 7, 1864.
   Columbia *Daily South Carolinian*, May 25, 1864, 2: col. 2–5.
30 (*OR*, XXXVI, part 1, 1069) Report of Col. James R. Hagood, 1st S.C.

31 Regimental strength and casualty return for the 2nd Rifles are from Alexander Papers #7, Southern Historical Collection, Special Collections Department, U.N.C., Chapel Hill.

32 The Richmond *Daily Dispatch*, May 10, 1864, 1: col. 3.

33 Columbia *Daily South Carolinian*, May 26, 1864, 3: col. 3.

34 Charleston *Mercury*, May 24, 1864, 2: col. 4.

35 Alexander Papers #7, Southern Historical Collection, Special Collections Department, U.N.C., Chapel Hill.

36 List of Casualties in the 8th Regiment Georgia Infantry During the Year 1864. Microfilm Publication M836, Confederate States Army casualties: Lists & Narrative Reports 1861–1865. Roll 7.

37 Casualties for the 9th, 11th and 59th Ga. are from a letter by Captain Sam D. Cockrell, 9th Ga., to *The Sentinel*, May 30, 1864, 1: col. 5.

38 (Simpson 1970, 402)

39 To date, Simpson's work on the Texas Brigade is the most thorough done on those regiments. I have chosen to use the figures he arrived at as the best of several choices. (Simpson 1977, 535)

40 The casualties of the 15th Georgia were reached by subtracting the casualties of the other regiments from the totals given in Alexander's Papers. The casualties for the brigade come from the same source.
Alexander Papers, #7, Southern Historical Collection, Special Collections Department, U.N.C., Chapel Hill.

41 Unless otherwise stated, the troop strengths are from *The Atlas to Accompany the Official Records.*

42 (Jones 1987, 198)

43 *The Sentinel*, Richmond, May 16, 1864, 2: col. 1.

44 *The Dispatch*, Richmond, May 17, 1864, 2: col. 5.

45 Robert J. Driver, Jr., *58th Virginia Infantry* (Lynchburg: H. E. Howard, Inc., 1990), 61.

46 *Daily Intelligencer*, May 27, 1864, 3: col. 2.

47 On May 5, the 31st Ga. lost 6 killed, and 46 wounded.
Letter, May 5, 1864, in the Savannah *Republican*, May 10, 1864, 1: col. 3.
The regiment lost 6 killed and 26 wounded on May 6, 1864.
Daily Intelligencer, May 27, 1864, 3: col. 3–4.

48 The 4th Va. had under 100 men present.
James I. Robertson, Jr., *The Stonewall Brigade*, (Baton Rouge: Louisiana State University Press, 1963), 220. Diary Entry, May 5, 1864, SGM Joseph McMurran, Accession #22076, Virginia State Archives, Virginia State Library, Richmond.

49 (Wallace 1988, 56)

50 Regimental strengths, excluding the 3rd N.C. are from:
McHenry Howard, "Notes and recollections of Opening of the campaign of 1864," *Papers of the Military Historical Society of Massachusetts*, IV, 92–93.

51 *Daily Confederate*, Raleigh, May 23, 1864, 2: col. 4.

52 (Ibid., May 28, 2: col. 4.)

53 *Richmond Enquirer*, May 20, 1864, 1: col. 4–5.

54 *The Sentinel*, May 17, 1864, 2: col. 5.

55 (Armstrong 1990, 76)

56 Letter from Capt. Edward M. Alfriend, Co. E, 44th Va.
The Sentinel, June 1, 1864, 1: col. 4.

57 (*48th Va.* 1989, 70–71)

58 *Richmond Whig*, June 16, 1864, 2: col. 5–6.

59 Napier Bartlett, *Military Record of Louisiana* (Baton Rouge: Louisiana State University Press, 1964), 17.

60 *Daily Intelligencer*, May 29, 1864, 2: col. 2.

61 (Jordan 1993, XIII: 28)

62 *The Daily Confederate*, Raleigh, May 24, 1864, 2: col. 3–5.

63 Henry W. Thomas, *History of the Doles-Cook Brigade, Army of Northern Virginia* (Atlanta: The Franklin Printing and Publishing Co., 1903)

64 Montgomery *Daily Register and Advertiser*, May 21, 1864, 1: col.6.

65 Montgomery *Daily Advertiser*, May 27, 1864, 2: col. 2.

66 Lt. Robert E. Park's Co. had 1 man wounded.
Montgomery *Daily Advertiser*, May 30, 1864, 2: col. 2.

67 Casualty returns are from *Alabama Historical Quarterly*, Vol. 39, 134.

68 Casualties for the 9th and the 11th Ala. are from the Montgomery Daily Advertiser, June 19, 1864, 2: col. 3.

69 Montgomery *General Advertiser*, May 30, 1864, 1: col. 3.

70 *Richmond Whig*, May 16, 1864, 2: col.5.

71 "Report of General William Mahone," SHSP, 6:85.

72 *Daily Richmond Examiner*, May 31, 1864, 1: col. 4–5.

73 Alexander Papers #7, Southern Historical Collection, Special Collections Department, U.N.C., Chapel Hill.

74 Francis F. Fleming, *Memoir of Captain C. Seton Fleming of the Second Florida Infantry, C.S.A.* (Jacksonville, Fla.: 1881. Reprint: Alexandria Va., 1985), Appendix J.

75 2nd and 11th Miss. totals are from:
Richmond Enquirer, June 7, 1864.

76 Company B, 42nd Miss. lost 10 out of 24 men, killed and wounded on May 5.
(Dunlop 1988, 371)

77 According to Clark, III:305, the 55th North Carolina had 340 present for duty. The casualty tabulations are from Weymouth T. Jordan, Jr., (comp.), *North Carolina Troops 1861–1865 A Roster* Vol. XIII, Infantry (Raleigh: Division of Archives and History, 1993), 401.

78 (Clark 1901, II:416)

79 *The Daily Confederate*, Raleigh, May 17, 1864, 1: col. 1–2.

80 Adjutant W. A. Knight, 27th N.C. in a letter said the regiment had 310 men present. He also sent a detailed list of casualties to the newspaper.
The Sentinel, May 31, 1864, 2: col. 7.

81 The 46th N.C. had 540 present.
(Clark 1901, III:75)

82 May 5: 5 killed; 86 wounded, 4 missing = 95.   May 6: 1 killed, 7 wounded, 1 missing = 9.
Raleigh *Semi-Weekly Standard*, May 24, 1864, 2: col. 4–6.

83 May 5: 3 killed, 20 wounded, 9 missing = 32. May 6: 5 wounded, 7 missing = 12.
From R. L. Reynolds, Adj., 40th Va.
The Sentinel, Richmond, June 23, 1864, 2:col. 5.

84 Letter from Adjutant Samuel D. Davis, 47th Va.
The Sentinel, May 30, 1864.

85 (O'Sullivan 1989, 69)

86 Richmond *Daily Dispatch*, May 26, 1864, 1: col. 7.

87 13th Ala., 1st, 7th, and 14th Tenn. totals are from:
Richmond Enquirer, June 4, 1864, 3: col. 4–5.

88 Brigade casualties are from :
J. H. Lane, "History of Lane's North Carolina Brigade," SHSP, 9:128.

89 *The Daily Confederate*, Raleigh, May 24, 1864, 2: col. 5.

90 (Caldwell 1951, 136)

91 Savannah *Republican*, May 21, 1864, 1:col. 3–4.

92 May 5: 4 killed, 14 wounded, 2 missing = 20. May 6: 20 killed, 59 wounded, 27 missing = 106.
Augusta *Daily Constitutionalist*, May 28, 1864, 1: col. 3–4.

93 Brigade casualties. This source was used to supplement the figures reported by McDonald.
Diary of Private James F. Wood, Co. F, 7th Va. Cav.
(McDonald 1907, 382–495)

94 Entry, May 6, 1864, Diary of Jasper Hause, Co. B, 11th Va. Cav., Microfilm Room, Alderman Library, University of Va., 9.

95 (Frye 1988, 65)

96 J. D. Fergusson, "Memoranda of the Itinerary and Operations of Major General Fitz Lee's Cavalry Division of the Army of Northern Virginia from May 4th to October 15th, inclusive," Munford-Ellis Family Papers, Thomas T. Munford Div. 1, Miscellany–Box 1, Civil War Mss., 1861–1865, Special Collections Department, Wliiam R. Perkins Library, Duke University, Durham.

97 *Richmond Enquirer*, May 20, 1864, 1: col. 4.

98 *The Sentinel*, Richmond, May 21, 1864, 1: col. 3.

99 May 6: 4 killed, 6 wounded. May 7: 7 wounded.
    Thomas P. Nanzig, *3rd Virginia Cavalry* (Lynchburg: H. E. Howard, Inc., 1989), 47.

100 *Daily Richmond Examiner*, May 17, 1864, 1: col. 5.

101 Company E, 4th Va. Cav. suffered these losses.
    Richmond Enquirer, May 17, 1864, 3: col. 4.

102 *Daily Richmond Examiner*, May 11, 1864, 1: col. 4.

103 "Barringer's N. C. Brigade of Cavalry," *The Daily Confederate*, February 22, 1865.

104 Approximate numbers.

105 The final totals do not agree with the specific killed, wounded, and missing because in some brigades they tallied all casualties together rather than under specific classifications.

IBLIOGRAPHY

Published Primary Sources

Adams, Z. Boylston. "In the Wilderness," *Civil War Papers Read Before the Commandery of Massachusetts, Military Order of the Loyal Legion of the United States*. II. Boston: 1900.

Albert, Allen D. (ed.) *History of the Forty-Fifth Regiment Pennsylvania Veteran Volunteer Infantry 1861–1865*. Williamsport, Pa.: Grit Publishing Co., 1912.

Anderson, John. *The Fifty-Seventh Regiment of Massachusetts Volunteers in the War of the Rebellion*. Boston: E. B. Stillings & Co., 1896.

Alexander, E. Porter. *Fighting for the Confederacy, The Personal Recollections of General Edward Porter Alexander*. Gary G. Gallagher (ed.) Chapel Hill: U.N Press, 1989.

Alexander, E. Porter. *Military Memoirs of a Confederate*. New York: Scribner's Sons, 1907.

Bartlett, Napier. *Military Record of Louisiana*. Baton Rouge: Louisiana State University Press, 1964.

Bates, Samuel P. *History of Pennsylvania Volunteers 1861–5*. 4 volumes. Harrisburg: S. Singerly Printers, 1869–70.

Baxter, Nancy Niblack (ed.) *Hoosier Farm Boy in Lincoln's Army, The Civil War Letters of Pvt. John R. McClure*. Privately printed, 1971.

Bennett, Edwin C. *Musket and Sword*. Boston: Coburn Publishing Co., 1900.

Bernard, George. *War Talks of Confederate Veterans*. Petersburg: Fenn & Owen, 1892.

Bidwell, Frederick David (comp.) *History of the Forty-Ninth New York Volunteers*. Albany: J. B. Lyon Co., 1916.

Bowen, James L. *History of the Thirty-Seventh Regiment Mass. Volunteers in the Civil War of 1861–1865*. Holyhoke, Mass.: Clark W. Bryan & Co., 1894.

Bowen, J. R. *Regimental History of the First New York Dragoons*. J. R. Bowen, 1900.

Brewer, A. T. *History of the Sixty-first Regiment Pennsylvania Volunteers 1861–1865*. 1911.

302

Brown, Henri LeFevre (comp.) *History of the Third Regiment, Excelsior Brigade, 72nd New York Volunteer Infantry, 1861–1865.* 1902.

Bruce, George A. *The Twentieth Regiment of Massachusetts Volunteer Infantry 1861–1865.* Baltimore: Butternut and Blue, 1988.

Burrage, Henry S. *History of the Thirty-Sixth Regiment Massachusetts Volunteers, 1862–1865.* Boston: Press of Rockwell and Churchill, 1884.

Caldwell, J. F. J. *History of a Brigade of South Carolinians Known First as "Gregg's:" and Subsequently as "McGowan's Brigade".* Marietta, Ga.: Continental Book Co., 1851.

Chamberlin, Thomas. *History of the One Hundred and Fiftieth Regiment Pennsylvania Volunteers, Second Regiment, Bucktail Brigade.* Baltimore: Butternut & Blue, 1986.

Cheney, Newel. *History of the Ninth Regiment New York Volunteer Cavalry, War of 1861–1865.* Jamestown: Martin Merz & Son, 1901.

Clark, Walter (ed.) *Histories of Several Regiments and Battalions From North Carolina in the Great War.* 5 volumes. Raleigh: E. M. Uzzell, 1901.

Cogswell, Leander W. *A History of the Eleventh New Hampshire Regiment Volunteer Infantry in the Rebellion War, 1861–1865.* Concord: Republican Press Assoc., 1891.

Commager, Henry Steere (ed.) *The Blue and the Gray.* Indianapolis: The Bobbs-Merrill Co., 1950.

Committee of the Regimental Association. *History of the Thirty-Fifth Regiment, Massachusetts Volunteers, 1862–1865.* Boston: Mills, Knight & Co., 1884.

Connor, Selden. "In the Wilderness," *War Papers Read Before the Commandery of the State of Maine, Military Order of the Loyal Legion of the United States.* Vol. IV. Wilmington, N.C.: Broadfoot Publishing Co., 1992.

Cook, Benjamin F. *History of the Twelfth Massachusetts Volunteers (Webster Regiment).* Boston: Twelfth (Webster) Regiment Association, 1882.

Cowtan, Charles W. *Services of the Tenth New York Volunteers (National Zouaves) in the War of the Rebellion.* New York: Charles H. Ludwig, 1882.

Craft, David. *History of the One Hundred Forty-First Pennsylvania Volunteers.* Towanda, Pa.: Reporter-Journal Printing Co., 1885.

Curtis, O. B. *History of the Twenty-Fourth Michigan of the Iron Brigade.* Detroit: Winn & Hammond, 1891.

Cutcheon, Byron M. *The Story of the Twentieth Michigan Infantry.* Lansing: Robert Smith Printing, 1904.

Dawes, Rufus R. *Service With the Sixth Wisconsin Volunteers.* Dayton, Ohio: Morningside Bookshop, 1984.

Dawson, Francis W. *Reminiscences of Confederate Service 1861–1865,* Bell I. Wiley (ed.) Baton Rouge: University of Louisiana Press, 1980.

Dickert, D. Augustus. *History of Kershaw's Brigade.* Dayton, Ohio: Morningside Bookshop, 1976.

Dobbins, Austin C. *Grandfather's Journal*. Dayton: Morningside Bookshop, 1988.

Dunlop, W. S. *Lee's Sharpshooters*. Dayton, Ohio: Morningside Bookshop, 1988.

Fleming, Francis F. *Memoir of Captain C. Seton Fleming of the Second Florida Infantry, C.S.A.* Jacksonville: 1881. Reprint, Alexandria, Va., 1985.

Foster, Alonzo. *Reminiscences and Record of the 6th New York V.V. Cavalry*. Alonzo Foster, 1892.

Galwey, Thomas Francis. *The Valiant Hours*. Wilbur S. Nye (ed.) Harrisburg: Stackpole, 1961.

Gavin, William G. (ed.) *Infantryman Pettit*. Shippensburg: White Mane, 1990.

Gordon, John B. *Reminiscences of the Civil War*. Dayton, Ohio: Morningside Bookshop, 1985.

Grotty, Daniel G. *Four Years Campaigning in the Army of the Potomac*. Grand Rapids, Mich.: Dygert Brothers & Co., 1874.

Hackley, Woodford B. *The Little Fork Rangers*. Richmond: The Dietz Printing Co., 1927.

Hadley, Amos (ed.) *History of the Sixth New Hampshire Regiment in the War for the Union*. Concord: Republican Press Assoc., 1891.

Hagemann, E. R. (ed.) *Fighting Rebels and Redskins: Experiences in Army Life of Colonel George B. Sanford 1861–1892*. Norman: University of Oklahoma Press.

Haines, Alanson A. *History of the Fifteenth Regiment New Jersey Volunteers*. New York: Jenkins & Thomas Printers, 1883.

Hale, Laura Virginia and Stanley S. Phillips. *History of the Forty-Ninth Virginia Infantry, C.S.A., "Extra Billy Smith's Boys"*. Lynchburg: H. E. Howard, Inc., 1981.

Howard, McHenry. *Recollections of a Maryland Confederate Soldier and Staff Officer*. Dayton, Ohio: Morningside Bookshop, 1975.

Howe, Mark DeWolfe (ed.) *Touched With Fire, Civil War Letters and Diary of Oliver Wendell Holmes, Jr. 1861–1864*. Cambridge: Harvard University Press, 1946.

Hunter, Alexander. *Johnny Reb and Billy Yank*. New York: The Neale Publishing Co., 1905.

Hutchinson, Nelson V. *History of the Seventh Massachusetts Volunteer Infantry in the War of the Rebellion of the Southern States 1861–1865*. Taunton, Mass.: Regimental Association, 1890.

Hyde, Thomas W. *Following the Greek Cross or Memories of the Sixth Army Corps*. Boston: Houghton, Mifflin and Co., 1894.

Isham, Asa B. "Through the Wilderness to Richmond," *Sketches of War History 1861–1865*. Vol. I. Cincinnati: Robert Clarke & Co., 1888.

Johnson, Robert U. and Clarence C. Buel (eds.) *Battles and Leaders of the Civil War*. Secaucus, N.J.: Castle.

Jordan, William C. *Some Events and Incidents During the Civil War*. Montgomery: The Paragon Press, 1909.

Kepler, William. *History of the Three Months and Three Years' Service of the Fourth regiment Ohio Volunteer Infantry in the War for the Union*. Cleveland: Leader Printing Co., 1886.

Kidd, J. H. "The Michigan Cavalry Brigade in the Wilderness," *War Papers Read Before the Commandery of the State of Michigan of the Loyal Legion of the United States*. Vol. I. Detroit: Winn & Hammond Printers, 1893.

Lloyd, William Penn. *History of the First Reg't Pennsylvania Reserve Cavalry*. Philadelphia: King & Baird, Printers, 1864.

Longstreet, James. *From Manassas to Appomattox*. New York: DaCapo Press, 1992.

McDonald, William N. *A History of the Laurel Brigade*, Bushrod C. Washington (ed.) Kate S. McDonald, 1907.

Meier, Heinz K. (ed.) *Memoirs of a Swiss Officer in the American Civil War*. Bern: Herbert Lang, 1972.

Mixon, Frank M. *Reminiscences of a Private*. Columbia: The State Co., 1910.

Mohr, James C. (ed.) *The Cormany Diaries, A Northern Family in the Civil War*. Pittsburgh: University of Pittsburgh Press, 1982.

Monteith, Robert. "Battle of the Wilderness and Death of General Wadsworth," *War Papers Read Before the Commandery of the State of Wisconsin, Military Order of the Loyal Legion of the United States*. I. Milwaukee: Burdick, Armitage & Allen, 1891.

Myers, Frank. *The Comanches: A History of White's Battalion, Virginia Cavalry*. Marietta, Ga.: The Continental Book Co., 1956.

Neese, George M. *Three Years in the Confederate Horse Artillery*. Dayton, Ohio: Morningside Bookshop, 1983.

Oates, William C. *The War Between the Union and the Confederacy*. Dayton: Morningside Bookshop, 1974.

Page, Charles D. *History of the Fourteenth Regiment, Connecticut Vol. Infantry*. Meriden: Horton Printing Co., 1906.

Peck, R. H. *Reminiscences of a Confederate Soldier of co. C, 2nd Va. Cavalry*. 1911.

Poague, William Thomas. *Gunner With Stonewall*. Monroe F. Cockrell (ed.) Jackson, Tenn.: McCowat-Mercer Press Inc., 1957.

Preston, N. D. *History of the Tenth Regiment of Cavalry New York State Volunteers*. New York: D. Appleton and Co., 1892.

Pyne, Henry R. *Ride to War, The History of the First New Jersey Cavalry*. New Brunswick: Rutgers University Press, 1961.

Rea, Lilian (ed.) *War Record and Personal Experiences of Walter Raleigh Robbins From April 22, 1861 to August 4, 1865*. (n.d.)

Roback, Henry (comp.) *The Veteran Volunteers of Herkimer and Ostego Counties in the War of the Rebellion: Being a History of the 152nd N.Y.V.* Little Falls: L. C. Childs and Son, 1888.

Rodenbough, Theodore F. (comp.) *From Everglade to Cain With the Second Dragoons.* New York: Van Nostrand, 1875.

Rozier, John (ed.) *The Granite Farm Letters: The Civil War Correspondence of Edgeworth & Sallie Bird.* Athens: University of Georgia Press, 1988.

Sawyer, Franklin. *A Military History of the 8th Regiment Ohio Vol. Infy.* Cleveland: Fairbanks & Co., 1881.

Scott, Kate M. *History of the One Hundred and Fifth Regiment of Pennsylvania Volunteers.* Baltimore: Butternut and Blue, 1993.

Scott, Robert N. (comp.) *The Official Records of the War of the Rebellion.* Vol. XXXVI, part 1. Washington, D.C.: U.S. Government Printing Office, 1887.

Seville, William P. *History of the First Regiment, Delaware Volunteers.* Longstreet House: reprint, 1986.

Silliker, Ruth L. (ed.) *The Rebel Yell & the Yankee Hurrah, The Civil War Journal of a Maine Volunteer.* Camden, Me.: Down East Books, 1985.

Smith, A. P. *History of the Seventy-Sixth Regiment New York Volunteers.* Cortland: 1867.

Sorrel, G. Moxley. *Recollections of a Confederate Staff Officer.* Jackson: McCowat-Mercer Press, 1958.

Stevens, C. A. *Berdan's Sharpshooters in the Army of the Potomac, 1861–1865.* Dayton, Ohio: Morningside Bookshop, 1984.

Stevens, George T. *Three Years in the Sixth Corps.* Albany: R. S. Gray, 1866.

Stiles, Robert. *Four Years Under Marse Robert.* New York: The Neale Publishing Co., 1903.

Stone, James Madison. *Personal Recollections of the Civil War.* Boston: 1918.

Survivors' Association. *History of the Corn Exchange Regiment, 118th Pennsylvania Volunteers.* Philadelphia: J. L. Smith, Publisher, 1888.

Tobie, Edward P. *History of the First Maine Cavalry 1861–1865.* Boston: Emery & Hughes, 1887.

Vautier, John D. *History of the 88th Pennsylvania Volunteers in the War for the Union, 1861–1865.* Philadelphia: J. B. Lippincott, 1894.

Walcott, Charles F. *History of the 21st Massachusetts Volunteers in the War for the Preservation of the Union, 1861–1865.* Boston: 1882.

Welch, Spencer Glasgow. *A Confederate Surgeon's Letters to His Wife.* Marietta, Ga.: Continental Book Co., 1954.

Weld, Stephen M. *Civil War Diary and Letters of Stephen Minot Weld 1861–1865.* Boston: Massachusetts Historical Society, 1979.

Westbrook, Robert S. *History of the 49th Pennsylvania Volunteers.* Altoona, 1898.

Weygant, Charles H. *History of the One Hundred Twenty-Fourth Regiment, N.Y.S.V.* Newburgh: Journal Printing House, 1877.

White, Russell C. (ed.) *The Civil War Diary of Wyman S. White.* Baltimore: Butternut & Blue, 1991.

Whitman, William E. S. and Charles H. True. *Maine in the War for the Union: A History of the Part Borne by Maine Troops.* Lewiston: Nelson Dingley, Jr. & Co., 1865.

REGIMENTALS – SECONDARY SOURCES

H. E. Howard, Inc.: Lynchburg, Va.

Armstrong, Richard L. *11th Virginia Cavalry,* 1989.

Musick, Michael P. *6th Virginia Cavalry.* 1990.

Nanzig, Thomas P. *3rd Virginia Cavalry,* 1989.

Reidenbaugh, Lowell. *33rd Virginia Infantry.* 1987.

OTHER REGIMENTALS

Carmichael, Peter S. *Lee's Young Artillerist.* Charlottesville: University Press of Virginia, 1995.

Collier, Calvin L. *"They'll Do to Tie To," The Story of the Third Regiment Arkansas Infantry, C.S.A.* Little Rock: Pioneer Press, 1959.

Gavin, William G. *The 100th Pennsylvania Volunteers, The Roundhead Regiment.* Dayton: Morningside, 1989.

Simpson, Harold B. *Hood's Texas Brigade: A Compendium.* Hillsboro: Hill Junior College Press, 1977.

Simpson, Harold B. *Hood's Texas Brigade: Lee's Grenadier Guards.* Dallas: Alcor Publishing Co., 1983.

Suderow, Bryce. *"Todd's Tavern, Va., May 5–8, 1864: Sheridan vs. Stuart: The Opening Round,"* unpublished monograph.

Swinfin, David B. *Ruggles' Regiment, The 122nd New York Volunteers in the American Civil War.* Hanover: University Press of New England, 1982.

Wert, Jeffrey D. *General James Longstreet: The Confederacy's Most Controversial Soldier–A Biography.* (New York: Simon and Schuster, 1993.

Wilkinson, Warren. *Mother, May You Never See the Sights I Have Seen.* New York: Quill, 1990.

Wyckoff, Mack. *A History of the 2nd South Carolina Infantry: 1861–65.* Fredericksburg: Sgt. Kirkland's Museum and Historical Society, Inc., 1994.

PERIODICALS, NEWSPAPERS – PRIMARY SOURCES

The Alabama Historical Quarterly

Vol. XXXIX, Nos. 1–4. Alabama State Department of Archives and History.

Confederate Veteran

Bradwell, I. G. "Gordon's Ga. Brigade in the Wilderness." XVI, 1908, 641–642.

Bradwell, I. G. "Second Day's Battle of the Wilderness, May 6, 1864." XXVIII, 1920, 20–22.

Flanagan, W. A. "Account of How Some Flags Were Captured." XIII, 1905, 250.

Gee, Leonard Grace. "The Texan Who Held Gen. R. E. Lee's Horse." XII, 1904, 478.

Heater, Jacob. "Battle of the Wilderness." XIV, 1906, 262.

Johnson, W. Gart. "Barksdale-Humphreys Mississippi Brigade." I, 1893, 206–207.

Parrent, E. "Dock". "General Lee to the Rear." III, 1895, 14–15.

Polley, J. B. "Texas in the Battle of the Wilderness." V, 1897, 290–293.

Vance, S. W. "Heroes of the Eighth Alabama Infantry." VII, 1899, 492–493.

White, E. V. Letter, IX, 1901, 167.

Grand Army Scout and Soldiers' Mail

"An Incident in the Battle of the Wilderness," January 12, 1884, 2.

Beech, John P. "Gallantry of the 4th New Jersey in the Wilderness: The Break in the Lines of the Sixth Corps," October 24, 1884, 1.

Blair, F. L. "That Incident in the Wilderness," February 9, 1884, 2.

English, Edmund. "More About That Incident in the Battle of the Wilderness," February 9, 1884, 2.

Hall, E. C. "In the Wilderness, Incident of That Battle Connected With the Sixth Corps," January 26, 1884, 2.

Walker, T. F. "Another Account of the 91st P. V.," October 18, 1884, 2.

The National Tribune

Barnes. "The Wilderness. Another Account of What Took Place at the Plank Road," August 6, 1891, 3.

Berry, Thomas S. "In the Wilderness: Second Brigade, Second Division, Sixth Corps, May 6, 1864," October 17, 1889, 5.

Brewer, J. H. C. "The Wilderness," June 14, 1882, 3.

Brice, Frederick. "Split His Head Open," May 30, 1918, 8.

Caril, Harrison. "Campaigning With Grant Through Virginia," April 9, 1925, 5.

Carter, Joseph F. "In the Wilderness. The controversy Between Carroll's and Leasure's Brigades," January 1, 1891, 4.

Carter, Joseph F. "In the Wilderness. The Troops at the Crossroads Saved by the Wall of Fire," April 7, 1892, 4.

Carter, Joseph F. "Leasure's Brigade, Another Account of the Fight at the Salient Angle," September 25, 1890, 3.

Cordrey, Francis. "The Wilderness. What a Private Saw and Felt in That Horrible Place," June 21, 1894, 3.

Crockett, Edwin. "First Time Under fire. Moving Into the Awful Hell of the Wilderness," May 5, 1904, 3.

Crockett, Edwin. "Turning the right Flank, May 6, 1864," October 10, 1889, 3.

Daniels, O. G. "At the Crossroads, The Charge Made by Carroll's Brigade," December 4, 1890, 4.

Davis, George E. "Faced 1,000 Rifles," March 5, 1925, 2.

Dickson, D. J. [No Title], March 12, 1891, 3.

Dunham, Samuel. "Death of General Hays. Where and How He Fell at the Battle of the Wilderness," November 12, 1885, 3.

Funke, C. G. "In the Wilderness. A New York Comrade Gives His Experience of fighting in the Woods and Brush," July 14, 1892, 4.

Goodrich, Ira B. "Helped Save the day. A Massachusetts Comrade's Testimony for Leasure's Brigade," April 30, 1891, 3.

Grant, L. A. "In the Wilderness," January 28, 1897, 1.

Griffin, Z. T. "The Wilderness. The Turning of the Right Flank, May 6, 1864," August 15, 1889, 3.

Haverly, William J. "The Wilderness. Turning the Right Flank, May 6, 1864," October 10, 1889, 3.

Haynes, Ashbury F. "How Haynes Won His Medal of Honor," October 21, 1926, 2.

"In the Wilderness," September 12, 1889, 1.

"In the Wilderness. Chapter XII of Lt. Kirk's History of the 4th N.Y.H.A.," September 19, 1889, 1.

Isham, Asa B. "Through the Wilderness to Richmond," June 5, 1902, 7.

Jeffers, C. T. "What the Gallant Ninth Corps Did," July 9, 1896, 1.

Kerr, Samuel C. "The Wilderness. Turning the Right Flank on May 6," July 11, 1889, 3.

Kilmer, George W. "With Grant in the Wilderness," July 17, 1924, 7.

McDonald, M. "March and Battle," April 2, 1896, 3.

Marsh, Edward C. "In the Wilderness. In the Hottest of the fight at Spotsylvania and Wounded at Bethesda Church," July 10, 1913, 7.

Miller, N. E. "The Wilderness. What the 20th Indiana Did at the Junction of the Brock and Plank Roads," January 21, 1892, 4.

Myerhoff, Charles H. "In the Wilderness. One of Carroll's Brigade Takes Comrade Carter to Account," December 3, 1891, 4.

Myerhoff, Charles H. "The Wilderness. The Charge of Carroll's Celebrated Brigade," October 23, 1890, 4.

Myers, Ephraim E. "Trials and Travels of the 45th Pa.," December 10 and 17, 1925, 3.

Nesbit, J. W. "Cross Roads in the Wilderness. The Bitter Fighting There, May 6, 1864," March 22, 1917, 7.

Norton, F. M. "That Tangle of the Wilderness," June 26, 1913, 7.

Parker, E. K. "In the Wilderness: Turning of the Right Flank, May 6, 1864," November 14, 1889, 3.

Payne, J. "The Wilderness. The Turning of the right Flank, May 6, 1864," July 18, 1889, 3.

Rhodes, J. E. "The Wilderness Campaign," March 24, 1910, 7.

Rogers, Earl M. "How Wadsworth Fell. His Death at the Battle of the Wilderness," December 24, 1885, 1.

Russell, George G. "From the Wilderness to Andersonville," October 22, 1925, 3.

Stevens, C. E. "Not a Fighting Regiment," October 10, 1908, 7.

Sudsburg, Joseph M. "In the Wilderness. The Colonel of the 3rd Md. Takes a Hand in the Controversy," January 15, 1891, 4.

Syphers, A. L. "In the Wilderness. Was the Right Flank Turned May 6?" June 13, 1889, 3.

Thompson, J. S. "Turning the Right flank, May 6, 1864," August 1, 1889, 3.

Walley, J. J. "In the Wilderness. Another Account of the Fight at the Angle," December 18, 1890, 4.

Wentz, A. "Closing Days of the War," January 28, 1904, 3.

Wright, Owen T. "Liked Gen. Grant's Story. One Who Was There Tells How He Was Taken in by the Johnnies," February 25, 1897, 3.

Our Living and Our Dead

Jones, Charles. "Historical Sketch," April 15, 1874.

Philadelphia Weekly Times

Bowles, P. D. "Annals of the War, Battle of the Wilderness, The Fourth Alabama Regiment in the Slaughter Pen on May 6, 1864," Saturday, October 4, 1884.

Rockingham Recorder

"Diary of W. H. Arehart," II, #3, October 1959, 148–155.

Southern Historical Society Papers

Bryan, Goode. "Report of General Goode Bryan," VI, 1878, 83.

Field, C. W. "Campaign of 1864 and 1865." XIV, 1886, 543–547.

Kershaw, Joseph B. "Operations of Kershaw's Division," VI, 1878, 81.

Lane, J. H. "History of Lane's North Carolina Brigade," IX, 1881, 124–129.

Perry, William F. "Reminiscences of the Campaign of 1864 in Virginia." VII, 1879, 49–63.

"Report of General James Longstreet," VI, 1878, 79.

Venable, Charles S. "The Campaign from the Wilderness to Petersburg." XIV, 1886, 522–527.

The United Service

Clarke, Augustus P. "A Cavalry Surgeon's Experiences in the Battle of the Wilderness," II, February, 1894.

NEWSPAPERS
The Atlanta Journal

McBride, A. J. "From the Chuckee to the Wilderness," June 29, 1901.

Walden, D. I. "Wounded at the Wilderness," February 23, 1901.

Atlanta *Southern Confederacy*. June 15, 1864, "Wofford's Georgia Brigade."

Augusta *Daily Constitutionalist*. May 28, 1864, 1:col. 3-4.

The Charleston Mercury. May 24, 1864, 2:col. 4; June 9, 1864, 1:col. 2.

The Columbia *Daily South Carolinian*. May 25, 1864, 2:col. 2-5; May 26, 1864, 3:col. 3.

The Daily Confederate (Raleigh). May 17, 1864, 1:col. 1-2; May 23, 1864, 2:col. 4; May 24, 1864, 2: col. 3-5; "Barringer's N. C. Brigade of Cavalry," February 22, 1865.

Daily Richmond Examiner. "The Fight Near Spotsylvania Court House Between Fitzhugh Lee and the enemy," May 11, 1864; May 17, 1864, 1:col. 5; May 31, 1864, 1:col. 4-5.

Daily Intelligencer. May 27, 1864, 3:col. 2; May 29, 1864, 2:col. 2; June 4, 1864, 1:col. 3-4.

Macon Daily Telegraph. June 21, 1864, 2:col. 2.

Montgomery *Daily Register and Advertiser*. May 21, 1864, 1:col. 6; May 27, 1864, 2:col. 2; May 30, 1864, 2:col. 2; June 19, 1864, 2:col. 3.

Raleigh *Semi-Weekly Standard*. May 24, 1864, 2:col. 4-6.

Richmond *Daily Dispatch*. May 10, 1864, 1:col. 3; May 17, 1864, 2:col. 5; May 26, 1864, 1:col. 7.

Richmond Enquirer. May 17, 1864, 3:col. 4; May 20, 1864, 1:col. 4-5; June 4, 1864, 3:col. 4-5; June 7, 1864; June 14, 1864, 2:col. 3.

Richmond Whig. June 16, 1864, 2:col. 5-6.

Savannah *Republican*. May 10, 1864, 1:col. 3; May 21, 1864, 1:col. 3-4.

The Sentinel, (Richmond). May 16, 1864, 2:col. 1; May 17, 1864, 2:col. 5; "The Second Virginia Cavalry in the Late fights," May 21, 1864; May 30, 1864, 1:col. 5; May 31, 1864, 2:col. 7; June 1, 1864, 1:col. 4; June 23, 1864, 2:col. 5.

MANUSCRIPT COLLECTIONS
Alabama State Archives, Montgomery, Alabama

Coles, R. T. "History of the 4th Alabama."

Duke University, Special Collections Department, William R. Perkins Library, Durham, North Carolina.

Buck, Samuel. "Recollections of an Old Confed," Samuel Buck Papers, ca. 1890.

Bush, A. Mc. Letter to General J. W. Hoffman, September 21, 1872, Winfield Scott Hancock Papers, 1863–1885.

Dudley, C. R. "What I Know About the Wilderness," Confederate Veteran Papers.

Elder, Henry G. Letter to General J. W. Hoffman, September 27, 1872, Winfield S. Hancock Papers, 1863–1885.

Ferguson, J. D. "Memoranda of the Itinerary and Operations of Major General Fitz Lee's Cavalry Division of the Army of Northern Virginia from May 4th to October 15th, inclusive," Munford-Ellis Family Papers, Thomas T. Munford Div. 1, Miscellany-Box 1, Civil War Mss., 1861–1865.

Graham, James A. Letter to his mother, May 9, 1864, James A. Graham Papers, 1861–1901.

Haskell, John Cheves. "Memoirs," John Cheves Haskell Papers, 1861–1865.

Hudgins, Francis L. "38th Georgia Regiment at the Wilderness," Confederate Veteran Papers, Battles 1861-1932 & n.d., Box 1.

Irvin, John. Letter to General J. W. Hoffman, November 9, 1872, Winfield S. Hancock Papers, 1863–1885.

Jones, Thomas G. Letters to John W. Daniel, February 29, June 20, and July 3, 1904, John Warwick Daniel Papers, 1849–1904, 22-G.

Johnson, Robert D. Report of Operations, January 1865, John Warwick Daniels Papers, 1849–1904, 22-G.

Johnson, Robert D. to John W. Daniel, undated note. John Warwick Daniel Papers.

Ragland, Ned R. Reminiscences, Confederate Veteran Papers, 1861–1932, Box 6.

Smith, W. W. Letter to John W. Daniel, October 24, 1904, John Warwick Daniel Papers, 1849–1904, 22-G.

Wheeler, W. H. "War Record of Reminiscences," W. H. Wheeler Papers.

Fredericksburg and Spotsylvania National Battlefield Park, Chatham Hall, Fredericksburg, Virginia.

Carter, William. Diary.

Peyton, George Quintus. "A Civil War Record for 1864–1865," 1906.

"Report of Henry Heth, Spring 1864 to October 1864," Mss., ANV, Leaders, Vol. 178.

Wilmer D. Martin Collection, Tucson, Arizona.

Martin, Alfred Thomas. Memoir, 38th North Carolina. With Permission.

Library of Congress, Manuscript Division, Washington, D.C.

Boteler, Alexander R. Diary.

Fisk, Wilbur. Co. E, 2nd Vermont, Diary.

Museum of the Confederacy, Eleanor S. Brockenbrough Library, Richmond, Va.

Green, Edward A. "The War of the Confederacy."

"Report of Major General Fitzhugh Lee of the Operations of His Cavalry Division, A.N.V., From May 4th 1864 to September 19th 1864 (both inclusive).

National Archives, Washington, D.C.

RG 94, OAG, Volunteer Organizations, Civil War Returns, Grand Army of the Potomac.

RG 27, Box 28, Nominal Casualties for the first Division, Cavalry Corps from May 4th to June 20th, 1864.

John M. Priest Collection, Boonsboro, Md.

Bowen, George A. Diary, 12th New Jersey.

The South Carolinia Library, University of South Carolina, Columbia, S.C.

Hagood, J. R. "Memoirs of the First South Carolina Regiment of Volunteer Infantry in the Confederate War for Independence from April 12, 1861 to April 10, 1865.

"Reports of Operations of Wade Hampton's Cavalry Division."

Bryce Suderow Collection.

Letter, F. M. Myers to His Parents, May 15, 1864.

United States Army Military History Institute, Manuscripts Department, Carlisle Barracks, Pa.

Daily, W. J. (Cpl.). Co. M, 6th N.Y. State Heavy Artillery, Diary, Jan. 2, 1864–May 30, 1864, Civil War Times Illustrated Collection.

Del Vecchio, Richard J. "With the First New York Dragoons: From the Letters of Jared L. Ainsworth," 1971, Harrisburg Civil War Round Table.

Eichelberger, Grayson M. "Memoirs," October 1912, Civil War Miscellaneous Collection.

Harris, Avery. "Personal Reminiscences of the Author From August 1862 to June 1865, War of the Rebellion," Avery Harris Papers.

Hoffman, Clement. Letters to his Mother, February 12, 1863–July 14, 1867.

Plumb, Isaac. Captain, Co. C, 61st N.Y. Vol. Inf., "Recollection of Life and service From Compiled records," Civil War Miscellaneous Collection.

Ressler, Isaac H. Co. L, 16th Pa. Cavalry, diary 1862–1865, Civil War Times Illustrated Collection.

Rucker, Samuel Burns. "Recollections of My War Record During the Confederacy," January 5, 1930, Civil War.

Thompson, Alfred. Letters and Diary, Jay Luvaas Collection.

Turner, Henry P. Diary, January 1–December 29, 1864, Civil War Miscellaneous Collection.

Webb, John G. Letter, May 7, 1864, Lewis Leigh Collection.

University of Georgia, Athens, Ga.

Hall, George W. Diary, 14th Georgia Volunteers, Georgia Room.

Johnson, Francis Solomon, Jr. Letter to Emily Hutchings, May 8, 1864, Special Collections Department.

University of Michigan, Michigan Historical Collections, Bentley History Library, Central Campus, Ann Arbor.

Kirk, Newton. "Reminiscences," Newton Thorne Kirk Papers, #1397, Archives and Historical Collections.

Rowe, James D. Letter, May 6, 1864.

University of North Carolina at Chapel Hill, Special Collections Department, Chapel Hill, North Carolina.

Alexander Papers #7.

Benson, Berry G. "Reminiscences of Berry Greenwood Benson, C.S.A." I, Berry G. Benson Miscellaneous Writings.

Goggin, James M. Letter to James Longstreet, August 10, 1887, Longstreet Papers.

"Report of Operations of Horse Arty., Comd. by Maj. Jas. Breathed from the 4th of May to the 31st of August 1864," Halsey Papers, #2447.

McDonald, E. H. McDonald Papers, 2131.

Proffitt, Alfred, Letters to R. L. Proffitt, May 8 and 12, 1864, Alfred Proffitt Papers.

Todd, Westwood A. Reminiscences, Vol. 1, part 2, Westwood A. Todd Papers.

Venable, Charles S. Letter to James Longstreet, October 21, 1877, Longstreet Papers.

University of Virginia, Manuscripts Department, Alderman Library, Charlottesville, Virginia.

Bumgardner, James. "The Fifty-Second Virginia," *Richmond Dispatch*, October 8, 1905, James Bumgardner Papers.

Couse, Catherine. Letter to Mr. and Mrs. H., May 4–20, 1864.

Garnett, Theodore. Memoirs.

Hawse, Jasper. Diary, Co. B, 11th Va. Cav., Alderman Library, microfilm.

Millam, B. K. Letter to John W. Daniel, John W. Daniel Papers, Acc.#158,5383, Box 24.

Virginia Historical Society, Richmond, Virginia.

Ball, William S. "Reminiscences."

Phillips, James Eldrid. "Memoirs," James Eldrid Phillips Papers.

Virginia Military Institute, Archives Department, Lexington, Virginia.

Pendleton, P. P. HQ, Horse Artillery, A.N.V.

"Reports of John J. Shoemaker and P. P. Pendleton, HQ, Horse Artillery, A.N.V."

Virginia State Archives, Richmond, Virginia.

Wood, James F. Diary, Company F, 7th Virginia Cavalry.

Virginia State Library, Richmond, Va.

Sale, John F. Diary, John F. Sale Papers.

Winthrop College

McDonnell, John Daniel. "Recollections of the Civil War," Archives and Special Collections Department.

REFERENCES

Beyer, W. F. and O. F. Keydel (ed.) *Deeds of Valor*. I. Detroit: Perrin-Keydel Co., 1907.

Hardee, W. J. *Rifle and Light Infantry Tactics, School of the Battalion*. II. Westport, Conn.: Greenwood Press, Reprint, 1971.

Medical and Surgical History of the Civil War. VIII. Wilmington, N.C.: Broadfoot Publishing Co., 1991.

Steere, Edward. *The Wilderness Campaign*. Harrisburg, Pa.: The Stackpole Co., 1960.

Troop Movement Maps, U.S. Department of the Interior, NPS, Division of Design and Construction, Eastern Office, 1962.

U.S. Department of the Army. *The Medal of Honor of the United States*. Washington, D.C.: U.S. Government Printing Office, 1948.

Howard Michael Madaus, Cody, Wyoming. Confederate Flags.

INDEX

C

G

T

U

V

W

Y